E L S

December 2002

Contract Actions in
Modern Employment Law:
Developments and Issues

Contract Actions in Modern Employment Law: Developments and Issues

Professor Ian Smith
MA, LLB, Barrister, Clifford Chance Professor of Employment Law,
University of East Anglia, Devereux Chambers, London

Nicholas Randall
LLB, Barrister, Devereux Chambers, London

Precedents and accompanying commentary by **Helen Milgate** MA, LLM, LLB,
Solicitor, Pinsent Curtis Biddle

Scottish contribution by **Rod McKenzie** LLB NP AICA, Solicitor,
Law Society of Scotland accredited specialist in Employment Law, Harper
McLeod

Butterworths
LexisNexis™

Members of the LexisNexis Group worldwide

United Kingdom	LexisNexis Butterworths Tolley, a Division of Reed Elsevier (UK) Ltd, Halsbury House, 35 Chancery Lane, LONDON, WC2A 1EL, and 4 Hill Street, EDINBURGH EH2 3JZ
Argentina	LexisNexis Argentina, BUENOS AIRES
Australia	LexisNexis Butterworths, CHATSWOOD, New South Wales
Austria	LexisNexis Verlag ARD Orac GmbH & Co KG, VIENNA
Canada	LexisNexis Butterworths, MARKHAM, Ontario
Chile	LexisNexis Chile Ltda, SANTIAGO DE CHILE
Czech Republic	Nakladatelství Orac sro, PRAGUE
France	Editions du Juris-Classeur SA, PARIS
Hong Kong	LexisNexis Butterworths, HONG KONG
Hungary	HVG-Orac, BUDAPEST
India	LexisNexis Butterworths, NEW DELHI
Ireland	Butterworths (Ireland) Ltd, DUBLIN
Italy	Giuffrè Editore, MILAN
Malaysia	Malayan Law Journal Sdn Bhd, KUALA LUMPUR
New Zealand	LexisNexis Butterworths, WELLINGTON
Poland	Wydawnictwo Prawnicze LexisNexis, WARSAW
Singapore	LexisNexis Butterworths, SINGAPORE
South Africa	Butterworths SA, DURBAN
Switzerland	Stämpfli Verlag AG, BERNE
USA	LexisNexis, DAYTON, Ohio

© Reed Elsevier (UK) Ltd 2002

A CIP Catalogue record for this book is available from the British Library.

ISBN 0 406 11841 8

Typeset by Kerrypress Ltd, Luton, Beds
Printed by Cromwell Press, Trowbridge, Wilts

Visit Butterworths LexisNexis *direct* at www.butterworths.com

Foreword

For the employment law practitioner, teacher and student the significance and effect of the contract of employment and its breach continues to grow in importance. It took 23 years before the power to confer jurisdiction on Employment Tribunals to hear breach of contract claims, first provided for in section 113 of the Industrial Relations Act 1971, was introduced. Now breach of contract of employment claims are a regular feature in tribunal cases.

The old principle that the manner of dismissal did not sound in damages at common law, nor form a head of compensation in unfair dismissal claims has now been revisited in the recent House of Lords decisions in the *BCCI* case (stigma damages) and in *Johnson v Unisys*.

Similarly, the old rule that an employee could not recover by way of damages discretionary benefits to which he was apparently not strictly contractually entitled is being eroded by cases such as *Clark v BET* and *Clark v Nomura*.

In such a climate of change this work provides a timely, comprehensive and thoughtful analysis of the present position with valuable pointers to the future.

His Honour Judge Peter Clark
Audit House
London
August 2002

Preface

The whole area of employment contracts and common law actions based upon them has been generating much interest lately, and it is hoped that this offering will be thought timely. Contract actions can be seen either as an adjunct to a statutory action or as an end in themselves. Either way, we continue to see serious case law often having to consider and define (or re-define) some surprisingly fundamental issues. Our aim is to analyse these developments and to point out what we see as the important issues and possibilities, hence the title of the book. With regard to possibilities, some are by now becoming fairly well established, whereas others may be viewed by the reader as being somewhere along a spectrum from the merely speculative through to the rantings of obviously deteriorating minds. Whatever the category concerned, we have tried to write a book that will be considered genuinely *interesting*. Moreover, it is a book that is actually intended to be read. One aim has been to integrate the substantive law and the available remedies, in a way which will be helpful to practitioners. To this end, in addition to our own contributions, Helen Milgate of Pinsent Curtis Biddle has contributed the precedents and accompanying commentary and Rod McKenzie of Harper McLeod has checked the work to ensure applicability in Scotland.

In places it has been necessary to lay down some basic principles, where that is essential to make sense of the more interesting material, but in other places it is largely assumed that the reader is aware of those basics and is wanting to see where developments from them may lead. We attempt to help the process of seeking answers to practical problems by considering such developments from first principles. We also try to point out where we see the potential flashpoints (actual or reasonably apprehended) for the future, up in our eyrie as editors of *Harvey*, staring down on the plains below. With regard to timing, we have had to press ahead while the Employment Bill 2002 was still before Parliament, especially as commencement dates were still uncertain, and with so much left to eventual Regulations. We have, however, referred to proposed changes in the Bill wherever relevant, as is the case with the Fixed term Employee (Prevention of Less Favourable Treatment) Regulations, in draft form at the time of writing.

One final point is worth a mention at the outset. The aim of the book is not to rehearse and rehash the thoughts and arguments of others. It can be argued that one curse of modern legal writing is to go down the route (seen often in social science writing) of compulsive citation of anything that moves. At best, that can produce dense and confusing text, difficult to read; at worst, it could be viewed as licensed plagiarism. We have been extremely sparing in citation, looking for a particularly high level of relevance. For better or for worse, these are our own ideas. Indeed, at the risk of giving a horrendous hostage to fortune for an evil-intentioned reviewer, we could each say, with Touchstone (As You Like It, V. iv) – 'an ill-favoured thing, sir, but mine own'.

Ian Smith
Nicholas Randall
Devereux Chambers
London
July 2002

Contents

Contents

12 The Scottish dimension   177

Precedents

Table of statutes

Table of statutory instruments

Table of European legislation

Table of cases

H

Decisions of the European Court of Justice are listed below. This decision is also included in the preceding alphabetical list.

Chapter 1

Introduction – the importance of contract actions

1.1   In the case that revolutionised the area of legal liability for references, Lord Slynn commented on 'the changes which have taken place in the employer and employee relationship, with far greater duties imposed on the employer than in the past, whether by statute or judicial decision, to care for the physical, financial or even psychological welfare of the employee'[1]. This area is an interesting example because traditionally there was *no* liability to the subject of a job reference (as opposed to its recipient), and yet within a space of only a few years it has become a highly contentious subject of legal debate. This pace of change is now normal in employment law. From the outside, as a matter of first impressions, this may appear largely as a result of legislation, with the enormous caseload on employment tribunals from complaints of unfair dismissal and the various forms of employment-related discrimination, the consistent impact of EC law and a full legislative agenda from all recent governments. This would seem to leave little scope for older forms of employment law based on the contract of employment, and contract-based common law causes of action.

Nothing could be further from the truth. The modern statutory rights have not replaced contractual rights, and the relationship between them can be a subtle one, as seen in the next chapter. In fact, interest in common law actions in employment law has never been greater. Paradoxically, when common law rights were all that the employee had (before the first of the modern statutes in 1963) there was very little litigation, with the law giving little job protection and employment disputes normally being resolved industrially rather than through the courts. With increased statutory protection, contractual rights become more realistically enforceable. Sometimes this will be as an adjunct to statutory actions, but employment lawyers also have to deal regularly with purely contractual disputes, either those actually arising or those which could possibly arise (thus giving rise to a need for advice in advance, as to drafting, procedures or tactics), especially with the growth of ever more valuable contractual benefits for employees, requiring contractual remedies for their enforcement. In many (though not all) sectors, employment is now a more formal relationship than in the past, and it is the contract that is at the heart of it.

Traditionally, a contract action had to be brought in the ordinary courts. Given the economics of this, the focus there would naturally be on large claims. These continue to be seen, in cases for example of the dismissal of executives or directors with serious common law claims. In some, even the greatly increased limits in unfair dismissal claims (standing at £52,600 for the compensatory

1

award and £7,500 for the basic award at the time of writing) would scarcely be adequate. On the other hand, more ordinary mortals could still gain through a common law action, for example where a test case is being mounted which, though in the form of an individual action, is actually meant to resolve a collective dispute[2], or where an individual is dismissed within the first year of employment and so cannot claim unfair dismissal.

1   *Spring v Guardian Assurance plc* [1994] ICR 596, [1994] IRLR 460, HL at 628, 474.
2   A good example is *Rigby v Ferodo Ltd* [1988] ICR 29, [1987] IRLR 516, HL where an individual's action for wages was used to attack a unilateral wage cut by the employer for the whole staff.

1.2   In the case of smaller claims, however, the major change in the last two decades has been in forum. It is now possible to bring such claims in employment tribunals, a widespread practice as shown by the statistics. Tribunals only have the jurisdiction that is given to them by statute. In two ways, this has always enabled contractual disputes to be considered. First, a contractual question can easily arise as an incidental question in a statutory action. Two obvious and fundamental examples are (a) where a tribunal has to decide whether or not an individual was an 'employee' at all, a key requirement for major statutory rights, and (b) whether an employer's conduct was in breach of the contract of employment (as to its express terms or, increasingly, any terms implied into it by law or factual inference) in a case where an employee is claiming constructive dismissal. Other examples will arise throughout chapters 2, 3 and 4. Secondly, questions as to what may or may not have been contractually agreed can be raised by an employee in an action under the Employment Rights Act 1996, ('ERA 1996' hereafter) s 11, the complaint being that the employer gave either no 'section 1 statement', or did but included inaccurate particulars[1]. Technically, some care is needed here because the section 1 statement is not per se the contract of employment; however, in many cases (where nothing else has been given) it is powerful evidence of the terms of the implied contract that lies behind it, and so the sorts of arguments that arise on a section 11 claim may well be indistinguishable from those which would arise in a purely contractual claim[2].

These longstanding cross-overs between the statutory and the contractual allowed disputes relating to the latter to be aired. What for many years the tribunals could not do was to award *remedies* for breach of contract. It was in this crucial area that our historically split jurisdiction was at its most unfortunate (eg on dismissal an unfair dismissal claim going to a tribunal but a wrongful dismissal claim or a claim for outstanding holiday pay having to go to a court). Two developments have affected this fundamentally. First, a tribunal can give contract-based remedies under Part II of the ERA 1996, under the guise of 'unlawful deductions from wages'. When this law was first introduced in the Wages Act 1986 (and many lawyers still refer to a 'Wages Act claim') it was only meant as a replacement for the ancient laws against certain fines or deductions from the wages of manual labourers (eg for poor workmanship or lateness to work) contained in the Truck Acts 1831–1944. Its aims were modest, and the then Department of Employment estimated that there might be about 400 cases per year. However, this area has seen the most remarkable development. The key point came when it was accepted that, in a considerable stretch to the English language, 'deduction' can include non-payment, especially in a dispute where the employer denies the employee's version of events or the contract and maintains that the employee has no right to the amount or benefit that he or she is claiming[3]. Moreover, 'wages' has been widely construed, though with limitation in the case of wages in lieu on dismissal[4]. Thus, a Part II (or 'Wages Act') claim can be used widely to bring before a tribunal a substantive breach of contract action, either during employment or on termination; such an action, simple in form, can raise seriously complex issues of law[5]. In a slight disparity with the original estimate, the ACAS annual report 2000–2001 showed a total of 39,464 'protection of wages' claims started before tribunals and received by them in their conciliation role.

1   It is government policy to raise the profile of the section 1 statement, as a means of trying to avoid later disputes spilling out into the tribunals. The Employment Bill before Parliament at the time of writing proposes a power for tribunals to increase awards in cases where no such statement has been given (with *no* requirement that the employee's claim was *caused* by the lack of written particulars).
2   For example, as with an action for wages (para 1.1, n 2 above) a s 11 action could be used to challenge a variation of contract, pushed through by the employer by the time-(dis?) honoured tactic of 're-issuing your statements' (see para 3.33 below).
3   The key EAT cases were *Alsop v Star Vehicle Contracts Ltd* [1990] ICR 378, [1990] IRLR 83 ('deduction' even where it was so large as to negate payment altogether) and *McCree v Tower Hamlets London Borough Council* [1992] ICR 99, [1992] IRLR 56 (phasing out a bonus held to be a 'deduction'); this approach was approved by the Court of Appeal in *Delaney v Staples* [1991] ICR 331, [1991] IRLR 112 (successful tribunal claim for £55.50 unpaid commission and holiday pay), and not challenged on further appeal to the House of Lords (n 4, below).
4   *Delaney v Staples* [1992] ICR 483, [1992] IRLR 191, HL (wages in relation to actual notice can be recovered under Part II, but not amounts payable in lieu after the ending of the contract). The latter category can now be recovered under the Extension of Jurisdiction Orders, below.
5   The leading TUPE case of *Wilson v St Helens Borough Council* [1998] ICR 1141, [1998] IRLR 706, HL (holding that a transfer-related variation of the contracts of those transferred is void) was in fact in the form of a Part II claim for reimbursement of payments under certain contractual terms which the transferee employer thought had been bargained away after the transfer. Whether those payments actually continued to be due raised extremely complex points under the TUPE Regulations and EC law.

1.3   The second development in relation to remedies was actually intended, and was a direct transfer of jurisdiction in certain common law claims to tribunals. Under the Employment Tribunals Extension of Jurisdiction (England and Wales) Order 1994[1] and the Employment Tribunals Extension of Jurisdiction (Scotland) Order 1994[2] proceedings may be brought in a tribunal in respect of a contract claim of an employee for the recovery of damages or any other sum if the claim is one in respect of which a court would have jurisdiction, and 'arises or is outstanding on the termination of the employee's employment'[3]. A claim for damages, or for a sum due, in respect of personal injuries is excluded[4], as are certain other specific claims which still belong in the ordinary courts[5]. There is a time limit of three months beginning with the effective date of termination (with the usual 'reasonably practicable' ground for extension)[6] and a monetary limit of £25,000 'in respect of a contract claim, or in respect of a number of contract claims relating to the same contract'[7]. The emphasis on termination means that this form of claim can be used to recover payments in lieu that should have been made, and that other amounts outstanding can be claimed directly, rather than indirectly through a Part II action. On the other hand, a Part II claim would not be subject to the monetary limit (in an extreme case) and, unlike an Extension Order claim, is not subject to a counterclaim by an employer[8]. As with Part II claims, Extension Order claims have become common, with the ACAS annual report 2000–2001 showing a total of 29,390 'breach of contract' claims started before tribunals and received by them in their conciliation role[9].

Quantitatively, therefore, the number of contract actions has increased substantially over the last decade and a half, and employment lawyers are now called on frequently to advise on the drafting of contracts and the possibilities of disputes arising from them. In an ideal world, this would mean that the law here was certain, but this is not an ideal world. One feature of this area is that some very basic concepts remain subject to litigation. Sometimes this is still to establish fundamentals, but we are also seeing constant attempts to refine and develop even those rules which seem reasonably clear. As long ago as a case in 1918[10] McCardie J commented that 'the principles [of wrongful dismissal] are but rarely revealed'. Today, with so much more emphasis on individualism in employment law (in relation both to terms of employment and disputes arising from them), such basic principles may be more often revealed, but they are still subject to major debate and closely fought over.

1   SI 1994/1623; see *Harvey on Industrial Relations and Employment Law* para R [778].
2   SI 1994/1624; see *Harvey* R [788].
3   Article 3 of each Order. A claim cannot be brought before the effective date of termination of the contract in respect of which it is made: *Capek v Lincolnshire CC* [2000] IRLR 590, CA. Likewise, the 'on termination' requirement means that there can be no claim in relation to post-termination liabilities (eg an agreement reached by the parties after the contract ended): *Miller Bros & Butler Ltd v Johnston* [2002] IRLR 386, EAT. In the case of the former problems, a Wages Act claim may still be necessary.
4   Article 3 of each Order. This should mean that, even if the law develops to allow personal injury damages for simple breach of employment contract (eg where a harassment case leading to psychological injury is pleaded as breach of trust and respect, see paras 4.8 and 6.4, below), such a claim would have to be brought in the ordinary courts. This is not the case in a discrimination claim.
5   Article 5 of each Order excludes claims in relation to living accommodation, intellectual property, obligations of confidence and covenants in restraint of trade.
6   Article 7(1), (3) of each Order. If there is no EDT, the period is three months beginning with the last day on which the employee worked in the employment which has terminated: art 7(2).
7   Article 10 of each Order. It is noticeable that this amount has not been increased in line with rises in the maxima for unfair dismissal and other statutory rights. The relationship between this capped common law action before a tribunal and the unlimited jurisdiction of a common law court could aggravate problems experienced here with issue estoppel and/or cause of action estoppel, especially where an applicant brings a claim before a tribunal and then discontinues it in order to pursue a larger claim elsewhere. Fortunately, the latest Court of Appeal decisions have shown a more liberal view of estoppel, especially where it is clear that the applicant did not intend to abandon his or her claim altogether: *Sajid v Sussex Muslim Society* [2001] EWCA Civ 1684, [2002] IRLR 113 (on just such facts), subsequently applied more generally in *Ako v Rothschild Asset Management Ltd* [2002] EWCA Civ 236, [2002] IRLR 348 in preference to the far more restrictive approach taken in *Lennon v Birmingham City Council* [2001] EWCA Civ 435, [2001] IRLR 826.
8   The right to counterclaim is given by art 4 of each Order and is subject to (a) similar restrictions as to subject matter as the claim itself, and (b) a time limit of six weeks from receipt of the originating application in respect of the contract claim, with the usual 'reasonably practicable' ground for extension (art 8). Once properly commenced, the counterclaim is an independent cause of action which can, if necessary, survive the demise of the original claim: *Patel v RCMS Ltd* [1999] IRLR 161, EAT.
9   The fact that such a claim is often added on to a primary statutory claim (especially unfair dismissal) is shown by a difference in tribunal statistics and ACAS statistics – the former count applicants whereas the latter count individual claims, and each year the latter give a very substantially larger figure than the former.
10 *Re Rubel Bronze & Metal Co Ltd* [1918] 1 KB 315.

Chapter 2

Common law and statutory claims

1 Introduction

2.1   It can take an effort now to envisage just how different employment law
was, no more than four decades ago. Modern statutory coverage only dates back
to 1963 with the first Contracts of Employment Act, the major innovations of
redundancy payments and unfair dismissal following in 1965 and 1971.
Although this is positively antediluvian in an employment law time scale, it
remains relatively recent in a normal historical sense. As late as 1959 it was said
in the Court of Appeal that 'a contract of service is but an example of contracts
in general, so that the general law of contract will be applicable'[1], and as late as
1969 it could seriously be argued before that court that any hiring of an
employee on an open-ended basis was in law a hiring for one year only, due to
the 'presumption of a yearly hiring' which had existed in agriculture in order to
secure year-long employment, and which was based on the annual hiring fair
(well known to Thomas Hardy readers)[2]. The British tradition was rooted firmly
in the 'voluntary principle' of abstention from involving the law (primarily at a
collective level, buttressed by the Trade Disputes Act 1906, but also strongly
affecting individual disputes too), giving primacy to collective resolution of
disputes. Such legal involvement as there was had, by the twentieth century
(except in times of war), become founded on the individual contract of
employment, usually at the expense of the reality in many instances of the
importance of collective determination of wages and other working conditions:

> 'In the end, accordingly, labour relations resumed the patterns of the
> Edwardian settlement. In the general run, rights enforceable in law existed
> only in the individual worker's contract with his employer. To this the courts
> had insisted on annexing conditions which guaranteed liberal values: no
> employee could be compelled to serve, no employer to keep in service; if
> either broke the contract, the remedy was not an injunction but only
> damages. Neither was entitled to substitute a third party for himself (by
> assignment of his interest) without the consent of the other. The employee's
> right to choose his employer – even a remote, abstract corporation – was
> said by Lord Atkin to constitute 'the main difference between a servant and
> a serf'[3].

By contrast, the last four decades (and particularly the last three) have seen a
pace of change that has ranged from consistent to frenetic, producing a level of
statutory coverage hardly imaginable at the beginning of that period. These

statutory rights and obligations have for the most part not replaced the employee's common law contractual rights, but rather have supplemented or added to them[4]; indeed, it is one of the themes of this book that in many ways they have strengthened those common law rights, and certainly led to a level of their enforcement far higher than when they were the employee's only rights.

It is important, therefore, to appreciate how the common law and statutory claims and rights interact. The relationship is a complex one and this chapter looks at four aspects of it – (1) where they must be contrasted, (2) where the statutory rights in fact rely on the common law, (3) the extent to which statutory rights overlay the common law,and (4) the possibility of moves to extend statutory coverage beyond those traditionally viewed by common law as employees.

1   *Laws v London Chronicle* [1959] 2 All ER 285, [1959] 1 WLR 698, CA, per Lord Evershed MR.
2   *Richardson v Koefod* [1969] 3 All ER 1264, [1969] 1 WLR, CA.
3   Cornish & Clark *Law and Society in England 1750–1959* (1989) p 353; chap 4 as a whole is highly recommended reading for a historical overview. See also Smith & Wood *Industrial Law* (7th edn, 2000) Butterworths, p 27 where, for example, the point is made that the Law Report Index 1951–1960 did not have a heading 'Employment'; in that period, only 30 employment-related cases were reported.
4   One notable exception here is the Transfer of Undertakings (Protection of Employment) Regulations 1981, SI 1981/1794 (under review, with a view to reform, at the time of writing) which can in fact cut across normal domestic contract law, especially in relation to post-transfer alteration of terms which has been held to be void if transfer-related, even where an agreement to that effect would be valid in contract law: *Wilson v St Helens Borough Council* [1998] ICR 1141, [1998] IRLR 706, HL; see *Smith & Wood* p 163. One way of putting this (only half facetiously) is that in a TUPE case, to adopt Lord Atkin's formulation (n 3 above), the employee wants to be a serf, not a servant – a servant may be more free but on a transfer may otherwise be short on remedies.

2   Common law and statutory claims contrasted

2.2   The most obvious contrast is between wrongful dismissal and unfair dismissal. Although the media can be trusted to get it wrong and use these phrases interchangeably, these are two radically different causes of action. Wrongful dismissal is the common law cause of action on termination which, as will be seen at length later, is basically a simple breach of contract action where the subject matter is the ending of employment by the employer, though with the complication that employment contracts differ from most other types by normally being terminable by notice. Indeed, it is around the non-giving of proper or any notice that the action normally revolves. This means that, except where the employer purported to dismiss for good cause but none existed, the substantive reason for the dismissal is irrelevant. Unfair dismissal, by contrast, is a statutory action involving an examination of the substantive reason for the dismissal and the fairness of the procedures by which it was effected[1]. Its principal features are that it is entirely laid down by statute (originally the Industrial Relations Act 1971, now the ERA 1996), it is brought before an employment tribunal, there are limitations on who can bring it (in particular, in most cases, a requirement of one year's qualifying employment), the burden of proof on fact is primarily on the employer, and the compensation that can be awarded is usually subject to a statutory maximum (the cap for the compensatory award, meant to reflect actual loss, having been raised from £12,000 to £50,000 in December 1999 and subjected to regular up-rating by the Employment Relations Act 1999 ('ERA 1999' hereafter)). On the other hand, wrongful dismissal is a common law action based on breach of contract, until 1994 it could only be brought in the ordinary civil courts and now can be brought there or in a tribunal[2], there are no limitations on locus standi and no qualifying period, the burden of proof is on the employee and compensation is not subject to statutory rules and maxima. The latter point might be an advantage in some cases, but usually damages then are severely limited by the common law rule that the prima facie measure is only wages during the notice period (given that that is technically all that the employee has lost), though it will be argued later that there are signs of some movement away from this strictness.

Two further differences are to be noted. The first is that if the employer dismisses on ground A which is insufficient but then discovers evidence of ground B which would be sufficient, that 'after-aquired evidence' can be used at common law to make a wrongful dismissal lawful[3], but cannot be used under the statute to make an unfair dismissal fair[4]; thus, the common law looks at the objective position under the contract in the court's own view, whereas unfair dismissal law looks at what was actually motivating the employer at the time of dismissal[5] (this meaning, at the latest, at the time of confirmation of the dismissal at an internal appeal[6]). The second difference is that the procedures adopted by the employer in coming to the decision to dismiss may be crucial in an unfair dismissal, for it was held at an early stage that a dismissal can be unfair purely procedurally[7], but in the past this has normally been an irrelevant factor in a wrongful dismissal action, which has looked only to the existence of an objectively sufficient level of gross misconduct to justify summary dismissal or (more usually) to whether proper notice was given. However, as we shall see later, in this area the difference may be diminishing in modern law, with more emphasis being placed on the question whether the employer's disciplinary procedures are themselves part of the contract; if so, to dismiss without proper recourse to them might make the dismissal wrongful, leading to damages (at least for the extra time it would have taken to dismiss properly[8]) or, in a few cases, to the enforcement of the contract by injunction (unless and until a proper procedure is used)[9], normally not an option open to a court.

1 See generally *Smith & Wood* chap 8 and *Harvey on Industrial Relations and Employment Law* Div DI, Butterworths.
2 Employment Tribunals (Extension of Jurisdiction) Order 1994, SI 1994/1623 (in Scotland, SI 1994/1624). If the claim is brought before a tribunal, there is a statutory cap of £25,000; see chap 1 above.
3 *Boston Deep Sea Fishing & Ice Co v Ansell* (1888) 39 Ch D 339, CA.
4 *W Devis & Sons Ltd v Atkins* [1977] AC 931, [1977] 3 All ER 40, HL.
5 This point was strongly re-emphasised in *Polkey v AE Dayton Services Ltd* [1988] AC 344, [1987] 3 All ER 974, HL, where it was said that in such a case there would be a finding of unfair dismissal, but that the after acquired evidence could be taken into account when fixing compensation.
6 *West Midland Co-operative Society Ltd v Tipton* [1986] AC 536, [1986] ICR 192, HL.
7 *Earl v Slater and Wheeler (Airlyne) Ltd* [1973] 1 All ER 145, [1972] ICR 508, NIRC, approved by the House of Lords in *W Devis & Sons Ltd v Atkins* [1977] AC 931, [1977] 3 All ER 40, HL. Note that the procedures in question (warnings, hearings, appeals) appear nowhere in statute, but were instead taken from the ACAS Code of Practice No 1, which had seminal importance here in imposing patterns of behaviour on personnel management; this Code was updated in 2000 as the ACAS Code of Practice on Disciplinary and Grievance Procedures. At the time of writing, the Employment Bill before Parliament proposes to enact a basic 'statutory procedure' whose use will, in effect, become compulsory, but also to reintroduce the 'it made no difference' defence (disapproved by the House of Lords in *Polkey v AE Dayton Ltd* [1988] ICR 142, [1987] IRLR 503) in relation to more sophisticated elements of an employer's own procedure.
8 *Gunton v Richmond-upon-Thames London Borough Council* [1980] ICR 755, [1980] IRLR 321, CA. The Employment Bill proposes to make the basic 'statutory procedures' (n 7, above) part of all

contracts of employment; this could have an interesting effect on wrongful dismissal, though the question whether more sophisticated procedures are contractual will remain subject to the existing law.

9   See chap 9. For a recent example, see *Peace v City of Edinburgh Council* [1999] IRLR 417, Ct of Sess (OH) where an interdict was granted to restrain the employer from using a recently-introduced disiplinary procedure which the employee argued was contrary to his existing contract which he had not agreed to vary.

2.3   The end result of these differences is that each cause of action must be considered separately, and that any given dismissal might be both wrongful and unfair, neither, wrongful but not unfair[1] or unfair but not wrongful. More generally, there can be a misfit not just between the two causes of action, but also between contractual and statutory rights generally, with the fact that the employee is contractually in the right not necessarily ensuring success in a statutory action. A longstanding example of this (dating back to the original Redundancy Payments Act 1965) is that an employee about to be made redundant from job A may be 'offered' suitable alternative employment by the employer in job B; if he or she unreasonably refuses, the sanction is loss of the redundancy payment[2] (thus showing that the term 'offer' is somewhat loaded). If job B is not within the employee's contract, the employee is contractually in the right to refuse it[3], but the statutory redundancy right may be lost anyway. A further example of this phenomenon concerns dismissals for suspected misconduct where the longstanding law is that, for the dismissal to be fair, it is only necessary for the employer to have a genuine belief in guilt (based on reasonable investigation)[4]; this rule (entailing a high level of subjectivity[5]) has never formed part of the law on wrongful dismissal (in a case where the employer has dismissed summarily for cause) where the question must be whether the gross misconduct has or has not been objectively established on a balance of probabilities. However, the clearest example (again showing a conflict with contractual rights generally, not just a difference from wrongful dismissal) arises in cases of business reorganisations where the employer eventually dismisses an employee who will not agree to change his or her contract in order to work pursuant to the new system (eg where shifts and/or payments are being changed). Here, in a purely contractual sense, the employee is in the right in standing on the contract and insisting on the ability not to agree a variation, *but* it has long been established that provided there is a strong business case for changes, attempts have been made to accommodate and/or persuade the employee, there has been full consultation and a fair procedure has been adopted generally, the dismissal can be fair, as being for 'some other substantial reason' within the unfair dismissal legislation[6]. As has recently been pointed out very clearly by Judge Clark in the EAT, the contractual lawfulness of an order to an employee (in this context, to change job content or organisation) will be of central importance in a wrongful dismissal action (if the employee is dismissed summarily for refusal) and indeed in any question of constructive dismissal (where the employee leaves rather than obey) because, as we shall see shortly, this also works on a contractual basis, *but* in an unfair dismissal claim it will be only one of several factors to be considered by the tribunal in applying a broader test[7].

1   See, eg, *Treganowan v Robert Knee & Co Ltd* [1975] ICR 405, [1975] IRLR 247 where the dismissal was not unfair, the proper notice had not been given, but the latter could (then – see para 2.2, n 2, above) not be awarded by the tribunal.

2   ERA 1996, s 141.

3   This is not affected by the broader approach now to be taken to the definition of 'redundancy' itself in the light of *Murray v Foyle Meat Co* [1999] ICR 827, [1999] IRLR 562, HL.

4   *British Home Stores v Burchell* [1980] ICR 303n, [1978] IRLR 379, EAT, one of the best known decisions in unfair dismissal law, approved by the Court of Appeal in *Weddel & Co v Tepper* [1980] ICR 286, [1980] IRLR 96 and *Foley v Post Office* [2000] ICR 1283, [2000] IRLR 827.

5   This element came under attack as part of the attempt to move away from the 'range of reasonable responses' test for unfair dismissal: *Haddon v Van den Bergh Foods Ltd* [1999] ICR 1150, [1999] IRLR 672, EAT; *Wilson v Ethicon Ltd* [2000] IRLR 4, EAT. However, orthodoxy was restored in relation to both the range test and *BHS v Burchell* in *Foley* (n 3, above) and *Whitbread plc v Hall* [2002] EWCA Civ 268, [2001] IRLR 275.

6   For the voluminous case law on this difficult area, see *Smith & Wood* pp 496–501 and *Harvey* Div DI, head 12A. This heading of fair dismissal was established early in the history of unfair dismissal in *RS Components Ltd v Irwin* [1973] ICR 535, [1974] 1 All ER 41, NIRC; a particularly good example is *Catamaran Cruisers Ltd v Williams* [1994] IRLR 386, EAT.

7   *Farrant v The Woodroffe School* [1998] ICR 184, [1998] IRLR 176, EAT; this is a particularly strong decision because the school, convinced that they had the contractual authority to order the employee on to the new system, had in fact dismissed him for *misconduct*, but in spite of this his claim failed and the dismissal was fair, for some other substantial reason, under the general test of reasonableness in the ERA 1996, s 98(4).

2.4   When one turns to discrimination legislation, the contrast with the common law on employment becomes if anything greater, because to a large extent this legislation enacts its own definitions and concepts. The application of one whole part of each of the Sex Discrimination Act 1975, the Race Relations Act 1976 and the Disability Discrimination Act 1995 to 'Employment' is little more than descriptive. Not only is the application of these statutes made deliberately wider than just to 'employees' in the common law sense (see below), but also one important facet of their interpretation in recent cases has been an emphasis on the 'protective intent' of the legislation (often justifying a broad and purposive interpretation), combined with an obvious impatience with defendant/ respondent arguments seeking to use common law principles which evolved in totally different contexts and would be capable of depriving employees of the protection that Parliament intended to give[1]. A prime example of this is the decision in *Jones Tower Boot Co*[2] that an employer could be liable under the vicarious liability provisions of the Race Relations Act 1976 for extreme racial harassment by fellow employees; the matter hinged on what was to fall within the phrase 'in the course of employment', used in s 32(1) to put liability on to an employer, subject to the 'reasonably practicable steps' defence in s 32(3). Had the traditional common law on vicarious liability (which also uses the phrase 'in the course of employment') been applied, the perpetrators would probably have been 'on a frolic of their own' and the employer not liable (as had been the decision in the EAT[3]), but the Court of Appeal held that the phrase was to be construed in an ordinary sense as it stood in the statute, in order to affirm the intended protection, and *not* by reference to the narrower common law sense. Arguably the result is that it means here little more than 'at work', with the whole emphasis thrown on to whether the employer can then establish the s 32(3) defence, eg by having had actively-enforced anti-harassment policies in place and taking complaints seriously. Other recent cases illustrate the point. For example, (1) liability under the Disability Discrimination Act 1995, s 12 for discrimination by a principal against a contract worker was held to lie on the true 'end user' of the services and the niceties of the contractual relationships in the case (involving a chain of contracts and a service company) were not allowed to obscure the statutory intent[4]; (2) a similarly broad approach has been taken under the Race Relations Act 1976, s 7 as to when a contract worker can be said to be 'supplied' to work 'for' a principal[5]; (3) the leading case on the Disability Discrimination Act 1995 generally makes it clear that in sickness dismissal cases (if the sickness constitutes a 'disability') it is not enough for the employer to show that the ordinary contractual sickness procedures have been applied, as they would have been to a non-disabled absentee, but instead the employer must go on to show justification for the action taken, within the parameters set by the Act itself[6].

These examples should show how common law and statutory actions can differ. A possible assumption, with some validity in the past, would be that a statutory right would almost always be preferable for an employee to rely on. However, given more recent developments in relation to common law contractual options, such an assumption may not now be accurate. To take one example, a common occurrence is the employee off sick for a long, continuous period, with a term in the contract providing for relatively generous contractual sick pay on top of statutory sick pay. Can the employer lawfully dismiss that employee *before* he or she exhausts the contractual entitlement to sick pay? In a statutory action for unfair dismissal, the received wisdom has always been that the fairness of a dismissal would not necessarily be affected by whether or not the employee had exhausted the sick pay[7], so that if the employer can show good business need to dismiss (especially in order to replace permanently) the employee will have little protection from the statute. However, in the light of what are generally known as the 'PHI cases'[8], it is increasingly being argued that to dismiss (even with lawful notice) where that has the effect of depriving the employee of the full benefit of the sick pay that, after all, the employer has *promised*, may be a simple breach of contract giving rise to an action for damages by the employee. Thus, a common law action (or, more realistically perhaps, the timely threat of it) may actually give more protection. In the light of an example such as this, those advising an employee may well wish to indulge in a certain amount of contractual lateral thinking as well as consulting the wording of the statute, and those advising an employer may wish to make doubly sure that contractual obligations are being fully discharged, as well as fair industrial relations procedures being observed.

1 A very similar approach can be seen in the modern case law on the Health and Safety at Work Act 1974. See in particular the extremely important decision of the House of Lords in *R v Associated Octel* [1997] IRLR 123, [1996] 4 All ER 846, HL imposing on employers (as a matter of policy, based on s 3 of the Act) widespread liability for the acts and omissions of their independent contractors, such as would *not* arise at common law under the doctrine of vicarious liability. The latter was not allowed to obscure the interpretation and application of the Act.

2 [1997] ICR 254, [1997] IRLR 168, CA. Work-related socialising was held to be capable of being in the course of employment in *Chief Constable of Lincolnshire Police v Stubbs* [1999] ICR 547, [1998] IRLR 81, EAT and *Sidhu v Areospace Composite Technology Ltd* [1999] IRLR 683, EAT. A similarly broad approach can be seen in *Burton v De Vere Hotels* [1996] IRLR 596, EAT (the 'Bernard Manning case') which shows that an employer can also be liable for the acts of third parties, against its own employees, if there is sufficient de facto 'control' over those acts; again, it is doubtful if there would be common law liability in such circumstances.

3 There have since been major developments in the law on vicarious liability in tort in the House of Lords decision in *Lister v Hesley Hall Ltd* [2001] UKHL 22, [2001] 2 All ER 769, [2001] IRLR 472 (particularly in relation to deliberate torts by an employee), moving away from the traditional tests based on employer authorisation, towards a broader test of a close connection with what the employee was employed to do. This moves closer to the discrimination test, but may still be narrower, in the sense of still looking at work/job content, not just hours and place of work; see [2001] NLJ 1154 and 1243.

4 *MHC Consulting Services Ltd v Tansell* [2000] ICR 789, sub nom *Abbey Life Assurance Co Ltd v Tansell* [2000] IRLR 387, CA.

5 *Harrods Ltd v Remick* [1998] ICR 156, [1997] IRLR 583, CA; *C J O'Shea Construction Ltd v Bassi* [1998] ICR 1130, EAT.

6 *Clark v Novacold Ltd* [1999] ICR 951, [1999] IRLR 318, CA.

7 *Smiths Industries Aerospace and Defence Systems Ltd v Brookes* [1986] IRLR 434, EAT. Note that if any question arose as to whether the sickness constituted a disability, other factors might now arise, see previous note.

8 Permanent health insurance. See para 4.29, below.

3   The interaction between statutory claims and the common law

2.5   The ERA 1996, the second major consolidation of individual employment law, gives rise to the most important interaction between the statutory rights contained in it and the common law lying behind those statutory rights, and does so indirectly, in the definition provisions in s 230. This defines an 'employee' (to whom most of the statutory rights belong[1]) as 'an individual who has entered into or works under (or, where the employment has ceased, worked under) a contract of employment', which is then simply defined as 'a contract of service or apprenticeship, whether express or implied, and (if it is express) whether oral or in writing'. There is thus *no* statutory definition of a contract of employment, even though it is the raft on which most of the statutory rights float. Instead, the definition is left to the common law, so that if anything goes wrong with the contract (in particular, by a finding that the contract was illegal or was frustrated by events) the statutory rights crash along with the purely contractual rights. Thus, even in the case of the assertion of an apparently purely statutory right before a purely statutory employment tribunal, a preliminary point may arise as to whether the applicant was an 'employee' under what the common law would accept as a contract of employment[2]. One side point in relation to this is that in such a case what the tribunal (or court) has to decide is whether the applicant comes within the common law concept of an 'employee'; if it decides that he or she does not do so, it does not have to go further and decide what the applicant *was*. In some cases, that can remain uncertain – a clear and uncontrovertible distinction between a wage-slave employee and a thrusting entreprenerial independent contractor may be too much to hope for, and as the law currently stands there is a distinct possibility of a black hole somewhere between the two. For example, in *Clark v Oxfordshire Health Authority*[3] it was held that a 'bank' nurse, being called on to work when necessary, was not the health authority's employee and so unable to claim unfair dismissal; quite what she *was* is an interesting question particularly as her pay had throughout been subject to PAYE, NI contributions and even to contributions to the NHS superannuation scheme. Likewise, in the leading House of Lords case of *Carmichael v National Power plc*[4] it was held that there was no single, overall contract of employment in the case of power station guides retained on a 'casual, as required' basis, due to lack of necessary, residual mutuality of obligations; what remains unclear from the decision is what their status was when actually working – was there an individual contract of employment each time they worked[5], or were they self-employed at all times, despite having been on the PAYE payroll? While it is true that the employment and tax positions do not in law have to be consistent (even though the tests appear to be similar, and precedents are sometimes used interchangeably), the inconsistency in cases like this is disturbing, with the individual being required to contribute to the public purse as an 'employee', but on termination having none of an employee's rights.

This dependence of statutory rights on a common law contractual basis has been carried through into some, though not the majority, of the recent legislation; in particular, it is found in the Maternity and Parental Leave Regulations 1999[6] and the Transnational Information and Consultation of Employees Regulations 1999[7]. Any liberalisation of the common law definition is now unlikely in the light of the regressive decision in *Carmichael* (above), and there is probably little mileage in trying to draw a distinction between the technical existence of an employment contract and the realities of an employment *relationship* (with rights attaching to the latter)[8], even though such a distinction appears to be drawn in some EC Directives[9], and is known to the Law of Tort in the 'borrowed servant' cases, where the lender employer remains the long-term employer under the contract of employment but the borrower employer may be vicariously liable for the negligence of the employee in the course of employment[10].

1 The principal exception is the right not to have unlawful deductions from wages, contrary to Part II of the Act; this originated in the Wages Act 1986, which used the wider definition of 'worker', which is continued in the ERA 1996 consolidation. After conflicting case law, it was held that there is no rule of public policy preventing a controlling director of a one-man company from being an 'employee' for the purposes of making an insolvency claim against the Secretary of State: *Secretary of State for Trade and Industry v Bottrill* [1999] IRLR 326, CA.

2 For a now-classic argument that employment law should cut loose from this contractual basis and produce its own, sui generis, definitions and bases, see Hepple 'Restructuring employment rights' [1986] 15 ILJ 69.

3 [1998] IRLR 125, CA.

4 [2000] IRLR 43, [1999] 4 All ER 897, HL.

5 As, for example, in *Hellyer Bros Ltd v McLeod* [1987] ICR 526, [1987] IRLR 232, CA.

6 SI 1999/3312; see the definitions in reg 2.

7 SI 1999/3323.

8 An attempt to draw such a distinction failed in a TUPE case where a teacher was faced with transfer (in fact, non-transfer!) to a newly established school with new governors, but still in a contractual relationship with the local authority; he was redundant and could not demand to be transfered under the Regulations to the new school, since there was no contract with the respective governors (even if there was an employment 'relationship') and the Regulations can only bite on such a contractual relationship: *Askew v Governing Body of Clifton Middle School* [1999] IRLR 708, CA. See also *Symbian Ltd v Christensen* [2001] IRLR 77, CA, in the context of a garden leave clause.

9 The Parental Leave Directive 96/34/EC (the Framework Agreement, cl 1(2)), Part Time Worker Directive 97/81/EC (the Framework Agreement, cl 2(1)) and the Fixed-Term Worker Directive 99/70/EC (cl 2(1) of the Framework Agreement, cl 2(1)) apply to workers who have an employment contract *or employment relationship*.

10 *Mersey Docks and Harbour Board v Coggins and Griffiths (Liverpool) Ltd* [1947] AC 1, [1946] 2 All ER 345, HL. In such cases the traditional test of 'control' is likely to be more important than in ordinary cases involving longer-term employment rights: *Sime v Sutcliffe Catering Scotland Ltd* [1990] IRLR 228, Ct of Sess (OH). Note however that the long-term employer may still have health and safety obligations *to* the employee, even while the latter is lent to another undertaking: *Morris v Breaveglen Ltd* [1993] ICR 766, [1993] IRLR 350, CA.

2.6   Three further areas of interaction are worth mentioning. The first is that, in cases of alleged gross misconduct, anything incorporated into the contract and/or disciplinary procedure identifying misconduct which may merit instant dismissal may well be important *evidence* in an unfair dismissal action; it is, however, no more than that and certainly cannot prevent a tribunal from going on to determine whether the employer behaved reasonably in *all* the circumstances[1]. Certain offences will almost always be dismissible, such as theft or violence[2], but an employer may wish to state expressly other forms of conduct which are wholly intolerable in the particular circumstances of that undertaking (eg breaches of hygiene requirements in a food processing firm). Employers sometimes worry that by setting out such grounds they are fettering their discretion, but it is fairly clear that (unless express wording is used excluding any other heads of misconduct) the view will be taken that all that the employer has done is to particularise certain important headings, while leaving it open to regard other, unforeseen, major transgressions as gross misconduct[3].

1 *Laws Stores Ltd v Oliphant* [1978] IRLR 251, EAT.

2 For a standard form of disciplinary procedure, see the ACAS handbook 'Discipline at Work' Appendix 3.

3 *Distillers Co (Bottling Service) Ltd v Gardner* [1982] IRLR 47, EAT; *Macari v Celtic Football &*
   Athletic Co Ltd [1999] IRLR 787, Ct of Sess. This point may be strengthened by wording such as
   'the employee is *liable* to instant dismissal' and 'offences warranting instant dismissal *include...*'

2.7   The second area is the statutory doctrine of constructive dismissal which
arises where (for unfair dismissal and redundancy purposes) the employee
terminates the employment by leaving, but argues that he or she was 'entitled to
terminate it without notice by reason of the employer's conduct'[1]. After some
initial uncertainty when the modern legislation was first introduced, the Court of
Appeal held in *Western Excavating (ECC) Ltd v Sharp*[2] that the basis of
interpretation of the crucial word 'entitled' is contractual, so that the employee
must show that the 'employer's conduct' in question was not just generally
unreasonable, but in law constituted a fundamental breach going to the root of
the contract. Thus, the exact *terms* of the contract of employment may be of great
importance in such a statutory claim, because the employer must be shown to
have been in definable breach of one or more of them. When *Western Excavating*
was first decided, it seemed likely to restrict severely the ambit of constructive
dismissal, essentially to cases where there had been some concrete breach of an
express term (eg by non-payment of wages), whereas one of the policy
objectives of having such a concept was arguably to prevent an employer from
goading the unwanted employee into resigning by a sustained campaign of
denigration or harassment (but with no major events capable in themselves of
being a definable breach of contract). A wide ambit was, however, preserved by
the sustained process (ever since) of the implication of wide-ranging *implied*
terms into all contracts of employment, such as to safeguard health and safety, to
provide a reasonably suitable working enviroment, to deal properly with
grievances and to treat the employee with trust and respect (see Chapter 4) –
breach of *these* can now support constructive dismissal. The term of trust and
respect has been the most important and has now received the stamp of approval
by the House of Lords[3]. In what is still one of the principal cases on the term[4],
Browne-Wilkinson P expressly accepted that the purpose of its development was
to counter the otherwise-restrictive effects of *Western Excavating*. Arguably this
has been one of the most productive areas of cross-fertilisation of common law
and statute in our employment law, seen mainly in the law of unfair dismissal,
but also more recently in moves towards the use of the idea of constructive
dismissal itself in common law actions for wrongful dismissal.

1 ERA, ss 95(1)(c) (unfair dismissal) and 136(1)(c) (redundancy payments).
2 [1978] ICR 221, [1978] IRLR 27, CA.
3 *Malik v BCCI SA* [1997] ICR 606, [1997] IRLR 462, HL.
4 *Woods v WM Car Services (Peterborough) Ltd* [1981] ICR 666, [1981] IRLR 347, EAT (upheld by
   the Court of Appeal). The EAT added that any breach of this implied term will constitute repudiation
   by the employer because it will go to the root of the contract, an approach reaffirmed in *Morrow v
   Safeway Stores* [2002] IRLR 9, EAT.

2.8   The third area of interaction is in effect in reverse, ie an effect of the
existence of the statutory rights on the development of the common law and
contractual rights. In *Johnson v Unisys Ltd*[1] the House of Lords had to consider
the soundness of an apparently large extention of common law damages into
areas of 'stigma' and 'manner of dismissal' by one of their own previous
decisions[2] which was being widely interpreted and relied upon. In holding that
stigma damages were not available on termination of employment, that the old
rule against damages for manner of dismissal remained good and that their
previous decision was confined to breaches of contract during employment, they
gave as a principal reason that it is the statutory action for unfair dismissal that

13

Parliament intended to be the vehicle for compensating employees on termination for such matters as 'manner of dismissal'[3], and that (crucially) the common law on contractual damages was not to be developed so as to outflank that statutory action (with the limitations placed on it by Parliament, particularly the qualifying period and the cap on the compensatory award). In the light of the discussion in the previous paragraph (the interaction between the implied term of trust and respect and the statutory action for constructive dismissal), *Johnson* cannot be seen as preventing any future such interaction, which has been so vital in the past. What it perhaps does do is to point out that somewhere there will be the proverbial line in the sand beyond which it can be contended that an argued-for development in the common law would not just develop and enrich a statutory action, but would instead negate or frustrate it, at which point the judges will feel obliged to reject it on that basis, as contrary to Parliamentary intent. Such a line in the sand could of course be anything but clear as to its location, and be hard fought over.

1   [2001] UKHL 13, [2001] ICR 480, [2001] IRLR 279.
2   *Malik v BCCI SA* [1997] ICR 606, [1997] IRLR 462, HL.
3   This was, to put it mildly, news to most employment lawyers. 'Manner' damages had always been ruled out as such by the leading authority of *Norton Tool Co Ltd v Tewson* [1972] ICR 501, [1972] IRLR 86, NIRC, but Lord Hoffman specifically said that that case was too narrow on the point, and that unfair dismissal is capable of compensating for 'distress, humiliation, damages to reputation in the community or to family life'. Further developments on this potentially radical departure are awaited with interest at the time of writing.

4   Statutory overlay of the common law

2.9   Given the long voluntarist approach to British industrial relations, the substance of contracts of employment (in the sense of the levels of pay and other terms and conditions set in them) has rarely been subject to statutory intervention, even in times of attempts by various governments to achieve incomes policies or pay restraint. Traditionally, the only such intervention was through Wages Councils, set up to establish minimum wages in a minority of industries (originally the 'sweated trades'), and certain devices to seek to require the payment of 'fair wages' in government contracts, or to attack pockets of low pay in an industry by requiring the payment of the 'going rate' for the job. There was certainly no question of a national minimum wage, or active wage-fixing by statute. However, even this minimal intervention was viewed as unacceptable by the Conservative government of Mrs Thatcher, to whom the only fair wage or going rate was that set by a free market in labour. The relevant provisions were therefore removed[1], leaving the Agricultural Wages Board as the only example of statutory intervention in wage fixing[2].

1   Employment Protection Act 1975, Sch 11 (enforcing the going rate within an industry) was repealed in 1980. The Fair Wages Resolution (applying to government contracts) was rescinded in 1982. Wages Councils were limited in 1986 and finally abolished in 1993.
2   This survived because technically it was not a Wages Council, having been set up under separate legislation. It is currently under review, partly because it arguably sits oddly alongside the National Minimum Wage 1998.

2.10   Statutory intervention in Britain, such as it has been, has largely taken a different form, namely placing certain requirements on the form of contracts of employment and imposing certain minimum standards. Occasionally, the contract has been the vehicle for imposing rules of social policy. Not surprisingly, however, this form of intervention was relatively late into the field. For much of the twentieth century, it was limited to the Truck Acts 1831–1940 (requiring payment in current coin of the realm and placing restrictions on deductions from wages). The Contracts of Employment Act 1963 was the first serious change, for the first time requiring a written statement of the major terms of employment (the 'section one statement'), fixing minimum periods of notice based upon length of service (one week's notice per year of employment, up to a maximum of twelve years) and laying down statutory rules on continunity of employment[1]. These provisions are still in force largely in their original format, though now contained in the ERA 1996[2]. To these have been added the following:

- statutory rules on an employee's rights during notice[3];
- updated rules on deduction from wages, replacing the Truck Acts legislation[4];
- a statutory 'equality clause' requiring the maintenance of equal pay and conditions between the sexes[5];
- a power for the Central Arbitration Committee to include better terms and conditions as a penalty on an employer for not divulging to a union certain bargaining information[6];
- special employment protection measures for shop workers and betting workers not wishing to work on Sundays[7];
- a general ban on any clause in a contract which purports to exclude or limit the operation of the ERA 1996 or to preclude a person from bringing proceedings under it to tribunal[8].

To these can be added the proposal in the Employment Bill (before Parliament at the time of writing) to deem the basic 'statutory procedures' for dismissal and grievances to be incorporated into all contracts of employment, with significant penalties on employers *or employees* failing or refusing to go through these procedures.

In addition, it goes without saying that if anything in a contract has an unlawful discriminatory effect, it can be challanged under the relevant discrimination Act, and indeed one could see the Transfer of Undertakings (Protection of Employment) Regulations[9] as the high point of statutory overlay, in their own highly specialised context, given that their whole rationale is to produce results contrary to those that would be reached under ordinary contract law (see para 2.1, note 4, above).

What all of these have in common is that they have little or nothing in common. Apart from the original 1963 Act (together with the statutory rights during notice) there has been little attempt at systematic statutory coverage of contracts of employment. One simple example of this is that if a lawyer is asked 'what is the position on holiday pay/Bank holidays/payment during sickness/pension rights?', the answer has almost always been that there is 'no law' on such matters – they are left entirely to coverage (express, implied or nil) in the individual contract, as a matter of agreement.

In the last two years, we have however seen several further examples of statutory intervention into freedom of contract, either directly (by provisions actually governing or limiting certain terms) or indirectly (by enacting a statutory right which, though operating independently, does act in an area traditionally left to contract, the prime example being the statutory right to minimum paid holidays).

1   Continuity rules have always been essential to protect employees reliant on continuous employment for qualification for or quantification of various rights. However, the rules are relatively technical and have no common law or equitable equivalent; thus, the EAT have reminded us that if the employer can organise its contractual arrangements in such a way as to fall outside the statutory rules, there is nothing to prevent it and continuity may well be broken: *Booth v United States of America* [1999] IRLR 16, EAT.
2   Written statements are in ss 1–7; minimum notice is in s 86; the continuity rules are in ss 210–219.
3   ERA 1996, ss 87–91.
4   ERA 1996, ss 13–27.
5   Equal Pay Act 1970, s 1.
6   Trade Union and Labour Relations (Consolidation) Act 1992, s 185. Note that this device was not adopted in the new laws on statutory recognition, enacted in ERA 1999.
7   ERA 1996, ss 36–43.
8   ERA 1996, s 203.
9   'TUPE' – SI 1981/1794.

(a)   The national minimum wage

2.11   The first and most obvious example comes from the enactment of a national minimum wage, one of the most distinctive contributions to employment law of the Labour government. Where the worker qualifies, they must be remunerated by their employer 'at a rate which is not less than the national minimum wage'[1]. If they are paid less, they are declared to be entitled *under their contract* to be paid the shortfall[2]. Given this formulation, there was no need for the Act to go further and provide a recovery procedure because the worker can simply sue for breach of contract in the ordinary courts or (under the ERA 1996, Part II) in an employment tribunal. What the Act does add to this is an enforcement power for an National Minimum Wage officer to require payment by an enforcement notice, backed by a power to sue on the worker's behalf on the event of non-compliance with a notice, though again the basis of such an action remains contractual.

1   National Minimum Wage Act 1998, s 1(1). Any provision in any agreement purporting to restrict this right is void: s 49. An irony here is that the legislation uses the individual contract as the vehicle for enforcing the minimum wage, when it is the contract itself which has failed to provide a reasonable wage.
2   National Minimum Wage Act 1998, s 17.

(b)   Working time legislation

2.12   Secondly, the Working Time Regulations 1998 enact four principal rights pursuant to the Working Time Directive 93/104/EC, relating to a 48 hour maximum average working week, limitations on night working, rest breaks and paid annual holidays; again, any attempt to contract out of these minimum protections is declared to be void[1]. There are, of course, very major 'derogations' whereby much the same effect can be achieved, though these tend to be by collective means (ie through a collective agreement or workforce agreement[2]), with the exception of the maximum working week provisions which can be disapplied quite simply by the worker's agreement in writing[3] (which may or may not be in the contract itself), a particularly weak form of protection which was weakened further at the end of 1999 by amending Regulations which dropped the detailed record-keeping requirement on the employer, which had originally been introduced as a necessary quid pro quo where such an opt-out was in operation. The provisions on rest breaks and minimum paid holidays are enforceable by an individual worker by an action before a tribunal, not based on contract, but they obviously affect terms and conditions by setting a floor. The case of paid annual holidays is an interesting example. The right (increased to four weeks from November 1999) may seem relatively unimportant in many employments which already comply with or exceed it (and the usual provision is enacted in the Regulations that any contractual holiday payments go towards discharging the statutory obligation and vice versa), but in two ways it could have a significant effect – (i) even where a contractual right already exists to at least four weeks, the Regulations provide that (in relation to the minimum four weeks) it is not now lawful for the parties to agree either to carry some of it over into the next holiday year or for the employer to 'buy out' any of that entitlement, so that in effect the employer is under an obligation to ensure that the minimum period is actually taken; (ii) the Regulations will have an impact where traditionally there was no holiday entitlement, especially in the myriad forms of 'casual work', especially since the original 13 week qualifying period was ruled by the ECJ to be contrary to the Directive[4] and was removed by amending Regulations, being replaced by a simple month-by-month accrual system at the beginning of employment[5]. The provisions on the 48 hour maximum and night working are stated by the Regulations to be amenable only to administrative enforcement by the Health and Safety Executive, thus emphasising the hybrid nature of these provisions, involving both employment law and health and safety law (the latter being, of course, the basis on which the Directive was passed by majority vote, against the UK's will). However, in a radical judgment in *Barber v RJB Mining UK Ltd*[6] Gage J held that the primary obligation on an employer in regulation 4(1) not to require a worker to work more than the statutory 48 hours (where that applies) is impliedly *contractual*, thus grafting on a common law breach of contract action at the suit of the worker, in addition to administrative enforcement, with the result that an employer cannot simply force the worker to exceed the limit, on the assumption that it cannot be sued, and on the basis that it can take upon itself the risk of prosecution. This novel contractual cross-over (which arguably applies also to the night work provisions) is fascinating, and may have wider implications as we shall see in Chapter 4.

1   Working Time Regulations 1998, SI 1998/1833, reg 35.
2   The Regulations also include the concept of a 'relevant agreement' which means a workforce agreement, a collective agreement forming part of the worker's contract *or* 'any other agreement in writing which is legally enforceable as between the worker and the employer' (reg 2(1)); the latter could simply mean a term in the contract of employment. However, relevant agreements tend not to be used to establish derogations as such, but rather to allow the parties to reach their own definitions on matters such as what constitutes working time and night time.
3   Working Time Regulations 1998, SI 1998/1833, reg 5, amended by the Working Time Regulations 1999, SI 1999/3372.
4   *R v Secretary of State for Trade and Industry, ex p BECTU* C-173/99 [2001] IRLR 559, ECJ.
5   Working Time (Amendment) Regulations 2001, SI 2001/3256, repealing the qualifying period in reg 13 of the 1998 Regulations and adding reg 15A ('Leave during the first year of employment').
6   [1999] ICR 679, [1999] IRLR 308, QBD. One result of the decision is that an employee being required to work beyond the statutory maximum could work out when, in the 17 week averaging period, he or she had *averaged* 48 hours per week and then lawfully stop working until the next period started.

(c)   Maternity and parental rights

2.13   A third example is to be found in the Maternity and Parental Leave etc Regulations 1999 which considerably simplified and rationalised the previous chaotic provisions on maternity and introduced the new EU-required right to parental leave[1]. When what is now called 'ordinary maternity leave' was introduced by the Trade Union Reform and Employment Rights Act 1993 (pursuant to the Pregnant Workers Directive 92/85/EEC) it operated on a basis of statutory continuation of the contract of employment (except for the purposes of remuneration) but serious problems remained in relation to the major, longstanding 'right to return' (up to 29 weeks after childbirth) which had always operated as a purely statutory scheme and had never explained what was to happen to the contract during absence. If the scheme worked as it should, that question was not relevant because of the special statutory rules allowing return and safeguarding continuity. However, the scheme was extremely complex and if an employee failed to comply, even on technical grounds, with the notification requirements she lost the right to return altogether. Where this happened, we saw consistent arguments that the courts should explore a contractual alternative, keeping the contract alive (often on parlous evidence, such as continued correspondence between the parties) so that there would be a common law right to resume employment. Sometimes such arguments succeeded and sometimes they failed[2], but the point is that they produced extreme complication and uncertainty, especially when allied to the classic problem of the employee who is ill at the due date of return. The latter point was subject to radical judicial revision (strongly in the employee's favour) shortly before the statutory changes[3], which involved statements by the Court of Appeal to the effect that the contract was 'suspended' during leave, being revived by the giving of the proper notices, followed by an equally radical reaction by the House of Lords (after the statutory charges, and so of little practical importance) denying the validity of any such analysis[4]. Hopefully such sophistry, the employment law equivalent of counting the number of angels that can dance on the head of a pin (fascinating but ultimately unfruitful), should now be a thing of the past because in the ERA 1999 and Regulations the government took an exceptionally 'first principles' approach. Not only is the draconian penalty of total loss of rights for failure to adopt the right procedure removed, but the approach of contractual continuation is adopted for *both* ordinary and 'additional' maternity leave (the old right to return); the wording adopted is significant, for there is now no reference to 'returning', but instead a simple provision in relation to both leaves that an employee who satisfies the relevant conditions 'may be absent from work'. Thus the complex provisions enacting a statutory right to return are no longer necessary, nor are special rules on an employee still ill at the end of the leave period, because now they are simply deemed to be still in employment but subject to the employer's normal sickness absence procedures. What the Act and Regulations do is to lay down what elements of the contract remain in being during the relevant leave – in the case of ordinary leave this continues to be the whole of the contract except any terms and conditions about remuneration[5] and in the case of additional leave it is (on the employer's part) the terms relating to trust and confidence, notice, redundancy compensation, and disciplinary and grievance procedures, and (on the employee's part) the terms relating to good faith, notice, disclosure of confidential information, acceptance of gifts or benefits and participation in any other business[6]. Terms and conditions on resumption of work are to be no less favourable than if she had not been absent, though with the distinction that during ordinary leave seniority and accruing rights continue to accrue[7] but during additional leave such matters are effectively frozen, reviving on resumption of work[8]. Thus, the previous controversies over contractual status of an employee on maternity leave should now be dead, and the new rules should be interpreted and applied de novo. Of course, many employments will continue to be covered by contractual maternity leave/pay schemes which, provided no less generous than the statutory scheme, will continue to take precedence; the Regulations repeat the pre-existing provision that where there is a statutory and a contractual right (in relation to ordinary or additional maternity leave or parental leave) the employee may 'take advantage of whichever right is, in any particular respect, the more favourable'[9].

1   The necessary changes were provided for in the Employment Relations Act 1999, Sch 4, Part 1. By contrast, the provision on time off for dependants (also required by the Parental Leave Directive 96/34/EC) was, in its eventual form, put into primary legislation (ERA 1996, ss 57A, 57B as inserted) and does not operate on contractual principles at all. Further major developments in the whole area of family-friendly policies are to be expected during the currency of this book, in the light of the Green Paper 'Work and Parents' (Cm 5005) and vires powers for further reforming regulations in the Employment Bill before Parliament at the time of writing.

2   See, eg, *Lewis Woolf Griptight Ltd v Corfield* [1997] IRLR 432, EAT adopting the contractual analysis and *McPherson v Drumpark House* [1997] IRLR 277, EAT and *Halfpenny v IGE Medical Supplies Ltd* [1998] IRLR 10, EAT strongly doubting it.

3   *Crees v Royal London Mutual Insurance Ltd* [1998] ICR 848, [1998] IRLR 245, CA.

4   *Halfpenny v IGE Medical Supplies Ltd* [2001] ICR 73, [2001] IRLR 96, HL.

5   ERA 1996, s 71(4),(5), as substituted by the ERA 1999.

6   Maternity and Parental Leave Regulations 1999, SI 1999/3312, reg 17. This regime also applies to parental leave.

7   ERA 1996, s 71(7).

8   Maternity and Parental Leave Regulations 1999, SI 1999/3312, reg 18. Again, the same provisions apply to parental leave. This approach of allowing accruing rights during ordinary leave (as required by the Pregnant Workers Directive 92/85/EEC) but not during additional leave was held by the ECJ (in the context of a contractual maternity scheme widely used in the public sector) *not* to infringe EC law: *Boyle v Equal Opportunities Commission* C-411/96 [1999] ICR 360, [1999] IRLR 717.

9   Maternity and Parental Leave Regulations 1999, SI 1999/3312, reg 21. In re-enacting the exact wording of this longstanding provision, the effect is presumably to continue in effect the difficult decision in *Bovey v Board of Governors of the Hospital for Sick Children* [1978] ICR 934, [1978] IRLR 241, EAT, to the effect that there must be limits on the extent to which the employee may pick-and-mix, in spite of the phrase 'in any particular respect'.

(d)   Whistleblowing

2.14   A fourth example is a provision inserted into the ERA 1996 by the Public Interest Disclosure Act 1998. Better known as the 'Whistleblowers Act', the latter was initially a private member's Bill which was adopted by the government; it gives important new statutory protection to employees making 'protected disclosures' in a manner set out in the legislation. As part of this protection it is provided that any agreement is 'void in so far as it purports to preclude a worker from making a protected disclosure'[1]. This is aimed, inter alia, at banning the sort of 'gagging clause' in a contract of employment that gave rise to demands for the legislation in the first place. This could be an important statutory restriction on the use of confidentiality clauses in contracts, especially as early case law has given a wide interpretation to the Act's provisions generally[2].

1   ERA 1996, s 43J, added by the Public Interest Disclosure Act 1998, s 1.

2   See in particular *Parkins v Sodexho Ltd* [2002] IRLR 109, EAT where it was held that a complaint about a breach of the applicant's contract of employment could constitute a complaint of a failure 'to comply with any legal obligation' and hence a 'protected disclosure' under the legislation.

(e)   Part-time working

2.15   A fifth example, placing restrictions on the use of a whole class of contracts (unusual in UK law), is the law required in order to comply with the Part Time Workers Directive 97/81/EC. This took the form of a 'framework' Directive, negotiated by the EU social partners; this provenance had the effect of making parts of it vague and aspirational. The first half is a relatively precise requirement of laws to stop discrimination against part-timers, but the second half is far more nebulous, seeking to make the social partners within the member state take practical measures to increase the status of part-time work within an

19

organisation, at all levels, in an attempt to change a prevalent attitude that part-timers are only peripherals, not part of the core staff. Needless to say, the form of this half of the Directive (whatever its merits) was bound to lead to problems of implementation in a member state such as the UK with a literally-minded legal system.

The Part-time Workers (Prevention of Less Favourable Treatment) Regulations 2000 enact the first, legally precise, half of the Directive. The first point to note is that, in a change from the original draft Regulations, they apply to 'workers', not just to 'employees' (see head (5) below). Such a worker (simply defined as one who is not a full time worker, having regard to the custom and practice of that employer[1]) has a right not to be treated by his employer less favourably than the employer treats a comparable full-time worker[2], as regards the terms of his contract or by being subjected to any other detriment by any act, or deliberate failure to act, of his employer[3]. A *pro rata temporis* principle may be applied[4] and the question of overtime is specifically addressed[5] but apart from these provisions any discrimination in terms of employment on the basis of being part-time (such as, obviously, the old practice of having a 'part-timer's rate' per hour or per piece) is unlawful, unless it can be objectively justified[6]. A worker may present a complaint of unlawful discrimination to an employment tribunal which, if it finds the complaint well founded, may make a declaration as to the worker's rights, order a payment of compensation (of a just and equitable amount, having regard to the infringement of the rights and loss attributable to it, including expenses reasonably incurred and loss of any benefit which the worker may reasonably have expected but for the infringement), and/or recommended action to be taken by the employer to obviate or reduce the adverse effects of the infringement[7]. What effect is all of this likely to have on contract terms? In practice, most reputable employers have known for years that you do not treat part-timers on anything less than a pro rata basis, quite simply because of the possibility of a challenge on the basis of indirect sex discrimination. To that extent, the Regulations in many cases will simply be confirming existing positions and best practice. However, they will give a further weapon against certain uninformed employers who have continued with age-old practices of treating part-timers less than pro rata *and* in doing so will provide a *simpler* action to a tribunal (actual or, probably more importantly, threatened) directly under the Regulations themselves, rather than going through the hoops of a sex discrimination action.

It is, however, when one turns to the second, aspirational part of the Directive that the potential impact becomes more difficult to assess in this country. How is it to be implemented? The ERA 1999 gave powers to produce a Code of Practice on part-time work, but the government soon announced that that is not to be done, at least in the near future. Instead, the DTI produced a non-statutory document 'Part-time work: the law and best practice'. The first half of this gives guidance on the Regulations. It is the second half that is meant to enact the second half of the Directive, on improving the lot generally of part-timers. Leaving aside any question whether, if ever challenged, this format would be sufficient to constitute proper implementation of the Directive, the simple point here is that the advice given as to best practice is in wide terms. Under headings such as 'widening access to part-time work', 'recruitment', 'making a wider range of jobs available part-time', 'jobsharing', 'requests to increase or decrease hours' and 'other measures to facilitate part-time working', this advice goes well beyond purely statutory rights or obligations and tends to view part-time working as an inherent part of modern ideas on flexible working, distinctly abutting on to government policies on family-friendly policies. Treating part-timers as valued, central employees (at all levels of the organisation) can be seen in issues such as auditing jobs to be advertised to see if they could be offered on a part-time or jobsharing basis (even if that has never been done before) and making training available to part-timers (generally, but also to put them into the starting blocks for any full-time work becoming available). Certain HR ideas of 'core' and 'peripheral' staff hardly feature here.

What might be the effect of this best practice guidance? To a black letter lawyer, it may appear little more than pious *excreta tauri*, admittedly well-intentioned, but not law. However, amid the shifting sands of modern employment law that may be too hasty a dismissal of its importance. A little lateral thinking may show significant possible effects for employers. Could the guidance constitute at least *evidence* in some other context or claim? Perhaps the most pressing issue covered by the guidance is whether a full-time employee should be allowed to go part-time; the obvious example is whether a full-time worker should be allowed to return from maternity leave on a part-time basis. Hitherto there has been no legal right to do so, *but* there have been cases where the worker, faced with an outright refusal for no articulated reason, has claimed that this constitued indirect sex discrimination[8]. Alternatively, what about an employee consistently turned down in a manner making her position untenable; could she leave and claim constructive dismissal? In either of these cases, the best practice guidance on taking seriously requests to change to part-time working could be prime evidence for the complainant, thus achieving legal significance, even though still not constituting a legal right. In particular, it could be evidence against a defence of justification in an indirect sex discrimination case or of manifestly unreasonable behaviour destroying trust and respect by the employer in a constructive dismissal case. In the specific context of parental rights and family friendly policies, the Employment Bill 2002 will enact a new statutory right for a parent of a child under 6 (18 if disabled) to request a change in hours of work, time when work is to be done or place of work, and not to be refused except on enumerated grounds[9]; however, even in advance of that employment lawyers may already have felt obliged to advise employer clients that, although there was currently no right to it, an employer who refused *for no good reason* might be at risk legally in some other way. To put it simply, in an area covered by the guidance (requests for jobsharing being another example) a straightforward 'No' may be becoming dangerous; what the prudent employer needs to be able to say is 'No, because...', thus laying out in advance the sort of justification that is now arguably becoming necessary for legal safety. Indeed, the guidance itself sets out factors which the employer may want to take into account when faced with such a request. Bringing this back to the theme of this part of this chapter, what this speculation may show is the beginnings of an element of overlay of the common law not just by statute, but by non-statutory 'best practice' guidance. In such an area, there would still be no contractual right to what the employee requests, but the employer's response may be conditioned by extrinsic consider-ations of such best practice, which would thus become the major determinative factor, rather than strict contractual rights. The more we see relatively vaguely-drafted framework Directives being produced in the future, only really amenable to transposition in this country in this guidance format, the more prevalent this factor may become[10].

1   Part-time Workers (Prevention of Less Favourable Treatment) Regulations 2000, SI 2000/1551, reg 2(2).
2   There must be a comparison with a full-time worker under the same type of contract, employed by the same employer (note the absence here of any reference to 'associated employers'), engaging on

the same or broadly similar work, and based at the same establishment (though with a possibility of a cross-establishment comparison if there is no full-time worker at that establishment): reg 2(4). There are, however, two exceptions – where the worker has either changed to part-time working from full-time or has returned part-time after taking absence from full-time work, he or she may compare their part-time terms and conditions with their own previous full-time ones: regs 3,4.

3   Part-time Workers (Prevention of Less Favourable Treatment) Regulations 2000, SI 2000/1551, reg 5(1).

4   Regulation 5(3). Thus, obviously, a half-time worker may be paid half the wages of a full-time worker, but not one-third.

5   A part-time worker is not entitled to overtime on any hours above the part-time hours; the only entitlement in the Regulations is to overtime rates payable for hours for which a full-time worker would be entitled to them: reg 5(4).

6   Regulation 5(2). Justification is not defined, but the DTI Guidance Notes to the Regulations suggest that less favourable treatment will only be justified on objective grounds if it can be shown that it (1) is to achieve a legitimate objective, for example a genuine business objective, (2) is necessary to achieve that objective, and (3) is an appropriate way to achieve that objective. Arguably, it is difficult to see this defence applying widely, especially in basic matters such as pay rates per hour or per piece, especially given the protective intent of the directive. It may be that the objective justification defence will have more applicability in relation to the Fixed-Term Worker Directive (below), especially in the case of very short-term employments.

7   Regulation 8(1), (7)-(10). Compensation is not to include injury to feelings: reg 8(11). Mitigation and contributory fault apply: reg 8(12),(13). If an employer fails without reasonable justification to comply with such a recommendation the tribunal may award extra compensation: reg 8(14). There is a three month limitation period on a claim, subject to a discrimination-style 'just and equitable' power to extend: reg 8(2)–(5). On a complaint, it is for the employer to identify the ground for the less favourable treatment or detriment: reg 8(6).

8   This has a long pedigree, going back to *Home Office v Holmes* [1984] ICR 678, [1984] IRLR 299, EAT where it was held that there was indirect discrimination which on the facts was not justified. However, some of the impact was lessened by the subsequent decision in *Greater Glasgow Health Board v Carey* [1987] IRLR 484, EAT (on similar facts to *Holmes*) that justification had been established by the employer. There is an interesting summary of the case law on refusal of a request to work part-time in Annex E of the Green Paper Work and Parents (Cm 5005, December 2000); see also *Lockwood v Crawley Warren Group* [2001] Emp LR 322, EAT where a refusal to consider converting a job to homeworking (for a female employee experiencing problems with child care arrangements) was treated as akin to a change to part-time working, ie requiring objective justification to be shown.

9   This new right was added to the Bill as clause 47; much remains to be done by Regulations, including setting out a specific procedure to be adopted. One speculative point is whether eventually the restriction to parents will be dropped and the right given to any employee, showing that it is really part of the government's overall flexibility agenda, even though it starts out as a family friendly policy.

10   For any Trekkies amongst our readers, this may best be summed up in the phrase 'It's law, Jim, but not as we know it'.

(f)   Fixed-term contracts

2.16   Finally, mention may be made of one development in the pipeline at the time of writing, which again will place restrictions on the use of a whole class of contracts. This is the Fixed-Term Worker Directive 99/70/EC, which arguably may have more of an impact on UK employment law, which so far has not seen an impact of domestic and EC discrimination law on fixed-term contracts akin to that which has been so evident on part-time work[1]. This Directive, again the result of a framework agreement between the social partners, starts off with a general principle of non-discrimination on the basis of being a fixed-term worker unless different treatment is justified on objective grounds. In addition, however, the Directive has a second aim of establishing 'a framework to prevent abuse arising from the use of successive fixed-term employment contracts or relationships'. To that end, member states must have or introduce 'one or more of the following measures – (a) objective reasons justifying the renewal of such contracts or relationships; (b) the maximum total duration of successive fixed-term employment contracts or relationships; (c) the number of renewals of such contracts or relationships'. Clearly, the adoption of any one of these is capable of having a significant effect in an industry or sector that has traditionally used fixed-term contracts on any consecutive or renewal basis. Draft Fixed-term Employee (Prevention of Less Favourable Treatment) Regulations 2002 and consultation documents at the time of writing propose a similar regime to that in the Part-time Worker Regulations 2000 in relation to non-discrimination, namely a right not to be treated less favourably than a comparable permanent employee, subject to a defence of justification. Three significant points of detail are worth noting here – (a) these Regulations are restricted to coverage of fixed-term *employees* because (unlike the Regulations on part-timers) they were *not* extended to 'workers' in the light of the consultation exercise; (b) the Regulations adopt the Directive's definition of a fixed-term contract as covering not just time-limited contracts but also what UK law has always known (and excluded) as 'purpose' or 'task' contracts (and, significantly for the question of statutory overlay, the Regulations will also amend existing domestic legislation, for example on unfair dismissal and redundancy, to include coverage of such non-time-limited contracts); (c) in a late amendment the Regulations provide that, in determining whether a fixed-termer has been treated less favourably than a permanent employee, the employer will be able to rely on their contracts *as a whole*, thus enabling a 'package' approach (vital where a fixed-termer is in fact paid *more*, to reflect their non-eligibility for certain benefits) which is not permissible under the Part-time Worker Regulations 2000 or, indeed, under longstanding UK equal pay law where an applicant can require equality on a term-by-term basis. Even without recourse to such a package approach, it may well be that there are potentially more arguments on justification *as such* here than in the context of part-timers, particularly in relation to very short-term contracts, which are not really amenable to the inclusion of longer-term benefits available to permanent employees (eg pension rights, sickness benefits)[2]. In relation to a new law on successive fixed-term contracts, the proposal is to have a rule that any person kept on such contracts for four years or more is to be deemed to be a permanent employee, unless the employer can objectively justify keeping him or her on such contracts. This would be quite an innovation in our employment law which hitherto has not used as a remedy the deeming of one kind of contract to be another. Clearly, one crucial point here is how 'successive' contracts are to be defined, so that an employer may not use artificial gaps between contracts to defeat the Regulations. After some debate at consultation stage, the government decided not to enact some form of specific and acertainable 'linking rule' (such as that in statutory sick pay law, where two periods of illness not more than 8 weeks apart are deemed to be one), but instead proposes to adopt the ordinary continuity of employment rules in the ERA 1996[3]. While these have the advantage of flexibility and an existing anti-avoidance purpose, they do import considerable uncertainty as to what *length* of gap will be permissible, especially when applying the Delphic phrase 'temporary cessation of work'[4]. Once all these laws are in place, employers will have to audit not just the terms and conditions of those on fixed-term contracts, but also their *use* of such contracts, especially on any successive basis[5].

1 *Whiffen v Milham Ford Girls' School* [2001] EWCA Civ 385, [2001] IRLR 468 (indirectly discriminatory to make all fixed-appointment teachers redundant first, and only then apply selection criteria to the permanent staff) is a rare example.
2 Although not specifically mentioned in the Draft Regulations, cl 4(4) of the framework agreement annexed to the Directive clearly envisages the use (or continued use) of 'period-of-service qualifications' for particular conditions of employment, provided the same for fixed-term and permanent workers (or objectively justified, if different).

3 Sections 210–219; see *Smith & Wood* pp 147–159 and *Harvey* Div CI.
4 As pointed out in para 2.10, n 1, above, however, the case of *Booth v United States of America* [1999] IRLR 16, EAT shows that protection of employees is not perfect here and that a determined employer may still be able to break continuity deliberately (particularly by arguing that the work is still there, but was not given to that employee in the gap period, given that it is the work that must be temporarily ceased, not its distribution to one individual – the facts of *Booth* itself). One interesting speculation is whether, if an employer in the future pulled such a flanker under the Regulations by reliance on *Booth* it could be argued that the Directive had not been properly transcribed into the Regulations, and/or that *Booth* (even if continuing to be an authority on continuity generally) should not apply to continuity under the Regulations.
5 Given that it is also proposed to repeal the ability of an employer to get the employee to sign away redundancy rights in a fixed-term contract of two years or more (ERA 1996, s 197(3)–(5)), employment lawyers advising employer clients may increasingly have to question *why* they are still using such contracts – what do they think that they are still getting out of them? The cumulative effects of the new Regulations may mean that there is little to gain.

(g) Summary

2.17 To sum up on the question of statutory overlay, it has tended in the past to be largely piecemeal, and during the period of Conservative administrations from 1979 to 1997 the tendency was to reduce it, though with more latterly the constant threat of a pull in the opposite direction from the EU, with the previous government's opt out from the social chapter looking increasingly fragile. With the change of government in1997 and the UK's opting back into ideas of 'social Europe' that tension largely disappeared. However, it can fairly be said that the incoming (New) Labour government did not have a major agenda of consistent reforms in the employment sphere, certainly few that had featured largely in election pledges(a feature also of the 2001 election). The White Paper 'Fairness at Work' only appeared a year after the 1997 election[1] and was quite adamant that the new government was 'committed to maintaining the key elements of the employment legislation of the 1980s', and would seek to attain an inherently difficult balance between fairness to employees and flexibility and efficiency for employers. To say that the suggested reforms to individual rights were 'tinkering' would be unfair, but it can be argued that this was no agenda for a consistent and wide-ranging extension of statutory rights for employees, and there was certainly no 'big idea' behind it, with one possible exception explored below. Perhaps one could best characterise the individual rights chapter of the White Paper as aiming to redress a perceived imbalance against employees in certain areas of employment law, and to address a list of perceived abuses of the existing law. The significance of this becomes clearer when (a) the various strands are put together and (b) the increasing intervention of EC employment-related Directives is added. Thus, for example, the White Paper expressed the hope that abuse of 'nil hours contracts' (a matter of some controversy at the time) would be dealt with indirectly by a combination of new national law on the minimum wage and implementation of the EC Working Time Directive[2], rather than any more radical attempt to ban them by legislation. Thus, statutory overlay of contracts of employment has increased significantly in the term of office of the present government; while this has been step-by-step, and not as part of any grand plan (as can be seen from even a cursory glance at the table of contents of the ERA 1999), it is not 'piecemeal' in the way that previous intervention tended to be, and the overall effect is likely to be significant, requiring considerable rethinking by employers of certain employment practices, with the promise of more to come, as can be seen from the Fixed-Term Worker Directive and acute controversy (at the time of writing) over proposals for a new Agency Worker Directive.

1   Cm 3968. Contrast this with the incoming Labour government in 1974, whose first Act on to the statute book was the Trade Union and Labour Relations Act 1974, repealing the previous Conservative government's Industrial Relations Act 1971.
2   Paragraph 3. 15. By contrast, Ireland banned such contracts by statute, though the necessary drafting was long and complex.

5   Extending statutory coverage

2.18   There was one potential 'big idea' in the 'Fairness at Work' White Paper[1] but, although a regulatory power to achieve it is enacted in the ERA 1999, it is unclear at the time of writing how the government will exercise that power. The idea is to extend the coverage of standard employment rights (principally those in the ERA 1996, especially unfair dismissal) to a wider class than just those working under a contract of employment. The problem of the middle ground between an 'employee' as classically defined and an independent contractor in business on their own account is well known, and has been growing with the general increase of flexible forms of contracting, and the decline of traditional employment patterns in some areas.

The idea is not a new one, and a wider definition has existed in certain specific areas for many years. Trade union legislation uses the concept of 'worker', defined as 'an individual who works, or normally works or seeks to work (a) under a contract of employment or (b) under any other contract whereby he undertakes to do or perform personally any work or services for another party to the contract who is not a professional client of his'[2].

Discrimination legislation defines 'employment' in similarly wide terms as 'employment under a contract of service or apprenticeship or a contract personally to execute any work or labour'[3]. The provisions on unlawful deductions from wages (originally in the Wages Act 1986 and now in the ERA 1996, Part II) apply to 'workers' under a slightly extended version of the trade union law definition[4]. The Transfer of Undertakings (Protection of Employment) Regulations 1981 use the term 'employee' but define it as working 'for another person whether under a contract of service or apprenticeship or otherwise but does not include anyone who provides services under a contract for services'[5]. While these definitions contain certain differences, with the Wages Act 1986 definition arguably coming closest to reflecting the actual problem here and the Transfer of Undertakings (Protection of Employment) Regulations 1981 ('TUPE') definition perhaps being the least expansive (with its exception of *anyone* under a contract for services), the point remains that for a long time now the concept of an expanded definition has been with us, though the case law to date has been relatively scarce[6]. In addition to this, however, the issue has now become topical again because of the use of similar formulae in the present government's legislation. The Public Interest Disclosure Act 1998, operating as it does through amendments to the ERA 1996, adopts the latter's definition when it uses the term 'worker' in its protection for whistleblowers and, of greater significance, the National Minimum Wage Act 1998[7], the Working Time Regulations 1998[8] and the Part-time Worker (Prevention of Less Favourable Treatment) Regulations 2000[9] specifically adopt that 'Wages Act 1986' definition[10], word perfect, and so utilise what is argued above to be the most comprehensive wording to date. It is this point particularly that was picked up in the White Paper when suggesting legislation enabling the government to 'extend the coverage of some or all existing employment rights by regulation'.

Such a power is now given by the ERA 1999, s 23 which permits the Secretary of State by order to extend any right under that Act itself, the Trade Union and Labour Relations (Consolidation) Act 1992, the ERA 1996 or any instrument made under the European Communities Act 1972, s 2(2) to individuals of a specified description. This is an extremely wide power; on the one hand it could simply be used to include certain categories of employees currently excluded or it could be used for a major expansion of employment protection into the difficult middle ground. Unfortunately, the Parliamentary debate on the provision was not particularly illuminating on the latter, getting bogged down on the employment status of vicars (!) and on the question of specific existing exclusions; the relevant minister's principal contribution was to promise consultation on use of the power, though he did hint at one point at a possible differential approach, saying that while the government wanted to rationalise statutory coverage, it might still be appropriate for different definitions of 'worker' to be used for different purposes[11].

Thus, the section's power is capable of several quite different uses. In favour of the more radical approach of a general extension of statutory coverage to anyone providing personal service (other than by way of a profession or business), it could be argued that not only would this be in line with the government's overall fairness at work agenda, but that it is now necessary for legislation to have this effect, since the courts recently have shown that they are unlikely to carry on extending employment status, particularly since the rather regressive decision of the House of Lords in *Carmichael v National Power plc*[12], refusing to accept a 'casual, as required' power station guide as an employee, in spite of a relatively longstanding relationship and the payment of PAYE and NI contributions.

1   Paragraph 3. 18.
2   Trade Union and Labour Relations (Consolidation) Act 1992, s 296.
3   Equal Pay Act 1970, s 1(6)(a); Sex Discrimination Act 1975, s 82(1); Race Relations Act 1976, s 78(1); Disability Discrimination Act 1995, s 68(1) (though without the words 'or labour'). Note that (a) these definitions do not include the rider 'who is not a professional client of his' and (b) this legislation also contains several specific extension provisions, eg in relation to contract workers.
4   ERA, s 230(3); the extension here is to 'any other contract, whether express or implied and (if it is express) whether oral or in writing, whereby the individual undertakes to do or perform personally any work or services for another party to the contract whose status is not by virtue of the contract that of a client or customer of any profession or business undertaking carried out by the individual'. See the recovery of unpaid commission by a self employed investment consultant in *Robertson v Blackstone Franks Investment Management Ltd* [1998] IRLR 376, CA.
5   SI 1981/1794, reg 2 (1). These Regulations of course come from an EC Directive and under such Directives employment status is left to member states, not being an area for harmonisation.
6   When the matter arose recently in *Sheehan v Post Office Counters Ltd* [1999] ICR 734, EAT (sub-postmaster held not to be within the definition in the disability legislation) the court went back to *Mirror Group Newspapers Ltd v Gunning* [1986] ICR 145, [1986] IRLR 27, CA as the leading case, with its emphasis on whether personal service was the dominant purpose of the contract in question. In *Murray v Newham Citizens Advice Bureau* [2001] ICR 708, EAT an applicant for a post as a trainee, unpaid voluntary adviser with the CAB was held to come within the protection of the Disability Discrimination Act 1995. Perhaps most significantly, in *Byrne Bros (Farmwork) Ltd v Baird* [2002] IRLR 96, EAT it was held (in that sanctum sanctorum of dodgy self-employment, the building industry) that a Sch D taxed self-employed subcontractor was a 'worker' and so able to claim paid annual holidays under the Working Time Regulations.
7   Section 54. There is a clear policy objective here to have width of approach and coverage, to stop bad employers undercutting the good, and to prevent the former from hiding behind technicalities of 'employee' status.
8   Regulation 2(1).
9   Regulation 2(1).
10 See n 4, above.
11 HC SC E, 2 March 1999, cols 233–240. An example of this has turned out to be the use of 'worker' for part-timers but 'employee' for fixed-termers. Consultaion in fact began in July 2002 (URN 02/1058), but at a very preliminary and tentative level.

12 [1999] 4 All ER 897, [2000] IRLR 43, HL; see para 2.5, above and para 3.6, below. See also *Clark v Oxfordshire Health Authority* [1998] IRLR 125, CA where a PAYE and NI paying 'bank' nurse working only for one authority was held not to be an employee.

2.19   What would be the effect of such a legislative shift? At the moment, the definition of 'employee' is an exclusive one, in that if the individual cannot come within it they are excluded from employment rights depending on that status, regardless of what else they may or may not be. The wider 'worker' definition, by contrast, is basically inclusive, in that it includes the individual unless they come within a category clearly intended to be outwith it, the overall effect being potentially to encompass the difficult middle ground, including some of those who are technically self-employed but hardly at the cutting edge of venture capitalism[1]. On that point, one current buzz-phrase is worth noting. In the comprehensive DTI guidance on both the minimum wage and working time (and also in the Parliamentary debate on the ERA 1999, s 23) the point is made that the wider 'worker' definition should have the effect of including anyone providing personal service 'except the *genuinely* self employed'. This homely phrase may be as close as you can get in principle. Clearly any new such formulation would still raise major problems of definition (shifting from 'was there a contract of employment' to 'was this person genuinely self employed', prompting questions as to economic realities, whether they were running a truly independent business, or just adopting the status for tax reasons), and would be no panacea for all ills - for example, a casual worker, even with the new status, could still have problems with continuity of employment if claiming major statutory rights which have qualifying periods[2]. However, the overall inclusive effect of a new definition could well be worth these new problems, and would significantly extend the sort of statutory overlay that we saw in the previous section of this chapter. While it is true that persons in the middle ground who are currently outside the 'employee' definition may have common law contractual rights (on the assumption that there is *some* form of contract there), it may be that extension of statutory rights would in practice have the parallel effect of making employers treat their contractual rights more seriously too, in much the same way as this book argues that contractual rights and actions have come more into prominence in the case of employees in recent years. This would be particularly the case if the Part-Time Worker Directive and the Fixed-Term Worker Directive (with the possibility in the wings at the time of writing of an Agency Worker Directive) were effective in their overall aim of increasing the status of such work within an organisation, so that such workers along with others potentially enfranchised by an extended statutory definition would no longer simply be consigned to that pejorative category of 'peripherals'.

1   See particularly *Byrne Bros (Farmwork) Ltd v Baird* [2002] IRLR 96, EAT, para 2.18, n 6, above, where it was held that the building subcontractor could in no realistic sense be said to be genuinely in a business of his own.
2   *Booth v United States of America* [1999] IRLR 16, EAT (paras 2.10, n 1 and 2.16, n 4, above) is a recent reminder that continuity is a purely statutory concept, and that if the statute does not specifically prevent it the employer may still take steps to ensure that continuity is broken.

Chapter 3

The contract of employment

1 Introduction

3.1   In spite of the increasing statutory overlay, both domestic and EU-inspired, noted in the previous chapter, the corner stone of individual employment law remains the equally individual contract of employment (still occasionally referred to by the more archaic term contract of service)[1]. This has several immediate effects on the legal position and rights of the employee. The first is that the relationship is essentially a personal one. This very traditional view[2] may wear a little thin where the employer is a large corporation, and over-emphasis on it has in the past been criticised as one of the reasons for lack of development of effective remedies of reinstatement[3] or enforcement of the contract. However, it remains strong, for example in the longstanding rule that at common law (ie not taking into account the separate operation in some cases of TUPE) an employee cannot be transferred from one employer to another without his or her consent[4]. A second effect is that certain general doctrines of the law of contract will be applicable, examples being the rules on capacity, illegality, frustration and restraint of trade[5]. It may be that courts and tribunals will need to take into account the specific employment context in which these doctrines are being applied, because (being doctrines that arose primarily in the area of commercial contracts) an excessively purist (or, alternatively, unthinking) application may well produce a result that is either wildly unrealistic or manifestly unfair in terms of employment realities or practical employment relations[6]. Moreover, this point also means that employment cases are always potentially subject to a priori contract-based arguments; for example, any attempt by an employer to put into a contract an obligation on the employee to make certain payments in the case of certain defaults or transgressions might be met by arguments that it constituted an illegal penalty clause under general contract law[7]. Likewise, there has occasionally been speculation that there may be some mileage in the Unfair Contract Terms Act 1977 in the employment context, (though in general this has come to little[8]) and that there may be employment-related aspects to the Contracts (Third Party Rights) Act 1999[9]. A third effect is that rules of construction in ordinary contract law may be relevant in a dispute over the meaning of a contract of employment. In one sense this could be unfortunate if it led to an overly-strict regime of interpretation once the contract has been reduced to writing. In *Hooper v British Railways Board*[10] a sick pay term had been incorporated into contracts of employment from a collective agreement, but in wording from that agreement that was ambiguous and capable of producing a result which the employers argued they had certainly not meant; however, when

29

the matter was litigated, the Court of Appeal refused to accede to the employers' argument that the contract clause should be interpreted in the light of its origin in the relative informality of a non-legally-binding collective agreement, and held instead that normal, relatively strict canons of interpretation of written agreements were to be applied instead. Clearly, views and emphases may vary on a matter such as this and arguably Lord Hoffman's views in *Carmichael v National Power plc*[11] (at least in relation to the *existence* of a contract of employment, and arguably then in relation to its interpretation) lean more towards looking beyond the strict wording to the parties' other dealings at the time of contracting *and* to their dealings and understandings since (which had not been thought relevant by the Court of Appeal in *Hooper*). Perhaps what we are looking at is an inherently variable standard, with more scope for a purely contractual approach where the relationship is relatively formal, with the parties being expected to get the eventual drafting right (as part of the overall moves in modern employment law towards more formal contracts, often drafted with legal advice), whereas a case like *Carmichael* concerned a particularly loose and ill-defined relationship, on a much older and more traditional model, where it made more sense to look at the terms in the light of the parties' conduct.

1   One variant of this, mentioned in some of the statutory definitions of employment, is a contract of apprenticeship. Although traditional apprenticeships are now relatively rare (being largely replaced by various modern training schemes), they can still exist and when they do there may be additional rules to apply to them (for example as to written form, service and training requirements and limitations on the power to dismiss): *Wallace v C A Roofing Services Ltd* [1996] IRLR 435,QBD. Renewed significance has been given to apprenticeship because of references to it in the national minimum wage legislation, particularly in relation to exclusion from entitlement of apprentices under 26 in their first year of training, see *Edmunds v Lawson* [2000] IRLR 391, CA (pupil barrister over 26 not entitled to the minimum wage).

2   Blackstone refers to master and servant as one of the principal personal relationships in private law, along with husband and wife and parent and child: 1 Bl Comm 422.

3   For a recent example, see *Wood Group Heavy Industrial Turbines Ltd v Grossan* [1998] IRLR 680, EAT where re-engagement was refused because of a continuing breakdown of trust and confidence (employers still believing in employee's guilt of the offence; dismissal only held unfair on procedural grounds).

4   *Nokes v Doncaster Amalgamated Collieries Ltd* [1940] AC 1014, [1940] 3 All ER 549, HL, applied in the context of a tort action for damages for personal injury in *Bolwell v Redcliffe Homes Ltd* [1999] IRLR 485, CA.

5   Restraint of trade is not a purely contractual doctrine, being rooted primarily in public policy based on freedom of trade and competition; thus, for example, an individual aimed at by an agreement between employers that unlawfully restrains trade can challenge that agreement under restraint law even though not a party to it: *Eastham v Newcastle United Football Club Ltd* [1964] Ch 413, [1963] 3 All ER 139. The detailed law on restraint of trade is outside the scope of this book; see Smith & Wood *Industrial Law* (7th edn, 2000) Butterworths, pp 96–105, *Harvey on Industrial Relations and Employment Law* Div A4; Brearley and Bloch *Employment Covenants and Confidential Information* (2nd edn, 1999) Butterworths.

6   The doctrine of illegality has to be handled carefully, otherwise an employee taking a minor payment 'in hand' (ie without payment of tax) could be denied all employment rights, statutory and contractual; see *Smith & Wood* pp 92–96. The doctrine of frustration can mean that a contract is terminated by operation of law, thus negating any dismissal-based rights, see chap 7 below.

7   *Giraud (UK) Ltd v Smith* [2000] IRLR 763, EAT.

8   It was held for the first time in *Brigden v American Express Bank Ltd* [2000] IRLR 94, QBD that the Act can apply to an employment contract (entailing the strange idea of an employee being a 'consumer') but the action failed because the Act attacks *exclusion* clauses (not generally unfair ones) and it was held that the clause in question (no access to disciplinary procedures in the first two years of employment) was not an exclusion clause, but rather was a clause defining the employment relationship. This is likely to be the case with nearly all clauses usually found in an employment contract. *Quaere*, however, whether the Act could be used to attack a 'unilateral variation' clause put into the contact by the employer, ostensibly giving it the unrestricted right to change terms at any time, see para 3.12, below.

9   This Act, amending the law relating to privity of contract, at first sight has little to do with employment. It is, however, not limited to commercial contracts and could apply to a term in an

employment contract intending to confer a benefit on a third party (eg medical or insurance cover for or use of a company car by a spouse). From an employer's viewpoint, it may be important to ensure that enforceable third party rights are not created inadvertently; careful drafting could be essential here, see precedents 32 and 33, below, and see generally Milgate 'Third party-rights' Employment Law Journal, May 2000, p 5.

10 [1988] IRLR 517,CA; on incorporation of collective agreements, see para 3.21, below.
11 [1999] 4 All ER 897, [2000] IRLR 43, HL, see para 2.5, above.

3.2   In addition to this general point about the strictness of approach, there may be other, particular canons of interpretation that could be put to good use, especially by an employee wishing to mitigate the effects of a term drafted by an employer who had the economic upper hand at the time of contracting. There may be scope for use of the *contra proferentem* rule (for example where the employer has been seeking to limit or negate potential liability) at least as a last resort, and actual use has been made of the general rule of construction that a party should not be allowed to gain from his own misdeeds. In *Levett v Biotrace International plc*[1] a managing director's contract included an extremely valuable share option, which was expressed to lapse if he became subject to the firm's disciplinary procedures and his contract was terminated. Three years into the contract, he was disciplined but then dismissed summarily in circumstances which were admitted to have been wrongful. The firm argued that the lapse clause still applied, being widely enough drafted, but the Court of Appeal upheld the ex-employee's argument that the clause must be read as only applying where the disciplinary proceedings resulted in a *lawful* termination; otherwise, the firm would be able to profit from its own wrongful action. Interesting though this is, such a 'rule' at present remains only one of construction, capable of being negated by clear express wording to the contrary[2], *unless* a court in the future could be persuaded to elevate such a rule to one of law, either on a loose analogy with the special status now arguably being given to the implied terms of trust and respect and health and safety[3], or on a closer analogy with the longstanding rule of public policy that a restraint of trade clause becomes invalid if the employee is wrongfully dismissed[4]. The Achilles' heel of the latter argument may be that public policy has already influenced the law on restraint clauses at a prior stage by declaring them prima facie void (subject to employer justification) which arguably makes it easier to apply this wrongful dismissal rule, than in the case of a perfectly lawful share option clause (where, the employer would argue, it can be left entirely to the parties to spell out exactly when the right is to lapse, if necessary including a case where the employee is wrongfully dismissed).

1   [1999] ICR 818, [1999] IRLR 375, CA; see chap 5 below.
2   See *Micklefield v SAC Technology Ltd* [1990] IRLR 218, Ch D, also discussed in chap 5 below.
3   See chap 4, below.
4   *General Billposting Co v Atkinson* [1909] AC 118, HL; in *Rock Refrigeration Ltd v Jones* [1997] ICR 938, [1996] IRLR 675 the Court of Appeal thought obiter that this rule may now be too sweeping, but felt obliged to follow it as a matter of precedent. Given that it applies, any attempt by the employer to provide that the clause would apply on dismissal 'howsoever caused' would be invalid where the dismissal was wrongful.

3.3   Two further points are made by way of introduction. The first is that, whereas the contractual base of employment is of great importance, the form of the agreement generally is not, and there is little legal control over or predetermination of the substantive terms and conditions of employment (subject now to the national minimum wage, the basic restrictions on working time and the proposal in the Employment Bill 2002 to incorporate basic disciplinary and grievance procedures into all contracts of employment, as seen in the previous chapter). With regard to form, writing has never been a general legal requirement, and indeed the standard definition in various statutes on employment refers to a contract 'whether express or implied, and (if it is express) whether oral or in writing'. The only legal requirement arises separately by statute, which is that an employee must be given, not later than two months after the beginning of the employment, a *statement* in writing (a 'section 1 statement') setting out various basic terms of employment[1]. It is trite law that such a statement is not in itself a contract of employment, but remains evidence of the terms; the importance of this distinction is that it leaves it open to one of the parties (particularly the employee) to argue that the statement is inadequate or inaccurate, not properly reflecting what was agreed, whereas once a formal contract is signed there will be much less scope for any such arguments[2]. In reality, of course, in many cases the statement will be the only evidence, with the employee having worked pursuant to it for a significant period, and its terms will correspondingly increase in weight. On the other hand, if an employer wishes to put clear obligations on to an employee going beyond the statutory matters (eg a strong confidentiality clause or a restraint of trade clause) then a full contract is necessary. Arguably, the idea of the section 1 statement comes from an earlier era[3] of large-scale collective determination of terms and conditions between employers and unions, ensuring that the individual employee at least received some formal notification of the results. To that end, the legislation as originally enacted allowed large-scale reference even in the statement to 'other documents' (in particular, the ruling collective agreement), which merely had to be kept open to inspection. In a small but significant change in 1993 (prompted by ensuring the compliance with Directive on information concerning employment conditions, 91/533/EEC, with which the UK largely complied anyway) the previous government changed the drafting so that now, under the ERA 1999, s 2(4), most of the major terms must be set out specifically 'in a single document'[4]. This can be seen as reflecting (and/or possibly encouraging) the major moves away from collective determination and towards individual contracting that have been such a feature of the last two decades.

The second and final point is a more general one. We have seen that the contractual base for employment can mean the sudden appearance of 'first principles' arguments based on common law principles; we have also seen that much of the substance of the major terms of employment is left to the parties themselves (so that, for example, a book such as this is not full of chapters on 'The law on holiday pay' or 'The law on sickness absence'). The emphasis legally has to be on the framework set by the law, in which the parties actually contract. Moreover, this area is a mixture of under-litigation in the past of some remarkably basic concepts and growing interest now in some cutting edge developments particularly in relation to common law damages. The result generally is that it can be a major mistake in this field to assume that a simple question will necessarily give rise to a simple answer.

1   ERA 1996, s 1; see *Harvey* Q [625] for the matters to be included.
2   See generally *Smith & Wood* p 84.
3   'The past is a foreign country; they do things differently there': L P Hartley, The Go-Between, Prologue.
4   On the technical level, this poses problems – what is one document? Is it enough to set terms out in, say, a company handbook provided it is served individually on the employee along with a statement referring to it? The Employment Bill before Parliament at the time of writing proposes a further change, making it clear that the particulars can be given in the form of a contract or letter of appointment; the s 1 particulars are to be emphasised even more by the Bill, as a way of trying to stop litigable disputes arising in the first place.

2 Developments in employment status

3.4 It is not proposed here to set out the basic law on defining a contract of employment and differentiating it from a contract of services. The well known history of this fundamental point is set out elsewhere[1] – from the original control test, through Lord Denning's test as to whether the individual was integrated into the business, to the current approach of weighing up all the relevant factors, now taking in not just physical factors such as methods of payment and supply of equipment but also possibly wider 'economic realities' factors (chance of profit, risk of loss; was he or she in business on his or her own account?) and ideas of mutuality of obligations. It is an area where a definition can only get you so far, after which (to use the standard lawyer's escape clause) it is all a question of fact, with the decision having to be made on an objective assessment, even if that entails in the longer term an ex post facto change to what had previously been understood to be the tax/NI position, possibly (in a case of reassessment from Schedule D to Schedule E) at considerable expense to all sides[2]. The aim here is instead to consider five developments in recent years which seem to be shaping this vital area.

1   See *Smith & Wood* pp 9–16; *Harvey* Division A1A (3). One unfortunate tendency lately has been for the higher courts to look for 'dominant' or 'defining' aspects, without which there *cannot* be a contract of employment: mutuality of obligations in *Carmichael v National Power plc* [2000] IRLR 43, [1999] 4 All ER 897, HL, personal service (in particular, no power to delegate) in *Express & Echo Publications Ltd v Tanton* [1999] ICR 693, [1999] IRLR 367, CA and good old control in *Montgomery v Johnson Underwood Ltd* [2001] EWCA Civ 318, [2001] IRLR 269. However, this search for the philosopher's stone, to turn factual dross into judicial gold, tends to appeal less at EAT level where these issues arise regularly and are less amenable to such first principles solutions; see the 'explanation' of *Tanton* in *MacFarlane v Glasgow City Council* [2001] IRLR 7, EAT and *Byrne Bros (Farmwork) Ltd v Baird* [2002] IRLR 96, EAT, though cf *Lincolnshire County Council v Hopper* (2002) Times, 17 June, [2002] All ER (D) 401 (May), EAT where the EAT held that the power to dismiss is a *sine qua non* of an employment relationship.
2   See, eg, *Young & Woods Ltd v West* [1980] IRLR 201, CA where Ackner LJ said that the 'employee' had won a 'hollow, indeed an expensive, victory', being successful in the unfair dismissal claim but facing a hefty tax bill on being retrospectively re-classified on to and reassessed under Schedule E. A good example of the necessary objective weighing of multiple factors is *Hall v Lorimer* [1994] ICR 218, [1994] IRLR 171, CA confirming for tax purposes the self-employed status of a freelance vision mixer.

(a)   A question of fact

3.5 The first is the continuing emphasis, recently strengthened, on the factual nature of the question. Not only is this important in explaining the nature of the enquiries to be made, but also of course it has the vital procedural consequence (in any statutory action depending on the contractual status of the applicant) of making it a matter purely for the employment tribunal, with little chance of an appeal (restricted to points of law), except on the highly restricted ground that the tribunal's decision was so wrong as to be perverse. Some disquiet was caused on this point in *Davies v Presbyterian Church of Wales*[1] which seemed to suggest that the question of employment status was one of law (and so fully reviewable on appeal), but the relevant dicta were soon 'explained' in later cases as only encompassing a case where the whole contract was contained in a written instrument (in that case, the church's rulebook)[2]. This view can also be seen in the speech of Lord Hoffman in *Carmichael v National Power plc*[3], which concentrates on the fact/law distinction. Thus, orthodoxy and the dominant factual nature of the question have been reasserted, and whereas Lord Irvine LC in this case spelled out why the court thought that the 'casual, as required' power station guides were not 'employees', Lord Hoffman went further and held not just that the Court of Appeal decision to the contrary was wrong, but that that court had itself been wrong to intervene and reverse the original decision of the employment tribunal on a question of fact. This approach was strengthened by two other significant aspects of his speech. The first was that, far from being a case of a contract wholly discernible from one written document, this was said to be a classic example of having to look to several sources to discern the whole agreement, some of which (particularly post-agreement conduct) would not normally be relevant in traditional contract law:

> 'I think that it was open to the tribunal to find, as a fact, that the parties did not intend the letters to be the sole record of their agreement but intended that it should be contained partly in the letters, partly in oral exchanges at the interviews or elsewhere, and partly left to evolve by conduct as time went on'[4].

This judicial approval for a highly practical approach is welcome, as is further guidance on the second aspect of the speech, namely the vexed question of the weight to be given to the parties' own statements and understandings of the position. While it is obvious that they cannot just call an arrangement 'self employment' (in the usual example) and get away with it, sometimes a court has gone as far as to say that the parties' own views are totally irrelevant[5], as the Court of Appeal had done here, or at best as a 'tie-breaker' in a particularly difficult case[6]. Lord Hoffman sought to give more weight to such matters, at least as a factor for consideration:

> 'The evidence of a party as to what terms he understood to have been agreed is some evidence tending to show that those terms, in an objective sense, were agreed. Of course, the tribunal may reject such evidence and conclude that the party misunderstood the effect of what was being said and done. But when both parties are agreed about what they understood their mutual obligations (or lack of them) to be, it is a strong thing to exclude their evidence from consideration'.

1 [1986] ICR 280, [1986] IRLR 194, HL.
2 *Hellyer Bros Ltd v McLeod* [1987] ICR 526, [1987] IRLR 232, CA; *Lee v Chung* [1990] ICR 409, [1990] IRLR 236, PC.
3 [1999] 4 All ER 897, [2000] IRLR 43, HL.
4 This approach to post-agreement conduct was adopted and applied by the Court of Appeal in *Stevedoring & Haulage Services Ltd v Fuller [2001] EWCA Civ 651*, [2001] IRLR 627, though (perhaps typically in this area) another division of the Court of Appeal held contemporaneously in *Dunlop Tyres Ltd v Blows* [2001] IRLR 629 that one still has to start from the ordinary contract law rule *against* the use of post-agreement conduct, unless the specific exception of ambiguity of the documentary evidence applies. The difference of approach is notable; *Carmichael* is not cited in *Dunlop*, but is relied on expressly in *Stevedoring*.
5 *Ferguson v John Dawson & Partners (Contractors) Ltd* [1976] 3 All ER 817, [1976] IRLR 346, CA, though note the strong dissent by Lawton LJ who would have allowed a larger element of self definition.
6 *Massey v Crown Life Insurance Co* [1978] ICR 590, [1978] IRLR 31, CA.

(b)   The flexible workforce

3.6   The second development has been the response of the courts to the ever-increasing flexibility and diversity of the workforce. It is a very obvious point, but to keep the legal concept of employment based on the model of a male working nine-to-five in a steel works with reasonable de facto job security until retirement age would soon lead to the legal disenfranchisement of large numbers of persons in the labour market, who used to be termed 'atypicals' but who are now all too typical of the jobs actually being created[1], not to mention any larger questions of indirect sex discrimination inherent in any 'two tier workforce' of core staff and peripheral staff. To give an idea of the scale of these shifts, research in 1998 showed that there were 6.6m part-time workers (comprising 1.3m men, 8% of the male workforce, and 5.3m women, 44% of the female workforce) and 1.8m temporary workers (8% of the workforce), more evenly split between the sexes[2]. Moreover, with the decline of traditional heavy industries, the nature of many employers has also changed, though it still came as a distinct surprise in 1998 when research on the small firm exemption in the Disability Discrimination Act 1995 found that one million employers in the private sector (95% of the total number of employers in the UK) employing 4.5m workers were firms employing less than 20 people[3]. Encouraging diversity was not only the policy of the previous government, but also featured strongly in the present government's 'Fairness at Work' White Paper. The general movement in the case law has tended to be towards including the more diverse patterns of hiring within the ambit of 'employment', starting with homeworkers[4]; although this is actually a rather old form of working, this could have modern significance when the homeworker in question is no longer a sewer of buttons or embroiderer of socks, but instead one of a new sophisticated breed of 'teleworker' utilising the new technology. Moreover, as seen in the previous chapter, part time workers and fixed term workers benefit from two EC Directives and enacting legislation. It is, however, in the area of casual work that most of the difficulties have arisen. As with homeworkers, the development of the idea of 'mutuality of obligations' and one overall 'global' or 'umbrella' contract seems to provide the means of including such workers, especially when working for the same employer with some regularity. However, the actual decisions have been less successful from the individual's point of view. In the well known older case of *O'Kelly v Trusthouse Forte plc*[5] 'regular casual' waiters were held not to be under overall contracts of employment. In such circumstances, there can be a secondary question whether there are individual employment contracts each time the casual works, but then of course the problem becomes lack of continuity of employment, as in *McLeod v Hellyer Brothers Ltd*[6] where fishermen consistently signing on for voyages with the same trawler company over a period of years were held at the end of that period to have been under separate contracts, with no continuity and therefore no statutory rights. More recently, the position of casual workers has continued to be made uncertain by the development of the idea (qualifying the general test of weighing up all the factors or 'badges' of employment) that there may be certain irreducible minima for the existence of any form of employment contract. In *Express & Echo Publications Ltd v Tanton*[7] it was held by the Court of Appeal that an obligation to render personal service (as opposed to a power to delegate) was a basic obligation in any contract of employment as a matter of law, lack of which could *of itself* rule out such a contract; in other words, all factors are equal but some are more equal than others. This particular point may be relatively esoteric in relation to most casual work (which will obviously involve personal service) and has to some extent been resiled from subsequently, but a more likely hurdle may be a similar 'basic obligation' approach to mutuality of obligations.

In *Clark v Oxfordshire Health Authority*[8] a 'bank' nurse, taking work when it was offered, with no entitlements between engagements, but subject to national pay rates, PAYE and NI deductions when working, was held by the Court of Appeal not to have been under a global contract of employment (necessary for her to claim unfair dismissal), in spite of working for one authority for three years, with only fourteen weeks in total between engagements. The basis of the decision was lack of mutuality of obligations throughout the *whole* period of the engagements. At the time, it could be argued that it was a rather retrospective decision, paying too much attention to the gaps and suggesting that there could only be an employment relationship if, for example, there was some form of retainer payment; it is, after all, the gaps that are inherent in the casual work, and what the concept of the global contract was trying to alleviate[9]. Such an approach seemed validated when, shortly afterwards, *Carmichael v National Power plc* went to the Court of Appeal[10] and it was held that the power station guides did qualify as employees. In this apparently well-reasoned majority decision, the gaps were filled by a highly purposive use of implied terms, namely reciprocal terms that under this 'casual, as required' agreement the employer impliedly undertook to offer each guide a reasonable amount of the work available and the guide undertook to accept a reasonable amount of the work offered. This seemed to offer a constructive way forward in casual work cases, at least where there is a history of consistent engagements. However, as pointed out above, this decision was reversed, and its reasoning comprehensively rejected, on further appeal to the House of Lords. Lord Irvine, giving the principal speech, based this strongly on lack of mutual obligations; it was interpreted as a deliberately loose agreement, with flexibility suiting both sides, giving rise at most to moral obligations. Citing the well-known passage from Stephenson LJ in *Nethermere (St Neots) Ltd v Gardiner*[11] on mutuality and the decision in *Clarke* (above), he refers to 'an absence of that irreducible minimum of mutual obligations necessary to create a contract of employment'. The irony here is that the idea of mutuality of obligations as an important factor was originally developed in order to *extend* employment status into (deserving) cases of non-standard working patterns (hence the importance also of being able to look at post-contractual conduct, and to use a large measure of hindsight), whereas here it is arguably being used to restrict any such extensions. Of course, the exact impact of *Carmichael* may take a long time to establish. It was followed by the Court of Appeal in *Stevedoring & Haulage Services Ltd v Fuller*[12] where redundant dockers were re-engaged on a casual basis, their letter of appointment specifically stating that no mutual obligations were to arise on either side and that any engagements were to be ad hoc. The court held that they were therefore not employees, in spite of evidence that in practice they had worked consistently (on, in effect, a rota system) for three years, usually being used in preference to agency labour; this was not allowed to outweigh the specific written provisions at the outset. This was clearly in line with the *Carmichael* ethos, but of course other questions about *Carmichael's* longer term influence remain – for example, does it mark a line in the sand stopping further expansion of employment status for casuals, or could it be used by employers to try to *reverse* certain past extensions (eg in relation to homeworkers)? Could a tribunal distinguish it in a casual work case where there was a more definable duty on the worker to turn up when called (or would the concept of mutuality also require a clearer obligation on the employer to offer at least a minimum amount of work, which could wreck the economic basis of the casual engagement from the employer's point of view?). Where would 'nil-hours' contracts fit into this? All of these uncertainties add to the argument put forward in the previous chapter that, if a way forward for casual workers is required, it now lies in the legislative route, by an exercise of the government's power in the ERA 1999, s 23 to extend the coverage of some or all statutory employment rights to persons other than 'employees'.

1   For a recent discussion of this point, see Fredman, 'Labour law in flux: the changing composition of the workforce' (1997) 26 ILJ 337.
2   [1998] Labour Market Trends 600.
3   Disability Discrimination Act 1995: the Employment Provisions and Small Employers (DFEE, 1998).
4   *Airfix Footwear Ltd v Cope* [1978] ICR 1210, [1978] IRLR 396, EAT; *Nethermere (St Neots) Ltd v Gardiner* [1984] ICR 612, [1984] IRLR 240, CA.
5   [1983] ICR 728, [1983] IRLR 369, CA.
6   [1987] ICR 526, [1987] IRLR 232, CA.
7   [1999] ICR 693, [1999] IRLR 367, CA; interestingly, the obligation of personal service was seen as the obverse of the implied term of trust and respect. This decision must now be seen in the light of its 'explanation' by the EAT in *MacFarlane v Glasgow City Council* [2001] IRLR 7 and *Byrne Bros (Farmwork) Ltd v Baird* [2002] IRLR 96, in order to preserve a more flexible approach and to avoid undesirable results (in particular, an employer cynically including a wide 'delegation' clause into an otherwise perfectly normal contract, in order to avoid employment status 'as a matter of law').
8   [1998] IRLR 125, CA.
9   The actual decision in Clark was to remit the matter to a tribunal to consider whether there was an individual contract of employment during each hiring. If so, could the nurse then claim statutory continuity of employment under the ERA 1996, s 212(3), (6)(b) (temporary cessation of work) as in *Flack v Kodak Ltd* [1986] ICR 775, [1986] IRLR 255, CA which itself concerned a highly irregular pattern of work for one employer over a considerable period of time?
10 [1998] ICR 1167, [1998] IRLR 301, CA.
11 [1984] ICR 612, [1984] IRLR 240, CA. The case is a difficult one because, although the law is subject to important development, the strong impression is that, if deciding it afresh, the judges would have held the homeworkers not to be in employment but (given their decision on the factual nature of the question) they were obliged to leave alone the tribunal decision in their favour.
12 [2001] EWCA Civ 651, [2001] IRLR 627, CA. The EAT had held for the dockers, using implied terms similar to those used by the Court of Appeal in *Carmichael*, but this was completely disapproved on further appeal.

(c)   Employment through third parties

3.7   The third development is renewed interest in the status of persons employed through a third party. An ancient version of this is the gang master system in agriculture[1], but increasingly we are seeing the use of intermediaries, either for the financial purposes of the person hired out or because of a perception by the hirer that increasingly the only safe way to make regular use of non-core staff is through some sort of agency. With regard to the former, the use of service companies (set up to 'employ' and hire out one consultant, especially in the IT area) is currently under attack by the Inland Revenue[2]. With regard to the latter, employment agencies have hitherto featured remarkably little in decided cases. The Employment Agencies Act 1973 used to contain a licensing system, but this was abolished in1994 by the previous government as a deregulatory measure and replaced with a much looser protective regime. The employment status of a person supplied through an agency arose in *McMeechan v Secretary of State for Employment*[3], but in a relatively unusual context of an insolvency claim against the Secretary of State in relation to outstanding pay for the last job the worker was sent on before the agency became insolvent. The question was whether the worker was the 'employee' of the agency. The simple point behind the decision is that there are no straightforward rules either way. In a normal agency agreement (with no obligations to offer or accept any particular work) it may well be that there is no general contract of employment between the agency and the worker[4] due to lack of mutuality (a point now underscored by *Carmichael*) but on the facts here the court held that when the worker was actually on an assignment there were sufficient factors pointing towards an employment relationship (powers of discipline and dismissal, grievance procedure, hourly pay rates with deductions for bad timekeeping, work or misconduct) to establish a contract of employment with the agency for the particular hiring; moreover, this could be so even when both general and particular hirings were apparently under the same general terms, which had to be considered separately in each context. This decision meant that the worker won his case, because all that was necessary was a contract during the last hiring; on the other hand, a wider claim for unfair dismissal or redundancy rights would depend instead on the general hiring position where the position would probably be the opposite, though ultimately that would depend on the facts of an individual case. Thus in the subsequent case of *Montgomery v Johnson Underwood Ltd*[5] the Court of Appeal held that an agency-provided part time worker was not an employee of the agency (for the purposes of an unfair dismissal action) because of lack of control, supervision or direction by the agency once she had been supplied to the client company. This perhaps points to the nub of the modern problem here; in many instances, agencies end up being little more than initial *recruiters* of individuals who then work on a long term basis for the client (particularly if they are good and their skills are in demand). They then start to look very similar to the client's ordinary employees (especially as good HR practice tends to be to try to 'integrate' them into the workforce, an unconscious echo of Lord Denning's contribution to the tests for employment). It was on this basis that the real bombshell was dropped in *Motorola Ltd v Davidson*[6] where the EAT held that, over a period of two years, an agency-provided mobile phone repairer had transmuted into an employee of the client company, especially as his termination was effected under the company's own disciplinary procedures. His claim for unfair dismissal lay against the company, not the agency (which had withered away to little more than a conduit for payment). The problem is, however, that Motorola could be a very fragile authority because (for whatever reason) argument before the EAT was restricted to the question whether there was sufficient control to make an employment relationship possible. This point was subsequently picked up by a differently constituted EAT in *Esso Petroleum Co v Jarvis*[7] where a tribunal had found no contract between agency worker and client but an evolved employer-employee relationship. The EAT took the straightforward view that if there was no contract between them, there could be no contract of employment. Thus the orthodox view prevailed, that the agency worker had no claim for redundancy rights against the client, and *Motorola* given a very limited interpretation. At present, therefore it can be argued that there are no clear answers, though it should be pointed out that the particular legislation on discrimination[8], national minimum wage[9] and working time[10] does specifically cover 'contract' or 'agency' workers. The White Paper 'Fairness at Work' promised a review of the law on employment agencies, and the power to do so by regulations was enacted by the ERA 1999, Sch 7; major concerns were expressed by the government in relation to charges levied by agencies and the need to strengthen inspection and offences[11], and these are dealt with by amendments to the Employment Agencies Act 1973. Of greater possible impact on the question of employment status, however, is the new power to regulate 'the way in which and the terms on which services may be provided by persons carrying on such agencies and businesses'. At the time of writing, it remains to be seen to what use this will be put. In addition, any moves under the ERA 199, s 23 (above) to extend employment status more widely could have interesting effects in this area too.

1   The tax and employment position here can be complex. If the gang master merely organises labour for a farm and works himself as part of the gang, tax liability for PAYE on earnings is on the farm: *Andrews v King* [1991] ICR 846, [1991] STC 481, Ch D. But what is the employment status (if any) of the gang members? What if the gang master has greater control over a regular gang?

2   Welfare Reform and Pensions Act 1999, s 75. In the current jargon, these are referred to as 'IR 35 cases'.

3   [1997] ICR 549, [1997] IRLR 353, CA.

4   *Wickens v Champion Employment* [1984] ICR 365, EAT, not doubted on its facts in *McMeechan*.

5   [2001] EWCA Civ 318, [2001] IRLR 269, CA.

6   [2001] IRLR 4, EAT. To the contrary is the decision of a different EAT in *Hewlett Packard Ltd v O'Murphy* [2002] IRLR 4 that a computer specialist operating through his own service company (see n 2, above) who was hired to the client through an agency did not transmute into an employee of the client. *Motorola* was not cited and it may well be, as put by the learned editor of the IRLR, that in *Hewlett Packard* there was simply one party too many (the service company).

7   [2002] All ER (D) 112 (Jan). One unresolved point is to what extent, on other facts, there could be seen to have been a variation (or even novation) of the contractual positions, to show an implied contract between agency worker and client. After all, a contract of employment does not have to be in writing.

8   Sex Discrimination Act 1975, ss 9 and 15; Race Relations Act 1976 ss 7 and 14; Disability Discrimination Act 1995, s 12. See *Abbey Life Assurance Co Ltd v Tansell* [2000] IRLR 387, CA for a broad, purposive interpretation of the latter.

9   National Minimum Wage Act 1998, s 34.

10   Working Time Regulations 1998, SI 1998/1833, reg 36.

11   There is no proposal to go back to the old licensing system.

(d)   Relationship with tax law

3.8   The fourth development is that we may be seeing increasing divergence between employment status for employment law purposes and for tax purposes. Such a divergence has long been seen with the law of tort, especially in the 'borrowed servant' cases, ie where general employer A lends an employee to employer B, during which time the employee injures a third party. Here, it may well be that it is B who is vicariously liable for damages to the third party (primarily on the ground of control at the time of the accident), whereas it remains clear that for the purposes of contractual and statutory employment law rights it is A who remains the 'employer'[1]; indeed, where the injury in question occurs to the borrowed servant himself, A may still be liable for the damages[2]. In the context of tax law, it is of course always open to Parliament to enact specific provisions addressing particular tax collection problems (eg in relation to employment agencies) which will then operate independently of normal employment status. That aside, the normal assumption in the past has been that employment status for tax and employment law purposes was subject to basically similar rules, the so-called 'badges of employment'. In many cases that will continue to be so (with some tax cases continuing to be cited in employment law works as general authorities), but it may be that we are starting to see more cases of divergence, especially in the area of sporadic or short-term employments. To take the examples given above, *Clark* (the bank nurse) and *Carmichael* (the power station guide) were both subject to PAYE and NI contributions while working, but were not 'employees' with employment law rights; similarly, members of an agricultural gang are taxable through the engaging farmer but have little chance of being considered the farmer's 'employees' (indeed, the system is there to avoid just that). In a sense, this has always been a possibility because status for one purpose does not formally determine it for another, hence the rule that tax/NI treatment of an individual whose status is being tested in employment law is only *one* factor. However, it may be that some of the recent, more restrictive, case law is showing the point up in higher relief.

1   *Mersey Docks & Harbour Board v Coggins & Griffiths (Liverpool) Ltd* [1947] AC 1, HL; *Denham v Midland Employers' Mutual Assurance Ltd* [1955] 2 QB 437, particularly at 443–444, per Denning LJ.
2   *McDermid v Nash Dredging & Reclamation Co Ltd* [1987] AC 906, [1987] 2 All ER 878, HL; *Morris v Breaveglen Ltd* [1993] ICR 766, [1993] IRLR 350, CA.

(e)   Future trends

3.9   The fifth and final point is more speculative. It concerns the perception among employers of the direction being taken in this area, and the question whether in the longer term it is worth continuing to use certain forms of engagement to try to avoid employment rights. Even with classic self employment, there has always been the known danger of unfortunate and expensive fallout if they get it wrong and it is later challenged. Further, it can be the case that status can change over time so that, for example, the person (eg an IT specialist) initially taken on from the open market as a 'consultant' but in fact getting all the work he or she wants from that one firm, and over a period of time becoming more and more integrated into the normal everyday running of the business, may imperceptibly transmute into an employee, whose position then needs to be regularised in case of any future disagreements. When this is added to (a) continuing developments in taxation policy and legislation, (b) the odd high profile case of an employer's ace wheeze to beat employment law not working[1], (c) the general direction of the government's fairness at work policy, allied to EU developments and (d) the high profile of many cases under discrimination law which operates under wider principles anyway, a picture can emerge that suggests that now may be the time to rethink certain more traditional hiring practices, in the direction of more formal, non-casual employment, in an old phrase 'through the books', in order to be ready for the law and realities half way through the new decade. While an employment lawyer can still be called on to give detailed advice as to whether an old practice can still technically be relied upon (and it must be accepted that the effect of *Clark, Carmichael and Stevedoring & Haulage Services* may well be to give at least a temporary respite from further legal developments in the area of casual work), it may increasingly be that what an employer really wants to know is the arguments for and against changing practices to be in fact ahead of the game[2], basically as a business decision, not a strictly legal one. This sort of prevalence of appearance and perception over strict legal reality is hardly unknown in employment law. It was arguably strong during the 1980s (after such a radical change of government in 1979, and particularly after the 1983 election) and, in a rather different way, we seem to be going through another phase of it now.

1   In *Brown v Chief Adjudication Officer* [1997] ICR 266, [1997] IRLR 110 the Court of Appeal had little difficulty in striking down the device of putting an employee on to 'daily contracts' (for 9 months!) to avoid matters such as statutory sick pay. In another high-profile case, a well known fast food retailer stopped putting its staff on to 'nil hours contracts' which said that, although on shift, they would only be paid when there were customers to be served, but this time because of press naming and shaming rather than legal challenge.
2   One analogous example of this is the number of recognition deals with unions concluded by employers 'voluntarily', in advance of the coming into force of the new statutory recognition procedure in the Employment Relations Act 1999; in the period from January to October 1999, 75 new deals were made, 90% in the private sector and 85% covering pay and other terms and conditions: Focus on Recognition (TUC; 2000).

3   Terms of the contract of employment

(a)   Express terms

3.10   In one sense there is little to say in relation to express terms, in that their substance is principally left to the parties and most disputes will revolve around questions of interpretation in the light of the particular facts, as in most breach of contract actions in the general law. Movements in the last three decades towards formalisation of the employment relationship naturally make the use of clear express terms desirable in most cases. Certain principal terms of employment must be at least evidenced in writing, as we saw earlier in this chapter, but this is as far as the law goes. Consistency is obviously important, and one well known practical problem arises where an employer unthinkingly gives a new employee a standard-form contract which fails to take into account certain particularities or unusual aspects of his or her hiring[1].

1   See, eg, the 'PHI' cases where the existence of valuable insurance rights were not reflected in the basic contracts given, leading to an acute clash between the two; see para 4.29, below.

3.11   Three particular points of some uncertainty in relation to express terms are to be noted. The first is whether the employer can draft a written contract so as to be exhaustive, thus ruling out any further implied terms. A contract in such terms ('this agreement records the entire agreement between the parties') succeeded for the employer in *Morley v Heritage plc*[1]; the contract set out holidays and holiday pay but made no provision for payment in lieu of any holidays not taken on termination. The Court of Appeal rejected the employee's claim for such payment under an implied term. Although the exclusivity clause played an important part in the decision, it is not clear that it was the sole reason for it, indeed it was combined in the judgments with the fact that the holiday provisions as they stood were entirely workable (albeit not to the employee's liking), so that it could be held that there was no *need* to imply a term. Thus, it may be that the real importance of an exclusivity clause is to defeat an argument for an implied extension or restriction of an express provision on grounds of business efficacy, where that existing provision can stand alone. On that analysis, the result might be different if the substantive provision made no sense on its own; an even more interesting case would be where an oral agreement had been struck but the eventual written contract omitted an important provision (without there being any evidence of the employee having agreed to that omission by way of variation) – in such circumstances the effectiveness of an exclusivity clause might be doubtful, on the basis that the whole contract was not to be found purely in the written document (see Lord Hoffman's views in *Carmichael v National Power plc*, above).

1   [1993] IRLR 400, CA.

3.12   The second point, of particular topicality, concerns flexibility clauses. The whole idea of flexibility is a major concept in modern employment law, and was one of the themes of the White Paper 'Fairness at Work'. In principle, there is an inherent tension between it and a written contract of employment, since one of the functions of the latter is to define the intended relationship, ie. to reduce it to certainty. The question therefore is to what extent an employer can use the contractual terms to enshrine flexibility. There are two ways in which this could be done. First, there could be a clause expressly obliging an employee to be flexible in relation to a particular matter, in particular job content (though a mobility clause could also be seen as an older form of flexibility clause). If drafted in a way that makes practical sense, there is no reason why such a clause should not be enforceable; although such clauses are now less important in redundancy law[1], they may still serve an important function in widening managerial prerogative and in making an employee refusal to transfer on to work covered by the clause potentially misconduct. Secondly, it could be done indirectly, by a more generalised clause in the contract either making it clear that a certain matter remained within the managerial prerogative, or alternatively by putting the matter into the contract but giving the employer a right of unilateral variation. There is surprisingly little authority on such a fundamental point (marking a reversal of the usual requirement of bilateral change of a contract). Such authority as there is has tended to uphold such clauses. In *Airlie v City of Edinburgh District Council*[2] the terms of a bonus scheme provided for consultation with the workforce before any changes, but affirmed the management's ultimate right to adapt it; the necessary consultation having taken place but ended in a failure to agree, the EAT upheld the management's right then to introduce variations. *Wandsworth London Borough Council v D'Silva*[3] is an example of the other technique, of keeping a matter non-contractual. Certain sub-rules on staff sickness (especially on the triggers for review procedures) were kept in a code of practice, which on the facts was held by the Court of Appeal to be intended to be non-contractual, so that the employers could lawfully amend the provisions in question. The employers had argued in the alternative that, even if the rules were contractual, other provisions in the contract reserved to them a power of unilateral variation. Although it was not necessary to decide the point, Lord Woolf MR did address what is really the ultimate point here – will a unilateral variation clause always work? He stated that:

> 'The general position is that contracts of employment can only be varied by agreement. However, in the employment field an employer or for that matter an employee can reserve the ability to change a particular aspect of the contract unilaterally by notifying the other party as part of the contract that this is the situation. However, clear language is required to reserve to one party an unusual power of this sort.'

On balance, he thought that such a power might have been made out in relation to procedural rules such as those in issue in the case, but drew a possible distinction with a case where the claimed power was to vary substantive employee rights under the contract:

> 'To apply a power of unilateral variation to the rights which an employee is given under this part of the code could produce an unreasonable result and the courts in construing a contract of employment will seek to avoid such a result.'

Seeking to avoid manifest unfairness by interpretation is thus a course open to a court or tribunal, and it may well be that it will decline to find a right of unilateral variation from vague wording in the contract or from a course of dealing between the parties, as in *Lee v GEC Plessey Telecommunications*[4] (employee contractual redundancy rights could not be removed unilaterally by reliance on a reference in the contract to the power of the employer to issue 'general instructions and notices') and *Davies v Hotpoint Ltd*[5] (reference to 'approved short time' in a term coming from collective bargaining interpreted as meaning agreed with the union, not as giving the employer the sole right to 'approve', ie. enforce, it). Important though this point is, however, it would not necessarily meet the ultimate form of this problem, which would arise where a harsh and unreasonable result was produced by a clear and unequivocal contractual right of unilateral variation. Contractual orthodoxy would require its approval, and pure interpretation would not help. At present, there would appear to be no basis upon which to strike down such a clause on general grounds of public policy, but one possibility would be to seek to control and limit its operation by invoking the implied term of trust and respect, so that the clause could not be used in such a way as to breach that term and destroy the basis of the contract; this would be a serious step, but it is after all the way that the courts have limited the operation of apparently unrestricted contractual mobility clauses[6]. For this to happen, however, it has to be accepted that at least this implied term has an effect over and above that of most implied terms, because the result would be to qualify (possibly even negate) a clear express term. This brings us neatly to the next point.

1 This is since the 'contract test' for redundancy (ie has all the work the employee could be made to do under the contract gone?) was disapproved, being replaced by a straightforward causative test under the plain wording of the ERA 1996, s 139 (1): *Murray v Foyle Meats Ltd* [1999] ICR 827, [1999] IRLR 562, HL, approving the redefinition by Judge Clark in *Safeway Stores plc v Burrell* [1997] ICR 523, [1997] IRLR 200, EAT.

2 [1996] IRLR 516, EAT.

3 [1998] IRLR 193, CA; see also *Cadoux v Central Regional Council* [1986] IRLR 131, Ct of Sess.

4 [1993] IRLR 383, QBD.

5 [1994] IRLR 538, EAT. See also *Securities and Facilities Division v Hayes* [2001] IRLR 81, CA where the court, echoing distinctly the views of Lord Woolf above, refused to find that a government agency employee's contract impliedly allowed a unilateral change to a subsistence allowance.

6 See para 3.13, below. Alternatively, could the Unfair Contract Terms Act 1977 be used to attack an unreasonable unilateral variation clause? It is suggested that this is unlikely for the reasons given in para 1, n 8, above, ie such a clause may or may not be unfair, but it is not an *exclusion* clause. On the other hand, there might be more mileage in an argument that, although it is not an exclusion clause, it could still be seen as a clause seeking to alter the basic obligations of the parties.

3.13   The third point of uncertainty in the modern law is whether an employer (to put it most bluntly) now has to exercise its contractual rights reasonably. In traditional contract law there is only one answer – unless the term in question itself refers to reasonableness, there is *no* such obligation on a contracting party; contractual wording means what it says and, once signed to, can be enforced[1]. This, however, along with much of basic contract law, ignores any imbalance in contracting power such as can easily exist in an employment relationship. In the light of this, there have been significant developments in the context of contracts of employment, but they must be treated with some care. To take a concrete example, can an implied requirement of reasonable exercise be read into an apparently unrestricted mobility clause? If mobility is not covered by the contract at all but becomes so important that a term has to be implied, then a court or tribunal may well define it in such a way as to give the employee some protection, in particular by a requirement that the employer gives reasonable notice of the move[2]. However, the crux comes if there is an express term with no mention of area or the giving of notice. In the key case of *United Bank Ltd v Akhtar*[3] the EAT upheld a claim of constructive dismissal where an employee (subject to such a clause) was told to move from Leeds to Birmingham in six days' time, and was refused any postponement on the basis of his personal circumstances. This was achieved by (a) implying a term of reasonable notice and (b) more fundamentally finding that this reliance on the black and white of the clause was a fundamental breach of the term of trust and respect. Both grounds are controversial, but it is the second that would establish a broader principle. In the words of Knox J's judgment:

> 'We take it as inherent that there may well be conduct which is either calculated or likely to destroy or seriously damage the relationship of trust and respect between employer and employee which a literal interpretation of the written words of the contract might appear to justify, and it is in this sense that we consider that in the field of employment law it is proper to imply an overriding obligation [of trust and respect] which is independent of, and in addition to, the literal interpretation of the actions which one permitted to the employer under the terms of the contract.'

The point could hardly be explained more clearly. However, the question remains whether this can be elevated into a positive obligation on an employer always to exercise contractual rights reasonably. When this was put directly to it in *White and Reflecting Roadstuds Ltd*[4], the EAT seemed to take fright and objected to any such positive formulation (holding that an employee subjected to a contractually-valid transfer to a lower-paid job could not claim constructive dismissal). However, it is strongly arguable that *White* does not negate *Akhtar* because at the end of his judgment in the former Wood P suggested that in a case of 'capricious' reliance on a contractual term the employee could still rely on the implied term of trust and respect. This whole matter raises the question whether we now have certain 'overriding' implied terms, which is considered immediately below. In the context of express terms, the situation can perhaps be summed up in this way – (1) there is probably no single, overall, positive principle that an employer's express rights under the contract must be exercised reasonably *but* any oppressive or (manifestly) unreasonable exercise to the employee's significant disadvantage could be argued to be breach of the implied term of trust and respect, provided the complaint is phrased properly in terms of that implied obligation (ie reaching the same result by a less direct route); (2) in practice, the effect of cases like *Akhtar*, and the fact that the implied term of trust and respect is now so well known, could have an influence greater than in strict law because of the uncertainty caused – if an employer asks a legal adviser 'Can I insist here on the precise wording of this clause?' the advice may have to be that the employer would be contractually in the right but that if the employee was disproportionately affected it could not be ruled out that the employee (or ex-employee in a constructive dismissal case) might challenge the employer's actions as breach of trust and respect. Again, the negative formulation may be tactically important[5], but the overall effect no less real for it.

1   For an application of this straightforward approach in employment law (in the context of an unrestricted mobility clause), see *Rank Xerox Ltd v Churchill* [1988] IRLR 280, EAT. The decision in the case now cannot be supported because of the disapproval of a purely contractual test for place of work (in redundancy law) in *High Table Ltd v Horst* [1998] ICR 409, [1997] IRLR 513, CA.
2   *Prestwick Circuits Ltd v McAndrew* [1990] IRLR 191, Ct of Sess; though cf the earlier, stricter decision of the Court of Appeal in *Courtaulds Northern Spinning Ltd v Sibson* [1988] IRLR 305.
3   [1989] IRLR 507, EAT.
4   [1991] ICR 733, [1991] IRLR 331, EAT.
5   Although usually expressed in the negative, it has been held that the implied term of trust and respect can be positive in substance: *BG plc v O'Brien* [2001] IRLR 496, EAT, upheld by the Court of Appeal [2002] EWCA Civ 379, [2002] IRLR 441; see para 4.48, below.

(b)   Implied terms

3.14   It is when we turn to implied terms that we see some of the principal divergences between basic contract law and modern employment law. Commercial contract law essentially does not like implied terms – the parties are expected to get it right, tests are evolved (the 'business efficacy' test and the 'officious bystander' test) to allow the implication of terms but only as a last resort, and the whole matter is backed by the rule that ultimately a wholly unclear contract may be void for uncertainty. Arguably, none of these can be allowed to operate in unrefined form in the law relating to contracts of employment, where (a) the eventual written instrument will often not be the only source of the contract (as Lord Hoffman has recently emphasised in the *Carmichael* case, above), (b) there has always been far more need for implied terms to perfect agreements, especially where a whole topic has never really been thought through by the parties but later becomes a key point in a legal dispute, and (c) the end result of an informal agreement being void for uncertainty is simply not an option in the realities of an employment relationship, especially a longstanding one. These points in turn must be seen against the background of inequality of bargaining power between employer and employee in most forms of employment, as shown inter alia by the way in which an employer will often seek to keep certain benefits (especially their quantification) discretionary, in a way that would rarely arise or even be thought possible in a commercial contract; discretionary bonuses or commissions are a good example and have featured in some of the recent case law where the law is being developed to put brakes or restrictions on the exercise of such discretions. In the light of all of this, it is necessary to consider three aspects of the implied term – real implied terms, characteristic or default terms, and the argument that some of the latter may now have overriding effect.

(I)   REAL IMPLIED TERMS

3.15   It of course remains perfectly possible for a 'real' implied term to be found in a contract of employment, in the sense of being founded on the actual or supposed intent of the parties, applying the classic contract law tests. As a matter of law, the relevant exercise is to apply those tests, the rest being a question of fact, on which views can differ markedly as in any such contractual dispute. A good example of this is *Ali v Christian Salvesen Food Services*[1] where an annualised hours contract had been adopted, through negotiations with the recognised trade unions, requiring a set number of hours in the pay year at basic rates, after which higher rates were payable. The problem was that no mention was made of what was to happen where an employee left part-way through the year, having done hours in excess of the normal, but not having reached the number required for premium payments. In the case, an employee made redundant half way through the year in these circumstances brought a Wages Act 1986 claim for certain premium rates, arguing that there was to be implied a term granting such rates pro rata in the case of an early leaver. The EAT agreed with the employee and implied such a term on ordinary principles (finding on the facts that it was an unintended gap in the scheme that needed filling). However, the Court of Appeal allowed the employers' appeal and, on equally ordinary principles, found that the natural inference was that the matter had deliberately been omitted from the scheme (as being too complicated or too controversial) which, after all, had been freely negotiated in a collective agreement, and so there was no need to supplement it with an implied term and the result was that in the case of premature termination the loss was left to lie where it fell.

1   [1997] ICR 25, [1997] IRLR 17, CA (reversing the EAT: [1996] ICR 1, [1995] IRLR 624).

3.16   Even in the area of genuine implied terms, however, contracts of employment have at least two peculiarities. The first is that in certain employments in certain circumstances there will be a ready-made source of material for implication, namely custom and practice. This famous industrial relations phrase has a long history, and can be seen as an essential element of the old voluntary system of legal abstentionism, being itself a form of self-regulatory law-substitute. As such, there were always tensions on the cusp with written contracts, the contract law position being that custom and practice could not negate a written term, but the practical position being that much could be done by allowing custom and practice to 'interpret' a written term[1]. In practice, there is less scope today for arguments on custom and practice due to the increased formality of the employment relationship, certainly in relation to traditional areas for its application such as payment methods and working practices. There is, however, one area where it can cause complicated arguments; this arises where an employer adopts a 'policy' on the matter. As we shall see below, the policy approach may be used in order to keep the matter non-contractual and therefore in the management's prerogative, but what is the position if that policy is applied frequently? Will there come a time when employees can argue that it has in fact been incorporated into their contracts on the basis of custom and practice? In *Quinn v Calder Industrial Materials Ltd*[2] the employers had paid enhanced redundancy terms on four occasions between 1987 and 1994 (pursuant to a policy document primarily for management's guidance, but informally known to employees), though on each occasion as a result of an individual decision by higher management. When the applicants were made redundant in 1994, no enhancement was offered; the applicants argued that it was contractually due to them, by reason of established custom and practice. Rejecting their applications on the facts, the EAT held that two important factors will be (a) whether the policy has been drawn to the attention of employees and (b) whether it has been followed without exception for a substantial period; however, Lord Coulsfield added that the ultimate question is whether these factors (along with other circumstances) demonstrate that the employers intended the policy to have contractual effect (which could be seen as an interesting contemporary example of the basic contract law requirement of intent to create legal relations).

1   *Dunlop Tyres Ltd v Blows* [2001] EWCA Civ 1032, [2001] IRLR 629, CA. For consideration of the old case law on custom and practice, see *Smith & Wood* p 116. The phrase normally used is that the custom must be 'certain, general and reasonable'. In *Henry v London General Transport Services Ltd* [2002] EWCA Civ 488 [2002] IRLR 472, the incorporation of changes into individual contracts through collective negotiations was established on the basis of traditional dealing.
2   [1996] IRLR 126, EAT, citing Browne-Wilkinson J's judgment in *Duke v Reliance Systems* [1982] IRLR 347, EAT (concerning retirement age). See also the similar decision on similar facts in *Warman International v Wilson* [2002] All ER (D) 94 (Mar) and the refusal to incorporate a security of employment statement into the employment contracts on the basis of custom and practice in *Hagen v ICI Chemicals and Polymers Ltd* [2002] IRLR 31, QBD.

3.17   The second peculiarity is that the *basis* for implication is arguably broader than in ordinary commercial contracts. Against the background of the increased need for implied terms generally and the practical inapplicability of the doctrine of uncertainty, it can be argued[1] that a court or tribunal may need to go beyond supposed subjective intent, the officious bystander and business efficacy, and look more at the overall relationship and (the acid test) what it would be reasonable to imply. This is a difficult area, because a direct argument that a term should be implied simply on the ground of reasonableness might be too much for a court or tribunal to swallow[2]; equally, the more that the argument in favour of implication can be cast in terms of the traditional tests, the safer the ground will be. However, it may be that ideas of 'necessity' of implication (taken from the business efficacy test) have a wider meaning here when dealing with an obvious gap in a relatively informal contract. The case of *Mears v Safecar Security Ltd*[3] can be seen as sanctioning this wider approach, even though a particularly strong dictum that in a particularly ambiguous case a court may have to 'invent' a term to resolve the matter was latter criticised as too extreme[4]. On the other hand, in *Courtaulds Northern Spinning Ltd v Sibson*[5] where the point at issue was location in a contract that was silent on the matter Slade LJ put it this way:

'[I]n cases such as the present where it is essential to imply some term into the contract of employment as to place of work, the court does not have to be satisfied that the parties, if asked, would in fact have agreed the term before entering the contract. The court merely has to be satisfied that the implied term is one which the parties would probably have agreed if they were being reasonable'.

In relation to both custom and practice and this arguably wider approach to implication, there may be two further divergences from strict contract theory. The first is that (particularly in relation to custom and practice) a relevant factor may be the expectations of (and employer behaviour towards) *other* employees, not just the one claiming the right, especially where the argument is that that employee took the employment subject to existing practices[6]. The second is that (as seen above) it may also be necessary to look at what happened in practice *after* the commencement of the employment.

1   *Smith & Wood* p 108.
2   The authority against simple reasonableness that is usually cited in the cases is *Liverpool City Council v Irwin* [1977] AC 239, [1976] 2 All ER 39, HL.
3   [1982] ICR 626, [1982] IRLR 183, CA. The case in fact concerned a statutory action concerning the written statement of terms and conditions required under what is now the ERA 1996, s 1, but that should make no difference to the applicable principles.
4   *Eagland v British Telecommunications plc* [1993] ICR 644, [1992] IRLR 323, CA.
5   [1988] ICR 451, [1988] IRLR 305, CA.
6   See *Sagar v H Ridehalgh & Son Ltd* [1931] 1 Ch 310, CA, one of the leading cases, where a weaver was deemed to accept employment subject to deductions from pay for bad workmanship which were applied to other weavers in that mill.

(II)   CHARACTERISTIC OR DEFAULT TERMS

3.18   The term 'implied term' has a secondary meaning. It is also used to denote a term which the courts or tribunals will read into all contracts of employment simply because of their nature, and with little or nothing to do with the individual parties. If we had a sui generis Law of Employment, these would simply be viewed as legal incidents of it, but as we persist in using a contractual analysis, they are dressed up as implied terms on employer and employee. To that extent, they are more 'imposed' terms than implied terms, and their existence has little or nothing to do with the classic tests for a "real" implied term considered above[1]. Acceptance of this separate role for implied terms can be traced back at least to *Lister v Romford Ice and Cold Storage Co Ltd*[2] (concerning the obligation to insure) and *Sterling Engineering Co Ltd v Patchett Ltd*[3] (concerning common law rights to inventions). In the latter, Lord Reid said:

> 'Strictly speaking, I think that an implied term is something which, in the circumstances of a particular case, the law may read into the contract if the parties are silent, but it would be reasonable to do so; it is something over and above the ordinary incidents of the particular type of contract. If it were necessary in this case to find an implied term in that sense I should be in some difficulty. But the phrase "implied term" can be used to denote a term inherent in the nature of the contract which the Law will imply in every case unless the parties agree to vary or exclude it.'

The latest word on the matter has come in *Malik v BCCI*[4], where the House of Lords gave its full approval to the evolution of the implied term of trust and respect, in which Lord Steyn referred to this form of implied term as creating 'default rules', and as operating as 'a standardised term implied by the law', that is, a term which is said to 'be an incident of all contracts of employment'. The particular terms in question, either well established or still arguable, are set out in Chapter 4.

1   See, eg, *Scally v Southern Health and Social Services Board* [1991] ICR 771, [1991] IRLR 522, HC at 781 and 525, per Lord Bridge for a clear explanation of the difference.
2   [1957] AC 555, [1957] 1 All ER 125, HL.
3   [1955] AC 534, [1955] 1 All ER 369, HL.
4   [1997] ICR 606, [1997] IRLR 462, HL.

(III)   OVERRIDING TERMS?

3.19   The particularly controversial point that follows on from the discussion of characteristic terms is whether some of them are taking on the nature of 'overriding' terms. This raises two separate but linked questions. Answers in the affirmative to either would again mark a significant departure from contract law orthodoxy.

The first question is whether such a term may be used in order to cut down or even negate an express term of the contract, especially one giving an apparently unlimited power to the employer. The two implied terms to date which seem to be in contention for being given this effect are the obligations on the employer to treat the employee with trust and respect and to take reasonable care to safeguard the employee's health and safety. It is the former that has figured most prominently, with a particularly marked effect on the law of constructive dismissal (though *Malik* of course showed its ability to stand alone as the basis for a common law action for damages, even though it was ultimately unsuccessful on its facts[1]) and, as considered above in relation to express terms, the key case has been *United Bank Ltd v Akhtar*[2], where Knox J referred to the 'overriding obligation' of trust and respect which must be applied in addition to the literal interpretation of the contract. This was in the context of a mobility clause, but a similar idea had previously been used to qualify an apparently unqualified disciplinary power[3], and was subsequently used to like effect in relation to a power to suspend an employee[4] and even in that sanctum sanctorum of the purest strains of contract and equity, the administration of occupational pension schemes[5]. The implied term of health and safety was at issue in *Johnstone v Bloomsbury Health Authority*[6] which concerned a legal challenge by a junior doctor to excessive hours being required of him under his contract. The three judgments in the Court of Appeal covered a full spectrum. Leggett LJ (dissenting) gave a straightforward contract answer, that the doctor had signed the contract and so had to abide by it. Browne-Wilkinson V-C found a middle way by stressing that the mandatory hours were only 40 per week; the remaining 48 were 'on call' and in the employers' discretion, and it was that discretion that could be made subject to the implied term. Stuart-Smith LJ, however, went furthest and held that the whole contractual right to demand up to 88 hours per week had to be exercised subject to other contractual rights, especially the implied obligations relating to health and safety. This first question is thus capable of differing views; in the light of that, it may be advisable to cast those implied terms in a negative format – not that the employer *shall* act reasonably or promote health and safety, irrespective of what the rest of the contract says, but that the employer will *not* use otherwise unrestricted powers in the contract so as to wreck the basis of the contract in trust and respect, or so as to endanger health and safety; to that extent, the fiction might be maintainable that the implied term is simply 'interpreting', or at the most 'qualifying' the express term[7]. Where does this lead? On the one hand, the decision of the House of Lords in *Johnson v Unisys Ltd*[8] (denying stigma damages at common law on termination of employment) may be seen as starting from contract orthodoxy that an implied term may not contradict an express term (so that, according to the majority, an express power of dismissal on notice was not to be subjected to the implied term of trust and respect). However, the reasoning in the case is complex and arguably ambiguous. Lord Hoffman for the majority states that proposition, but is soon into the grey area of what constitutes contradiction and what constitutes mere qualification or modification, stating that a modification by the term of trust and respect *would* have been possible, had it not been outweighed by the policy considerations that policing the manner of dismissal is now the function of the law of unfair dismissal, and that to develop a common law remedy would be contrary to Parliamentary intent (the ratio of the case). Lord Steyn, dissenting on the reasoning though concurring in the eventual result on the facts, envisaged a wider role for implied terms. This was partly on the basis that the rule in contract law against contradiction of an express term by an implied term applies primarily to implied terms of *fact*. He said that counsel for the employers' submission based on the contract rule 'loses sight of the particular nature of the implied obligation of mutual trust and confidence. It is not a term implied in fact. It is an overarching obligation implied by law as an incident of the contract of employment'. He had little difficulty from this standpoint in holding that to apply that implied term would not negate the express power to dismiss. One view of all this would be that the real distinction between these two principal speeches in the case is merely as to how quickly one should reach the conclusion that to apply the implied term would remain on the right side of the contradiction/qualification borderline. Outright contradiction would, however, remain out of bounds. On the other hand, if the courts were ever to develop a more general principle that one term of the contract (no matter how unequivocal) should not be exercised so as to prejudice rights or obligations under another term, that could have even broader implications, as can be seen from the 'PHI cases' cutting down on apparently unrestricted right to dismiss by notice, considered in Chapter 4 below[9].

1 *BCCI SA (in liquidation) v Ali (No 3)* [2002] EWCA Civ 82 IRLR 460.
2 [1989] IRLR 507, EAT.
3 *BBC v Beckett* [1983] IRLR 43, EAT; *Cawley v South Wales Electricity Board* [1985] IRLR 89, EAT.
4 *McClory v Post Office* [1992] ICR 758, [1993] IRLR 159, QBD.

5   *Imperial Group Pension Trust Ltd v Imperial Tobacco Ltd* [1991] ICR 524, [1991] IRLR 66, Ch
     D, a decision of Browne-Wilkinson V-C holding that the strict wording of pension fund deeds and
     rules is subject to an obligation of exercise in good faith and not so as to undermine trust and
     respect towards employee members and beneficiaries. This running together of trust and respect
     and more general ideas of 'good faith' dealing may be significant for future developments.
6   [1991] ICR 269, [1991] IRLR 118, CA.
7   Although a negative formulation may usually be advisable, the term of trust and respect can have
     a positive application if necessary: *BG plc v O'Brien* [2001] IRLR 496, EAT, upheld on appeal
     [2002] EWCA Civ 379, [2002] IRLR 441.
8   [2001] UKHL 13, [2001] ICR 480, [2001] IRLR 279.
9   See para 4.29, below.

3.20   The second question is whether the parties are now unable to contract out
of a term which may otherwise have overriding effect. In the case of most
characteristic terms, it is said in the leading authorities to be possible for the
parties to agree that they are not to apply; this can be seen in the dictum of Lord
Reid set out above, and also in Lord Steyn's speech in *Malik* where he said that
'Such implied terms operate as default rules. The parties are free to exclude or
modify them'. As seen above, in *Johnson v Unisys Ltd* the latter judge referred
to the term of mutual trust and confidence as an 'overarching obligation' and may
be seen to have posed a higher test for exclusion – 'It requires at least express
words or a necessary implication to displace it or cut down its scope'. However,
it is one thing to say that the parties could agree, in unusual circumstances, to
exclude or limit a term such as confidentiality or to provide wages (eg in cases
where it was accepted that the employee would continue with an existing
competing business, or where the employee would rely largely on tips or
commission), but quite another to say that the potentially overriding terms of
trust and respect and health and safety could be excluded. What would a tribunal
make of an express term that the employee would not be required to treat the
employee with trust and respect, or to take reasonable precautions to safeguard
health and safety[1]?

1   The real test would arguably be whether the term of trust and respect could be excluded, since the
     term of health and safety is at least buttressed by a major legislative scheme for protection of
     persons at work; in that context of health and safety, to allow a simple express exclusion could
     be seen as the reintroduction of the defence of *volenti non fit injuria*, which has largely been
     outlawed from the employment context (even in industrial injury cases) for many years, see *Smith
     & Wood* p 734.

(c)   Incorporated terms

3.21   Terms can be incorporated into contracts of employment from other
sources, either expressly or impliedly. In the past, this meant primarily from a
governing collective agreement which of course gave rise to the longstanding
dichotomy in employment law that the real substance of the negotiated term of
employment in question came from the collective level but in UK law the
collective agreement itself is legally unenforceable[1], so that the term could only
gain enforceability by being incorporated into an individual's contract of
employment. Before an amendment in 1993 (considered above) this dual system
was reflected in the statutory provisions (now) in the ERA 1996 requiring a
written notice of basic terms and conditions (the 'section 1 statement'), which
said that on any given topic the statement could refer to 'other documents', thus
giving a positive invitation to express incorporation of parts of a collective
government. Of course, in any business or sector affected by the consistent
moves towards more individual contracting, this particular question of
incorporation of agreements has become less applicable, and prima facie there

should be a 'purer' form of individual contracting in evidence. However, in many cases problems of incorporation will remain, though in a different form. Many contracts will not be wholly contained in one document, and the question today will often revolve around whether certain collateral matters or sources are *meant* to be contractual, ie whether they are incorporated. The sources of problems tend to be company handbooks, working rules, employer policies or codes, and disciplinary procedures. These will be considered below, in addition to the more traditional area of collective agreements.

1 Trade Union and Labour Relations (Consolidation) Act 1974, s 179.

3.22 Before doing so, one general point on incorporation should be made. This is that, once a term has been incorporated into a contract of employment from an extraneous source it has *independent* legal effect, and so continues to operate (unless and until varied or consensually terminated) even if the original source no longer exists. This was particularly important in times of significant levels of derecognition of trade unions and individualising of contracts – an employer could derecognise a union and tear up a collective agreement with legal impunity, but that did *not* mean that any terms of individual contracts incorporated from the agreement thereby lapsed and could be changed unilaterally; they still had to be varied by a level of consent sufficient to satisfy the requirements of contract law[1]. A recent example of this with a curious spin on it is *Whent v T Cartledge Ltd*[2] where council workers (whose contracts incorporate major terms from a ruling collective agreement as amended from time to time) were subject to a contracting out exercise and became employed by a private employer, under the terms of TUPE. They were told by their new employers that any union recognition and collective agreements in respect of them had lapsed, and that under TUPE their existing pay rate as at the date of transfer was protected, but nothing more. When, however, the relevant council collective agreement later raised wages, the employees successfully sued for the increase, even though their new employer was in no way involved in the bargaining – their contracts still (under TUPE) contained a clause that their pay was that set by the collective agreement as amended from time to time, and that was unaffected by the major organisation changes to which they had been subjected.

1 *Burroughs Machines Ltd v Timmoney* [1977] IRLR 404, Ct of Sess; *Robertson v British Gas Corpn* [1983] ICR 351, [1983] IRLR 202, CA; *Gibbons v Associated British Ports* [1985] IRLR 376, QBD.
2 [1997] IRLR 153, EAT. See, to similar effect, *Unicorn Consultancy Services Ltd v Westbrook* [2000] IRLR 80, EAT which raised the problem of what is to happen to a profit-related pay provision in an employment contract with employer A when the employee is TUPE-transferred to employer B.

3.23 Incorporation of collective agreements used to be common. The 1980s and early 1990s saw a substantial decline in the general levels of union recognition and collective bargaining, partly due to deliberate changes in employer practices and partly due to major structural changes in the economy. There are, however, currently signs of at least an arresting of the move towards flexibility and individual contracting, with the ERA 1999 instituting a new statutory recognition procedure, preceded by a sharp increase in voluntary recognition agreements in anticipation of its commencement[1], and enacting statutory protection against being forced out of collective determination and into individual contracts[2]. The strength of the latter is open to doubt because the provisions go out of their way to continue the lawfulness of 'sweetener payments', ie financial inducements to make such a move, so that arguably the case that caused the moves to amend the law would ironically still be decided the same way today[3]. Be that as it may, the question of incorporation of collective agreements remains a live one. Indeed, if moves continue towards more use of 'workforce agreements' in cases where unions are not recognised (or recognition is only partial), and towards more use on a voluntary basis (ie beyond the statutory purposes[4]), we may see questions also arising as to incorporation of elements of these agreements too.

1 See para 3.9, n 2, above.
2 ERA 1999, Sch 2 amended the provisions of the Trade Union and Labour Relations (Consolidation) Act 1992, ss 146[1984] ICR 612, [1984] IRLR 240, CA 148 on detriment against union members. ERA 1999, s 17 permits new laws making illegal detriment or dismissal for refusing to enter a new contract differing from the terms of an applicable collective agreement.
3 *Associated Newspapers Ltd v Wilson, Associated British Ports v Palmer* [1995] ICR 406, [1995] IRLR 258, HL. The ERA 1999 failed to repeal s 148(3) which permits sweetener payments provided they are not for the primary purpose of detering union *membership* itself; further, s 17(4) also states that such a payment will not offend the new laws on 'detriment' for refusing to change to individual contracts, again as long as there is no assault on actual union membership. See Randall & Smith *A Guide to the Employment Relations Act 1999* (1999) Butterworths, pp 16–17. These provisions will now have to be amended in the light of the decision of the ECHR that they infringe the Convention right to freedom of assembly and association: *Wilson v United Kingdom* (2002) Times, 5 July.
4 Consultation of the workforce (through elected representatives) is required by the laws relating to collective redundancies, business transfers and health and safety. There are significant 'carrots' for employers in the laws on working time and parental leave. Some employers may take the view that in the longer term it is preferable to have standing machinery for all these purposes, which could then be used voluntarily for other consultative and informational purposes. At the time of writing, there has been adopted Directive 2002/14/EC requiring more general informing and consulting of the workforce, though technically stopping short of a formal requirement of works councils.

3.24 Incorporation of agreements or parts thereof can be express or implied[1]. With regard to express incorporation, problems can arise as to which agreement of several is being referred to, and (once that is clear) which parts are or are not meant to be incorporated; these are fundamentally questions of fact and interpretation. There can, however, be more complex problems in relation to implied incorporation. Although again heavily factual, certain specific points tend to arise – the actions of the parties, and alleged customs and practices, may be important evidence, but there will also be a fundamental question whether the matter in question is *appropriate* for incorporation into an individual contract. This is based on the fact that collective bargains can serve two quite different functions – to set basic terms and conditions, but also to govern the collective relationship between employer and union; the theory is that only matters in the former category are appropriate for incorporation. The difficulty of applying this distinction can be seen from the example of redundancy clauses in collective agreements (the subject of much of the relatively sparse case law). While it may be that a clause quantifying individual entitlements to enhance redundancy payments could be incorporated (if the facts show the relevant intent to be bound), larger questions as to the handling of a redundancy may fall into the purely collective category, with selection criteria falling into a difficult grey area[2]. In the foundation case of *Young v Canadian Northern Rly Co*[3] the Privy Council declined to incorporate a clause setting out agreed seniority provisions for use in a redundancy. A very similar decision was reached in *Alexander v Standard Telephones & Cables Ltd (No 2)*[4], but in *Anderson v Pringle of Scotland Ltd*[5] the Court of Session found (in interim proceedings for an interdict) at least a prima facie case that a collective agreement term providing for LIFO selection on a redundancy *had* become part of the contract of the individual employee who was successfully challenging a merit/'brownie points' selection method used by the employer, in defiance of the agreement. Ultimately, the question has to be not just whether a particular agreement or clause has been applied in the past, but whether the facts as a whole show an intent to do so as a matter of contractual obligation. The situation is particularly well set out in a passage from the judgment of Hobhouse J in *Alexander*[6]:

> 'The so-called "normative effect" by which it can be inferred that provisions of a collective agreement have become part of individual contracts of employment is now well recognised in employment law. However, serious difficulties still arise because the principle still has to be one of incorporation into the individual contracts of employment and the extraction of a recognisable contractual intent as between the individual employee and his employer. The mere existence of collective agreements which are relevant to the employee and his employment does not include a contractual intent (see for example per Ackner LJ, *Robertson v British Gas* [1983] IRLR 302). The contractual intent has to be found in the individual contract of employment and very often the evidence will not be sufficient to establish such an intent in a manner which satisfies acceptable contractual criteria and satisfies ordinary criteria of certainty. Where the relevant subject-matter is one of present day-to-day relevance to the employer and employee, as for example wage rates and hours of work, the continuing relationship between employer and employee, the former paying wages and providing work, the latter working and accepting wages, provides a basis for inferring such a contractual intent. Where, as in the case of redundancy, the situation is one which does not have daily implications but only arises occasionally the inference will be more difficult to sustain.'

As pointed out above, where there has been incorporation (either express or implied), there can then be problems of interpretation and application. The case of *Hooper v British Railways Board*[7] decides that the fact that a particular contract term originated in a collective agreement does not justify any wider and more purposive interpretation than would normally be given in a contractual dispute. Further, the basis of the decision of the Court of Appeal in *Ali v Christian Salvesen Food Services Ltd*[8], reversing the decision of the EAT, was that a failure in a collective agreement to cover the question of early leavers under an annualised hours pay system (which was then incorporated into contracts of employment) meant that no term was to be implied because the omission was deliberate; arguably this might have ignored the realities that an omission in an agreement after collective negotiations might equally have been due to the matter not having been thought of at the time, not having been subject to final agreement in a time-limited exercise, or due to a desire to get to the pub before closing time. It is certainly arguable that there is scope for wider canons of construction where a contractual term (or lack thereof) owes its origin to a collective agreement, to take into account such eternal verities. If, however, the present law is still to apply, it can equally be argued that, if there is to be any sort of revival of collective negotiation of terms and conditions of employment in the light of the ERA 1999, there is much scope for a radical re-thinking of the ways in which collective bargains are phrased, with a need for more professionalism (in line with the more consumerist and 'new realism' approach of much of modern trade unionism) in their drafting with (dare one say) more legal involvement, and a greater emphasis on future enforceability of relevant terms, once incorporated into individual contracts.

1   For general coverage of the older law here, see *Smith & Wood* pp 112–116 and *Harvey* Div A2D
    (1). *Henry v London General Transport Services Ltd* [2002] EWCA Civ 488 [2002] IRLR 472 is
    a rare recent example of the incorporation of a negotiated agreement into individuals' contracts
    (based on a history of incorporation), against the objection of a significant number of individuals.
2   Procedures for resolving disputes were not incorporated in *NCB v NUM* [1986] ICR 736, [1986]
    IRLR 439, Ch D. On the other hand, in *City and Hackney Health Authority v NUPE* [1985] IRLR
    252, CA it was thought arguable on an interlocutory application that a Whitley Council clause
    concerning shop stewards was incorporated into an individual steward's contract.
3   [1931] AC 83, PC.
4   [1991] IRLR 286, QBD.
5   [1998] IRLR 64, Ct of Sess; *Alexander (No 2)* is not mentioned in the judgment.
6   At 292.
7   [1988] IRLR 517, CA.
8   [1997] ICR 25, [1997] IRLR 17, CA.

3.25   When one turns from incorporation of collective agreements to incorporation of terms from other sources, further considerations arise, though again based essentially on contractual intent. There is a longstanding question as to what elements of 'works rules' can achieve contractual status, and what elements remain subject to managerial prerogative. The obvious difference is that the former would require employee consent or (at least) assent in order to change, whereas the latter would be subject to unilateral change by the employer, though possibly now subject to the method of change not constituting a definable breach of the term of trust and respect as argued above. Old authority clearly establishes this distinction[1], but a modern case makes the point neatly. In *Dryden v Greater Glasgow Health Board*[2] an employee who was a heavy smoker left employment due to the progressive implementation by the employers of a no-smoking policy. Her claim of constructive dismissal was dismissed because (a) a no-smoking policy remained in the realm of working rules and gave rise to no arguments of breach of contractual entitlements, and (b) the way in which it had been introduced could not be said to have infringed the implied term of trust and respect.

1   *Secretary of State for Employment v ASLEF (No 2)* [1972] 2 QB 455, [1972] 2 All ER 949, CA.
2   [1992] IRLR 469, EAT.

3.26   The distinction between contractual terms and working rules has, however, potentially been made more difficult by an otherwise desirable development in personnel practice, namely the company or organisation handbook. In many ways this is a useful tool, encouraged by ACAS guidance as a way of increasing communication within an organisation. There is, however, a potential legal problem, in that a handbook will tend to include both contractually-binding matters and also matters of guidance/good practice which ultimately remain within the employer's prerogative. In a sense, the effect of a handbook is neutral, in that it merely puts into written form the basic realities, and leaves the matter to legal resolution on ordinary principles, as to which parts are meant to have contractual effect.

3.27   More recently, however, there has been a further refinement. This concerns the prevalence of employer 'policies' or various forms of codes of practice. Although such ideas originated largely in the area of health and safety, they have also figured largely in the area of discrimination law. The decision of the Court of Appeal in *Jones v Tower Boot Co Ltd*[1] increased their importance.

The statutory rules on vicarious liability[2] operate by making the employer liable for discriminatory acts (particularly harassment) by fellow employees 'in the course of employment', subject to the defence that the employer took 'such steps as were reasonably practicable to prevent the [fellow] employee from doing that act, or from doing in the course of employment acts of that description'. If one interpreted 'in the course of employment' in the way traditionally accepted by the common law on vicarious liability (as had been the case in the previous case law[3]) there would be the paradoxical effect that the more gross and 'personal' the harassment, the more likely it was to be construed as the employee acting 'on a frolic of his own', for which the employer would *not* be liable. However, *Jones* took the revolutionary step of deciding that the discrimination statutes were to be interpreted afresh and in the light of their protective intent, so that 'in the course of employment' now means little more than 'at work' in a purely factual sense. Thus, the employer is now likely to be prima facie liable for any work-related harassment by fellow employees[4], and so the emphasis is thrown heavily on to whether the employer can establish the defence (the burden of proof being reversed) that all reasonable steps were taken to prevent it. The starting point for this is likely to be the existence of appropriate policies, though it is equally clear that their observance and enforcement will be as important as their existence[5].

The policy or code of practice approach is thus common, but a question can arise whether such devices are incorporated into contracts, ie do they achieve contractual status? In the context of an action under one of the existing discrimination statutes (on sex, race and disability and in Northern Ireland, religion) this question is irrelevant, the focus being potentially on the existence of a policy and its enforceability in practice. However, the matter has arisen acutely in areas where there is currently *no* statutory coverage, but some think that there ought to be – in particular in areas of alleged discrimination on the basis of age or sexual orientation. These are not currently subject to domestic legislation, but some organisations will have equal opportunities policies which go beyond the present legal coverage and pledge the organisation not to discriminate on other grounds, particularly these two. The question then arises whether this is just well-meaning hyperbole *or* in fact a contractual entitlement, such that an employee alleging breach of the policy in his or her case could claim damages for breach of contract, even though subject to no statutory protection. At the time of writing, the cases to date have resulted in failure for the employees, though the reasoning has varied. In *Grant v South-West Trains Ltd*[6] an attempt to establish that an equal opportunities policy covering sexual orientation had contractual effect, so that refusal to grant travel facilities to a same-sex partner was a breach of contract, failed on the basis that the proper construction was that the policy was merely a statement of aims and aspirations, not a contractual obligation. A similar approach, in a less controversial context of a sickness absence policy code of practice, can be seen in *Wandsworth London Borough Council v D'Silva*[7]. On the other hand, in *Taylor v Secretary of State for Scotland*[8] the Inner House of the Court of Session accepted that an equal opportunities policy had become part of prison officers' contracts; however, when they sought to rely on a statement in the policy that the employers would not discriminate on the grounds of age in order to attack a decrease by the employers of the compulsory retirement age, the court held that as a matter of construction the policy (though contractual) was not strong enough to overturn a bona fide change of retirement age, which was construed as not involving an element of discrimination. The contractual effect of the policy had been accepted by the EAT below, and was not re-argued before the Court of Session (or, eventually, the House of Lords). However, that was based on the fact that, when introducing this policy, the employers had presented it as a substantive change to the employees' terms of employment, ie the employers themselves had raised the question of contractual incorporation, and were later hoist by their own petard. In a case without complication (such as *Grant*), the better view at present is that a matter kept purely as a question of policy or guidance probably will *not* be construed as part of the individual's contract[9].

1 [1997] ICR 254, [1997] IRLR 168, CA.
2 Sex Discrimination Act 1975, s 41; Race Relations Act 1976, s 32; Disability Discrimination Act 1995, s 58.
3 The law of vicarious liability is currently under change, towards a broader consideration of 'work connection', rather than the traditional approach of 'employer authorisation': *Lister v Hesley Hall Ltd* [2001] UKHL 22, [2001] 2 All ER 769, [2001] IRLR 472.
4 This has been extended to situations outside working hours, but still work-related, eg social activities organised in a working context: *Chief Constable of Lincolnshire Police v Stubbs* [1999] ICR 547, [1999] IRLR 81, EAT; *Sidhu v Aerospace Composite Technology Ltd* [1999] IRLR 683, EAT.
5 *Balgobin v London Borough of Tower Hamlets* [1987] ICR 829, [1987] IRLR 401, EAT.
6 [1998] IRLR 188, QBD. Note that this litigation was parallel to the main litigation (ultimately unsuccessful) before the ECJ trying to extend EC discrimination law to cover sexual orientation: C-249/96 [1998] ICR 449, [1998] IRLR 206, ECJ.
7 [1998] IRLR 193, CA.
8 [1999] IRLR 362, Ct of Sess, upheld by the House of Lords in a short judgment concerned purely with the question of interpreting the contractual terms: [2000] ICR 595, [2000] IRLR 502.
9 There are arguments that this could be unfair, especially where an employer adopts a 'policy' approach to major obligations (even statutory ones), leaving it open to argue later that it is not bound by such a policy if it does not live up to it; from a simple locus standi perspective, the employee's only chance of enforcement lies through the contract.

3.28   Finally on incorporation, a question can arise as to whether a disciplinary procedure has contractual effect. As before, this can be covered one way or another expressly, or can be left to be implied. The latter may be particularly the case if the procedure is set out in a company handbook, with other matters which are or are not contractual, thus leaving the matter ambiguous. Whether or not a disciplinary procedure has contractual effect ought to be irrelevant in an unfair dismissal action, where simply its existence is relevant and whether it has been fairly adhered to[1]. Likewise, a procedure may well set out offences potentially meriting summary dismissal, but even if that is contractual it will still only be evidence in an unfair dismissal case arising from such a dismissal, since the statutory action looks at the overall reasonableness of the employers' actions, not at the niceties of whether the dismissal was contractually sound[2]. Views tend to vary on the desirability from the employer's point of view of making a disciplinary procedure contractual. In its favour, it may be seen as indirectly strengthening it, and it is certainly the case that if an employer wishes to include a penalty (short of dismissal) that might otherwise be a breach of contract such as suspension without pay or disciplinary demotion, it is necessary to have that as part of the employee's contract. On the other hand, to make the procedure contractual increases the employee's rights to have it properly complied with; failure to do so has in the past led to an award of damages going beyond simple payment for the notice period (at least to the extent of adding on the time it would have taken to have gone through the procedure properly)[3], and in an extreme case to the possibility of a court order restraining disciplining or dismissal until the proper procedure is used[4]. In this context, it is of particular interest that the Employment Bill 2002, before Parliament at the time of writing, proposes to make the basic disciplinary and grievance procedures (set out in

Sch 2) part of all contracts of employment; it does *not* state what is to be the contractual status of more sophisticated procedures (even those which merely comply with the ACAS Code of Practice, which itself is more sophisticated than the Sch 2 procedures).

1   *Westminster City Council v Cabaj* [1996] IRLR 399, CA.
2   *Laws Stores Ltd v Oliphant* [1978] IRLR 251, EAT is a good example. Likewise, the fact that there is contractual power to impose a particular penalty does not mean that it will always be reasonable to do so: *BBC v Beckett* [1983] IRLR 43, EAT.
3   *Gunton v Richmond-upon-Thames London Borough Council* [1980] ICR 755, [1980] IRLR 321, CA; *Boyo v Lambeth LBC* [1994] ICR 727, [1995] IRLR 50, CA. Towards the end of his speech in *Johnson v Unisys Ltd* [2001] UKHL 13, [2001] ICR 480, [2001] IRLR 279, Lord Hoffman denies that disciplinary procedures (even if contractual) can 'create contractual duties which are independently actionable'. This seems to go against *Gunton and Boyo*, but (a) neither of those cases were cited, (b) the point had not been fully argued and (c) his Lordship may have been envisaging some major contractual action for damages for the dismissal itself, not the far more restricted remedy in those two cases.
4   For a rare example see *Peace v City of Edinburgh Council* [1999] IRLR 417, Ct of Sess (OH) where an interdict was issued restraining the employer from using a new disciplinary procedure which the employee claimed he had never agreed to as a replacement for the procedure in his original contract. Note that this was not actually a dismissal case. See para 10.6, below.

4   Notice provisions

(a)   Introduction

3.29   One of the principal peculiarities of employment contracts is that, unless clearly meant to be for a fixed term or to last until a certain event or eventuality, they are terminable by either side giving notice of termination. Most contracts will cover this matter expressly, but if this is not done the law will imply a term of reasonable notice, the quantification of which would then depend on the facts of the case such as the nature of the employment, seniority, any custom and practice and interval of payment[1]. Normally, notice is thus a matter of contract, but statute has intervened in three ways – (a) length of notice is one of the matters to be notified in writing to a new employee in the section one statement[2]; (b) minimum periods of notice are laid down, being one week for each year of employment up to twelve (in the case of dismissal by the employer) and one week (in the case of resignation by the employee), with both rights arising once the employee has been employed for one month[3]; (c) there are statutory rules on the rights of an employee under notice[4].

The common law doctrine of notice was responsible in the past (before the inception of unfair dismissal by statute) for a low level of job security – the employee could be dismissed for any reason or none (especially before statutory discrimination law) by being given notice *and* before the Contracts of Employment Act 1963 the notice period itself could be very short and status-based (not increasing with length of service). This could well have the effect of negating other express or implied employee rights under the contract, because if he or she tried to insist on them the result could be dismissal by notice which, provided of the requisite length, could not constitute wrongful dismissal – small wonder that the Donovan Commission[5] on industrial relations found that the traditional way to fight a dismissal was by industrial action, not recourse to the law (and so recommended an effective law on unfair dismissal in order to channel such disputes into the legal system). The doctrine of notice has had another, linked but separate, restricting effect on the usefulness of a common law action for dismissal. If the proper notice is not given (and summary dismissal for gross misconduct was not warranted), the dismissal is wrongful and the employee can sue for breach of contract. However, the traditional view has always been that the prima facie measure of damage is not the loss of livelihood or even the wages for the likely duration of the hiring (but for the dismissal), but is instead merely wages for what should have been the proper notice period, because on an ultra-logical approach (assuming that the employer at common law has an unfettered right to give notice without having to justify the reason) that is all that the employee has lost[6]. We shall see in the course of this book that there may be moves in the modern law of employment contracts to extend possible heads of damage, or to restrict the right to give notice if that would negate other vital aspects of the contract. However, the traditional view has in the past had a severely limiting effect, particularly when allied to relatively short notice periods. At one end of the spectrum, this emphasis on the notice period could be advantageous, in the case of a highly-placed employee on a high salary and a long notice period; for most ordinary mortals however, it was always a cause of little protection at common law.

Two particular aspects of the law on notice are worth special comment because of the interest being shown in them currently. These are the widespread practice of giving wages in lieu and the specialised form of notice known as a 'garden leave clause'.

1   A particularly notable (or notorious) example of this was Lord Denning MR's judgment in *Hill v C A Parsons Ltd* [1972] Ch 305, [1971] 3 All ER 1345, CA where he quantified reasonable notice for an engineer at six months, thereby quite fortuitously bringing him under new legislation that would protect him from the union pressure that had caused his dismissal!
2   ERA 1996, s 1(4)(e).
3   ERA 1996, s 86(1), (2). This minimum standard (dating back to the original Contracts of Employment Act 1963) does not prevent either party waiving his right to notice on any occasion or accepting a payment in lieu: s 86(3). Nor does it prevent either party terminating without notice by reason of the conduct of the other party, eg in a case of summary dismissal for gross misconduct, or constructive dismissal: s 86(6).
4   ERA 1996, s 87–91. These sections set out certain basic rights to pay and other contractual terms, but in doing so they only *define* contractual rights, and so the employee's remedy remains contractual, not statutory: *Westwood v Secretary of State for Employment* [1985] ICR 209, [1984] IRLR 209, HL (as the claim was contractual, the employee was still under an obligation to mitigate loss).
5   Report of the Royal Commission on Trade Unions and Employers' Associations (1968) Cmnd 3623.
6   One interesting gloss on this can be seen in *Silvey v Pendragon plc* [2002] EWCA Civ 784 [2002] IRLR 685, where a wrongfully dismissed employee successfully claimed the value of a contractual benefit that he *would have qualified for* if he had been given notice as required by his contract.

(b)   Wages in lieu

3.30   The giving of wages in lieu of notice has always been common, in order to remove the employee from the workplace immediately, while discharging the principal contractual obligation of paying wages for what would normally have been the notice period; extreme employer sensitivity to the integrity of its computer systems has only increased the need for instant departure of the employee once dismissal is decided upon. In the past, there has tended to be an assumption that payment of wages is inherently lawful, even if not provided for in the contract, because the main obligation on an employer under a contract is to pay wages (not to provide work) and so even if giving wages in lieu was technically a breach of contract, the 'damages' have already been paid, ie the wages that would have been earned if the notice period has been allowed to run[1]. What we have seen in recent years, however, is more emphasis on analysis of the legal position and the exploration of some of its more subtle aspects[2]. In particular, we have seen emphasis on the question whether to put an *express* term into the contract permitting payment in lieu. While the pros and cons may have been considered in each individual case, the general position is as follows. The advantages for the employer of an express in-lieu clause are – (a) a dismissal with a payment in lieu made under the clause is then lawful under the contract; (b) this means that any restraint of trade clause can continue to operate rather than being destroyed by a wrongful dismissal[3]; (c) the effective date of termination for statutory purposes is the date the wages in lieu are given, not the date the notice period would have expired; (d) if the effect of this earlier termination is to deprive the employee of the one year qualifying period for an unfair dismissal claim, the rule allowing the employee to claim this as a head of damage in a wrongful dismissal action[4] will not apply because the dismissal was lawful[5]; (e) a 'Wages Act' action (now Part II of the ERA 1996) will not lie in relation to any non-payment of the in-lieu amount in question because it does not represent 'wages' under a subsisting contract[6]. There are, however, two potential disadvantages to an express in-lieu clause, one each to employer and employee. An employer must realise that, as the dismissal with wages in lieu is lawful, any amounts not actually paid to the employee under the clause (once it has been relied on by the employer) can be recovered by the employee by an action in *debt*, rather than as damages; the crucial point about this is that the doctrine of mitigation does not apply to an action in debt, so that the full amount is payable even if the ex-employee obtained lucrative alternative employment elsewhere immediately[7]; had the dismissal been wrongful (for example, where there is a clause but the employer does not purport to rely on it, or as where there is no clause but the employer simply insists on paying in lieu) those new earnings would have been deductible from the employer's liability[8]. This could be a distinction of some importance for a highly paid employee on long notice, who is highly marketable elsewhere. On the other hand, the distinction between a contractual and a non-contractual payment in lieu can also affect the employee, because it is now established (after a surprisingly long period of uncertainty) that a payment in lieu under a contractual clause is subject to income tax in the hands of the ex-employee, who cannot claim the benefit of the £30,000 post-termination payments exemption[9]; a non-contractual (ie de facto) payment in lieu is not affected because it retains its character as damages, and so the valuable exemption can be claimed. The balance of advantage may thus have to be weighed carefully. One final point on in-lieu clauses is that in a worrying decision[10] the ex-President of the EAT Morison J, in one of his many leaving presents, suggested obiter that such a clause might be contrary to statute, on the basis that the provision stating that the minimum statutory notice periods do not prevent a party from waiving notice or accepting a payment in lieu[11] could be interpreted as being restricted to an ad hoc agreement to do so, and not applying to a formal agreement in advance. He did accept that any decision to that effect could now only be made by the Court of Appeal or above and when the appeal was heard in the case itself the point was not discussed; it is strongly suggested that such a decision should *not* be taken, because to do so would be highly unrealistic, given the prevalence of these clauses and the general desirability of having matters such as this clearly set out in the contract.

1 *Dixon v Stenor Ltd* [1973] ICR 157, [1973] IRLR 28, NIRC. Equally, there is no contractual breach by the employee if he or she takes new employment during what would have been the

notice period, even with a competitor (unless there is an actual breach of confidentiality): *Hutchings v Coinseed Ltd* [1998] IRLR 190, CA.

2   See particularly the speech of Lord Browne-Wilkinson in *Delaney v Staples* [1992] ICR 483, [1992] IRLR 191, HL, setting out a four-fold categorisation of payment-in-lieu cases (see *Smith & Wood* p 369); this was for the immediate purpose of determining whether a failure to pay in lieu was a 'deduction' for the purposes of the Wages Act 1986, but can be viewed as a wider statement of principle.

3   *Rex Stewart Jeffries Parker Ginsberg Ltd v Parker* [1988] IRLR 483, CA.

4   Such a possibility has been mooted obiter for some years, and was finally accepted in *Raspin v United News Shops Ltd* [1999] IRLR 9, EAT. See *Smith & Wood* p 393.

5   *Morran v Glasgow Council of Tenants' Associations* [1998] IRLR 67, Ct of Sess.

6   *Delaney v Staples* [1992] ICR 483, [1992] IRLR 191, HL. Such amounts now can be claimed before a tribunal as amounts outstanding on termination, under the Extension of Jurisdiction Orders.

7   *Abrahams v Performing Right Society* [1995] ICR 1028, [1995] IRLR 486, CA. The case of *Gregory v Wallace* [1998] IRLR 387, CA may seem to contradict this, but is in fact consistent with it and explicable on the basis of a specific clause in the contract allowing alternative work in what would have been the notice period. *Abrahams* has strange dicta suggesting no duty to mitigate even where the action is for damages, but these are best tactfully forgotten (and were side-stepped in *Gregory*).

8   *Cerberus Software Ltd v Rowley* [2001 EWCA Civ 78, [2001] ICR 376, [2001] IRLR 160 where there was an in-lieu clause in permissive terms ('the employer *may* make a payment in lieu') but it was not used by the employer who purported to dismiss summarily for gross misconduct; this was untrue, the dismissal was wrongful and so the employee was under a duty to mitigate.

9   *EMI Group Electronics Ltd v Coldicott (Inspector of Taxes)* [1999] IRLR 630, [1999] STC 803, CA. This has been extended to a case where the employer gives notice under the contract and then negotiates a sum in settlement of the employee's rights (including to a payment in lieu): *Richardson (HMI) v Delaney* [2001] IRLR 663, Ch D.

10 *Cerberus Software Ltd v Rowley* [1999] IRLR 690, EAT (reversed on appeal, see n 8, above).

11 ERA 1996, s 86(3), see para 3.29, n 3, above.

(c)   Garden leave clauses

3.31   Turning to the question of garden leave clauses, these operate by way of maximising the effect of a notice provision. In order to restrict the chance of a key employee going to work for a competitor while still in possession of current business or research knowledge, the idea is to put him or her on to a long notice period with an express stipulation that during it they will not be required to work for the employer, will be paid everything due under the contract, and will not work for anyone else during the notice period[1]. Such an arrangement must be done by express terms, because the Court of Appeal in *William Hill Organisation Ltd v Tucker*[2] stated that such a controversial arrangement would not be implied. The idea of garden leave was evolved to meet the problem that classic restraint of trade clauses are difficult to get right and, if excessive, immediately become void, so that the employer is left with no protection at all. The idea was that a garden leave clause would be viewed more favourably by a court because the hardship to the employee was far less – under a restraint clause the ex-employee is without the job and cannot take other employment in his or her chosen field, whereas under a garden leave clause the employee is still being paid, possibly handsomely. Moreover, the device seemed to have the best of all possible worlds because in one reported case where the employer had imposed too long a period of garden leave the court cut it down and enforced what would have been reasonable[3], something a court will not normally do with an over-long restraint clause. However, from the start the courts had made clear that enforcement would not be automatic; the remedy is an injunction which is discretionary and so an order might be refused if there was insufficient evidence of potential detriment to the employer[4]. Moreover, the idea that because the employee was being paid he or she could have no complaint could be too simplistic, because the effect of a long period of neutralisation could be the wasting of the employee's expertise or knowledge to an unconscionable extent, ie there could well be cases where after a while the money was secondary to the employee's interest in remaining employable. The case of *William Hill* (above) fired two shots across the bows (in addition to holding against any question of implication, in the absence of express stipulation). First, the court seemed to widen the ambit of cases where the employee can claim a genuine interest in carrying on with the work itself, not just receiving income[5]. Secondly, a dictum by Morritt LJ at the end of his judgment is capable of casting doubt on the basic idea that a garden leave clause is more likely to succeed than a restraint clause:

> '[I]f injunctive relief was sought then it had to be justified on similar grounds to those necessary to the validity of the employee's covenant in restraint of trade. The court should be careful not to grant interlocutory relief to enforce a garden leave clause to any greater extent than would be covered by a justifiable covenant in restraint of trade entered into by an employee.'

Further developments here are awaited with interest. Is this just a warning of a more discretionary attitude to enforcement or could it mean, more literally, that an employer seeking to enforce a garden leave clause will be required to go through the hoops normally associated with justifying a restraint clause? If so, there would need to be more emphasis on the exact nature of the interest to be protected, the geographical extent and the length of time, against a background of increased unwillingness by a court to sever objectionable elements or to rescue an over-long clause by cutting it down at enforcement stage[6]. The exact effects of *William Hill* remain to be explored; at the very least it shows that garden leave clauses are not an automatic panacea for an employer, who may need to be able to show that the protection sought is no more than is demonstrably necessary, bearing in mind also the employee's interest in the work as well as the money.

1 *Evening Standard Co Ltd v Henderson* [1987] ICR 588, [1987] IRLR 64, CA (one year clause enforceable against a newspaper production manager); *Euro Brokers Ltd v Rabey* [1995] IRLR 206 (six month clause enforced against a money broker).
2 [1998] IRLR 313, CA.
3 *GFI Group Inc v Eaglestone* [1994] IRLR 119. Likewise, in *Symbian Ltd v Christensen* [2001] IRLR 77, CA the width of an anti-competition clause was cut down and an injunction granted on that lesser basis.
4 *Provident Financial Group plc v Hayward* [1989] ICR 160, [1989] IRLR 84, CA.
5 See para 4.3, below.
6 Arguably such a view would be contrary to the *fons et origo* of garden leave clauses (*Evening Standard Co Ltd v Henderson* [1987] ICR 588, [1987] IRLR 64, CA) and beg the question when it would ever be possible to have a valid garden leave clause.

5   Variation of contracts of employment

3.32   The law lying behind the practical realities of variation of contracts of employment can be easy to state but difficult to apply. This is an area where the contractual analysis remains strong, so that what must be shown is some form of assent. What form that takes can vary, and the problems can arise from the simple homely truth that contracts are static but jobs are not. Failure to change contracts when jobs have moved on and evolved can lead to the highly undesirable position in which an elderly contract no longer reflects current working practices, a recipe for legal difficulties if and when a litigated dispute arises.

Consensual variation is only necessary if the practice or benefit being changed itself is contractual. Matters remaining non-contractual, and so in the managerial prerogative, can be changed by managerial decision, though there are signs of the law evolving so that an exercise of such discretion must not be such as to breach the employment relationship[1]. Another approach by an employer might be to accept that a certain matter is contractual, but write into the contract a power of unilateral variation; as seen earlier this chapter, it is likely that such a clause would have to be clear and unambiguous, and that a court or tribunal would, if necessary, construe it narrowly.

One of the advantages for an employer having a recognised trade union representing a particular set of employees is that change can be channelled through that one avenue. Where it is clear, especially through a history of dealings leading to contractual changes, that re-negotiated terms and conditions are to become new terms of individual contracts, the employees will be deemed to have agreed to the changes. This may be obvious in good times, when the changes are improvements from the employees' perspective; it may be crucial if in bad times the union agrees to poorer terms, because it may then be difficult for individuals to object individually[2], even if they are not actually members of the union. The overall advantages of such a system are such that some employers may want to keep it, even if union membership among the employees has decreased markedly, even to a small minority. However, in many instances such a decline in membership over the past two decades has led to a move away from collective bargaining, on to a basis of individual contracting. While this may have all sorts of economic advantages for an employer (and fit in with more current ideas of human resource management) it does store up problems legally in relation to contractual change. If such an employer, having moved to individual contracts, later says to the lawyer 'How do I now change terms and conditions lawfully?' the lawyer will have to answer 'Individually'.

Of course, in many cases that will not be a realistic option and employers will seek to find some form of 'collective' change, even though the collective machinery itself has gone. Two well-known employer wheezes need to be considered at this point, to show the legal pitfalls.

1   See, eg, the change to a no smoking policy in *Dryden v Greater Glasgow Health Board* [1992] IRLR 469, EAT.
2   *Henry v London General Transport Services Ltd* [2002] EWCA Civ 488 [2002] IRLR 472. In the context of a collective agreement for increased pay but on the basis that it is not to be pensionable, see *South West Trains v Wightman* [1998] PLR 113, considered in chap 5 below.

3.33   The first tactic is for the employer to 'propose' a change, leaving it for the employee to object; absence of objection will then be argued to be consent through acquiescence. This is a not uncommon tactic (sometimes done by 're-issuing section/statements' or 'up-dating contracts'). There is no legal right of unilateral variation, but on the other hand there is also no legal requirement that 'consent' be positive, let alone joyous. This is therefore a tactic that may work, depending on economic realities, as much as legal arguments. There are, however, at least three potential problems legally. The first is that the result can remain open-ended for some time, rather than achieving the desired finality. While it is true that an employee faced with major change (of immediate impact) such as an amended shift pattern will have to make up his or her mind quickly whether to go along with it, in a case of a change to terms and conditions only having a longer-term effect (eg sickness benefits) there is well-known authority that a court or tribunal may be much more reluctant to find acquiescence from simple silence, especially where the reason for that silence may have been a basic desire to keep the job[1]. There could therefore be an argument by the employee some considerable time later that they did not really consent to the change at the time, and that the old term should therefore continue to apply. The second problem is that there may be active opposition by employees. Here, the employees may continue to work under protest and then use a common law action to challenge the validity of what the employer claims was a variation. Where the change in question has entailed a fall in take-home pay, one tactic used to good effect in the past has been for the employees to wait for a period of time and then bring an action for arrears of wages[2], claiming the net decrease either in an ordinary breach of contract action in the civil courts or, increasingly, as an unlawful 'deduction from wages' (under the ERA 1996, Part II) in an employment tribunal. Although the basis for either action is the individual's contract, such a method of objection may in practice be more likely if the employees in question are acting together, especially where backed by their union. The third problem could arise if the employee is so unhappy with the purposed changes that he or she would rather lose the job than accept them. Here, the ultimate weapon of the employee is to leave and claim constructive dismissal, based on the employer's contractual breach in forcing through the change without consent. The actual argument for constructive dismissal will be relatively clear, but it is not all simple for the employee because the fact the there is a constructive dismissal does not necessarily mean that it will be held to have been unfair. If the employer can show strong business need to make the changes and the adoption of fair procedures to try to obtain the workforce's agreement (especially if it can also be shown that the majority have agreed), then the dismissal of objecting individuals may ultimately be held to have been for 'some other substantial reason' and fair[3]. This will normally involve the employer actually dismissing the employees in question, but can also apply to a case of constructive dismissal[4]. If, however, the employer has simply tried to force through the 'proposed' changes with little by way of consultation or other fair procedure, it is likely that the eventual dismissal will be both constructive and unfair.

1 *Jones v Associated Tunnelling Co Ltd* [1981] IRLR 477, EAT.
2 The leading case is *Rigby v Ferodo Ltd* [1988] ICR 29, [1987] IRLR 516, HL. The employees may not continue eto work under protest indefinitely; after a certain period they will be deemed to have acquiesced, particularly if acts are done which are inconsistent with continued opposition: *Henry v London General Transport Services Ltd* [2002] EWCA Civ 488 [2002] IRLR 472.
3 *Catamaran Cruisers Ltd v Williams* [1994] IRLR 386, EAT and *Farrant v Woodroffe School* [1998] ICR 184, [1998] IRLR 176, EAT are good examples.
4 *Savoia v Chiltern Herb Farm Ltd* [1982] IRLR 166, CA.

3.34 The second tactic for insisting on a change of terms can feature prominently in employer mythology. It is quite simply to serve notice of termination of the existing contract (of the necessary lawful length) and then immediately 're-engage' the employees on the new terms. In the opinion of some managers, this seems to be thought foolproof, and arguably (on ordinary contractual principles) it should have the effect of bringing about the desired contractual changes[1]. However, there are two possible ramifications under statute that should make the employer have second thoughts. The first is that there could be an action for unfair dismissal by the affected employees. This may seem strange, given that they are still working for the same employer (albeit on the new terms), but it is the case that there can be a dismissal from a particular *contract*[2]; if that is held to have been unfair (as it may well be in the case of highly unilateral action by the employer[3]) it may be that a tribunal would seek to fix compensation by reference to the loss sustained by the employees in having to accept the new terms. The second intervention of statute has come more recently in *GMB v Man Truck and Bus UK Ltd*[4] and involves the law on consultation on collective redundancies. Following a merger of two firms, the new employer sent letters to all employees giving notice to terminate, with offers to re-engage on the new terms on which they were insisting. The union representing the employees made a complaint to a tribunal of failure to consult on impending redundancies (of 20 or more), contrary to the Trade Union and Labour Relations Act 1992, s 188. This seems odd – how could the employees be 'redundant' when they were still employed? The answer was that the Trade Union Reform and Employment Rights Act 1993 substituted a new and specific definition of 'redundancy' for these purposes, in order to bring the UK provisions into line with EC law. All that this requires is a 'dismissal for a reason not related to the individual concerned'. That, according to the EAT, was satisfied here. The employees were thus 'redundant' for the purposes of s 188, there had not been the necessary consultation with the union (not surprisingly, given the employer's attempts to force the change through) and so the union had a good claim for protective awards for the individual employees. Given that the maximum protective award is 90 days' pay per employee, this highly inventive use of a complaint of failure to consult should be a considerable disincentive to use of the fire-and-rehire tactic on any collective basis, involving serious numbers of employees.

1   This was assumed to be the case in the context of changing terms after a TUPE transfer in *Wilson v St Helens Borough Council* [1998] ICR 1141, [1998] IRLR 706, HL.
2   *Hogg v Dover College* [1990] ICR 39, EAT; *Alcan Extrusions v Yates* [1996] IRLR 327, EAT. These cases are particularly strong because the employers did not expressly dismiss the workforce; they did, however, unilaterally impose changes so fundamental that the tribunals held that this alone amounted to the termination of the original contracts, amounting to 'dismissals' within (now) the ERA 1996, s 95(1)(a) ('the contract under which he is employed is terminated by the employer'), then held them to have been unfair.
3   *Quaere* whether it could be argued here that there is a breach of the term of trust and respect (affecting the fairness), where the employer tries to 'bounce' the employees into continuing on significantly different terms. If on the other hand employees seek such a change by strike action, the common law is of little help to them (there being no general concept of suspension of contract, in spite of Lord Denning's views in *Morgan v Fry* [1968] 2 QB 710, [1968] 3 All ER 452, CA). The House of Lords in *Johnson v Unisys Ltd* [2001] UKHL 13, [2001] ICR 480, [2001] IRLR 279 held that the term of trust and respect does not apply on termination, but it could be argued that that should not apply here where any 'termination' is both technical and tactical.
4   [2000] ICR 1101, [2000] IRLR 636, EAT. The case concerned consultation with a recognised trade union. However, lack of such a union will not now resolve this point for an employer since, it will be recalled, the collective redundancy laws were remodelled in 1995 to extend the obligation to non-unionised workplaces through the device of elected employee representatives.

Chapter 4

Implied terms in contracts of employment

1 Introduction

4.1 It is now necessary to consider in more detail the implied terms that are generally referred to as 'characteristic' or 'default' rules of contracts of employment in general. The first two parts of the chapter concern the well established implied obligations on employers and employees, with emphasis on recent developments. The third part looks at five areas of uncertainty where the law is still evolving, possibly in the direction of further implied obligations, of wider or narrower ambit. This is an area of law that has seen significant development, and is likely to see more in the future, either in the purest context of breach of these obligations giving rise to a common law action of sorts, or as the essential contractual background to a claim of constructive dismissal for the purposes of a statutory action for unfair dismissal.

2 Implied obligations on employers

(a) Payment of wages

4.2 The general obligation on an employer under a contract of employment is to pay the wages due, on the due date. Forms of remuneration are not generally governed by the law and will usually depend on what the parties have agreed, even to the extent of agreeing no wage as such, but instead relying on some other form of remuneration such as commission or piece rates[1]. Of course, in relatively poorly paid employment the employer will now have to ensure that the hourly rate does not fall below the national minimum wage; this may involve complicated averaging (having first decided on what basis under the National Minimum Wage Regulations 1999 that averaging is to be done), but provided this can be done and shows a result in compliance with the statutory minimum, the law is not further involved in the form the pay takes[2]. Statutory intervention is confined to a certain measure of protection from unnotified deductions from pay[3], and a requirement of an itemised pay statement[4].

Once outside the area of pay, there is relatively little scope for characteristic terms. In areas such as sick pay, holidays and lay-off pay, the emphasis is on specific coverage in the contract either through express terms or 'real' implied terms. With regard to sick pay, there is no presumption in favour or against, if the contract is silent, and so a court or tribunal will have to consider all the circumstances of the individual case[5]. Likewise with holidays, there are no particular default rules at common law (though there are now the provisions in the Working Time Regulations 1998 for a minimum of four weeks' paid annual leave, which may not be carried forward or bought out); indeed, there is not even any particular presumption that contractual holiday pay accrues and is payable pro rata on leaving part-way through the holiday year[6]. Payment during lay off has never been subject to satisfactory and consistent case law, and such as there is has tended to rely on factual implication and/or custom and practice; in the absence of any such implication, the practical route is to look at the various statutory provisions (in employment law and social security law) that impact on the laid-off worker, rather than any inherent common law protection.

With regard to pay, however, the obligation is a particularly strong one. This means that any failure to pay that which is contractually owing[7], or any particular element of it, is likely to be viewed as a fundamental breach of contract entitling the employee to walk out and claim constructive dismissal, as the Court of Appeal have recently reminded us in *Cantor Fitzgerald International v Callaghan*[8]. It is possible that there could be a de minimis exception, though it could be argued to the contrary that if there is the necessary intention to refuse payment the amount should be irrelevant; on the other hand, it may be that simple lateness in paying (eg due to an employer's cash flow problems or extraneous factors) might or might not be a fundamental breach[9]. In general, however, pay (including additional amounts such as bonus or commission) is likely to be such a basic element of the contract that any interference with it by the employer will be legally dangerous.

1   See generally Smith & Wood *Industrial Law* (7th edn, 2000) Butterworths, pp 172–177.
2   Ironically, the oldest legislation on individual employment law, the Truck Acts 1831–1940, did just this in one historically important way, by providing that a manual labourer had a right to payment in 'current coin of the realm' (to prevent abuse of payment in tokens to be spent in the employer's own 'tommy shop'); this eventually was inconsistent with moves towards cashless pay, which was facilitated first by the Payment of Wages Act 1960 and then by the repeal of the Truck Acts themselves by the Wages Act 1986.
3   ERA 1996, Part II, ss 13–27.
4   ERA 1996, s 8.
5   *Mears v Safecar Security Ltd* [1982] ICR 626, [1982] IRLR 183, CA.
6   *Morley v Heritage plc* [1993] IRLR 400, CA.
7   This of course is likely to be the key question – what payment *does* the contract require? This will be a heavily factual question, possibly more difficult in the case of supplementary or additional elements of remuneration than in the case of basic pay. An ex gratia bonus will not normally be contractual, but what if a clear pattern of such awards has been established (eg in fact based on company performance)? See para 9.5, below. It is unlikely that a court or tribunal would find an implied right to a pay rise as such: *Murco Petroleum Ltd v Forge* [1987] ICR 282, [1987] IRLR 50, EAT.
8   [1999] ICR 639, [1999] IRLR 234, CA, disapproving *Gillies v Richard Daniels & Co* [1979] IRLR 457, EAT which had suggested it remained a question of degree. The decision in *Cantor Fitzgerald* is a strong one, not concerning basic pay, but the tax efficiency (or otherwise) of only one (loan-based) element of a salary package; further, the alleged breach was being used by the employees to escape a restraint of trade clause, in order to go to work for a competitor.
9   *Adams v Charles Zub Associates Ltd* [1978] IRLR 551, EAT, not doubted in *Cantor Fitzgerald*.

(b)   Provision of work?

4.3   The general rule has always been that the employer's basic obligation is to pay wages, *not* to provide work to do[1]. For this reason, the assumption is usually made that a suspension with pay is inherently lawful (indeed, recommended in the ACAS Code of Practice in cases of suspected misconduct, to allow time for reasonable investigation), and that in the case of dismissal with wages in lieu it will either be impliedly permitted under the contract[2] or, if not so permitted (expressly or impliedly), of little practical consequence because the employer has paid anticipatory damages (wages during the notice period) and, as there is no right actually to work, there will normally be little or nothing left for the ex-employee to sue for.

To this general rule of no obligation to provide work, the courts evolved certain necessary exceptions relating to performers who have an interest in publicity as well as pay, piecework/commission workers who need at least a modicum of work in order to earn their pay, and an ill-defined category of professional office-holders[3]. An attempt by Lord Denning MR in *Langston v AUEW*[4] to erect a common law 'right to work' which would have effectively reversed the general rule fared badly. Its context was certain cases where the real target was a trade union exercising its influence against non-members in the period before the highly restrictive trade union laws of the 1980s outlawed such practices, and to that extent it soon became passe and largely forgotten, especially as the end result of the remission of Langston's case itself to the NIRC[5] was a much narrower decision based on the existing exceptions, rather than the application of any new, generalised principle. The question lay dormant in the case law for quarter of a century, though in the latter part of that period there were occasional press reports of employees seeking to rely on a right actually to perform their work, in particular when suspended for an unreasonably long period of time because of a complaint against them, without the matter being properly resolved by the employer. Indeed, one can argue that in our long hours, work-obsessed culture the idea that the employee's only interest is in pay, rather than high-profile work, 'results' and career advancement (plus the possibly disastrous effects of being kept away from work where it was at the cutting edge of technological, medical, business or other developments), was looking rather old fashioned. This point arose before the Court of Appeal in *William Hill Organisation Ltd v Tucker*[6], in the specific context of garden leave, but raising the provision of work issue incidentally. The simple starting point about this case is that the employers had neglected to put an express garden leave clause into the contract. Thus, when the employee left giving only one month's notice, rather than the long period of six months in the contract, the employers (seeking a restraining injunction) had to argue that there was an implied garden leave obligation, given that they were prepared to pay him for the full six months and could insist on him doing no work for them or anyone else during that period.

1 *Collier v Sunday Referee Publishing Co Ltd* [1940] 2 KB 647, [1940] 4 All ER 234.
2 *Konski v Peet* [1915] 1 Ch 530. If wages in lieu are permitted by the contract there is no breach by the employer (sufficient to found constructive dismissal) even if the employee loses financially by not working out the notice (eg by not earning commission): *Marshall (Cambridge) Ltd v Hamblin* [1994] ICR 362, [1994] IRLR 260, EAT.
3 See *Smith & Wood* p 120 for the old case law on these exceptions.
4 [1974] 1 All ER 980, [1974] ICR 180, CA.
5 [1974] ICR 510, [1974] IRLR 182, NIRC.
6 [1998] IRLR 313, CA. For garden leave generally, see para 3.31, above.

4.4 Reopening the question of provision of work in relation to the latter part of this argument, the court held that the argument would only hold good if there was indeed *no* obligation to provide work as well as pay. Traditionally, that would have been little problem, but Morritt LJ (giving the judgment of the court) said that 'as social conditions have changed, the courts have increasingly recognised the importance to the employee of the work, not just the pay'. Having reviewed the older case law, he went on to cast the law here in broader, more generally applicable terms. Although accepting that the answer lies in construction of the individual contract rather than in any broader 'right to work', he held that in this case (concerning a senior manager of 'spread betting'), there *was* an implied obligation to allow the employee to perform his work (including during the notice period), for three reasons – (1) the employee's post was a specific and unique one, which he had been instrumental in setting up; (2) the skills necessary for the post required frequent exercise for their enhancement and preservation; (3) the terms of the contract generally were consistent with such an obligation, particularly the terms requiring the employee to work such hours as were necessary to do the job, assigning a broad range of duties, providing for training and career development, and giving only a limited power of suspension in disciplinary cases. There was thus no scope for an implied garden leave obligation on the employee. At its narrowest, the decision means that an express garden leave clause is necessary whenever it is arguable that the employer is obliged to provide work as well as pay, and indeed as a matter of practice such an express clause is now always desirable.

However, the effects of the case may be much wider on the general principle. Ground (1) is possibly narrowing and (as the judge accepted) infinitely arguable, but it is ground (2) (particularly in conjunction with some rather generalised arguments on ground (3)) that is potentially of greatest significance (especially if (1) and (2) are to be interpreted disjunctively). In modern employment circumstances, especially in rapidly-evolving high-tech industries or professions, arguments on this basis could be raised much more often than under the old 'exceptions' basis (performers, pieceworkers, etc). These points have not yet been explored further at the time of writing, but could be pointing significantly in a new direction, leading to a requirement for more and clearer coverage of exact contractual rights and obligations in cases possibly covered by the new dispensation; for example, it may no longer be safe to *assume* an inherent right to suspend with pay or to give wages in lieu of notice, rather than putting these clearly into the contract.

(c) Health and safety

4.5   The employer's duty of care towards an employee in the law of tort is well established, requiring reasonable care to provide (1) safe premises, (2) safe equipment, (3) competent and safe employees and (4) a safe system of work in all the circumstances[1]. While the first two primarily concern the static condition of the workplace (the traditional concern of industrial safety legislation), the other two may involve more 'active' duties with more overlaps into employment law. The third may require positive disciplining or even dismissal of an unsafe employee (presumably being a good defence to an unfair dismissal action by the dismissed source of danger, provided properly handled). The fourth, a safe system of work, was in the past often little more than a make-weight at the end of a pleading, but with the broader approach now taken to combating general employment risks (including to health and welfare, not just safety from accidents) it has taken on greater significance, capable of calling into question ways of *managing* workforce health and safety[2], for example in the topical area of work-related stress injuries[3].

In addition to the general tortious duty of care, these obligations also exist as an implied term in the contract of employment. Normally this has little direct effect on a personal injury action, once injury has occurred, and its main effect in employment law tends to lie in peripheral areas, such as the obligation on the employer to take health and safety complaints seriously (see below). However, it may (untypically) assume more direct importance in at least three ways. First, it was relevant in *Matthews v Kuwait Bechtel Corpn*[4] in a case of an industrial injury suffered while working abroad, where the relevant private international law rules on jurisdiction would not allow an action to be brought in England for a tort, but would for a breach of contract. Secondly, in *Bernadone v Pall Mall Services Group Ltd*[5] it was relevant to an important recent extension of the coverage of TUPE, so that a subsisting civil action for damages for an industrial injury against employer A is automatically transferred as a liability to employer B where there is a TUPE transfer. This reasoning was facilitated by the fact that employer A's liability was not just in tort, but also arose under the implied term of reasonable safety in the employee's contract, and so capable of transferring along with other contractual duties and liabilities under the wide wording of regulation 5(2). Thirdly, the existence of this particularly important characteristic obligation on the employer has raised the question whether it is an 'overriding' obligation, ie. one which cannot be expressly excluded, and which must not be breached even where the employer seems to have an express contractual power to do so[6].

1   *Wilsons & Clyde Coal Co Ltd v English* [1938] AC 57, HL is the locus classicus. The evolution of this 'personal' liability on the employer (along with separate tort of breach of statutory duty) was of great historical importance because it outflanked the highly restrictive doctrine of common employment (from *Priestley v Fowler* (1837) 3 M & W 1) which had held back the development of industrial injury litigation for most of the nineteenth century. The four-fold classification of duties was later the model for the Health and Safety at Work Act 1974, s 2 (duties to employees), though that is only capable of administrative or criminal enforcement.
2   This is particularly important because the Management of Health and Safety at Work Regulations 1999, SI 1999/3242 (replacing the original 1992 Regulations) do not support civil liability, see reg 22. At the time of writing, this exclusion is under review.
3   The initial and ground-breaking case of *Walker v Northumberland County Council* [1995] IRLR 35, [1995] 1 All ER 737 was based entirely on failure to provide a safe system of work at common law; see also *Cross v Highlands and Islands Enterprise* [2001] IRLR 336, Ct of Sess (OH). The law here was comprehensively reviewed by Hale LJ in *Sutherland v Hatton* [2002] EWCA Civ 76, [2002] IRLR 263 (see particularly the guidance set out at para 43) in a way that lessens liability on employers who have sought to take the issue seriously. Ironically, the first post-Sutherland case in the Court of Appeal (*Young v Post Office* [2002] EWCA Civ 661, [2002] All ER (D) 311 (Apr)) upheld an award of damages, but on facts very similar to those in *Walker*.
4   [1959] 2 QB 57, [1959] 2 All ER 345, CA.
5   [2000] 3 All ER 544, [2000] IRLR 487, CA.
6   See para 3.19, above.

(d)   Suitable working environment

4.6   As seen above, modern health and safety law looks beyond pure accidents, and is now capable of dealing with longer term health and welfare risks of employment. One possible way of expressing that is to say that the emphasis now is on looking at the safety of the whole working *environment*, not just at the dangers of one-off accidents. Wording covering that environment has always been in the Health and Safety at Work Act 1974, s 2 (basic duties towards employees) and, of even greater long-term significance, it features in the EU power giving competence in the area of health and safety[1]; with regard to the latter, it was one of the reasons why the UK government lost its challenge to the legality of the Working Time Directive[2], passed by majority vote as a health and safety/working environment measure when the UK had sought to block it (as an employment measure requiring unanimity). This general movement towards a wider view of health and safety has now percolated into individual employment law with the promulgation of a characteristic term that the employer will provide and monitor for employees, so far as reasonably practicable, a working environment which is reasonably suitable for the performance by them of their contractual duties. This was established in *Waltons & Morse v Dorrington*[3] where a relatively longstanding employee of a solicitors' firm was moved to work close to three heavy smoking solicitors. The employee, a non-smoker, was subject to considerable discomfort; after several complaints to little avail, she was told to put up with it or leave. She left and successfully claimed to have been constructively dismissed, the employers having been in breach of this implied term of suitable working environment. Clearly, the term originates in standard health and safety law (citing the Health and Safety at Work Act 1974, s 2), but as Morison P pointed out this is a significant extension beyond the long established implied term of health and safety, since it may apply more generally to the welfare of employees at work, without having to show a direct connection to their health or *actual* injury or deterioration of health. The ambit of this new term is a matter for debate (on the assumption, it is argued justifiably, that it is not confined to cases of smoking at work) and further case law is awaited. It certainly appears to be very open-ended, though much will depend on the nature of the work in question. Its potency may well be increased when allied to the next implied term (to take complaints seriously, a further important factor in *Waltons & Morse*). On a broader view, it can be seen to be in line with much of the modern EU-led law on health and safety, particularly the generally-applicable rules in the 'Six Pack'[4], with the strong emphasis on establishing and managing safe systems (eg in relation to manual lifting and VDU use) and major requirements of risk assessment techniques, both generally (under the Management of Health and Safety Regulations 1999) and more specifically in areas such as the provision and use of personal protective equipment, lifting techniques and analysis of workstations for VDU operators[5].

1   Article 118A of the Treaty of Rome, inserted by the Single European Act; see now art 137 of the Treaty as revised by the Treaty of Amsterdam ('improvement in particular of the working environment to protect workers' health and safety').
2   *United Kingdom v EU Council* C-84/94 [1997] ICR 443, [1997] IRLR 30, ECJ.
3   [1997] IRLR 488, EAT.
4   This term refers to the six sets of Regulations first issued in 1992 which enact the Health and Safety Framework Directive, 89/391/EEC and its five 'daughter' Directives on workplaces, work equipment, personal protective equipment, manual handling and VDU equipment; see Smith, Goddard, Killalea & Randall *Health and Safety: the Modern Legal Framework* (2nd edn, 2000) Butterworths. The Framework Directive itself, with the broadest across-the-board duties on all employers, was enacted in the Management of Health and Safety Regulations, which were reissued in a slightly expanded form in 1999.
5   In trying to establish a practical balance on stress cases in *Sutherland v Hatton* [2002] EWCA Civ 76, [2002] IRLR 263, the Court of Appeal laid considerable emphasis on the burden on the employee to *divulge* to the employer what is going wrong, before harm becomes foreseeable by the employer; *quaere* whether this flies in the face of the modern EU approach in the Six Pack with its requirements of proactive risk assessment by employers. Is it proper for the common law to diminish the protection for employees set out in Directives and endorsed by Parliament?

(e)   Taking grievances seriously

4.7   A failure to act on a genuine grievance raised by the employee has long been considered to be a breach of contract in two specific areas – (1) health and safety complaints, where failure to act could be a breach of the general implied term of health and safety[1] and (2) sexual harassment, where failure to take a complaint seriously could be a breach of the implied term of trust and respect[2]. However, in *W A Goold (Pearmak) Ltd v McConnell*[3] the EAT took the opportunity to consolidate these strands and formulate them into one generalised implied term that an employer will deal with employee grievances reasonably and promptly. In the case, two salesmen (under an informal contract with no grievance procedure) wished to complain about changes in working methods which had an adverse effect on their commission; discussions with the managing director resulted in nothing, and when they wished to see the company chairman he was unobtainable. It was held that this justified them in leaving and claiming constructive dismissal, which the tribunal held to have been unfair. A full grievance procedure has not hitherto actually been legally obligatory, but this case showed that in effect the common law was ahead of the statutory provisions, to the extent that an employer could still be at a practical disadvantage if there was no procedure by which a grievance can be raised and dealt with 'reasonably and promptly'. Moreover, this development is now backed by (a) the reissuing of the original ACAS Code of Practice No 1[4], which now covers grievance procedures, again stressing how important it is not just to have one but also to ensure that it works as quickly and painlessly as possible, and giving guidance on what will normally be expected in a reasonable and fair procedure, and (b) the proposal at the time of writing in the Employment Bill to enact a minimum 'statutory procedure' for grievances which is to go into all contracts of employment, with penalties before a tribunal for either party not using it as appropriate.

1   *BAC Ltd v Austin* [1978] IRLR 332, EAT. This is now backed by legislative protection for employees making health and safety complaints, providing that dismissal for such a reason is automatically unfair: ERA 1996, s 100. Presumably this could render unfair a *constructive* dismissal where the employee had left, as in *BAC v Austin*, because of lack of action on the complaints. Note that health and safety is also one of the matters covered by the Public Interest Disclosure Act 1998.

2   *Bracebridge Engineering Ltd v Darby* [1990] IRLR 3, EAT; here the harassment was so gross (in fact amounting to a serious sexual assault) that it was clear that failure to investigate it properly could make the employee's position untenable, hence grave enough to breach the term of trust and respect. See also, to similar effect, *Reed v Stedman* [1999] IRLR 299, EAT, which contains useful guidance on harassment. This is particularly important because it has since been held that failure to deal properly with a complaint of harassment is not per se sex discrimination: *Coyne v Home Office* [2000] ICR 1443, [2000] IRLR 838, CA.

3   [1995] IRLR 516, EAT, approved and applied in *Waltons & Morse v Dorrington* [1997] IRLR 488, EAT.

4   Code of Practice on Disciplinary and Grievance Procedures (ACAS, 2000). The code also gives guidance on the statutory right to be accompanied at a grievance hearing by a fellow worker or trade union representative, enacted by the ERA 1999, ss 10–15.

(f)   Trust and respect

4.8   Potentially the most wide-ranging characteristic term in a modern employment contract is the term of trust and respect. While in one respect it may be said to have an ancient ancestor in the law of 'servile incidents' (that a contract of employment may not contain terms that are so excessively harsh, one-sided or personally onerous as to be contrary to public policy[1]), this term has evolved on its own, primarily in the context of the statutory concept of constructive dismissal, though its approval at the highest level was ironically in a common law action for damages. Its formulation has tended to vary. Sometimes it is put in a positive way, as an obligation to treat the employee with trust and respect; although this tends to be a useful shorthand, it may be more prudent in certain contexts to express it negatively as an obligation on the employer not to conduct itself in a manner likely to destroy or seriously damage the relationship of trust and confidence between employer and employee without reasonable and proper cause[2], especially as the current state of authority (as we saw in Chapter 3) is against taking it as far as a rule (which might be more in line with a positive formulation) that an employer must always behave reasonably, even when exercising otherwise unequivocal contractual rights[3]. This cautious approach to the sort of active interventionism possible by reliance on the term can also arguably be seen in the judgment of the Inner House of the Court of Session in *Macari v Celtic Football and Athletic Co Ltd*[4] where it was held that an employee could not refuse to obey a contractually lawful order simply on the ground that he or she considered that the order was given in bad faith, *but* that if the alleged bad faith went so far as to *deliberately* embarrass or harm the employee it may be that that would (independently) be construed as a breach of the implied term of trust and respect. It may, however, be argued that this shows too timid an approach in concentrating on deliberate mistreatment, and that there is no reason why the original bad faith should not itself be sufficient, especially as it has been held in the context of constructive dismissal that a breach of the term is *per se* repudiatory, leaving no room for arguments as to how bad the misconduct was[5].

From cases such as these it is arguable that the employee can get to the desired destination provided that the right path is chosen. Also of interest for the purposes of this book, versions of the term have recently made their appearance in the area of remedies. In *Wood Group Heavy Industrial Turbines Ltd v Crossan*[6] a continuing lack of trust on the part of the employer was held to be a good reason not to order re-engagement of an unfairly dismissed employee; this was a case where the misconduct dismissal was unfair procedurally, but the employers still had a genuine belief in his substantive guilt of the alleged misconduct. In the area of damages for wrongful dismissal, the term was used in *Clark v BET plc*[7] to particularly inventive effect. The normal rule is that the wrongfully dismissed employee can only claim damages for amounts contractually due under the contract of employment, so that traditionally amounts such as ex gratia bonuses have not been recoverable. In this case, however, a highly rewarded chief executive whose overall package was made up largely of pay increases and bonuses voted to him on the yearly performance of the company (and on three years' notice which was not given) was awarded a reasonable estimation of what those increases and bonuses would have been, had the company continued to act towards him in good faith. The judge refused to work on the assumption that the employers could have acted in bad faith and awarded him nil (under the plain wording of the contract). Also in the area of remedies, we have seen an extension of the term of trust and respect even into the sphere of personal injury damages. This is particularly likely to arise where treatment of the employee in clear breach of the term leads to psychiatric injury. This extension was held to be possible by the House of Lords in *Waters v Metropolitan Police Comr*[8] as an adjunct to a common law negligence action (based on a failure by the employer to take proper action to protect the employee from harassment). *Gogay v Hertfordshire County Council*[9] was the first decision directly on the point, awarding damages for inter alia personal injury (in the form of a recognised psychiatric condition) caused by breach of the term of trust and respect when a local authority suddenly and dramatically failed to support a care worker employee when unfounded allegations of child abuse were made against her.

1   See 16 Halsbury's Laws 19 for the old case law.

2   This formulation was used by Lord Steyn and Lord Nicholls in *Malik v BCCI SA (in liquidation)* [1997] ICR 606, [1997] IRLR 462, HL. In *Johnson v Unisys Ltd* [2001] UKHL 13, [2001] ICR 480, [2001] IRLR 279 Lord Steyn adopted the positive formulation of 'the employer's obligation of fair dealing', but when subsequently in *BG plc v O'Brien* [2002] EWCA Civ 379 [2002] IRLR 441 a tribunal referred to an obligation on the employer to deal in a 'fair and even handed manner' the Court of Appeal disapproved it and stated that the *Malik* formulation should be used. The 'without reasonable and proper cause' qualifications was included in early formulations of the term in *Courtaulds Northern Textiles v Andrew* [1979] IRLR 84, EAT and *Woods v WM Car Services (Peterborough) Ltd* [1981] ICR 666, [1981] IRLR 347, EAT (upheld by the Court of Appeal on other grounds: [1982] ICR 693. [1982] IRLR 413) and adopted by Lord Steyn in *Malik v BCCI SA (in liquidation)* [1997] ICR 606, [1997] IRLR 462, HL. It was specifically relied on by the EAT in *Hilton v Shiner Ltd* [2001] IRLR 727 in a case where the employer had good reason to remove the employee from cash handling duties, even though prepared to keep him in employment; in *BG plc v O'Brien* it was given an objective interpretation, so that the fact that the employer had made a genuine mistake (as to the employee's status) did not constitute reasonable and proper cause.
3   *White v Reflecting Roadstuds Ltd* [1991] ICR 733, [1991] IRLR 331, EAT; see para 3.13, above. In an appropriate case, however, the term can have a positive effect in substance: *BG plc v O'Brien* [2001] IRLR 496, EAT (upheld by the Court of Appeal on other grounds, see n 2, above). For discussion of the evolution of the term generally, see Lindsay J, 'The implied term of trust and confidence' (2001) 30 ILJ 1.
4   [1999] IRLR 787, Ct of Sess.
5   *Morrow v Safeway Stores plc* [2002] IRLR 9, EAT.
6   [1998] IRLR 680, EAT.
7   [1997] IRLR 348, QBD; see para 9.5, below. See also *Clark v Nomura International plc* [2000] IRLR 766, QBD where a similar result was reached (awarding what the employee said should have been given under a discretionary bonus scheme) but on different grounds, more akin to administrative law ideas of perversity or irrationality. The Court of Appeal in *Mallone v BPB Industries plc* [2002] EWCA Civ 126 [2002] IRLR 452 adopted the *Clark v Nomura* reasoning (see para 5.5, below).
8   [2000] IRLR 720, HL
9   [2000] IRLR 703, CA.

4.9   As is well known, the term of trust and respect was primarily evolved to repair the damage potentially done to the law of constructive dismissal by the decision of the Court of Appeal in *Western Excavating (ECC) Ltd v Sharp*[1] which decided (after a period of conflicting decisions below) that to be 'entitled' to leave employment the employee must show a breach of contract by the employer, not just unreasonable behaviour. Although this was not particularly drastic where the employee left in response to some definable breach of an express term (eg a refusal to pay, or a unilateral pay decrease), it could have been extremely limiting in cases where the employer uses much more subtle, undermining tactics to make the employee's position so unacceptable that they are goaded into leaving, but without ever being in overt breach of contract. Arguably, as a matter of policy, such cases are clearly meant to be covered by the statutory concept of constructive dismissal (itself a significant and deliberate extension of normal ideas of dismissal) and the response of the EAT was to develop the implied term of trust and respect, a breach of which will now constitute the necessary contractual breach 'entitling' the employee to leave[2]. This process of development was perfected, and set out overtly, in the seminal judgment of Browne-Wilkinson P in *Woods v W M Car Services (Peterborough) Ltd*[3] and it has been one of the most significant sustained developments in the modern employment law. It finally received the unequivocal approval of the House of Lords in *Malik v BCCI SA (in liquidation)*[4]. This was a common law action for damages for 'stigma' to relatively senior employees of the failed bank, allegedly wrecking their future prospects in the job market[5]. Much of the case is concerned with whether such damages can in law be granted (see Chapters 6 and 9 below), but in order to establish a cause of action in the first place the

73

ex-employees relied on the fraudulent conducting of the business constituting breach of the implied term of trust and respect. In this they were successful. Both speeches (by Lords Nichols and Steyn) approved the evolution of the term, with Lord Steyn putting it thus:

> '[T]he implied obligation as formulated is apt to cover the great diversity of situations in which a balance has to be struck between an employer's interest in managing his business as he sees fit and the employee's interest in not being unfairly and improperly exploited. The evolution of the implied term of trust and confidence is a fact. It has not yet been endorsed by your Lordships' House. It has proved a workable principle in practice. It has not been the subject of adverse criticism in any decided cases and it has been welcomed in academic writings. I regard the emergence of the implied obligation of mutual trust and confidence as a sound development.'

In addition to this general, and welcome, approval, the case also established two potentially important sub-rules – (1) the harsh or oppressive (or, as here, fraudulent) conduct by the employer does not have to be specifically aimed at the employee in question, provided that the actual result is to destroy or seriously damage the relationship of trust and confidence; (2) there is no need for the employee to have been aware of the conduct while in the employment, but rather he or she can still sue for damages afterwards (though of course in these circumstances the employee would not be able to claim constructive dismissal because of the causative requirement that an employee must leave in response to the employer's conduct). To these expansive sub-rules, however, there must now be added a restrictive one. In the subsequent House of Lords decision in *Johnson v Unisys Ltd*[6] it was held (Lord Steyn dissenting) that it is *not* appropriate to apply the term of trust and respect to the *termination* of employment. This was in the context of restricting 'stigma' damages to breaches of contract during employment (as in *Malik* itself) and, crucially, denying them as a possibility in wrongful dismissal cases[7]. It is, however, determined as a general principle, in Lord Hoffman's words:

> 'I rather doubt whether the term of trust and confidence should be pressed so far. In the way it has always been formulated, it is concerned with preserving the continuing relationship which should subsist between employer and employee. So it does not seem altogether appropriate for use in connection with the way that relationship is terminated'.

Whatever the arguments for or against such a limitation as a matter of policy, it does raise an acute problem of interpretation – what does 'on termination' mean? In the case itself the point at issue was the mechanism of the dismissal itself, where the rule makes sense. However, the problem is whether it can be stretched backwards in time, applying to the events leading *up to* termination. This could mean that there was no obligation of trust and respect in conducting disciplinary procedures. The Court of Session (OH) reacted strongly against such an interpretation in *King v University Court of the University of St Andrews*[8] where an employee was permitted to challenge in a common law action alleged flaws in procedure amounting to breaches of the implied term. The defenders had relied on *Johnson v Unisys* to stop such an argument but the court held that the 'on termination' limitation only applies once the decision to dismiss has been taken, *not* to an earlier stage of deciding whether or not to dismiss, where the term can still have valuable work to do. On the other hand, the Court of Appeal in *Eastwood v Magnox Electric plc*[9] took the opposite view and projected the 'on termination' limitation backwards into the process *leading up to* termination ('part of the circumstances attending the dismissal'), ruling out reliance on the implied term in a common law action based on allegations of seriously bad treatment and victimisation (leading up to stress-related illness, depression and inability to work) which were the back-drop to the employee's eventual dismissal. While this involves a measure of hindsight unusual at common law (what if the bad treatment had *not* led to dismissal?), at least this case *was* concerned with a common law claim where the damage of a wide approach may be containable. The problem would be if it spilled out into the statutory context, because any idea that the term of trust and respect cannot apply to events which later result in termination could be disastrous for the law relating to constructive dismissal (in the unfair dismissal context) which in practice is the true home of the term and where it is of greatest use in countering unacceptable conduct by the employer. At the time of writing, this is a major problem arising from *Johnson v Unisys Ltd*, which is in urgent need of resolution.

1 [1978] ICR 221, [1978] IRLR 27, CA.
2 The requirement for the breach to be serious enough for the employee, objectively, to be able to conclude that the employer was repudiating the contract was emphasised by the NICA in *Brown v Merchant Ferries Ltd* [1998] IRLR 682, but in *Morrow v Safeway Stores plc* [2002] IRLR 9 the EAT took a more purist approach and held that if the conduct is serious enough to undermine trust and confidence or to destroy or damage the employment relationship it will necessarily be serious enough to repudiate the contract. One particular category of case here, long accepted as constructive dismissal, is where an incident not particularly important or devastating in itself might be sufficient if the 'final straw' of a course of conduct by the employer: *Lewis v Motorworld Garages Ltd* [1986] ICR 157, [1985] IRLR 465, CA.
3 [1981] ICR 666, [1981] IRLR 347, EAT (upheld by the Court of Appeal on other grounds: [1982] ICR 693. [1982] IRLR 413); this judgment, from arguably the best EAT President we have had, still repays reading.
4 [1997] ICR 606, [1997] IRLR 462, HL. In his speech, Lord Steyn cited with approval an article on the development of the term: Brodie 'The heart of the matter: mutual trust and confidence (1996) 25 ILJ 121. For the same author's reaction to the case, see Brodie 'Beyond exchange: the new contract of employment' (1998) 27 ILJ 79.
5 The claim eventually failed on its facts before Lightman J who held that the necessary causative damage had not been proved: [1999] 2 All ER 1005, [1999] IRLR 226, upheld on appeal [2002] EWCA Civ 82 [2002] IRLR 460.
6 [2001] UKHL 13, [2001] ICR 480, [2001] IRLR 279.
7 See para 9.5, below.
8 [2002] IRLR 252, Ct of Sess (OH). *R (Arthurworrey) v Haringay London Borough Council* [2001] EWCA Admin 698, [2002] ICR 279, QBD can be seen as adopting a similar approach, though not expressly.
9 [2002] EWCA Civ 463 [2002] IRLR 447.

4.10 The implied obligation will of course apply (or be argued to apply) to a myriad of circumstances, success or failure being largely a question of fact for the tribunal, with correspondingly restricted chances of reopening the matter on appeal[1]. Moreover, it is by now a particularly well known requirement, of which an employer's personnel advisers will be rightly nervous; as argued in the previous chapter, this factor may in practice be just as important in making employers reflect on *how* they exercise their black-and-white rights under a contract of employment as the more difficult legal question whether this particular term is now strong enough to have an actual overriding effect over an express term of a contract. A particularly good example of (to put it neutrally) the implied term's 'supplementing' role is the decision in *French v Barclays Bank plc*[2] which not so many years ago would have been thought impossible. A bank manager required to relocate from Oxford to Essex was granted a discretionary interest-free bridging loan. Having bought a house in Essex on the strength of the valuation of the Oxford house, the latter was hit by a housing market slump and he could not sell it for the original valuation. After several months in this situation, the bank decided that it could not continue with this expensive loan and so told him that he must start paying interest on it or sell the house at the new, lower price. Unable to afford the interest, he sold it for a significantly lower amount, but then sued the bank for that amount (plus interest). Clearly, he had no contractual right to have this discretionary loan *but* both the trial judge and Court of Appeal held for him on the basis that (although granting the loan was discretionary) to seek to change the terms once granted in this way was a breach of the term of trust and respect, especially as the bridging loan was not an ordinary commercial one, but rather was part and parcel of arrangements made to facilitate their order to him to change his location under the mobility clause in his contract.

1   *Woods v W M Car Services (Peterborough) Ltd* [1981] ICR 666, [1981] IRLR 347, EAT (upheld by the Court of Appeal on other grounds: [1982] ICR 693. [1982] IRLR 413) is itself a very good example of this, at both EAT and CA stages. Reliance on the term has even been seen recently in the area of summary dismissal, see para 8.8, below.
2   [1998] IRLR 646, CA, the case of a bridging too far.

3   Implied obligations on employees

(a)   Obedience

4.11   The obligation on an employee to obey a lawful order is perhaps the most fundamental of all; after all, the original 'control' test for the existence of a contract of employment in the first place looked at whether the employer could tell the employee what to do *and* how to do it. The word 'lawful' is traditionally put before the word 'order', but it is a term of art, meaning simply that the order was within the legitimate scope of the contract. This is a question of interpretation, and it may mean that certain orders of a particularly personal nature (eg appearance, length of hair) could be challenged as 'unlawful' in this sense, unless the work is such as to make the matter in question relevant. This contractual basis for a lawful order has always been subject to two separate common law rules – (1) the employer may not order the employee to do something illegal[1]; (2) the employer may not order the employee into danger[2].

The case law on this area at common law is sparse, probably for three reasons. First, any cases arising on refusal of orders are now far more likely to raise questions of unfair dismissal and to be dealt with in a tribunal. Moreover, any case of ordering an employee into danger could now raise serious issues of health and safety law, within the background the special protection given in unfair dismissal law to an employee making health and safety complaints, or even leaving and/or refusing to return to work where there is 'serious and imminent' danger, or taking other 'appropriate steps to protect himself'[3]. Secondly, questions of personal orders tend to arise in the context of 'dress codes', etc, in sex discrimination cases, which continue to arise with some regularity[4], and may take on even more life under the Human Rights Act 1998, in particular under Article 10 of the incorporated European Convention, concerning freedom of expression[5]. Thirdly, at the time when the only remedies at common law were contractual (ie before the introduction of unfair dismissal in

1971) the voluntary principle held sway and so any problems arising were likely to have been resolved by industrial means rather than legal.

1   See, eg, the order to falsify accounts in *Morrish v Henlys (Folkstone) Ltd* [1973] 2 All ER 137, [1973] ICR 482, NIRC (an unfair dismissal case).
2   The danger must be immediate: contrast *Ottoman Bank v Chakarian* [1930] AC 277, PC and *Bouzourou v Ottoman Bank* [1930] AC 271, PC.
3   ERA 1996, s 100(1)(c)–(e). The first cases on this section have applied it widely; see in particular *Harvest Press Ltd v McCaffrey* [1999] IRLR 778, EAT which applied it to threats of physical violence at work, not just dangerous premises or plant.
4   In spite of the leading cases tending to uphold different employer-imposed dress codes, provided equally onerous between the sexes: *Schmidt v Austicks Bookshop Ltd* [1978] ICR 85, [1977] IRLR 360. EAT; *Burrett v West Birmingham Health Authority* [1994] IRLR 7, EAT; *Smith v Safeway plc* [1996] IRLR 456, CA.
5   The case law from the European Court of Human Rights on this point is fairly inconclusive – in *Stevens v United Kingdom* (1986) 46 DR 245 it was accepted that dress can be a form of self-expression, but in *Kara v United Kingdom* [1999] EHRLR 232 the court held that an employer had lawful grounds to require a transvestite not to wear clothing of the opposite sex to work. At the very least, however, the coming into force of the Act is likely to reopen some of these questions and probably to require a higher level of *justification* by the employer of any limitations or rules imposed. Also, it will not be necessary to attack them through *sex* discrimination.

4.12   What can an employee do if faced with an unlawful order, ie one in some way contrary to the contract? Useful guidance has been given on this recently by the Inner House of the Court of Session in *Macari v Celtic Football and Athletic Co Ltd*[1], ironically (in the light of the last points made above) a wrongful dismissal action. A football manager was summarily dismissed for being, the employers claimed, in flagrant breach of his contract and orders given to him under it (primarily concerning moving to live nearer his work and to attend full time to his duties). The manager argued that he was not in breach of contract because the orders in question had been given in bad faith, primarily aimed at producing a situation in which he would leave or be dismissed. The trial judge found against the manager, as did the Court of Session on appeal[2]. As stated above, the court held that a lawful contractual order does not become unlawful (and therefore ignorable by the employee) if given in bad faith; however, the circumstances of the giving of the order can be such as to constitute a breach of the implied term of trust and respect by the employer, which was held to have been the case here. That did not, however, decide the case in the manager's favour. The breach of the implied term by the employer would have justified the manager in leaving and suing for damages, *but* in fact he had remained in employment, drawing his salary but still not obeying the orders. That, the court held, was not an option – the fact that the employer was in breach did *not* justify the employee in refusing to comply with his duty of obedience; indeed, it was that refusal that then formed the basis for the employers' *lawful* summary dismissal of the employee. Thus, the grafting on of the term of trust and respect to the purely objective contractual question of whether the order is within the scope of the contract (the motive being irrelevant) does help the employee up to a point, but the tactics then adopted have to be chosen with care; staying under protest for a reasonable period may be possible (as with constructive dismissal), but not staying on with a pick-and-mix attitude to what obligations to observe. As with constructive dismissal again, the ultimate protection for the employee is the 'nuclear option' of leaving, in order to preserve both common law and statutory rights. A general comment on modern employment law, shown by this point among others, is that the rights and protections given to employees tend to be heavily based on dismissal or resignation (ie accepting loss of employment), with substantially less emphasis on protection during employment. Perhaps this is inevitable, and in the present circumstances it does have a certain logic – the whole point about destroying trust and confidence is that it makes the employee's position intolerable and further employment impossible, so there can be little scope for the employee to seek to stay on, on his own terms.

1 [1999] IRLR 787, Ct of Sess.
2 As the Lord President put it in his judgment, 'The Lord Ordinary assoilzied the defenders and the pursuer has reclaimed'. What else?

(b) Exercising care

4.13 The ancient authority of *Harmer v Cornelius*[1] decided that an employee seeking or taking on a skilled job impliedly warrants that he has the necessary skill to perform it. Given the development of the general law of negligence in the last century, it is not surprising that this has been extended to a duty of *care* on the part of the employee. An employer could be prejudiced by a breach of this in two ways – the breach could cause damage directly to the employer, or it could cause harm to a third party, for which the employer is vicariously liable. The duty of care in the first category is established by *Lister v Romford Ice & Cold Storage Ltd*[2]. The case of *Janata Bank v Ahmed*[3] is an extremely rare example of an employer actually relying on this duty in order to sue the employee for damages (as opposed to dismissing). It was argued for the employee that this action should not now lie, and that the employee should only be liable for incurring the employer in vicarious liability, but this argument was rejected. With regard to such an action for vicarious liability, the key question is whether the employer (having recompensed the third party) can sue the employee for contribution or an indemnity. In spite of arguments that this would be contrary to the theory behind vicarious liability (respondeat superior), this is legally possible, either at common law or under the Civil Liability (Contribution) Act 1978, and indeed *Lister* itself was an example of it, though on unusual facts suggesting collusion (the employee had made the company liable vicariously by running over a third party, his own father). Normally, although the law here is complex[4], the matter does not arise in practice, because it is not in the employer's interest to sue its own employee. There remains, however, a danger that a third party other than the employer might be subrogated to the employer's right to an indemnity against the employee: the Court of Appeal managed to prevent this happening in *Morris v Ford Motor Co Ltd*[5], but only because there was no express subrogation clause in the relevant commercial contract and the court would not imply one. The law here, if ever tested, is unsatisfactory but nothing has been done to change it. One way forward would be to impose an obligation on the employer to deal with all matters of insurance (in particular, public liability); the House of Lords refused to do so in *Lister* in 1957 but the question is whether a different attitude might now be taken, see below.

1 (1858) 5 CBNS 236.
2 [1957] AC 555, [1957] 1 All ER 125, HL.
3 [1981] ICR 791, [1981] IRLR 457, CA.
4 For a full consideration, see *Smith & Wood* pp 131–133.
5 [1973] QB 792, [1973] 2 All ER 1084, CA.

(c) Adaptation to new methods or techniques

4.14 A major conceptual problem in the law on contracts of employment is that jobs and work can change (never more rapidly than at the present), whereas the effect of a contract of any kind is to set down rights and obligations as at one time. To some extent, an employer can try to pre-empt this problem by drafting so as to import a level of flexibility, but in the nature of things that cannot always be an answer. One way forward would be to develop an implied term that the employee will make reasonable adaptations. The only reported case on this so far is *Cresswell v Inland Revenue Board*[1] where Walton J accepted such a term, thereby holding that the Inland Revenue were acting within their contracts in requiring its officers and clerks to operate a new computerised system of PAYE administration. This is consistent with (a) the fact that many questions of work *methods* will remain within the managerial discretion[2], (b) the approach taken in redundancy law that that law is not meant to stifle innovation and so serious changes of methods or techniques can be made without changing the actual job in question, for redundancy purposes[3], and (c) the fact that even the TUPE regulations have some flexibility built into them, with the concept of 'economic, technical or organisational reasons'. On the other hand, a point will still come where the changes in method are so great that they cross over the line of constituting a new *job*[4]; in that case, presumably the implied term of reasonable adaptation will cease to apply and the employer will need to obtain the employee's consent to a variation of contract; moreover, questions of redundancy may also arise. One important rider to the implied term was added in *Cresswell*, which was that the employer in such a case (in order to rely on the term) must provide the necessary training or retraining; this would be particularly important if the question arose in the statutory context of unfair dismissal, concerning a later dismissal for incapability.

1   [1984] ICR 508, [1984] IRLR 190.
2   See para 3.25, above.
3   *Chapman v Goonvean and Rostowrack China Clay Co Ltd* [1973] 2 All ER 1063, [1973] ICR 310, CA; *Johnson v Nottinghamshire Police Authority* [1974] 1 All ER 1082, [1974] ICR 170, CA; *Lesney Products Ltd v Nolan* [1977] ICR 235, [1977] IRLR 77, CA.
4   See the change of need from plumbers to heating engineers in *Murphy v Epsom College* [1985] ICR 80, [1984] IRLR 271, CA.

(d) Fidelity and co-operation

4.15   An employee owes an employer a common law duty of fidelity, which may be breached by action inconsistent with the express or implied terms of the contract of employment, causing injury to the employer. As with questions of obedience to lawful orders, this duty may be relevant in both contractual actions and statutory actions for unfair dismissal. The case law tends to crystallise into three main applications, two longstanding and one more recent.

The first application is that the employee must not put himself into a position of a conflict of interests with the employer's business. The taking of secret commissions, or indeed bribes, eg from the company's suppliers or potential suppliers, would come into this category, as could blatantly inconsistent personal share holdings. Both of these points can be seen in the leading case of *Boston Deep Sea Fishing & Ice Co v Ansell*[1], which also established the common law rule that such conduct may still justify dismissal even if it only came to light after termination – an important point in this context where this is likely to be the case. The case involved a managing director, where standards of fidelity may be even higher because of certain fiduciary duties on directors, but the general principle applies to ordinary employees too, and can certainly cover a case of misuse of employment position to make a personal profit[2].

1   (1888) 39 Ch D 339, CA.
2   See, for a bizarre example on its facts, *Reading v A-G* [1951] AC 507, [1951] 1 All ER 617, HL.

4.16 The second application is that in certain circumstances there will be a duty on the employee not to engage in competitive activities with the employer. One starts from a presumption that an employee's extra-work activities are his or her own business, so that any general restraint on these would need to be the subject of an express clause in the contract. However, there may be cases where these activities become in competition with the employer, causing damage, and can be restrained by injunction[1]. Most of the recent cases in this area have concerned not a common law or equitable claim, but rather the question under unfair dismissal law as to when it is fair to dismiss an employee for *intending* to leave and set up in competition or join a competitor. Unless the matter is complicated by questions of confidential information (see below), merely planning to do so may not be sufficient to justify a pre-emptive dismissal[2]. However, any extra elements of soliciting customers or other staff[3], or tendering for contracts[4], prior to leaving may put the employee in breach of the implied duty of fidelity. Returning to common law enforceability, the decision of the Court of Appeal in *J A Mont (UK) Ltd v Mills*[5] is a clear and factually interesting reaffirmation that once employment has ended, public policy (based on traditional laissez-faire ideas) requires that the implied obligation not to compete is no longer enforceable; any such obligation must be express, in a restraint of trade clause, and if (as in the case) that clause is too wide and is held to be void the ex-employee is free to compete as and when desired.

1   *Hivac Ltd v Park Royal Scientific Instruments Ltd* [1946] Ch 169, [1946] 1 All ER 350, CA remains the leading case.
2   *Laughton and Hawley v Bapp Industrial Supplies Ltd* [1986] ICR 634, [1986] IRLR 245, EAT. See also *Wallace Bogan & Co Ltd v Cove* [1997] IRLR 453, CA where solicitors within a firm, intending to 'swarm' out and set up a new practice, played it entirely by the book, avoiding any actions before leaving which could have been in breach of contract.
3   *Marshall v Industrial Systems and Control Ltd* [1992] IRLR 294, EAT.
4   *Adamson v B & L Cleaning Services Ltd* [1995] IRLR 193, EAT.
5   [1993] IRLR 172, CA. The judge at first instance had sought to develop the law to take a more flexible view, allowing restraint of post-termination competition in certain cases, but this was strongly disapproved by the Court of Appeal.

4.17 The third application is that an employee who has discretion in organising work must exercise that discretion so as to promote the employer's business, not so as to frustrate it. This point is not just more recent than the first two, but is subtly different; the first two are essentially negative in character (what the employee must *not* do), but this point raises the question as to the extent of any positive obligation of co-operation on the part of the employee. It can also be said of it that it arises from a particular context (of 'guerilla' industrial action) and is closely tied in with the remedies available to the employer in that situation. At the heart of it is the question of whether employees can always take lawful industrial action by performing only their strict contractual duties, a tactic variously known as working to rule, working to contract or withdrawal of good will. The question of a duty of co-operation was broached nearly three decades ago in *Secretary of State for Employment v ASLEF (No 2)*[1], but in a very different industrial context, under long-repealed legislation and with considerable variations in the three judgments. The modern case that has revived the issue is *British Telecommunications plc v Ticehurst*[2]. A manager took part in industrial action, first by way of a go-slow and work-to-contract, then by way of a rolling campaign of strikes. When the question arose as to whether she was in breach of contract, the Court of Appeal held that her actions were indeed a breach of the implied obligation to serve the employer faithfully within the requirements of the contract. Where an employee such as her has a discretion in organising work (in particular giving instructions to others and supervising their work) that discretion has to be exercised faithfully in the interests of the employers. This could mean that although each action could have been literally within the contract, there could still be breach of the implied term if they were done 'not in the honest exercise of choice or discretion for the faithful performance of her work but in order to disrupt the employer's business or to cause the most inconvenience that can be caused'. The bottom line in relation to remedy means that an employer, faced with such action, is not restricted to the previously-accepted action of docking a proportion of wages representing service not rendered[3], but can go further and state that it is not prepared to accept this defective performance, issue an ultimatum requiring full performance by a certain date, and if the action continues pay *nothing*, even for work actually done by the employee[4]. While it may be that in employments with very defined duties and little autonomy and/or discretion a work to rule, etc, may still be argued to be contractually lawful, this decision does suggest a significant difference wherever those elements do exist, which is likely to be increasingly the case in modern employment conditions.

1   [1972] 2 QB 455, [1972] 2 All ER 949, CA.
2   [1992] ICR 383, [1992] IRLR 219, CA.
3   *Sim v Rotherham Metropolitan Borough Council* [1986] ICR 897, [1986] IRLR 391; *Miles v Wakefield Metropolitan District Council* [1987] ICR 368, [1987] IRLR 193, HL.
4   See, to like effect, *Wiluszynski v London Borough of Tower Hamlets* [1989] ICR 493, [1989] IRLR 259, CA. This stringent approach is reinforced by the fact that UK law does not accept a 'suspension' theory in the case of an industrial dispute. Protection for striking employees exists in the event of a dismissal (especially, now, in the first 8 weeks of the dispute) but that does not feed back into the contractual position.

4.18   One final question in relation to the implied duty of fidelity generally (in a sense following on from the last point, concerning the extent to which the duty may be cast in positive terms) is that the law has always been unclear and difficult on the extent to which an employee has a duty to *disclose* breaches of that duty. The starting point has always been the decision of the House of Lords in *Bell v Lever Bros Ltd*[1] that an employer could not recover a golden handshake payment to an employee on finding out later about undisclosed misconduct. Directors may be under fiduciary duties, but an ordinary employment is not a contract *uberrimae fidei*, even at the stage of hiring; on the other hand, positive misrepresentation or fraud in order to obtain employment may be a good ground for dismissal[2] and so an employer has much to gain by asking the right questions. Clearly, the line can be thin here, and the decision of the Court of Appeal in *Sybron Corpn v Rochem Ltd*[3] is a highly illustrative case, with a very useful summary of the law; moreover, holding that the employers could in fact recover the termination payments because of after-acquired knowledge of the employee's misdeeds, the Court of Appeal decided that there *is* a duty to disclose the fraudulent misconduct of other, subordinate employees with whom the employee in question had acted, even if that indirectly meant disclosing his own misconduct. It was further suggested obiter that there may also be a duty to disclose the employee's own misconduct if fraudulently concealed. This meant that *Bell v Lever Bros Ltd* could be distinguished, although factually not a million miles from the conduct of the employee in this case. As soon as an employee acts in concert with others, or goes beyond simple non-disclosure and enters the area of deliberate concealment, this case could be of considerable use to the employer.

1   [1932] AC 161, HL. There is a particularly useful restatement of these principles by Elias J in *Nottingham University v Fishel* [2000] ICR 1462, [2000] IRLR 471, QBD, which shows that a realistic view is to be taken of an employee's obligations, which are not normally of a fiduciary nature.

2   *Birmingham District Council v Beyer* [1977] IRLR 211, [1978] 1 All ER 910, EAT. Note, however, that there is no obligation to disclose a conviction that is 'spent' under the Rehabilitation of Offenders Act 1974, unless the post in question comes under the Exemptions Order 1975, SI 1975/1023.

3   [1983] 2 All ER 707, [1983] IRLR 253, CA.

(e) Confidentiality

4.19   Of all the areas of the implied obligations on employers, this is perhaps where the employer has most to gain by covering the matter expressly, so as to make the application and extent of the obligation as clear as possible. However, certain excesses by certain employers in doing so have led to a legislative reaction in the Public Interest Disclosure Act 1998 to give certain protected rights of disclosure to whistleblowers. Longer standing legislative intervention covers two specific areas abutting on to confidentiality, namely the ownership of patents on inventions made by an employee at work and the similar problem of the ownership of copyright[1]. The common law now has little role in these areas.

The question therefore arises as to the extent of the *residual* implied duty of confidentiality, in the absence of express coverage (by a confidentiality clause during employment or a restraint of trade clause afterwards) or statutory coverage. The importance of such an implied obligation was stressed in the old authority of *Robb v Green*[2]. However, the modern law is that there is a major difference between the obligation during employment (where it applies to any confidential information belonging to the employer, if necessary covering matters in the employee's own knowledge and skills) and the remaining obligation after employment which is much narrower. The leading authority is *Faccenda Chicken Ltd v Fowler*[3] where the point is made succinctly by Neill LJ as follows:

'The implied term which imposes an obligation on the employee as to his conduct after the determination of the employment is more restricted in its scope than that which imposes a general duty of good faith. It is clear that the obligation not to use or disclose information may cover secret processes of manufacture such as chemical formulae, or designs or special methods and other information which is of a sufficiently high degree of confidentiality as to amount to a trade secret. The obligation does not extend, however, to cover all information which is given to or acquired by the employee whilst in his employment, and in particular may not cover information which is only "confidential" in the sense that an unauthorised disclosure of such information to a third party while the employment subsisted would be clear breach of the duty of good faith'.

The categories potentially covered post-termination and the factors determining them were then set out:

'(a) The nature of the employment. Employment in the capacity where "confidential" material is habitually handled may impose a high obligation of confidentiality.

(b) The nature of the employment itself. . .information will only be protected if it can properly be classed as a trade secret or as material which, while not properly to be described as a trade secret, is in all the circumstances of such a highly confidential nature as to require the same protection as a trade secret. Whether the employer impressed on the employee the confidentiality of the Information[4]. Whether the relevant information can be easily isolated from other information which the employee is free to use or disclose'.

One way of looking at this is that it is only in effect the categories that can validly be covered by a restraint of trade clause that are subject to the continuing obligation. The reference in (b) to matters which, while not a 'trade secret' as such, merit equivalent protection is important because a restriction to trade secrets as traditionally envisaged would be too narrow (applying to essentially physical matters and processes), at least in large areas of the knowledge-based economy[5]. This is, however, an area likely to produce considerable difficulties in definition and application – what is confidential *enough* to merit continuing protection? In *Johnson & Bloy (Holdings) Ltd v Wolstenholme Rink plc*[6] information concerning the making of certain kinds if ink and their drying agents was held to be protectable, whereas in *Brooks v Olyslager OMS(UK) Ltd*[7] the making of statements by a recently-dismissed managing director to an investment banker as to the ex-employer's financial difficulties and over-optimistic budgets was held not to breach the post-termination duty of confidentiality.

1 Patents Act 1977, ss 39–41; Copyright, Designs and Patents Act 1988, s 11; see *Smith & Wood* pp 143–145.
2 [1895] 2 QB 315, CA; see the reaffirmation of this authority in *Roger Bullivant Ltd v Ellis* [1987] ICR 464, [1987] IRLR 491, CA.
3 [1986] ICR 297, [1986] IRLR 69, CA. See Brearley and Bloch *Employment Covenants and Confidential Information* (1999) Butterworths, chaps 3, 5.
4 There may, however, be cases where the confidentiality is either sufficiently implicit or well known to override this requirement: *Lancashire Fires Ltd v S A Lyons & Co Ltd* [1997] IRLR 113, CA.
5 Certainly in relation to trade secrets and potential misuse of customer connections; restraint of trade has recently been extended to cover protection against solicitation of staff/fellow employees (*Dawnay Day & Co Ltd v De Braconier d'Alphen* [1997] IRLR 442, CA; *T S C Europe (UK) Ltd v Massey* [1999] IRLR 22, Ch D) but it is difficult to see this new head of protectable interest coming within the implied term.
6 [1987] IRLR 499, CA.
7 [1998] IRLR 590, CA.

4.20   There can of course be an overlap here with the law on competition with the employer, considered above, where we saw that in general the implied duty not to compete does not survive termination of the contract (hence the need for a valid restraint of trade clause). An employer might, however, seek to object to post-termination competition on the basis that use of trade secrets or confidential information makes that competition unfair. In the case of confidential information the position is again difficult because of employee arguments that what is being used is simply his own knowledge (albeit gained in previous employment). In practice, much may depend on how underhand the ex-employee was in *obtaining* the information in question. In particular, any element of deliberate gathering of information shortly before leaving and/or *physical* carrying away (traditionally in the form of copied files, documents, lists of customers, etc, but now of course in various computerised forms) will weigh strongly against the employee[1]. On the other hand, it has been stressed that this does *not* give rise to a rule of law that the ex-employee is always allowed to use whatever he managed to carry away in his head[2]. Instead, the matter remains a wide one of fact, though capable of producing narrow distinctions. Thus, for example, in *Sanders v Parry*[3] an assistant solicitor leaving the practice to set up on his own, having taken active steps to take with him a major client (whose affairs he had been dealing with) was held to be in breach of the implied duty of good faith, whereas in *Wallace Bogan & Co v Cove*[4] solicitors in a similar situation of leaving their firm to set up independently did nothing during employment to overstep the mark and only approached clients of the old employer after leaving, in the light of which they were held not to be in breach and so their actions could not be restrained by the old employer.

1 This is the particular significance in the modern cases of the frequently cited old authority *Robb v Green* [1895] 2 QB 315, CA.
2 *Johnson & Bloy* [1987] IRLR 499, CA, per Parker LJ, disapproving a suggestion to the contrary in *Balston Ltd v Headline Filters Ltd* [1987] FSR 330.
3 [1967] 2 All ER 803, [1967] 1 WLR 753.
4 [1997] IRLR 453, CA.

4.21 The final point to note on confidentiality is the position of the 'whistleblower', ie the employee who breaches confidentiality for arguably good reasons in the public interest. The common law accepted this as an exception to the normal rule, certainly where it was criminal activity being divulged, eg to a regulatory or enforcement body[1]. This matter is now largely covered by the Public Interest Disclosure Act 1998; this primarily operates by putting specific employment protection provisions into the ERA 1996 to protect against detriment to the employee, and making any dismissal automatically unfair (with no limit on the compensatory award), provided (a) the disclosure relates to one of the specified matters (covering criminal offences, failure to comply with a legal obligation, miscarriage of justice, health and safety breaches, environmental damage or a cover-up of any of these) and (b) the employee goes about it in the prescribed way (with disclosure to the employer itself first, and to the press last). Any contractual provision (ie confidentiality or 'gagging' clause) is 'void in so far as it purports to preclude the worker from making a protected disclosure[2]. Technically, the Act does not govern the position where a civil action is brought by the ex-employer for an injunction to prevent breach of an express or implied duty of confidentiality, but it may well be that in future the common law defence of public interest to such an action will be developed in the light of, and to be in line with, the rules laid down by Parliament in the Act (rather than by further argument over the pre-existing case law), especially as any express clause must now be shown not to infringe any of the rights in the Act, and it is difficult to imagine the implied obligation being allowed to be wider than an express stipulation.

1 *Initial Services Ltd v Putterill* [1968] 1 QB 396, [1967] 3 All ER 145, CA; *Lion Laboratories Ltd v Evans* [1985] QB 526, [1984] 2 All ER 417, CA; *Re a Company's Application* [1989] ICR 449, [1989] IRLR 477.
2 ERA 1996, s 43J, added by the ERA 1999.

4 Areas of uncertainty or development

(a) References

4.22 What legal duties surround the giving of references? A straightforward application of the law on negligent misstatement suggests a tortious duty of care by the giver of a reference to its recipient; indeed, those are the facts of *Hedley Byrne & Co Ltd v Heller & Partners Ltd*[1], the leading authority, albeit that the reference there was a commercial one relating to credit-worthiness, rather than an employment reference. Thus it is possible that a negligent reference on an employee (or perhaps a deliberately glowing reference aimed at getting rid of an unsatisfactory employee) could lead to liability on its maker if the new employer can show resultant loss. However, in the context of the employer-employee (or ex-employee) relationship the more pertinent question is whether an *employee* prejudiced by a negligently bad reference could sue the employer, eg for loss in not being able to get another job. In a significant development, the House of Lords in *Spring v Guardian Assurance plc*[2] held that such an action can lie, both as a tortious remedy and as an application of the employer's implied duty of care under the contract. Naturally, the normal hurdles of a negligence action have to be surmounted (even when considering the action as contractual, because the implied term is to exercise reasonable care not to cause harm), and this may well be factually difficult in any given case, not least because (a) traditionally most employers and referees have operated on the basis of confidential references (a practice which may now be subject to challenge under the Data Protection Act 1998) and (b) the employee must prove that any negligence on the part of the employer caused his or her loss, which may be difficult when failing to get a job for which there were many applicants. Be that as it may, the principle was established in *Spring* (either as an extension of *Hedley Byrne* or as a general application of the modern 'fair, just and reasonable' incremental approach to extending tortious liability). It was given an interesting interpretation in *Bartholomew v London Borough of Hackney*[3], as to how full and fair a reference needs to be. The ex-employee had been accused of financial irregularities; when he claimed race discrimination his claim was settled on the basis of severance and termination of the disciplinary procedure. A prospective new employer requested a reference which was given, stating that he had taken voluntary severance while suspended for gross misconduct and that the charges had lapsed on dismissal. The job offer was withdrawn in the light of this and the ex-employee sued the employer. The Court of Appeal held against him, on the basis that the obligation on the employer is to give a reference that is in substance true, accurate and fair, not giving a misleading impression. This formulation, taken from defamation law, means that it does not necessarily have to be as full and comprehensive as the employee might want. On the facts here, the reference was true, and not as a whole inaccurate or misleading and so passed this test. Indeed, to have failed to mention the unresolved disciplinary proceedings might have breached the duty of care to the recipient. This specific question of the approach to be taken by a reference writing ex-employer to disciplinary investigations pending at the date of termination of the employment has proved troublesome. It was revisited by the Court of Appeal in *Cox v Sun Alliance Life Ltd*[4] where the reference mentioned (contrary to the intent of a negotiated settlement) allegations against the employee which has only surfaced shortly before termination, had not been properly investigated and (in particular) had never been properly put to the employee. This was held to fall on the wrong side of the line, *Bartholemew* was distinguished and the ex-employee's claim for damages (having lost an employment offer) was upheld. The reference here went beyond a straight factual statement of any pending proceedings, and strayed into the area of value judgments as to their likely outcome. Mummery LJ added the interesting gloss that in a case such as this an analogy can be drawn with the well-known rules on misconduct dismissals in unfair dismissal law in *British*

Home Stores v Burchell[5], to the effect that a reference should only refer to the likely result of pending proceedings if there has been reasonable investigation leading to a positive belief in guilt; after all, that would have been the test in any unfair dismissal case had the employee not left but had been dismissed for misconduct on completion of the proceedings.

1   [1964] AC 465, [1963] 2 All ER 575, HL.
2   [1994] ICR 596, [1994] IRLR 460, HL.
3   [1999] IRLR 246, CA, applied in *Kidd v Axa Equity & Law Life Assurance Society plc* [2000] IRLR 301, QBD; see also, in the context of a constructive dismissal claim, *TSB Bank plc v Harris* [2000] IRLR 157, EAT.
4   [2001] EWCA Civ 649, [2001] IRLR 448.
5   [1980] ICR 303n, [1978] IRLR 379, EAT, recently reaffirmed in *Post Office v Foley; HSBC Bank plc v Madden* [2000] ICR 1283, [2000] IRLR 827, CA and *Whitbread plc v Hall* [2001] EWCA Civ 268, [2001] IRLR 275.

4.23   There is, however, one major point of uncertainty left – does the employer *have* to give a reference? Can all the above simply be avoided by refusing to act as a referee? In the past it has generally been assumed that there is no implied obligation on the employer. But this was put into doubt in *Spring* by dicta by Lord Woolf that in certain circumstances (where references are known to be an essential requirement of recruiting) there may now be such an implied obligation. The problem is to know how far this goes. On the one hand, the case itself concerned employment under the LAUTRO rules with their mandatory references, so seen in that light the dicta may be of narrow application. On the other hand the remarks in question are expressed in more general terms, arguably not restricted to the facts of the case, which would suggest a wider application, the arguments centring on how necessary/expected the references are in the industry or sector in question. This point awaits resolution. In the meantime, one category has been established, quite separately under statute, where a refusal of a reference is legally dangerous, namely where the refusal is in retaliation for a sex discrimination complaint made by the ex-employee. The Sex Discrimination Act 1975 did not seem to cover this form of victimisation because its wording did not obviously cover discrimination against ex-employees after termination. However, in *Coote v Granada Hospitality Ltd*[1] the ECJ held that the refusal was contrary to the Equal Treatment Directive, in the light of which the EAT at the resumed hearing re-interpreted the Act to cover cases such as this[2]. There is, however, a problem because a refusal on *racial* grounds is not covered; normally of course the two discrimination statutes are construed and applied in *pari materia, but* the Race Relations Act 1976 is not underpinned by equivalent EC law, and there is Court of Appeal authority that the Act in its terms cannot apply to post-termination discrimination[3]. This was reaffirmed subsequently by the Court of Appeal in *Rhys-Harper v Relaxion Group plc*[4] where it was held that neither the Sex Discrimination Act nor the Race Relations Act 1976 can in general apply to post-termination actions; *Coote* was construed as establishing an exception only in cases of victimisation because of the employee having brought proceedings for sex discrimination[5]. If that is the reason for the refusal of a reference for the ex-employee it remains unlawful, but there is no wider rule.

1   C-185/97 [1999] ICR 100, [1998] IRLR 656, ECJ.
2   [1999] IRLR 452, EAT.
3   *Post office v Adekeye* [1997] ICR 110, [1997] IRLR 105, CA (post-termination appeal hearing not covered). See also *Nagarajan v Agnew* [1994] IRLR 61, EAT (giving a *bad* reference for an ex-employee not covered).

4 [2001] EWCA Civ 634, [2001] IRLR 460.
5 Ie under the Sex Discrimination Act 1975, s 4.

(b) Advising or warning of rights; insuring

4.24 Common law duties to warn an employee of health and safety risks are well known in the law of tort and in personal injury litigation[1], but the extent to which there may be any implied duty to do so in relation to the employee's wider interests (particularly financial) has proved troublesome recently. So has the question whether the employer should insure the employee, but that has a longer record of difficulty.

In *Scally v Southern Health and Social Services Board*[2] health board employees were subject to a statutory superannuation scheme under which, for the first year of its operation, they could make additional contributions to purchase 'added years' if they were not otherwise able to work for the 40 years necessary for the full pension. Four doctors missed out on this opportunity, not having been informed of their right to do so, and brought actions against the board, inter alia for breach of contract in not informing them of their rights. The House of Lords upheld their contractual claim. Drawing on the distinction in *Lister v Romford Ice & Cold Storage Co Ltd*[3] between a genuine implied term and a characteristic or imposed term, Lord Bridge (giving the judgment of the court) said that there was no basis for the former, but upheld the claimants' claim of a term of the latter kind, in these terms:

'I would define it as the relationship of employer and employee where the following circumstances obtain: (1) the terms of the contract of employment have not been negotiated with the individual employee but result from negotiation with a representative body or are otherwise incorporated by reference; (2) a particular term of the contract makes available to the employee a valuable right contingent upon action being taken by him to avail himself of its benefit; (3) the employee cannot, in all the circumstances, reasonably be expected to be aware of the term unless it is drawn to his attention. I fully appreciate that the criterion to justify an implication of this kind is necessity, not reasonableness. But I take the view that it is not merely reasonable, but necessary, in the circumstances postulated, to imply an obligation on the employer to take reasonable steps to bring the term to the employee's attention, so that he may be in a position to enjoy its benefit.'

This was at the time quite a surprising decision, one peculiarity of which is that (given that it is a characteristic term, not one genuinely implied from the individual facts) it is formulated with such precision. It is at the opposite end of a long spectrum from a term as general as, say, trust and respect, and reads like a term invented to deal with one particular case. This of course poses a difficulty in trying to determine how widely it is likely to be applied in other cases. Two subsequent cases suggest not very widely at all. In *University of Nottingham v Eyett*[4] the claimant was a university employee who could retire after 60 on an average final salary basis. The details were set out in an explanatory booklet that he had been given. Shortly after reaching 60, he enquired of the university what his pension would be if he retired at a certain date; he was given an accurate figure and retired at that date. He later found out that if he had waited for a further month his entitlement would have been higher. He brought a complaint to the pensions ombudsman who held in his favour (on the basis that the employers

87

should have informed him of this difference) but on appeal to the Chancery Division Hart J allowed the employers' appeal. He held that there was no breach of the implied term of trust and respect in these circumstances, and distinguished *Scally* as a case where the employee was ignorant of his rights and had no means of finding out. That was not the case here, and there was no positive obligation on the employers to alert the employee to a possible financial mistake; essentially, it was for the employee to organise his own affairs and he had the means to do so. In *Hagen v ICI Chemicals and Polymers Ltd*[5] employees faced with being the subject of a transfer of undertakings alleged that they had relied on statements and reassurances by the transferor employer that certain terms (especially relating to pensions) would be protected. When this proved not to be the case, they sued the employer for damages for negligent misstatement and for breach of implied contractual duties, including a duty to take all reasonable steps to ensure that employees were made aware of the true position in regard to their pension rights and other contractual benefits and entitlements. In a magnum opus Elias J held that there was no positive duty on the employer to make employees aware of their pension rights or other contractual terms. *Eyett* was followed and *Scally* again distinguished. The employees in fact succeeded on negligent misstatement, in that it was fair, just and reasonable to allow a duty of care to arise in a TUPE case such as this and reasonable and foreseeable reliance had been shown[6]. Moreover, a parallel contractual duty of care was established (though, as in *Scally*, on very specific grounds[7]). However, what this all suggests is that *if* important statements are made by an employer to employees (who rely on them to their detriment) a duty of reasonable care arises, but there is no positive duty *to make* such statements for employees to rely on.

Obviously there will be many possible variations in cases such as these, on grounds of lack of knowledge and means of knowledge, or even existence of rights and quantification of rights. Taken together, however, the effect of *Eyett* and *Hagen* may be that there is little scope for extension of *Scally*, especially if that would involve a positive duty of best advice, except where provided for specifically in regulatory provisions or by statute.

1   See, eg, *Pape v Cumbria County Council* [1992] 3 All ER 211.
2   [1991] ICR 771, [1991] IRLR 522, HL.
3   [1957] AC 555, [1957] 1 All ER 125, HL, see para 3.18, above.
4   [1999] ICR 721, [1999] IRLR 87. In *Outram v Academy Plastics* [2000] IRLR 499 the Court of Appeal refused to allow liability in tort (for negligently failing to advise an employee as to options under the pension scheme) to be any wider than this liability under the contract of employment and its implied terms. In the pre-*Scally* case of *Reid v Rush & Tompkins Group plc* [1990] ICR 61, [1989] IRLR 265 the Court of Appeal had held that there was *no* obligation on an employer to advise the employee to insure against economic loss while working abroad.
5   [2002] IRLR 31, QBD.
6   Even here the case was unusual, because on the facts the employees could show causation, ie that if they had not had the reassurances they would have collectively opposed the transfer and that the likelihood was that such opposition would have stopped it. In many cases, of course, employees would *not* have such influence, they would have to go with the transfer anyway, and so causation would not be shown and a claim would fail.
7   The implied duty was said to arise where (1) the employer is proposing that the employees transfer their employment, (2) the transfer will impact upon the future economic interests of the employees, (3) the transfer will be unlikely to take place if a significant body of the employees object, (4) the employer has access to certain information unavailable to the employees, and (5) the employer knows that its information or advice will carry considerable weight with the employees.

4.25   Turning to the question of insurance, there has here been a history of a restrictive approach. In *Lister v Romford Ice & Cold Storage Co Ltd* (above) one way out of the complicated questions of subrogation and indemnities (where an employee has incurred the employer in vacarious liability to a third party) suggested by the employee was that the employer should be under an implied duty to deal with all matters of insurance while the employee was at work. This, however, the House of Lords by a 3-2 majority refused to do, at least to any greater extent than was required by law; the practical problem is, of course, that this excludes general public liability. Would a court now view the matter differently, in the light of changed circumstances since 1957 and the *possibly* wider approach taken in *Scally*, especially if work-related insurance were viewed as something essentially within the purview of the employer? The immediately pre-*Scally* decision of the Court of Appeal in *Reid v Rush & Tompkins Group plc* suggests not[1], but then again that involved an employee sent to work abroad and suffering economic loss (albeit arising from physical injury) in circumstances potentially so diverse (according to Gibson LJ) as to require the matter to be covered, if at all, by legislation, akin to that applying to road traffic.

1   [1999] ICR 721, [1999] IRLR 87.

(c)   Confidentiality towards employees

4.26   The duty of confidentiality by an employee is well established and set out above, but is there any reciprocal duty of confidentiality by the employer *towards* the employee? Two cases in the 1990s raised this issue in specific contexts, and arguably it is now coming to the fore on more general grounds, and we can expect further developments.

In *Dalgleish v Lothian and Borders Police Board*[1] civilian employees of a police force obtained an interim interdict restraining the force from complying with a request from a local council for their names and addresses, as part of a campaign to track down non-payers of the community charge. This was partly on the basis that an agreement between the force and employee representatives on use of personal information had arguably been incorporated into the petitioners' contracts, but also on the basis that in any event it was also arguably that the names and addresses were held only for the purposes of the relationship of employer and employee, and that any use beyond that could be prevented on general grounds of confidentiality. The general law of confidence remains difficult and underdeveloped and this judgment (being only at interim stage) did not need to take it any further, but there is a particularly interesting reference to *Robb v Green*[2], a leading case on the duty of confidentiality on an employee, suggesting a parallel duty on an employer at common law.

The second case was a particularly high-profile one in the press, between a female Assistant Chief Constable and her employing police force, alleging sex discrimination. As part of this litigation generally, *Halford v United Kingdom*[3] concerned her complaint to the European Court of Human Rights that telephone calls from work and home has been intercepted by her employers. The court held that the interceptions at work (in a manner unregulated by domestic law) constituted a violation of article 8(1) of the European Convention on Human Rights (right to respect for private and family life, home and correspondence) and disapproved an argument by the UK government that an employer should be able to monitor such calls without the prior knowledge of the employee. As the employer was a public body, there was a direct right not to have this interference, under article 8(2); lack of a domestic remedy for her meant that the UK were also in breach of article 13 (effective remedies).

While it would be premature to see this as the inception of a new 'right to privacy', the whole question of the treatment of employees at work in relation to surveillance, personal privacy and investigation has taken on considerable topicality since *Halford*. This has been increased most recently by the impact of new forms of communication, particularly e-mail and the Internet. Serious developments are likely here in the near future, for four reasons – (1) the incorporation of the Convention into domestic law by the Human Rights Act 1998 which means that we can expect more actions relying on it, either directly or through the general obligation on a tribunal or court to take Convention rights into account when deciding cases arising under other legal provisions (eg unfair dismissal and discrimination laws)[4], (2) the extended coverage of the Data Protection Act 1998, with the prospect (at the time of writing) of new codes of practice from the Commissioner on the use of personal data by employers, including employee surveillance (eg of e-mails); (3) the enactment of the Telecommunications (Lawful Business Practice)(Interception of Communications) Regulations 2000[5] which appear to be more indulgent in what they permit an employer to do by way of surveillance than the Commissioner's original Draft Code of Practice; (4) increased emphasis on employers using modern technology to have clear policies on the use and abuse of e-mail and the Internet, to make clear to employees what the basic rules are, primarily for disciplinary purposes[6] and to minimise the risk of the employer being vicariously liable for abuse (eg discrimination, harassment, defamation, breach of third party confidentiality, possession of pornography), but also possibly at the same time to delimit private from work use, and to set out what may or may not be done by way of the former[7]. All of those matters may well have a serious bearing on any further developments of the general law on confidentiality. Of more direct importance to this book, it will be interesting to see if these developments lead to the inception of a characteristic implied term in contracts of employment relating to employee confidentiality and privacy (a route not actually taken in *Dalgleish*).

1   [1991] IRLR 422, Ct of Sess (OH).
2   [1895] 2 QB 315, CA; see para 4.19, above.
3   [1997] IRLR 471, ECtHR.
4   As stated above, the issue was relatively simple in *Halford* because the employer was a public body. However, it has been held that the substance of the art 8 right is capable of applying to commercial activities/premises (*Niemietz v Germany* (1992) 16 EHRR 97), and so these indirect forms of enforcement will have potential. After considerable initial hype, the effects of the Human Rights Act 1998 on employment law generally have been predictably few, but the area of employee privacy may see developments. Will supermodels continue to fare better than footballers playing away?
5   SI 2000/2699.
6   The original, and still leading, case on computer misuse took a stringent line, considering that it will normally justify instant dismissal (even in the absence of financial gain): *Denco Ltd v Joinson* [1991] ICR 172, [1991] IRLR 63, EAT.
7   On a narrow view of the law so far (including *Halford*) it may be open to the employer simply to *ban* private use, so that no reasonable expectation of personal privacy can arise at all. If, however, use is permitted, arguments are now arising that an employer ought to provide a secure private facility somehow, if necessary by separate equipment not subject to monitoring.

(d)   An implied obligation to obey the law?

4.27   Should there be an implied obligation on the employer to, in effect, obey the law? In one sense, this would appear to be simply tautologous, and of little practical use, given that most legal obligations have their own form of enforcement which are the right way to do it, rather than through the contract. Thus, the EAT had little hesitation in disapproving an argument that there was an implied contractual right for an employee not to be unfairly dismissed[1].

However, this question has been raised recently in a high-profile case concerning the enforceability of a specific provision, but possibly containing indications for the future.

In *Barber v RJB Mining (UK) Ltd*[2] there was a dispute between mine owners and pit deputies over what the latter claimed were pressures to continue working beyond the average 48 hours per week introduced by the Working Time Regulations 1998; the deputies had refused to sign an opt-out agreement as part of a current pay dispute. The 48 hour week provisions in regulation 4 state that a worker's time is not to exceed an average of 48 hours for each seven days in a reference period (para (1)), and that the employer must take reasonable steps to ensure this. Crucially (and reflecting the hybrid nature of the backing Directive as being partly a health and safety matter and partly an employment matter) the Regulations provide that these provisions (along with those on night working) are only subject to health and safety enforcement; no individual cause of action to a tribunal is provided (though it is for the other major provisions on rest breaks and paid holidays). Thus, under the Regulations an employer could decide to run the risk of a health and safety prosecution, relying on the fact that the individuals concerned could not challenge any breaches. However, in this case Gage J held that regulation 4(1) imposes a *contractual* obligation on an employer not to require more than an average of 48 hours per week; breach of this could be challenged by an individual in a contract action. He made a declaration to this effect, adding for good measure that in the circumstances this meant that once an employee had done enough hours in the 17-week reference period to average 48 per week he could stop working and lawfully refuse to resume until the next reference period. This case, notable though it is, does not establish any single overarching term of observance of the law, and is partly explained in the judgment by detailed statutory interpretation of regulation 4[3], aided by the fact that the Regulations are of course the result of a Directive, to which reference could be made on the question of whether the Regulations alone provide the effective enforcement required by EC law. However, other parts of the reasoning are in broader terms which could perhaps be used in other contexts. Having established the separate nature of regulation 4(1), the judge said:

'It seems to me clear that Parliament intended that all contracts of employment should be read so as to provide that an employee should work no more than an average of 48 hours in any week during the reference period. In my judgment, this is a mandatory requirement which must apply to all contracts of employment. The fact that para(1) does not state that an employer is prohibited from requiring his employee from working longer hours does not in my view prevent that paragraph from having the effect of placing an obligation on an employer not to require an employee to work more than the permitted number of hours. Such an obligation is in keeping with the stated objective of the Directive of providing for health and safety of employees'.

This adoption of a contractual route was essential in the case because the judge went on to state that he would *not* have allowed an action in tort for breach of statutory duty to have been founded on regulation 4.

1   *Focsa Services (UK) Ltd v Birkett* [1996] IRLR 325, EAT; (the employee lacked the qualifying period of service for a claim for unfair dismissal). This is very much in line with the reasoning of the House of Lords in *Johnson v Unisys Ltd* [2001] UKHL 13, [2001] ICR 480, [2001] IRLR

279 that unfair dismissal rules (eg in relation to the qualifying period and the statutory cap on compensation) are not to be outflanked by the development of a common law action for, in effect, unfair conduct by the employer at the time of dismissal.
2   [1999] ICR 679, [1999] IRLR 308, QBD.
3   The principal point was that regs 4(1) and 4(2) were to be read disjunctively – reg 4(2) introduces the statutory scheme of health and safety enforcement, but reg 4(1) is separate and mandatory, allowing forms of enforcement other than that set out in the Regulations.

4.28   Thus, there are at least straws in the wind pointing towards the evolution of a term to comply with relevant legal (especially statutory) requirements[1], at least where they are 'mandatory' in nature (as in *Barber*) and also where there is not a stronger case that any remedies provided by the statute are meant to be exhaustive, leaving no room for the grafting on of contractual relief[2] (thus meeting the authority given above that there is no contractual right not to be unfairly dismissed – certainly where the aim of a contract action would be to evade the statutory requirement of qualifying service). If there were to be further developments here, what would be the effect? In an area like this it is inherently difficult to speculate, because the real significance would be that such an argument would be *available*, for use in diverse situations. However, three possibilities are suggested. The first is that the new implied term could be used again (as in *Barber*) to fill in apparent gaps in enforcement. One example here might be the Management of Health and Safety at Work Regulations 1999. At a late stage in the passage of the original 1992 Regulations, the then government acceded to suggestions by employers and put in a provision stating that these Regulations (unlike the rest of the Six Pack) do *not* support civil liability; thus, we have statutory provisions of great importance (especially on risk assessment and the general organisation of work safety) which cannot found an action for breach of statutory duty. There are moves afoot to change this eventually by legislation, but in the meantime might reasoning akin to that in *Barber* fill this gap, by making observance of these requirements an implied contractual obligation, so that injury caused by non-observance could be breach of contract[3]? The second possibility is that a new implied term could *supplement* existing enforcement machinery. Some legislation gives considerable protection to an employee from particular detriment and (particularly) dismissal for claiming rights under it, but there might be cases where the employee is not in this *in extremis* position, but still wants the benefit of the rights. The Public Interest Disclosure Act 1998 is one such, with heavy emphasis on negative obligations on an employer not to discipline or dismiss an employee for making a protected disclosure. Might there arise a case where for some reason an employee wishes to exert a more positive right *to* disclose, which could be guaranteed more clearly by an implied obligation on the employer to abide by the provisions of the Act? The third possibility is that a new implied term could be used in constructive dismissal cases, where an actual *or threatened* breach by the employer of the statutory right in question could, as a breach of this term, justify the employee in walking out. In many cases, this could presently be squeezed under the implied term of trust and respect, though in some ways that fits more neatly where the real cause for objection by the employee is the *way* in which the employer acts; a new term could more neatly fit the case where it is purely the *fact* of actual or threatened breach of the legal provision that causes the employee to leave.

One final question is posed. If there were significant developments in this direction, could they be taken beyond domestic statutory obligations and apply (most radically of all) to Directives? Could it be argued that, where a Directive or part thereof (eg the provisions of the second half of the Part Time Workers

Directive requiring the employer to give consideration to matters such as transferring from part-time to full-time and vice versa, and giving part-time workers access to training and career development) is directly relevant to a particular employment, observance of that Directive or part becomes an implied obligation under the contract (especially where domestic law remedies are absent or not particularly strong or there is some other reason to argue that the Directive has not been properly implemented into domestic law)? This would be a radical departure, because a contractual rights analysis could effectively extend direct enforcement of Directives to the private sector, making the individual private employer liable for breach of contract, rather than the government under a *Francovich* action[4]. This would not be for the faint-hearted.

1   In *Gogay v Hertfordshire County Council* [2000] IRLR 703, CA it was common ground between the parties that there was an implied term 'that the [public sector] defendants would not act otherwise than in accordance with their relevant statutory powers' (para 21). By contrast, in *Bernadone v Pall Mall Services Group Ltd* [2001] ICR 197, [2000] IRLR 487 the Court of Appeal disapproved the opinion of Blofeld J at first instance that there is an implied term that the employer will comply with the law on compulsory insurance against work-related accidents.
2   In that context, note the ERA 1996, s 205 which limits the remedy for most parts of the Act to the actions specifically laid down in the statute, before an employment tribunal.
3   It is established that an industrial injury case can lie in contract if for some reason a tort action is not available: *Matthews v Kuwait Bechtel Corpn* [1959] 2 QB 57, [1959] 2 All ER 345, CA. One other way to avoid the current exclusion of civil liability in the Management Regulations may be to argue that the major requirements such as risk assessment are now so embedded in good practice that a failure to comply with them constitutes common law negligence; see Smith, Goddard, Killalea & Randall *Health and Safety, the Modern Legal Framework* (2nd edn, 2000) Butterworths, p 30. There are signs of this in the judgment of Lord Macfadyen in *Cross v Highlands and Islands Enterprise* [2001] IRLR 336, Ct of Sess (OH).
4   A *Francovich* action was approved in the case of non-implementation of the Working Time Directive in the UK in *R v A-G for Northern Ireland, ex p Burns* [1999] IRLR 315.

(e)   An implied obligation not to use one contractual provision to negate rights under another?

4.29   In traditional contract law, a contract is a series of promises and counter-promises which stand or fall individually, the ultimate question being whether one party is in the right or wrong under the particular clause in question. This is normally a question of objective interpretation[1]. However, recent case law has questioned whether a court might take a wider view and hold that an employer may not use an apparently unrestricted power in one part of the contract as a means of frustrating the employee's normal expectations (or, indeed, rights) under another part. This raises questions similar to those surrounding the possibly overriding effect of the term of trust and respect[2], and indeed that may be its starting point, especially where the question is how an employer's discretion under a term in the contract is to be exercised. In *Mihlenstedt v Barclays Bank International*[3] the Court of Appeal held that where an employer's ill health early retirement scheme gave the employer a discretion to decide whether certain criteria were met (in, it has to be said, an exceptionally difficult case factually) there was an implied obligation on the employer to exercise it properly and in good faith, in the light of the medical opinions it had received; there was no overriding power to exercise the discretion simply so as to refuse the application for its own reasons.

The matter has, however, been taken significantly further in what have become known as the 'PHI' cases. In *Aspden v Webbs Poultry and Meat Group (Holdings) Ltd*[4] the claimant was a senior manager who had had offered to him when considering taking up employment a permanent health insurance (PHI) scheme of a particularly generous nature – if incapable of work for over 26 weeks he was entitled to ¾ salary until death, retirement or ceasing to be an employee. However, the problem was that this in fact acted as something of an 'add-on', because on taking up employment he was simply given a standard form contract which made no mention of the PHI scheme and was potentially inconsistent with it. In particular, it provided for ordinary sickness dismissal procedures (for dismissal in case of long-term sickness after exhausting sick pay) and an apparently unrestricted power on either side to give three months' notice of termination. When the employee later became ill (after altercations with the firm over reorganisations) the employers suspected that the illness may have been exaggerated, and so exercised their ordinary power of dismissal by notice *before* he could qualify for the PHI benefits. The employee brought an action for wrongful dismissal, which on ordinary principles would have been unmaintainable (contractual notice having been given). However, Sedley J held that there was here an implied term that, except for summary dismissal for cause, the employer would not terminate the employment while he was incapacitated in such a way as to deprive him of the benefits of the PHI scheme. The judge acknowledged that he was operating on the very margins of contract law, but felt able to do so because otherwise to exercise the apparently unrestricted right at common law to dismiss with notice would have completely negated the PHI scheme which was an integral part of his employment, albeit operating unfortunately separately. This very creative judgment was subsequently followed by the Court of Session[5] and approved obiter by the Court of Appeal[6]. It was subject to one refinement, in that the continuing power to dismiss must be construed as applying to gross misconduct *and redundancy*, because in neither case is dismissal being used to frustrate the PHI scheme rights[7]; however, the general principle was not denied. Indeed it was arguably taken further in *Villella v MFI Furniture Centres Ltd*[8] where the employee had already qualified for the PHI benefits and the judge held that the implied term also meant that the employers would not terminate the employment so as to frustrate the benefits *in payment*, obviously a vital matter for the employee, and particularly unfortunate for the employer because their insurance policy did terminate entitlement on the ending of employment, but no such stipulation appeared in the contract between the employer and employee, and it was held that the employer could not take advantage of the term in the insurance contract to terminate the employee's contract[9]. Of course, there may be scope for the employer to tailor the express provisions of a scheme to try to pre-empt some of these points, though by doing so they may rob it of its attraction as a headhunting device[10]. What they may not do is to hold it out as a valuable asset and then try to negate it later under other, unconnected, provisions in the contract, especially notice.

1   For a recent example, see *Macari v Celtic Football and Athletic Co Ltd* [1999] IRLR 787, Ct of Sess (IH) where the court refused to find mutually-reliant terms in a contract, so that the fact that the employer was in breach of the term of trust and respect did not permit the employee to disobey otherwise lawful orders.
2   See paras 3.19 and 4.8, above.
3   [1989] IRLR 522, CA.
4   [1996] IRLR 521, QBD.
5   *Adin v Sedco Forex International Resources Ltd* [1997] IRLR 280, Ct of Sess.
6   *Brompton v A O C International Ltd* [1997] IRLR 639, CA.
7   *Hill v General Accident Fire and Life Assurance Corpn plc* [1998] IRLR 641, Ct of Sess.
8   [1999] IRLR 468, QBD.
9   For good measure, the judge held that a defence of frustration through long-term ill health could not apply here, because the very existence of the PHI scheme meant that ill health was not an unforeseen eventuality.

10 The other possibility is, of course, to discontinue offering PHI schemes altogether, as being legally too open-ended. The main problem seems to be that they were taken up too readily, without their overall legal effects being thought through.

4.30   What is the overall effect of this? It is generally thought to be significant in the whole area of sickness, including the application of ordinary sickness absence and pay schemes. Not long ago, it would have been thought that the existence of a relatively generous sickness scheme (eg three months full pay, followed by three months half pay) would have had no effect on the employer's normal power to dismiss by notice. If, say, the latter was one month, the assumption would have been that if it was urgent to replace, then the employer could give the one month notice *within* the six month sick pay period, and that no question could arise of wrongful dismissal. In other words, the two sets of terms on sickness and notice would have operated independently. Now, however, in the light of the PHI scheme cases it may be that the only safe advice is not to give the notice to expire at any time before expiry of the sick pay entitlement, because the modern tendency is to view the two terms as interlinked, and to be construed together. After all, in simple terms, the employer has envisaged the possibility of sickness of that length and has promised to pay during it. The big question, however, is whether an even more general principle can be discerned from all of this, going beyond sickness schemes, and applying wherever reliance by the employer on one particular (apparently unrestricted) contractual power may prejudice an employee's rights under an equally important aspect of the contract[1]. Even more broadly, could it be argued that such an unrestricted power should not be allowed to negate a fundamental tenet or purpose of the contract? To take one concrete example, what would happen if an employer took on an employee in order to bring with him or her the custom of a particular client with whom they had dealt in the past, only then (once the custom was obtained) to give that employee notice of dismissal? In traditional contract law the employee would have no complaint, but could it be argued now that the notice power was subject to an implied limitation that it would not be exercised (other than for gross misconduct or redundancy) to terminate the employment while the employer continued to gain the economic advantages of that customer, who was the raison d'etre of the hiring? Further developments here would be both interesting and important, but would carry with them one major complication – the courts would, most unusually, have to grapple with the problem of awarding *general* damages for wrongful dismissal, rather than just working out what was owed for the notice period, as in the past. This is a particularly good example of the possible developments, of a fundamental nature, that are happening and being discussed in the modern law of employment contracts, and that are the subject of this book.

1   There are strong signs of this in the very recent decision of Elias J in *Jenvey v Australian Broadcasting Corpn* [2002] IRLR 520, QBD, where an employee successfully argued for an implied term that, in the event of an impending redundancy situation, the employer would not dismiss him for another reason, simply in order to deny his contractual entitlement to enhanced redundancy benefits.

Chapter 5

Share schemes and pensions

1   Introduction

5.1   Although a consideration of the application of implied terms arising out of the modern contract of employment is generally dealt with elsewhere in this book[1] it was felt that a separate chapter dealing with the specific context of share schemes and pensions was justified. This is because the application and effect of these implied terms is to a certain extent modified by the unique structural nature of these benefits. Four principal themes can be identified:

(a)   first of all share schemes and pensions involve freestanding obligations on employers which are often separate and distinct from the contract of employment itself[2]. Accordingly the impact of the relevant contractual terms on the dispute between the parties tends to be indirect rather than direct;

(b)   the application of the relevant terms tends to operate in circumstances in which the contract of employment itself is no longer subsisting[3]. This will often be because the issues either arise on the termination of employment or even many years later where the relevant individual has retired[4];

(c)   in the context of share schemes and pensions different jurisdictional issues arise to those encountered in mainstream employment law. Most pensions disputes, for example, are now litigated before the Pensions Ombudsman[5] or, on appeal, in the Chancery Division. Accordingly many of the decisions in this area are made in conditions which lack any form of input from an 'industrial jury' and where the decision takers are often considering the issues before them without a traditional employment law background. This tendency has often led to a degree of conflict between decisions in the pensions field and those dealing with unfair dismissal in particular[6]. By way of contrast it has been in the field of share schemes and pensions that there has been a perceptible shift towards the development of quasi public law concepts in the field of private law rights[7]. This tendency again appears to be driven at least in part by the jurisdictional background of the decision takers; and

(d)   when considering share scheme and pensions disputes the courts are often faced with circumstances in which employees have what are perceived as accrued rights over and above those which flow from the normal relationship of employer and employee. By way of example an option which has been granted under a share scheme will often be portrayed as an accrued right of the employee which should only be removed in clear circumstances. Similarly pension entitlements are now generally accepted as arising by way of delayed remuneration for work *already* performed[8]. In this respect again we can see that different considerations arise particularly regarding the way in which employers should approach the exercise of any discretion available to them under schemes or where they are seeking to discontinue the operation of any such scheme[9].

The structure of this Chapter is to consider various aspects of the interrelationship between the contract of employment and share schemes and pensions in the context in which they arise. Accordingly share schemes and pensions shall be considered separately although there is likely to be a degree of overlap between the two. Indeed one of the striking aspects of modern development in these areas is the degree of cross fertilisation which has taken place across these disciplines.

1   See chap 4.
2   See for example *Levett v Biotrace International plc* [1999] ICR 818, CA.
3   This provides an interesting contrast to the comments of Lord Hoffman in *Johnson v Unisys Ltd* [2001] UKHL 13, [2001] ICR 480 where he considers that the implied term of trust and confidence is only of utility during the currency of the employment relationship: see further chap 3.
4   See for example *Imperial Group Pension Trust Ltd v Imperial Tobacco Ltd* [1991] 1 WLR 589 in which Browne-Wilkinson V-C effectively extended the reach of the implied term of good faith not only to employees but also to former employees who had retired.
5   The powers and jurisdiction of the Pensions Ombudsman are set out at Part X of the Pension Schemes Act 1993. An appeal on a point of law lies to the Chancery Division of the High Court from a determination of the Ombudsman: Pension Schemes Act 1993, s 151(4).
6   A striking example is the difference in approach of the Chancery Division and the EAT in the cases of *University of Nottingham v Eyett* [1999] ICR 721 and *BG plc v O'Brien* [2001] IRLR 496 as to the question whether the implied term of trust and confidence places a positive obligation on an employer.
7   See in particular the concept of the 'reasonable expectations' of the parties as developed in *Equitable Life Assurance Society v Hyman* [2002] 1 AC 408.
8   Indeed this concept of delayed remuneration lies at the root of the ECJ jurisprudence on equal treatment in the context of pension schemes (see *Barber v Guardian Royal Exchange Society* [1990] ICR 616).
9   Interestingly though, although this concept was a particular driving force behind many of the earlier decisions in the *National Grid* case the House of Lords considered that no distinction should be drawn between contributory and non-contributory pension schemes (see [2001] ICR 544).

2   Share schemes

5.2   Share schemes have become a popular method of rewarding employees both for their performance and loyalty to the employer. Such schemes have the considerable advantage of linking rewards to overall company performance and potentially carry with them not only lucrative benefits but also considerable tax advantages for the parties[1]. Typically such schemes operate through the mechanism of an option being granted to an employee to purchase shares at a particular price. This option is normally purchased for a nominal consideration but if the share price increases in value over a nominated period it may result in a considerable profit to the employee when exercised. However, such schemes are complex in nature and will often leave to the employer considerable scope for the exercise of discretions as to when and to what extent an employee may exercise an option. These discretions are typically exercised through the mechanism of a remuneration committee.

Share scheme conflicts will often arise on the termination of employment. This is because it is common for share schemes to restrict the way in which options can be exercised depending upon the circumstances of departure. Typically options can be exercised in full where departure arises by reason of death, injury, retirement or redundancy (so called 'innocent reasons'). By way of contrast a dismissal 'for cause' will often lead to the immediate lapse of all unexercised options. In between there is a large category of reasons for departure which can vary from those which are the equivalent of innocent reasons which would normally not justify any restrictions on entitlement (ie on a business reorganisation but where the technical definition of redundancy has not been met) to those which fall just short of dismissal for cause (ie serious underperformance through lack of effort) and many shades in between. It is in these 'grey area' cases that scheme rules tend to provide for employers, or a committee acting on their behalf, to exercise 'an absolute discretion' as to when and to what extent the options can be exercised.

In the context of share schemes and employment disputes two principal issues arise, namely (a) the validity of attempts by the employer to restrict claims for damages arising from alleged breaches of the share scheme rules or the contract of employment; and (b) challenges to the exercise of a discretion on 'good faith' grounds.

1   For a fuller treatment of the structure of share schemes see *Harvey on Industrial Relations and Employment Law* Div B, and *Employee Share Schemes* (Ed, David Pett) Sweet & Maxwell.

(a)   Restrictions on damages for wrongful dismissal

5.3   The first example of the interaction between the contract of employment and share schemes is where attempts have been made to restrict the ability of wrongfully dismissed employees to exercise options already granted or to claim damages for breach of contract arising from the failure to be awarded further share options during the relevant notice period. This question typically raises issues relating to the construction of exclusion clauses which are often contained in both the contract of employment and the share scheme rules. If the employer is to achieve its purpose careful drafting is necessary. This is because the courts will apply the general rule of construction that a document will be construed in a manner which prevents a party from taking a benefit from its own wrong. This rule of construction is well established and has been recognised by the House of Lords in *Alghussein Establishment v Eton College*[1]. A review of the facts in *Alghussein* also illustrates the extremely robust nature of the principle and the fact that the courts will be willing to go to great lengths, including a departure from relatively clear wording, in order to achieve its aim. However, it is generally accepted that the rule is only a rule of construction and not a rule of law as such[2]. Accordingly it follows that the parties are free to exclude its operation but only by the use of clear and unambiguous language. An example of a case in which the employer achieved this result in a share scheme context is *Micklefield v SAC Technology Ltd*[3]. In that case the employee was awarded an option under the relevant scheme and gave notice of his intention to exercise it. However, before the option became due he was wrongfully dismissed[4]. He accordingly claimed damages for wrongful dismissal including an element in respect of his inability to exercise his option[5]. The employer relied upon the following exclusion clause:

'If any option holder ceases to be an executive for any reason he shall not be entitled, and by applying for an option an executive shall be deemed irrevocably to have waived any entitlement, by way of compensation for loss of office or otherwise howsoever to any sum or other benefit to compensate him for the loss of any rights under the scheme.'

A number of points of interest arise from the decision of the court that the employer could rely upon the provision in question. First of all the court was persuaded that the provision did not fall foul of the rule in *Alghussein* because it did not permit the party to take advantage of its own wrong but rather limited its liability for that wrong. Secondly, the court held that the wording of the provision was sufficient to rebut the rule of construction in any event. This was because the provision could only be referring to circumstances of wrongful dismissal since it referred to compensation for loss of office or otherwise howsoever.

There must be some doubt as to whether *Micklefield* would be decided in the same way in the modern climate. Two criticisms of the reasoning of the court can be made. The first is that the contention that it only seeks to limit the liability for a wrong, rather than permitting the party to take advantage of it, appears open to criticism particularly when it is understood that the share scheme contract is a separate contract albeit linked to the employment relationship. It follows that *all* liability under the share scheme contract was excluded. Secondly, there is considerable scope for arguing that the wording of the exclusion clause was insufficient to rebut the operation of the rule. Indeed on one reading of the decision in *Alghussein* the specific wrong must be identified in order to rebut the principle and words of general application will not suffice. It follows that an attack on such exclusion clauses may well succeed in the modern climate of employment law which is hostile to the removal of such accrued rights particularly where the options are granted as an important part of the individual's remuneration package.

A modern example of a similar provision being side stepped by the courts is *Levett v Biotrace International plc*[6]. In *Levett* the scheme rules contained a provision which provided for options to lapse when an individual became subject to the company's disciplinary procedures and his contract of employment was subsequently terminated. The employee did become subject to the relevant disciplinary procedures and was wrongfully dismissed by the employer without a payment in lieu of notice. He claimed damages for wrongful dismissal and sought a declaration regarding his rights under the share scheme. In finding for the employee the Court of Appeal made considerable use of the rule of construction that a party should not benefit from its own wrong. In particular the Court of Appeal held that the relevant provisions providing for a lapse of the options would only apply where the contract had been *lawfully* terminated. In addition where the employment contract contained a payment in lieu provision the dismissal would still be unlawful for these purposes unless the payment in lieu was made at the appropriate time under the contract.

Although *Levett* did not involve the consideration of an exclusion clause in the same terms as *Micklefield*[7] it is likely that the more robust approach of the Court of Appeal will be followed in the future. Accordingly any exclusion clauses would have to be drafted in very clear terms and identify the specific wrong which is in issue in order to have good prospects of being effective. Similarly if the employer is seeking to rely upon any payment in lieu provision it must be careful to ensure that its terms are properly complied with in full.

1   [1988] 1 WLR 587, HL.
2   See the comments of Lord Jauncey in *Alghussein* to this effect.
3   [1990] ICR 1002
4   To the extent that this contention was not in dispute for the purposes of the preliminary issue.
5   The relevant provision of the scheme rules was somewhat unusual as it provided for all options to lapse upon termination *'for any reason whatsoever'*.
6   [1999] ICR 818, CA.
7   The relevant provision in the *Levett* case had an exclusion which was in limited form *in respect of loss of rights to exercise an option after cessation of employment in circumstances otherwise permitted under the share option scheme rules.*

5.4   Additional difficulties which may arise on the construction of share schemes have been identified by the decision of the Court of Appeal in *Mallone v BPB Industries plc*[1]. In that case difficulties arose because of an administrative delay arising between the termination of the contract of employment on the one hand and the formal resignation of directorships under Italian law on the other. As is common with many share schemes the definition of employment for the purposes of identifying when options would lapse or become subject to the employer's discretion provided that employment shall not cease until all posts had been relinquished. The difficulty which arose in that case was that the employer had little option but to exercise its discretion on the termination of employment rather than wait for the administrative process to take its course since, if it waited, the employee would be able to exercise his options in any event. Although this argument was not advanced on behalf of the employee by way of any cross appeal the Court of Appeal felt it necessary to pass comment on the issue and concluded that if it had been necessary to decide the point it would have found that the earlier exercise of discretion was void. This is a further example which illustrates the general reluctance of the courts to adopt anything other than a purposive construction of scheme rules. Accordingly where, as may often be the case, there is a delay between the termination of employment and the effective resignation of a directorship the employee may be able to obtain full advantage and exercise options which he knows will be subject to some discretion if he delays.

By way of comment it is clear that any exclusion clauses contained in share schemes or the contract of employment will not operate so as to limit any claim arising by way of unfair dismissal. This is because any such provision *whether contained in a contract of employment or not* is void[2]. In addition for the purposes of unfair dismissal it will be no defence for an employer to argue that the loss under the share scheme arises not under the contract of employment but under a separate contract because of the wide nature of the employment tribunal's jurisdiction to assess compensation[3].

1   [2002] EWCA Civ 126 [2002] IRLR 452.
2   ERA 1996, s 203.
3   This is because the assessment of loss is directed at fixing a sum which is *just and equitable* having regard to the loss sustained by the employee *in consequence of the dismissal* and is not restricted to losses arising directly under the employment contract.

(b)   Good faith

5.5   Probably the most striking area in which implied terms impact upon share schemes is that of the application of good faith principles to the exercise of employer discretions. Although it is debatable as to whether these terms arise under the share scheme itself or are derived indirectly from the underlying contract of employment these distinctions are now of little relevance in view of the modern development of the law. This can be seen from the general cross fertilisation of ideas and principles from pensions cases such as *Imperial Group Pension Trust Ltd v Imperial Tobacco Ltd*[1] and *Mihlenstedt v Barclays Bank International Ltd*[2] through to wrongful dismissal and bonus cases such as *Clark v BET*[3] and *Clark v Nomura International plc*[4]. Perhaps inevitably these principles have also made their way into the judicial control of share scheme discretions. All of these cases deal to a certain extent with the practical mapping out of the concept of *fair dealing* which is said to be a necessary adjunct to the employment relationship[5].

A clear example can be gleaned from the development of the test of *perversity* for controlling an employer's discretion when dealing with a bonus payment in *Clark v Nomura International plc, supra*. Within a short space of time this proposition, which was not necessarily uncontroversial in itself, became embedded in the law relating to share schemes as considered by the Court of Appeal in *Mallone v BPB Industries plc*[6] with potentially far reaching effects. *Mallone* concerned an employee who was dismissed in circumstances in which the employers had considerable reservations regarding his performance as the Managing Director of its Italian subsidiary. The court considered that these reservations about performance were valid and held in good faith. However, the court still felt able to interfere with the employers' exercise of its 'absolute discretion' under the share scheme rules to cancel the employee's options. This was so despite the fact that the employee received a very substantial sum by way of compensation for loss of office under Italian law. This result was achieved under the guise of the perversity test incorporated from *Clark v Nomura*.

What is of central importance is the fact that the perversity test has a substantially different impact in a share scheme case. The normal bonus case will involve the assessment of the individual's performance throughout a relatively short period, commonly one year. The difficulty with replicating this principle to share schemes is that the options under such schemes may be granted over a number of years and may also take several years before they mature and become exerciseable. That was the case with Mr Mallone who had a number of options which had matured but which he had not exercised as well as some options which had been granted to him but were not yet exerciseable. The Court of Appeal effectively held that when exercising a discretion in such cases the employer has to have regard for the full period of employment in question. Accordingly it would be perverse in these circumstances to eliminate all of the options in circumstances in which concerns over performance only related to the later periods of employment. It is in this area that we can begin to see the development of quasi public law principles of proportionality and legitimate expectation into areas of private law. This may also have a serious impact not only on the substance of any discretion which is exercised but also in the manner in which it is exercised. The Court of Appeal made some comment in *Mallone* regarding the lack of contemporaneous documentation dealing with the way in which the discretion was exercised. Accordingly it is probably now incumbent upon an employer to set down in clear terms not only the result of any exercise of discretion but also the approach taken and the factors taken into account. This requirement is likely to be fuelled not only by the application of the perversity test but also because, on one view, the effect of exercising a discretion to refuse the exercise of an option may well be akin to the removal of a property right. If this analysis is adopted by the courts then it may well raise the stakes even higher and the argument that an employee is entitled to some input into the decision making process itself may flourish.

What does now appear clear is that considerable care must be exercised by employers when both drafting and implementing share schemes. The courts have two powerful weapons available to them in the form of the rules of construction and the test of good faith which enable them to interfere with discretions and decisions which, although taken in good faith in the sense of an absence of malice, may nevertheless lead to results which may be perceived as being unduly harsh on the employee.

1   [1991] ICR 524.
2   [1989] IRLR 522.
3   [1997] IRLR 348.
4   [2000] IRLR 766.
5   See in particular the comments of Lord Steyn in *Johnson v Unisys Ltd* [2001] UKHL 13, [2001] ICR 480.
6   [2002] EWCA Civ 126 [2002] IRLR 452.

3   Pension Schemes

5.6   When considering the impact of the contract of employment on pension schemes it is important to analyse the basic structure of the legal relationships which are created. There can often be a degree of confusion as to whether particular rights arise under the contract of employment or not. The best analysis to date can be found in the judgment of the Privy Council in *Air Jamaica Ltd v Joy Charlton*[1]. In that case Lord Millett considered that although it was possible for a pension scheme in theory to be established by way of a contract between employer and employee, that would generally be very unusual. The normal position where a scheme operates through the mechanism of a trust scheme[2] is that individuals do not have *contractual* rights to their pensions as such. However, perhaps somewhat confusingly, Lord Millett went on to indicate that their rights are 'derived from their contracts of employment as well as from the trust instrument'. He also accepted for the sake of completeness that although the entitlements arise by way of trust under the pension scheme the 'company's obligation to deduct contributions from members and to pay them to the trustees together with its own matching contributions, is contractual'[3].

Although Lord Millett's analysis is helpful it falls short of a full analysis of the pension relationship. In particular it fails to recognise the modern tendency for the employer to reserve to itself many of the central obligations under the scheme rather than leaving such matters to the trustees. In particular the *Air Jamaica* analysis does not mention the well established principle that when exercising its discretions and powers under a pension scheme the employer is controlled *not* by trust law concepts but by the implied term of good faith arising from the contract of employment[4]. In *Imperial Group Pension Trust v Imperial Tobacco Ltd*[5] Browne-Wilkinson V-C expressly commented that 'the pension trust deed and rules themselves are to be taken as being impliedly subject to the limitation that the rights and powers of the company can only be exercised in accordance with the implied obligation of good faith'[6]. It follows that if Lord Millett's analysis is taken at face value it may mask the real effect of the contract of employment on the pension relationship.

It is also of interest to note that Lord Millett comments that the obligation on the employer to make contributions to the scheme was 'subject to the power of the company unilaterally to discontinue the plan under the plan rules'. It is respectfully contended that such a bold statement is highly controversial and must depend upon the precise nature of the contractual obligation on the employer. It can be said with some confidence that any employer which has used its pension scheme benefits as a bargaining chip during pay negotiations may get a rude awakening on a claim for breach of contract if it unilaterally seeks to close a scheme at a later date since such agreements may be considered to have overriden the scheme rules or alternatively to be subject to a further implied term that the power to close the scheme will not be used to deprive the relevant employees of long-term participation in the scheme[7]. Furthermore, it is also likely that the court will be able to control the power of the employer to close a scheme through the *Imperial* implied term in circumstances in which the closure of a scheme is proposed for an illegitmate collateral purpose[8]. It follows that these matters are necessarily fact sensitive and the general statement of Lord Millett should be seen in this context.

1   [1999] 1 WLR 1399.
2   The requirement that such a scheme be established under trust is a normal requirement of the Inland Revenue before granting approval under the Income and Corporation Taxes Act 1988 (see further *Harvey* Div B).
3   See [1999] 1 WLR 1399 at 1408 (at B in particular).
4   See *Imperial* case at [1991] ICR 524 which since *Air Jamaica* has been formally approved by the House of Lords in the *BCCI* litigation: see para 4.9, above.
5   [1991] ICR 524.
6   See [1991] ICR 597H to 598A.
7   See in the context of employers being able to rely upon such provisions *South West Trains v Wightman* [1998] PLR 113 and *Trustees of the NUS Officials and Employees Superannuation Fund v Allen* [2002] PLR 93.
8   See further the *Imperial* case at [1991] ICR 524 where the release of a pension fund surplus was held to be an improper motive.

(a)   Implied term of trust and confidence

5.7   With regard to the implied term of trust and confidence it is of interest to note that three of the 'cutting edge' cases which were responsible for the development of law in this area involved pensions disputes: *Imperial, supra,* (regarding the treatment of scheme members in order to obtain a pension fund surplus) *Mihlenstedt v Barclays Bank International Ltd*[1] (nature of an employer's obligations when dealing with an application for an ill health pension) and *Scally v Southern Health and Social Services Board*[2] (the provision of information on potential benefits to members where that information not available from other sources and the obtaining of the benefit being dependent upon action being taken by the individual employee concerned). It is also of interest when considering these cases that two of the above clearly involved the extension of the protection of the implied term of good faith to circumstances in which the employment had been terminated (ie *Mihlenstedt* and *Imperial*). It follows that the obiter comments of Lord Hoffman in *Johnson v Unisys, supra,* regarding the inappropriateness of the application of the implied term of good faith to dismissal situations should be narrowly construed and is no basis for attacking the well established role of the implied term in the pensions context[3].

However, although several of the leading cases dealing with the extension of implied terms arose in the pensions context it is also clear that some of the more recent examples of attempts to hold back this development have occurred in cases involving appeals from the Pensions Ombudsman. The clearest example is the decision in *University of Nottingham v Eyett*[4]. In *Eyett* Hart J potentially restricted the operation of the implied term of good faith by suggesting that it was more difficult to establish a breach of the implied term where a positive obligation was being imposed on the employer. Although the judge did recognise that there could be circumstances in which the implied term *may* have a positive content the broad thrust of his reasoning was that such occasions would be rare. This potentially broad attack on the implied term of good faith has been effectively blocked by a later decision of the EAT in *BG plc v O'Brien*[5] in which the practical difficulties with *Eyett* were discussed. As the EAT commented it will often be possible to categorise a negative obligation as a positive one and vice versa. It followed that Hart J's comments in *Eyett* should not be taken as a general statement of the law and it now appears likely that the courts will not permit *Eyett* to be used as a way of reducing the content of the implied term of good faith in the future.

1   [1989] IRLR 522.
2   [1992] 1 AC 294; see para 4.24, above.
3   See further para 4.9, above.
4   [1999] ICR 721; see para 4.24, above.
5   [2001] IRLR 496, upheld on appeal [2002] IRLR 441, CA.

(b)   Advice and information

5.8   However it does now appear that the impact of the implied term on the provision of information in the pension schemes context has reached its high water mark. In *Scally*[1], the House of Lords held that there was an implied term which obliged the employer to provide information to its employees on certain pensions-related benefits. However, it appears as if this principle will now be restricted to the facts of that case, namely where the nature of the benefit in question depends upon positive action being taken by the employee and where it cannot be obtained from other sources.

In particular the courts have taken a robust approach regarding the provision of *advice* by employers and have flatly refused to imply terms to this effect (see *Outram v Academy Plastics Ltd*[2]). In addition there has been a relatively long line of cases in which arguments that employers have been in breach of the implied term by failing to provide pension information have floundered either on the basis that the complaint was really about advice rather than information or where the information provided was accurate albeit limited (see for example *NHS Pensions Agency v Beechinor*[3] and *Hamar v Pensions Ombudsman*[4]).

Although a claim relating to inadequate information succeeded in *Hagen v ICI Chemicals and Polymers*[5] that had little to do with the contract of employment or the rights arising from it. This is because Elias J felt able in that case to impose liability on a transferee employer for failing to provide accurate information on pension rights through the traditional route of negligent misstatement and misrepresentation.

It follows that with regard to the provision of information and advice there has been relatively little development in the law since *Scally* which must now be seen as a high water mark case.

1   [1992] 1 AC 294; see para 4.24, above.
2   [2001] ICR 367.

3   [1997] OPLR 99.
4   [1996] OPLR 55.
5   [2002] PLR 1.

(c)   Use of contractual terms to override the pension scheme

5.9   One further development in this field which is certainly worthy of note, not only in terms of its practical importance but also because it involves a clear degree of interraction between the individual contract and the pension scheme, is the increasing willingness of the courts to recognise that parties may utilise the contract of employment as a vehicle for overriding pension scheme provisions. The classic example arises where a pay rise has been awarded in circumstances in which the increase in pay is expressed not to be pensionable. In such cases the courts will prevent employees from contending at a later date that the scheme provisions should prevail. This result has been achieved through both the express terms of the contractual arrangement and through the use of an implied term that the employee would not make a claim for the higher rate of pension. This result has been achieved both where terms had been individually bargained (see *Trustees of the NUS Officials and Employees Superannuation Fund v Allen*[1]) and where they had been collectively bargained (see *South West Trains v Wightman*[2]).

As stated earlier in this Chapter it will be of interest to see whether the Courts will be willing to impose similar restrictions on reliance on the scheme rules in circumstances in which employees and not employers are seeking to rely upon the contractual provisions. This may well arise where employers seek to close final salary schemes in circumstances in which terms as to contribution rates and expectations have been resolved contractually by way of individual or collective negotiations.

1   [2002] PLR 93.
2   [1998] PLR 113.

Chapter 6

Remedies for breach of contract short of dismissal

1 Introduction

6.1 The common law has traditionally been reluctant to grant remedies which interfere with a subsisting employment relationship[1]. The justification for this reluctance has been said to relate to the difficulties which arise for the courts in policing any orders which may be made and the traditional refusal to enforce, by way of court order, the personal relationship inherent in the employment contract[2]. Furthermore, this reluctance has been bolstered by the many and widespread forms of statutory intervention which have made significant inroads into the subsisting employment relationship and which have, in turn, alleviated the need for any significant development of the common law[3].

Accordingly it can be seen common law remedies play only a limited role in controlling workplace relationships during periods in which the contract of employment subsists and this remains a fairly accurate summary of the modern law. However, this does not mean to say that there has been no development at all. In particular the last twenty years have seen considerable advances in the use of interim injunctions for both employers and employees to enforce contractual obligations in the context of a subsisting employment relationship[4]. In addition there have been some significant, if limited, developments in the availability of a damages claim for the breach of implied terms which arise in circumstances other than the termination of employment. In this Chapter we shall consider the main categories of contractual remedy which can operate in circumstances where a breach of the employment contract has taken place but where that breach falls short of termination.

1 Although there are some well established exceptions to this rule, two prime examples being a claim in debt for unpaid wages typically arising after a unilateral variation in terms by an employer and the strike injunction which, although obtained through an action against the relevant trade union, will indirectly bite on the individual contractual relationship.
2 For judicial discussion of these propositions see *C H Giles & Co Ltd v Morris* [1972] 1 WLR 307.
3 Many striking examples exist including the national minimum wage and the discrimination legislation in particular. These reforms are likely to reduce the scope for further development of common law remedies on the basis of the reasoning adopted by the House of Lords in *Johnson v Unisys Ltd* [2001] UKHL 13, [2001] ICR 480. See further para 4.9, above.
4 Most notably in the form of garden leave and the injunction to compel observance of disciplinary procedures in certain cases: see para 3.31, above and generally, chap 10, below.

2 Declarations

6.2 A declaration is a discretionary remedy which permits the court to pronounce on the precise content of the legal relationship between the parties. By its very nature it is rare to see circumstances in which a party to an employment contract will seek the remedy of a declaration in isolation from other remedies. One example may be where a view is sought on the respective obligations of the parties under a share or pension scheme[1] but even these circumstances will be rare and the courts will not grant such a remedy if the dispute between the parties is purely academic in nature or where, on a proper analysis, it has not yet crystallised in legal terms. It follows that the best option for both parties to the employment contract will often be to delay matters in the hope that the dispute is resolved through non legal means before seeking any form of declaratory relief from the court. Accordingly it is far more common to see the declaration deployed as a secondary form of attack in a wider dispute which will typically relate to a claim for damages or debt[2].

However, these limitations should not mask the effective nature of a declaration in the right case. A striking example is *Jones v Gwent County Council*[3] in which a declaration was obtained on a summary judgment application that a letter of dismissal was not valid and effective because it had been promulgated in breach of contract[4]. A modern example of the effective use of the declaration is *Barber v RJB Mining (UK) Ltd*[5] in which the relevant employees sought to enforce their entitlements under the Working Time Regulations 1998 through the mechanism of a declaration and certain injunctions. The declaration sought was that the workers 'need not work any hours at all until such time as their average working time fell within the limit imposed by regulation 4(1)'. It is instructive to note that the High Court granted the declaration but refused to grant injunctions which sought to prevent the employer from requesting that the employees worked in contravention of the Regulations. The reasoning of the court is of interest and illustrates not only the flexibility of the employment contract when enforcing statutory rights[6] but also the utility of a declaration as a method of achieving the underlying purpose of statutory provisions[7]. The court felt free to grant a declaration because this would provide assurance to each individual employee regarding their legal position. This would obviously be of importance to any individual who wished to refuse to work. However, the wider application for injunctive relief was refused on the basis that such orders would cause considerable disruption to the business of the employer and would remove the ability of each individual employee to decide how they wished to progress the dispute. *Barber* therefore provides an interesting example of a case in which declaratory relief was used as a way of asserting the legal interests of individual employees who were involved in a continuing dispute with their employer.

One further benefit of the declaratory remedy which is perhaps under-utilised at present is its use by the employer as a defensive weapon. In some respects this is the mirror image of the use to which the remedy was put in *Barber*. An example would be where a dispute has arisen between the parties which is not being actively pursued by workplace representatives but which is being used as a bargaining chip in continuing negotiations. If the employer is keen to see the matter resolved he may seek to use the remedy of a declaration as a means of putting an end to that dispute[8]. However, such an approach is not for the risk adverse and should be limited to the strongest of cases since it may well be preferable to seek a settlement through traditional industrial relations mechanisms.

It follows from the above that the remedy of the declaration remains something of a bit part player in the armoury of employment contract remedies: often effective as a secondary weapon but rarely utilised as a principal weapon in its own right.

1   One example would be *Levett v Biotrace International plc* [1999] ICR 818 but even in that case the declaration was sought under the terms of the share scheme but there was an accompanying claim for damages for wrongful dismissal.
2   In this regard we can see similarities with many statutory employment rights where a statutory declaration is often coupled with a right to compensation or payment.
3   [1992] IRLR 521.
4   Although the underlying reasoning of the decision is highly contentious and appears not to have been followed in subsequent cases it provides a helpful illustration of the declaratory remedy nonetheless.
5   [1999] ICR 679.
6   See further chap 10, below.
7   In passing it is worthy of comment that many statutory protections themselves grant to tribunals and courts the power to grant a declaration as a remedy.
8   Such an approach may also be taken where a claim has been made against the employer but the employees are dragging their feet on the prosecution of such a claim. In these circumstances it may be tactically astute for the employer to force the pace through a claim for a declaration and an application under CPR Part 24. In these circumstances a declaration may well be of more benefit than simply having the original claim dismissed under CPR Part 24.

3   Claim in debt

6.3   The claim in debt is one of the most useful remedies available to an employee for a breach of contract short of dismissal. The classic example of a debt action is where the employer seeks to impose a unilateral cut in pay in breach of contract. If that unilateral reduction is not accepted by the workforce and they continue to work under their original terms they can enforce those terms through the courts in a claim in debt[1]. The classic example of such a debt action is *Rigby v Ferodo Ltd*[2] in which the House of Lords upheld the employee's action in debt in precisely these circumstances. The major advantage to the employee of such a claim is that it avoids the requirement to bring the subsisting relationship to an end through a resignation in response to a repudiatory breach by the employer. This presents a significant advantage to the employee since it also removes the possibility of the employer justifying the reduction in subsequent unfair dismissal proceedings thereby limiting the employee to a claim for wrongful dismissal which will necessarily cover the period of notice under the contract alone.

Although it is arguable that the intervention of the statutory protections regarding deductions from wages has undermined the use of the common law remedy of the debt action a more realistic assessment is probably that the statutory provisions have reinforced the common law remedy rather than undermining it. The relevant provisions dealing with deductions are now contained in Part II of the ERA 1996[3] and they effectively provide the employee with a choice as to the jurisdiction in which he can bring such a claim. This choice will often make the action in debt or its statutory equivalent an even more realistic option. Although the statutory provisions are undoubtedly wider in their application[4] and cover more than just simple claims for breach of contract they nevertheless principally operate through the mechanism of the contract of employment itself[5]. It follows that the statutory provisions encompass claims of the type pursued in *Rigby v Ferodo*. It is also of interest to note that in this area the statutory equivalent of the contractual remedy of a declaration can also be claimed in the tribunal in the deductions from wages claim[6].

It follows that the debt action remains one of the most relevant forms of contractual remedy for breaches of contract short of termination. This relevance has been enhanced by modern developments in the jurisdiction of employment tribunals and the availability of a claim for unlawful deductions from wages which is also based upon the contractual obligations of the parties.

1   It is obviously necessary for the precise sum which is due and owing under the contract to be identified. If this is not possible the claim will be properly categorised as either a claim in damages or a claim for a *quantum meruit*.
2   [1988] ICR 29, HL.
3   These provisions were originally enacted in the Wages Act 1986 and a claim under the ERA 1996 provisions may still be referred to as a Wages Act claim.
4   See for example *New Century Cleaning Co Ltd v Church* [2000] IRLR 27, CA. By way of further comment the extension of the jurisdiction of employment tribunals into the sphere of breach of contract is of no assistance in this regard because the jurisdiction is expressly limited to claims which arise on the *termination* of employment (see para 1.3, above).
5   See further chap 1, above.
6   See the ERA 1996, s 24.

4   Damages

6.4   As has been mentioned above a claim for damages may have a role in circumstances in which a unilateral reduction in pay has been imposed by an employer in breach of contract but where the precise amount of the deduction in question is not capable of quantification. Furthermore there is also the availability of a claim for damages in other circumstances relating to remuneration where, for example, the employer has failed to exercise a valid discretion when considering a bonus payment or some such similar benefit[1]. In all of these examples there is no reason in principle as to why a claim for damages should not be brought during the subsistence of the employment relationship. In addition such claims are also likely to fall under the rubric of the statutory provisions on deductions from wages which are obviously capable of impacting on the continuing employment relationship[2].

Another example of an area in which opportunities for damages claims have arisen in the context of the continuing employment relationship is where a claim is made relating to a breach of the implied terms of the contract of employment. A clear example is the type of claim recognised by the Court of Appeal in *Gogay v Hertfordshire County Council*[3]. In *Gogay* the employee was a residential care worker who established a breach of the implied term of trust and confidence in circumstances in which she was suspended pending an investigation into an allegation of sexual abuse made by a young person in her care. The breach was established because the employee had been completely blameless, the allegations made fell short of sexual abuse and, in any event, she had previously brought her concerns about the individual child to the attention of her employer and had been given assurances about her conduct in that regard. As a result of the investigation *Gogay* was reinstated to her position but was initially unable to return to work because of the psychiatric injury suffered by her. The Court of Appeal upheld her claim for damages arising from the breach of the implied term of trust and confidence[4].

Importantly in *Gogay* the Court of Appeal upheld the damages award which had been made in the employee's favour. At first instance the Court had awarded the employee damages including an amount in respect of general damages for the psychiatric illness suffered by her. On appeal this award was challenged on the basis that such damage was not recoverable under the principle set out in *Addis v Gramophone Co Ltd*[5]. In upholding the employee's claim the Court of Appeal stressed that it would be inappropriate to draw any distinctions between the law of contract and the law of tort when assessing compensation for psychiatric injury. In addition it considered that the compensation sought in *Gogay* related not to hurt, upset and injury to feelings for which in general the law does not provide compensation but for a recognised psychiatric illness where it does. In addition the employer's reliance upon the decision of the Court of Appeal in *Johnson v Unisys*[6] was held to be of no assistance because the present case involved a breach of contract which arose not on termination but in circumstances in which the contract of employment was subsisting.

1   The availability of such claims has probably been enhanced as a result of the developments in the court's willingness to exercise control over such discretions: see further para 4.8 and chap 5, above.
2   Although the remedy is technically a statutory one.
3   [2000] IRLR 703.
4   It is relevant to state at this point that although the authorities now support the proposition that any breach of the implied term of trust and confidence must be repudiatory in nature it does not follow that an employee must resign in response to that breach. In certain circumstances they may elect to affirm the contract and sue for damages for the breach.
5   [1909] AC 488, HL. At the time of decision *Johnson v Unisys* had only been considered by the Court of Appeal: [1999] IRLR 90, CA.
6   [1999] IRLR 90.

6.5   It follows that it is now possible for an employee to claim damages for a recognised psychiatric injury sustained in circumstances which amount to a breach of the implied term of confidence. However, this principle does not extend to a claim relating to general injury to feelings where there is no evidence of a recognised psychiatric illness. In this respect a clear difference exists between statutory claims for discrimination which provide for general injury to feelings to sound in compensation and contractual claims arising out of breaches of implied terms. It is also of interest that part of the underlying rationale for the Court of Appeal's decision in *Gogay* was that such damages could be claimed because the relationship was a continuing one and the limitations inherent in *Johnson v Uniysys* did not apply. It is unlikely that there is any material in the House of Lords' subsequent consideration of *Johnson* to alter this approach. This is because to do so would undermine the core ratio of the earlier decision of the House of Lords in *Malik v BCCI SA*[1]. However these examples again highlight some of the difficulties with *Johnson* which are considered elsewhere in this book[2]. In particular it appears somewhat misplaced to prevent the development of the common law when termination is in issue because of the intervention of Parliament but to permit such development where the relationship is a continuing one even though there has been substantial statutory intervention in that area as well.

It is important to recognise that the *Gogay* principles will apply to any breach of the implied terms of the contract of employment and are not restricted in principles to breaches of the implied term of trust and confidence[3].

It is also relevant to note that although the decision of the House of Lords in *Malik* has potentially opened up broad areas of new liability for damages claims arising out of the breach of implied terms in the context of a continuing employment relationship this should not mask the considerable evidential difficulties which are associated with such claims. By way of example it will often be extremely difficult for employees to establish a recoverable loss in these circumstances[4]. Furthermore, it will also be necessary, in the light of *Gogay*, to establish that any injury to feelings amounts to a recognised psychiatric illness if it is to sound in damages.

1   [1997] IRLR 462, HL.
2   See para 4.9, above.
3   So for example a claim based upon the failure to deal promptly with a grievance will also be subject to the same rules: see further para 4.7, above.
4   The remedies hearing in the *BCCI* claims provides salutary reading in this regard: *BCCI v Ali (No 3)* [2000] ICR 1354, upheld on appeal [2000] IRLR 460, CA.

5   Injunctions

6.6   Although an interim injunction[1] is a well established remedy for an employer seeking to prevent post-termination breaches of the contract of employment by an employee, its use had previously been of limited utility during periods in which the contract of employment was subsisting. This is because compliance with the contract during these periods could normally be secured by the employer through the use of the disciplinary procedures under the contract. However, modern developments have led to an increasing use of interim injunctions as a way of keeping the contract alive at least to a limited extent[2]. This development has been achieved through two principal routes: the first is through injunctions which have been granted to prevent an employee from walking out without giving notice where the employer has undertaken to comply with all of its contractual obligations. The second relates to 'garden leave' injunctions where the employer typically relies upon an express term which permits the employment relationship to continue with its attendant obligations of good faith albeit that the employee is not required to be at work[3].

It is relevant to note that both approaches identified above proceed on the basis that the employee is not required to actually work for the employer during the period of restraint. Accordingly the traditional objection of the common law to the compulsion of personal service is removed. In addition the employer achieves its objective of preventing work for a competitor in the trade through the continuation of the implied terms which prevent such disloyal behaviour from the employee.

By way of example in *Evening Standard Newspapers Ltd v Henderson*[4] the Court of Appeal granted to the employer an injunction in circumstances in which a highly skilled employee was proposing to walk out of his employment without notice and join a competitor. The employer refused to accept the repudiation and undertook to pay all relevant contractual benefits during the notice period. During this period the employee would not be required to attend work. As the damage which the employer would suffer was impossible to quantify and the employee would not be reduced to a position of starvation or idleness the Court of Appeal granted the injunction. What is of relevance here is that it was expressly on the basis that the contractual relationship continued that the injunction was granted[5]. This therefore opened up a new route by which employers could obtain protection rather than relying upon the application of post termination covenants which can often be a hazardous exercise. Accordingly it became typical for employers to insert 'garden leave' provisions in contracts of employment which enabled the employer to effectively put the employee 'out of the game' during the notice period and either prevent the individual from working for a competitor or provide a sufficient breathing space for any confidential information in the possession of the employee to become stale.

However, the courts have subsequently imposed some limitations on the ability of the employer to enforce garden leave provisions. In particular there is no universal implied right in the contract of employment which enables the employer to insist on the employee remaining at home during the notice period. Whether such a result can be achieved in the absence of an express garden leave provision is obviously a question of fact in each case but if the particular individual can satisfy the court that they need to work in order to maintain their skills base such an injunction may well be refused[6].

1   For a detailed consideration of the law relating to injunctions see Brearly and Bloch *Employment Covenants and Confidential Information* (1999) Butterworths.
2   It is important to note that this does not mean that employees can be compelled to work. This is expressly prohibited by the Trade Union and Labour Relations (Consolidation) Act 1992, s 236.
3   For a detailed consideration of these types of claims see *Harvey on Industrial Relations and Employment Law* para A[597].
4   [1987] ICR 588, CA.
5   Interestingly there is no debate in the decision regarding the various theories of the impact of a repudiatory breach on the contract of employment: see further paras 7.2–7.4, below.
6   See *William Hill Organisation Ltd v Tucker* [1998] IRLR 313, CA.

6.7   Although an application for an injunction has been a relatively well established method of obtaining protection for an employer it was rare for employees to seek such a remedy[1]. This was because the relationship of trust and confidence will often have broken down between the parties[2], damages would normally be an adequate remedy for the employee and the court would not enforce a contract of personal service by way of specific performance. However, this did not mean that such injunctions could not be obtained in certain circumstances. One such example was *Hill v CA Parsons*[3] in which the Court of Appeal felt able to grant an injunction in circumstances in which there was a threat of dismissal made under trade union pressure. It followed that the employer retained his trust and confidence in the employee. Another relevant factor was that the employee would be denied the benefit of the protection of the unfair dismissal legislation which was about to come into force. In these fairly extreme circumstances the Court of Appeal felt able to intervene. However, it was often though that *Hill* was a case which was very much limited to its own facts and the implementation of the unfair dismissal legislation appeared to remove one of the central planks of the employee's argument on the balance of convenience.

1   There are the exceptional cases such as *Lumley v Wagner* (1852) 1 De GM & G 604 but these are unlikely to impact on normal employment relationships and are not considered in any detail here.
2   A factor which is also recognised as a ground for refusing to make an order of reinstatement or re-engagement in an unfair dismissal case: see further *Harvey* Div DI.
3   [1972] Ch 305; see para 10.4, below.

6.8   It followed that in the immediate aftermath of *Hill* there was relatively little development in the field of interim injunctions obtained by employees. However, a period of radical development later followed with a number of cases being brought seeking to ensure compliance with contractual disciplinary procedures. The landmark case was *Irani v Southampton and South West Hampshire Health Authority*[1] in which such an injunction was granted. *Irani* was an ophthalmologist who was employed on a part-time basis by a health authority. He had fallen out with a senior colleague and an ad hoc committee had determined that there were irreconcilable differences between the two colleagues and that Mr Irani should be dismissed. Mr Irani sought an injunction restraining dismissal on the basis that the Whitley Council disputes procedures which were incorporated into his contract of employment had not been complied with. In reaching its decision the court relied heavily upon the earlier reasoning in *Hill*. Of particular relevance was the fact that the court felt that the employer still maintained trust and confidence in the employee at least to the extent that his working standards were not in question. In addition the impact of dismissal on the employee was potentially substantial and may have restricted his ability to gain access to national health service facilities in the future.

Whether *Irani* would be decided in the same way today is in doubt. In the subsequent case of *Powell v London Borough of Brent*[2] the Court of Appeal gave some consideration as to what was required to be established in order to show that trust and confidence remained to the extent necessary to grant such an injunction. The court felt that two separate factors had to be considered, namely: (a) the question of the competence to do the job; and (b) the absence of friction at the workplace. In *Powell* both of these factors were satisfied but it is difficult to see how *Irani* could satisfy the second of the factors identified in view of the breakdown of the relationship with his supervisor.

However, the requirement that trust and confidence subsists between the parties has been diluted in two subsequent cases. In *Wadcock v London Borough of Brent*[3] the fact that the employee undertook to work normally as part of the terms of the order appeared to satisfy the relevant requirement even though there was some suggestion that the relationship had earlier broken down[4]. Furthermore, in *Robb v London Borough of Hammersmith and Fulham*[5] the Court recognised that it was not necessary for the employer to have trust and confidence in the employee in circumstances in which they were suspended from work and the limited purpose of the injunction was to ensure compliance with disciplinary procedures. In these circumstances the disciplinary process was still workable even where there was an absence of trust and confidence between the parties.

However the cases have not all been one way and it has proved extremely difficult for employees to advance beyond achieving compliance with contractual disciplinary procedures. A good example is *Alexander v Standard Telephones and Cables Ltd*[6] where the court refused to grant an application to secure compliance with an agreed redundancy selection procedure. The court refused the injunction on the basis that the terms were not apt for incorporation into the individual contract of employment as well as the traditional objections to interfering in a subsisting employment relationship.

It is also fair to say that the increase in unfair dismissal compensation limits may also have an impact in this area. This will particularly be so if the wider formulation of the just and equitable jurisdiction of the employment tribunal to award compensation suggested by Lord Hoffman in *Johnson v Unisys* is adopted[7]. If that was to be the case it would provide very powerful arguments for an employer who contends that the balance of convenience points against the granting of such an injunction. Accordingly it looks as if cases such as *Irani* and *Powell* may now represent the high water mark for development in this area.

1 [1985] ICR 590.
2 [1988] ICR 176, CA.
3 [1990] IRLR 223, Ch Div.
4 Although in principle this can be seen as an option it may well be difficult to satisfy evidentially particularly where an employer is asserting that the relationship has broken down for all future purposes.
5 [1991] ICR 514.
6 [1990] ICR 291.
7 [2001] UKHL 13, [2001] ICR 480. The suggestion being that the employment tribunal has jurisdiction to award compensation reflecting injury to feelings and loss of reputation.

6   Industrial action

6.9   One area which also appears closed to any further development in terms of injunctive relief is that of industrial action. Although there may have been some mileage in attempts to resurrect Lord Denning's contractual suspension theory in the aftermath of *Malik* this route now appears blocked by reason of the substantial statutory intervention in the area. The relevant reforms were introduced by way of additional unfair dismissal protections contained in the ERA 1999. In many respects the effect of these provisions is to produce a quasi suspension of the employment contract for an eight week period where the industrial action has been lawfully called. On any view in the light of *Johnson v Unisys* it appears as if this is now an area closed to future development.

Chapter 7

Termination of an employment contract

1 Introduction

7.1   It is natural to think of a contract of employment being terminated in one of three ways – by resignation by the employee with notice, by dismissal by the employer with notice, or, in a relatively extreme case of gross misconduct, by dismissal by the employer without notice; the last two are so important that they are dealt with separately[1]. However the vagaries and infinite varieties of both working life and the law of contract are such that other forms of termination may arise, which tend to be less common but potentially more troublesome. This chapter will consider termination by breach, frustration, mutual agreement, expiry of a fixed term or specific task and by insolvency. We shall see yet again that these tend in some ways to involve contract law with a difference, given that basic tenets of commercial contracts law may not fit the realities of the workplace, and will either need reshaping to fit the circumstances, or will cause unfortunate results.

1   For dismissal by notice, see para 3.20, above; for summary dismissal for gross misconduct, see chap 8 below.

2 Termination by breach: the elective/automatic controversy

7.2   The contract orthodoxy that a repudiatory breach by one party gives the innocent party the option to accept the repudiation and terminate the contract can be seen at work in the traditional common law approach to dismissal for gross misconduct, where the employee's serious misconduct permits summary dismissal by the employer, dispensing with the employee's normal right to notice[1]. While this may still be of great importance in a common law action for wrongful dismissal by a dismissed employee claiming that his/or her conduct did not merit such an extreme sanction, such a contractual analysis will not normally be particularly significant where the action being brought is a statutory action for unfair dismissal. Moreover, in anything less than a case of gross misconduct, the repudiation argument is not relevant – at common law, the employer could always dismiss by giving notice[2], and in practice such a 'standard' dismissal is likely to be subject to a challenge as unfair, with far more emphasis on the substantive allegations and whether a fair procedure was adopted by the employer than on the contractual niceties.

When the position is reversed, and one considers a case of repudiation by the employer, there is to a large extent a similar picture, in that in most cases the live question will be, not the purely contractual implications, but the statutory question whether the employer's misconduct was such as to repudiate the contract for the purpose of permitting the employee to leave and claim constructive dismissal[3]. Resignation (with or without notice) is usually fatal to an employee's statutory rights, but if constructive dismissal can be shown (the burden being on the ex-employee to do so), then an action for unfair dismissal (or a redundancy payment) can proceed as if it had been the employer who had dismissed.

It is when one turns to purely contractual consequences of employer repudiation that the problems arise. On ordinary principles, such repudiation would justify an employee in leaving immediately, without having to give contractual notice; in the highly unlikely event of the employer suing the employee for damages for lack of notice, this would be a defence, and in theory at least it means that the common law also recognises the concept of constructive dismissal, though this has hardly featured in the case law[4]. However, the position becomes much more complex when the opposite (and equally unusual) situation arises of an employee who wants to *stay* in the employment in spite of the employer's actions. If those actions amount to something short of dismissal, in theory the employee may decide against leaving, stay and sue for damages for the breach, but what if the employer's actions amount to a dismissal which breaches the contract (usually by not giving the requisite notice, but more recently with an emphasis on non-exhaustion of a contractual disciplinary provision)? Can the employee refuse to accept this and claim to keep the contract alive, if necessary by court order?

1 See para 8.5, below.
2 For possible moves towards restricting this wide right, see para 4.29, above.
3 ERA, ss 95(1)(c) (unfair dismissal) and 136(1)(c) (redundancy rights). Early in the history of the legislation it was held that the test for constructive dismissal is based on repudiatory breach, not just unreasonable conduct by the employer: *Western Excavating (ECC) Ltd v Sharp* [1978] ICR 221, [1978] IRLR 27, CA. The evolution of strong implied terms in the contract of employment, especially the term of trust and respect, has been vital in this context, see chap 4 above.
4 For a rare example, see *Bliss v South East Thames Regional Health Authority* [1987] ICR 700, [1985] IRLR 308, CA; also, there is an assumption that it applies at common law in the important TUPE decision in *University of Oxford v Humphreys* [2000] IRLR 183, [2000] 1 All ER 996, CA.

7.3   As a matter of ordinary contract law, if an officious bystander were to ask whether, to be effective, a repudiation by the employer has to be accepted by the employee, a lawyer would no doubt answer with a testy 'Oh, of course'. It is normal to cite at this point the dictum of Asquith LJ that an unaccepted repudiation is 'a thing writ in water'[1]. The idea that this orthodoxy is equally applicable to a contract of employment is the basis of the elective (or acceptance) theory. However, matters immediately become complicated when this is viewed against the background of (a) the normal rule on remedies that a court will not enforce a contract of employment and (b) the reality of life that once the employee is unequivocally sacked and placed (sometimes physically) immediately outside the barred gates by security staff before being able to put an avenging bug into the computer system, it makes little sense to stand there for however long shouting that he or she does not accept the repudiation and is still in employment. As we shall see in Chapter 10, this is an area dominated primarily by the law and practicalities of remedies, not by *a priori* arguments on principle, which makes it doubly difficult to see what the true principle is. The point is that in some cases the courts have tried to progress matters and have held that the rule against enforcement is so strong (as is the normal rule that even where a dismissal is clearly wrongful the employee's remedy lies in damages) that the employee *cannot* refuse to accept the employer's repudiation, because to do so leads into a legal cul-de-sac. This is the basis for the 'automatic' (or 'unilateral') theory that a repudiation of an employment contract (at least where it amounts to a purported dismissal) automatically terminates the contract, *in law* transforming the employee's remedy into an action for damages only:

> '. . .in the ordinary case of master and servant the repudiation or the wrongful dismissal puts an end to the contract, and the contract having been wrongfully put an end to a claim for damages arises. It is necessarily a claim for damages and nothing more. The nature of the bargain is such that it can be nothing more'[2].

In a legal culture where reinstatement is almost wholly unknown (in contrast to the position in other jurisdictions within the EU, the practical sense of this can be appreciated.

The elective versus automatic controversy is very well known and is well rehearsed elsewhere[3]. It has been going on for four decades, and indeed the authors of this book seem to have been talking about it forever, man and boy. It is still unresolved. One possible synthesis was to draw a distinction between the employment *relationship* (which automatically terminates because the employee cannot force the way in next day through security) and the employment *contract* which might technically subsist for some unspecified time into the future for certain collateral purposes[4]. Even so, if there was any hope that this could be used to claim wages into the future in debt, this was quickly squashed by a decision that even if the elective theory is applied the demise of the employment relationship is enough to bar such an action and convert it into an action for damages (thus, in particular, bringing in the requirement to mitigate)[5]; moreover, the distinction between an employment relationship and an employment contract, though arguably known to EC law[6], has been rejected recently as a useful legal device by the Court of Appeal in two different contexts[7].

Perhaps the key case is *Gunton v Richmond-upon-Thames London Borough Council*[8], both for demonstrating the difference of opinion, and for showing how little that difference may achieve in practice. It concerned a challenge to the validity of a dismissal without exhaustion of the proper contractual procedures. The claimant claimed that he had not accepted this repudiatory conduct. Did that open up a vista to the Elysian uplands of perpetual wages into the future? Not quite. Although there was a sharp disagreement in principle between Buckley and Brightman LJJ who adopted the elective theory and Shaw LJ who adopted the automatic theory, the end result was that they all agreed that there could be *no* open-ended claim for future wages. Once the normal rule on damages kicked in, the claim was one for wages during the notice period *plus* an amount representing wages during the time that it would have taken to have gone through the procedure *properly*. This latter was the sole advance in practice achieved by the case – while this in itself is of some importance, it is far removed from a radical remedy of positive enforcement of a contract of employment, either by injunction effecting reinstatement or some form of order enforcing employment benefits to some notional date in the future[9]. Even on its own restricted basis, *Gunton* has not had unanimous acceptance, and it may be significant that in *Boyo v London Borough of Lambeth*[10] the Court of Appeal only applied the narrow principle in *Gunton* because required to as a matter of precedent, and with considerable and expressed misgivings, not only stating their preference for Shaw LJ's dissenting approval of the automatic theory, but even doubting the soundness of the award of wages during the notional period of operation of the disciplinary procedure.

1   *Howard v Pickford Tool Co Ltd* [1951] 1 KB 417, at 421. The phrase is taken from the Roman poet Catullus who was referring, not to a contractual repudiation at common law (strangely) but, far more interestingly, to what a woman says to her lusty lover.
2   *Vine v National Dock Labour Board* [1956] 1 QB 658, at 674, [1956] 1 All ER 1 at 8, CA, per Jenkins LJ (upheld on appeal in the House of Lords).
3   See Smith & Wood *Industrial Law* (7th edn, 2000) Butterworths, pp 377–380; *Halsbury's Laws of England* (4th edn) (2000 reissue) para 452. The cases in favour of the elective theory are primarily *Decro-Wall International S A v Practitioners in Marketing Ltd* [1971] 2 All ER 216, [1971] 1 WLR 361, CA; *Hill v C A Parsons & Co Ltd* [1972] Ch 305, [1971] 3 All ER 1345, CA; *Thos Marshall (Exports) Ltd v Guinle* [1978] ICR 905, [1978] 3 All ER 193; *Gunton v Richmond-upon-Thames London Borough Council* [1980] ICR 755, [1980] IRLR 321, CA; *Dietman v Brent London Borough Council* [1987] ICR 737, [1987] IRLR 259. The cases in favour of the automatic theory are primarily *Vine v National Dock Labour Board* (n 2 above); *Denmark Productions Ltd v Boscobel Productions Ltd* [1969] 1 QB 699, [1968] 3 All ER 513, CA; *Sanders v Ernest A Neale Ltd* [1974] ICR 565, [1974] 3 All ER 327; *R v East Berkshire Health Authority, ex p Walsh* [1984] ICR 743, [1984] IRLR 278, CA; *Boyo v Lambeth London Borough Council* [1994] ICR 727, [1995] IRLR 50, CA.
4   *Delaney v Staples* [1992] ICR 483 at 489, [1992] IRLR 191 at 193, HL, per Lord Browne-Wilkinson.
5   *Marsh v National Autistic Society* [1993] ICR 453.
6   For example, both the Part-time Workers Directive 97/81/EC and the Fixed-term Workers Directive 99/70/EC refer to workers 'who have an employment contract or employment relationship'.
7   *Askew v Governing Body of Clifton Middle School* [2000] ICR 286, [1999] IRLR 708, CA (no TUPE transfer when a teacher remained under contract to the education authority but with a potentially changed employment relationship from School A to School B); *Symbian Ltd v Christensen* [2001] IRLR 77, CA (disapproving the view of the judge below that a garden leave clause ended the employment relationship but retained some form of shell of the employment contract).
8   [1980] ICR 755, [1980] IRLR 321, CA.
9   This is especially so in the light of later authority that a court will not, in these cases, speculate as to whether the missing disciplinary proceedings might actually have been decided in the employee's favour, and award damages for the lost chance of retaining the employment: *Focsa Services (UK) Ltd v Birkett* [1996] IRLR 325, EAT; *Janciuk v Winerite Ltd* [1998] IRLR 63, EAT.
10 [1994] ICR 727, [1995] IRLR 50, CA.

7.4   Where does all of this meandering leave us? Five particular thoughts are offered:

(1) The theoretical dispute between the automatic and elective principles arises in few cases, and is determinative of even fewer. One major reason for this is that even if the elective theory is adopted, it is subject to the caveat that in all but exceptional cases it will be easy to find actual acceptance by the employee, especially when he or she has little practical alternative[1].

(2) The elective theory has thus not been allowed to develop as a gateway to long-term general damages for wrongful dismissal, still less to the granting of injunctions to restrain dismissal. It will be argued in Chapter 10 that there is no general remedy of enforcement of contract, and that such cases as do exist of an element of enforcement have tended to enforce only certain incidental aspects of employment, or have involved arguments on acceptance or non-acceptance which were really concerned with another agenda or sub-plot.

Thus, one can argue that the real interest lies at the remedies end, in deciding when a court might be persuaded to grant an injunction[2], rather than in exploring even further the conceptual basis of automatic or elective effect.

(3) The one outstanding case of an actual enforcement of employment as such (by an injunction restraining a dismissal without notice) remains *Hill v C A Parsons & Co Ltd*[3] where Lord Denning MR (with the support of Sachs LJ, but against the strong dissent of Stamp LJ) *used* the concepts of non-acceptance by the employee and continuing mutual trust between the employer and employee to reach the desired result of an *extension* of the contract by the (deemed) notice period, quite simply in order to bring the claimant under the new provisions of the Industrial Relations Act 1971 which would protect him from the trade union pressure that was being put on the employer to be rid of him. Even this case, therefore, falls far short of legal protection of longer-term job security. Moreover, it is now possible to see *Hill's* case in its historical perspective, not just as a case really aiming the common law at perceived (pre-Thatcher legislation) abuse of trade union power, but as marking a possible move towards some common law restraint on unbridled dismissal, which was very quickly trumped by the arrival of the statutory action of unfair dismissal which turned out to be the real area for future development[4].

(4) Although the controversy over the automatic and elective theories has little practical effect per se, similar ideas can percolate into the statutory actions where, as always, it has been important not to let inappropriate contract theories jeopardise statutory rights and procedures. As pointed out elsewhere[5] a pragmatic and differential approach has had to be taken to these matters when applied to the law of unfair dismissal. With regard to the *definition* of dismissal, to apply the automatic theory (in reverse, ie to a repudiatory breach by the employee) would be disastrous, because it would legitimise 'self dismissal', ie where the employer could argue that the employee's conduct was so bad as to repudiate his contract, thus automatically terminating the contract without the need for the employer to do anything. This potential coach and pair through the statute was avoided by applying the *elective* theory, so that the misconduct of the employee repudiates the contract, which is ended by the employer accepting that repudiation and 'dismissing' within the statutory definition, thus not ruling out an unfair dismissal action[6]. On the other hand, to apply the elective theory to the rules on the effective *date* of dismissal would be equally disastrous, because it would allow an employee to bring a claim after the expiry of the three month limit for claims, simply by arguing that he had not 'accepted' the employer's repudiatory dismissal until some time later (ie within three months of bringing the claim). Here, it has been held that, for the sake of certainty, it is the *automatic* theory that must be applied to the date of dismissal, so that it is dated to the time of the employer's termination, regardless of any arguments as to the lawfulness of that termination at common law[7]. Thus, at least in these important statutory contexts, it is important *not* to have a clear choice made between the conflicting theories – each has its place.

(5) A final thought concerns our changing patterns of working. Ideas of the enforceability of employment contracts are based on larger ideas of the desirability of improving the job security of employees. Whether this can ever be done by the law in any long-term sense is debatable, with legal intervention being arguably of greatest effect in preventing or deterring hasty or unfair termination, and in ingraining in most respectable employers basic tenets of best practice of personnel management. We have seen that positive enforcement of continuing employment was not a feature of UK law, even in

times when a relatively high level of job stability and de facto security was the norm in many industries. Now that that picture has changed in significant parts of the economy (largely in the private sector), being replaced for good or ill by a far more transient workforce, with little loyalty on either side and an expectation of relatively frequent changes in job and employer, ideas of positive enforcement may seem not just impractical, but actually inappropriate. While one cannot generalise too much, it seems that there are increasingly large areas of employment where the very idea of trying to enforce a contract with one particular (reluctant, to say the least) employer would seem bizarre. Paradoxically, the automatic theory might be more appropriate in such a setting, namely that it is known in advance that no quarter is given on either side, that there is no retrieving the situation after the relationship has perished, and that the employee's real 'protection' lies in making the most financially out of the job during its currency, contracting where possible for the largest possible termination pay-outs, and keeping up skills that permit the rapid finding of new, replacement employment, with any question of the fairness of the termination being taken straight to a tribunal, with the increased cap on unfair dismissal compensation (at the time of writing, £52,600), and limitless compensation for any element of discrimination. Significantly, we shall see in Chapter 10 that most of the relatively few cases on enforcement of some element of the contract have arisen in the public sector; there is no purely legal reason for this, and it may be linked instead to the persistence in such quarters of older models of employment, a greater expectation of longer-term employment, and the existence of more complex procedures to be invoked when seeking to terminate employment.

1   This point was made strongly in *Gunton*, but again the issue is not entirely clear because in *Boyo* the court (especially Gibson LJ) were clearly less certain that this would always be the case, pointing to their fear that the elective theory *could* lead (in principle at least) to open-ended liability.
2   See chap 10, below.
3   [1972] Ch 305, [1971] 3 All ER 1345, CA.
4   If a flight of fancy may be permitted at this point, one could see *Hill's* case as the *Rylands v Fletcher* of employment law – a fascinating early decision which could have led in a totally new direction if it had been followed, but which for good historical reasons was not further developed, and which remains in force in its own restricted terms, to be relied on in a few cases but not the majority.
5   *Smith & Wood* p 380, adopting the analysis originally put forward in McMullen, 'A synthesis of the mode of termination of contracts of employment' [1982] CLJ 110.
6   *London Transport Executive v Clarke* [1981] ICR 355, [1981] IRLR 166, CA.
7   *Brown v Southall and Knight* [1980] ICR 617, [1980] IRLR 130, EAT; *Robert Cort & Son Ltd v Charman* [1981] ICR 816, [1981] IRLR 437, EAT. One consideration behind this is that the EDT (like continuity of employment) is a purely statutory concept, not amenable to being changed by the parties. The decision in *Lambert v Croydon College* [1999] ICR 409, [1999] IRLR 346, EAT contradicts this and may be dubious; an appellate level decision on this point would be useful.

3   Frustration of the contract of employment

7.5   Frustration is one of the ways in which a contract of employment may terminate by operation of law. This is a drastic result for the employee because it means that there is no 'dismissal' for statutory purposes, thus disentitling the employee to any right dependent on having been dismissed. This harsh outcome was recently reaffirmed in *G F Sharp & Co Ltd v McMillan*[1] where a sympathetic tribunal held that, although the employment contract of a joiner was frustrated by a lasting injury to his hand, he should at least receive payment for his notice period, but the EAT restored orthodoxy and held that a contract that has been frustrated cannot be relied on for *any* purpose[2]. The harshness is made worse by the fact that in many cases (though not, admittedly, in *Sharp*) frustration will be a defence thought up *ex post facto* by the employer's lawyer, once all the events have occurred, rather than having been a live issue at the time of dealing with the problem. It is a prime example of a purely contractual doctrine which ill fits employment, can do considerable damage to statutory rights and which, all other things being equal, would ideally not apply in employment law at all. Unfortunately, all other things are not equal because when such a head-on attack on the doctrine was made in one of the early cases (at least where the employment could be terminated by short notice anyway) it was rejected[3].

The doctrine of frustration therefore applies to employment contracts, principally in the two areas of sickness and imprisonment, which are well set out elsewhere[4]. The point that is made here is that the doctrine has already had to be amended in one way in order to fit employment law needs, and there are signs of a further refinement which, if eventually pursued seriously, could diminish some of the harshness that arises when the doctrine is applied to sickness cases. The existing amendment arose in relation to frustration through imprisonment of the employee, and the normal requirement that the frustrating event must not have been self-induced. Surely the imprisonment was self-induced by the employee and so, it was argued, could not be used by the employer. When this issue had to be faced in the Court of Appeal in *F C Shepherd & Co Ltd v Jerrom*[5] the majority (Lawton and Mustill LJJ) construed the rule to be that neither party can rely on their *own* misconduct to establish a defence of frustration; here, it was the employer relying on the employee's misconduct (offences of juvenile violence leading to a sentence to borstal), and so the doctrine could be applied to deal with the perceived merits of the case, in spite of the normal contract law view that there must not be self-induction on either part.

1 [1998] IRLR 632, EAT.
2 One possible complication may now arise, in a sickness frustration case, if the incapacity constitutes a disability within the Disability Discrimination Act 1995. Presumably the courts would not allow frustration to defeat a claim under that Act, just as they have not allowed the common law doctrine of illegality to defeat a statutory claim of sex discrimination: *Hall v Woolston Hall Leisure Ltd* [2000] IRLR 578, CA.
3 *Notcutt v Universal Equipment Co (London) Ltd* [1986] ICR 414, [1986] IRLR 218, CA, criticising *Harman v Flexible Lamps Ltd* [1980] IRLR 418, EAT. Similarly, the judgment in *Norris v Southampton City Council* [1982] ICR 177, [1982] IRLR 141, EAT that a contract is not frustrated by imprisonment was overturned by the Court of Appeal in *F C Shepherd & Co Ltd v Jerrom* [1986] ICR 802, [1986] IRLR 358, CA.
4 *Smith & Wood* pp 358–363; *Harvey on Industrial Relations and Employment Law* paras A[810] ff.
5 See n 3, above.

7.6 The other amendment, with considerable potential, concerns another basic rule of frustration, namely that the frustrating event must be unforeseen and unlooked-for. In the EAT in *Shepherd*, Waite P had held that there was no frustration because the juvenile's apprenticeship contract had contained a procedure for termination, capable of covering the misconduct in question; this meant that the eventuality was not unforeseen and so the contract was not frustrated. This approach was not adopted by the Court of Appeal, who held that the contract was frustrated, though Mustill LJ did say that 'the presence of a termination provision should inhibit the court from being too ready to find in favour of frustration'. This might be a useful indicator of emphasis, especially in a case where the form of misconduct in question was *specifically* covered by the contract (as opposed to just coming under a general 'you may be dismissed for gross misconduct' clause). However, the question whether frustration can actually be *defeated* by the foreseeability of the event in question has taken on more seriousness in the more controversial area of frustration by illness or injury. The question has been forced, as have others that we have seen[1], by the increased use of permanent health insurance (PHI) schemes in the contracts of more senior employees, providing for generous (sometimes remarkably generous) payments in the long term for lasting, debilitating illness. Could the existence of such a scheme in the individual employee's case mean that his or her contract could not be frustrated by a serious illness. This question arose as one of the employer's defences to a breach of contract action (based on the employers' withdrawal of PHI benefits) in *Villella v MFI Furniture Centres Ltd*[2]; Judge Green QC said:

'It is, of course, common ground that a contract of employment is capable of frustration by incapacity of sufficient duration to strike at the root of the contract. It is common ground that frustration terminates the contract on its own and independently of any intention, acceptance or indeed any activity by either party of any sort. [Counsel for the employee] concedes that if the contract had been frustrated that would be a leaving of service within the meaning of [the PHI scheme], but he has a short and, to my mind, complete answer to the submission that frustration occurred. . ..He points out that an occurrence which is both foreseen and provided for by the contract is incapable of being a frustrating event. The contract expressly foresaw and provided for long-term incapacity due to illness. It follows inevitably that the later occurrence of such long-term incapacity cannot frustrate the contract'.

At the time of writing, we have no appeal court ruling on this fascinating point, but the argument seems sound, and capable of constructive use on behalf of an employee. Indeed it is possible that there may be attempts to press it further – could it go beyond specific PHI schemes and even apply to an ordinary sick pay term in the contract, especially where it is relatively generous? We have already seen[3] that there is a growing school of thought that if, say, the contract promises sick pay for six months, it may now be thought to be a breach of contract to dismiss on ordinary notice (of, say, one month) within that period, thus depriving the employee of the benefit of the sick pay clause. Could that argument be taken further, to invalidate any claim by an employer that the contract was frustrated within that six months? The argument would again be that illness lasting at least six months was foreseen and provided for in the contract. Given the prevalence of contractual sick pay schemes, this would be a serious development. One counter-argument might be that PHI schemes and ordinary sick pay provisions are distinguishable, in that PHI schemes envisage permanent, disabling illnesses (which would otherwise potentially be frustrating events), whereas the aim of a sick pay provision is usually to maintain an element of income during *temporary* illness, the expectation being that normally the employee will return to the job; on that basis it might be argued that the existence of an ordinary sick pay provision should *not* rule out a finding of frustration in the event of a sudden, catastrophic illness or injury that removes all likelihood of return.

These matters are, of course, very uncertain, but the very fact that they are being discussed shows that the topic of frustration, relatively dormant for the last decade, could be about to see further development.

1 See para 4.29, above.
2 [1999] IRLR 468, QBD; the passage cited is at 474.
3 Paragraph 4.30, above.

4 Termination by mutual consent

7.7 Mutual consent to terminate is a possible way of ending a contractual relationship in ordinary contract law. In employment law, with major rights depending on the employee having been dismissed, the courts have consistently held that it should be found only rarely, and on clear facts[1]. Pressure by the employer to 'agree' to terminate may be seen by a tribunal as in fact a dismissal for statutory purposes, just as in the 'resign or be dismissed' cases. Rather like 'self dismissal', it is viewed as too simple a solution for the employer seeking to escape statutory liability; indeed, as in the case disapproving of self dismissal[2], it may be that a tribunal would strike down any apparent agreement to terminate without liability as an attempt to 'exclude or limit the operation of any provision of' the ERA 1996, and so void under s 203(1).

There is, however, one exception where mutual consent may be found at common law, and where s 203 would be held inapplicable. This is where there is a *genuine* severance agreement for valuable consideration, where it can be argued that the parties are assuming that *all* liabilities are being dealt with, so that to find afterwards that there was in law a dismissal (allowing claims for a redundancy payment or unfair dismissal) would simply be inappropriate. The leading cases are *Birch v University of Liverpool*[3] (where academics taking early retirement under a purely voluntary scheme offering financial inducements were not allowed to claim that they were dismissed, in order to claim in addition a statutory redundancy dismissal, which had not been envisaged under the settlement) and *Scott v Coalite Fuels and Chemicals Ltd*[4] (where employees already under notice for dismissal, who accepted a voluntary early retirement package, were again not allowed to claim a redundancy payment in addition). In cases such as this, mutual consent to termination is a useful device. The boundaries are narrow though, because on the opposite side of the line it has also been held that the existence of a dismissal (and normal redundancy rights) are not jeopardised by volunteering for redundancy or not objecting to it[5].

1 *McAlwane v Boughton Estates* [1973] 2 All ER 299, [1973] ICR 470, NIRC; *Lees v Arthur Greaves Ltd* [1974] 2 All ER 393, [1974] ICR 501, CA.
2 *Igbo v Johnson Matthey Chemicals Ltd* [1986] ICR 505, [1986] IRLR 215, CA.
3 [1985] ICR 470, [1985] IRLR 165, CA.
4 [1988] ICR 355, [1988] IRLR 131, EAT; see, to like effect in a case where an employee under threat of disciplinary action accepted a voluntary severance package, *Logan Salton v Durham County Council* [1989] IRLR 99, EAT.
5 *Burton, Allton & Johnson Ltd v Peck* [1975] ICR 193, [1975] IRLR 87, EAT, distinguished in *Birch* (n 3, above).

5 Termination by expiry or performance

7.8 One aspect of this country's more diverse and flexible workforce has been the increased use of fixed-term contracts. Where a contract is expressed to last until a certain date, it terminates automatically at common law on that date, without any need for notice or indeed any other action by the employer. Thus, at common law there is no dismissal. To counter such an obvious form of evasion of statutory rights based on dismissal, the employment protection legislation has always contained provisions deeming the expiry of a fixed term contract without renewal to be a 'dismissal' for statutory purposes[1]. This protection has in general been widely construed, as in the early case law holding that a fixed-term contract remains such, even if there is in fact a notice provision in it, allowing termination before the end of the fixed term[2]. This prevented a form of avoidance by putting the employee on to (ostensibly) a fixed-term contract but inserting a notice provision and then, when the term expired, arguing that it was not within the statutory definition of fixed-term contract, so that there was no dismissal at all (actual or deemed).

There is, however, one way in which the protection has hitherto been construed narrowly, which is in the requirement that, to be a fixed-term contract under the statute there must be a fixed termination date[3]; it may not be enough if the contract is simply expressed to be for a minimum period[4], but it may be sufficient if, though no terminal date is mentioned, the engagement is such that in practice its termination can be dated, as with the contract to teach a particular course at a college during an academic year in the leading case of *Wiltshire County Council v NATFHE*[5]. There could be a thin dividing line here, but one thing that is tolerably clear is that the statutory definition does not cover a 'purpose' or 'task' contract (eg employment until a particular building is demolished) and the case of *Brown v Knowsley Borough Council*[6] showed an extension to this, to cover the case where the employment is subject to an external condition which may or may not eventuate. In that case, a temporary teacher's contract was conditional on continuing sponsorship by outside bodies; when that dried up, it was held by the EAT that she had not been dismissed at all – there was no actual dismissal, the contract did not come within the statutory definition of a fixed-term contract, and at common law the contract came to an end automatically when the condition was no longer met. Thus, purpose or conditional contracts have always potentially been a way round the statutory protection because of their common law effect and the statutory requirement of a terminal date (actual or reasonably discernible). Fortunately, there has been no obvious evidence of widespread use of such contracts.

Fixed-term contracts as such have, however, been widely used, but two legislative developments (one actual and one in the pipeline at the time of writing) might diminish their attractiveness. The possible use of a fixed term contract in order to require the employee to sign away his or her statutory rights has been lessened by the repeal by the ERA 1999 of the power to exclude unfair dismissal rights in a fixed-term contract of one year or more[7]. The redundancy exclusion power in fixed-term contracts of two years or more remains in force at the time of writing, and we have been reminded recently of how effective that exclusion can be[8], but arguably the unfair dismissal exclusion was more potent as a factor in favour of fixed-term contracts, and that has now gone completely.

The development currently in the pipeline, as seen above[9], is the Fixed-term Worker Directive 99/70/EC, due for implementation in the Fixed-term Employee (Prevention of Less Favourable Treatment) Regulations 2002, in draft at the time of writing. Could this be used in future to attack any unconscionable use of fixed-term contracts (by relying on the common law position of automatic termination on expiry)? The first point to note is that the Directive adopts a significantly wider definition of 'fixed-term contact', including what in domestic law would be considered to be purpose contracts – 'fixed term worker means a person having an employment contract or relationship. . .where the end of the employment contract or relationship is determined by objective conditions such as reaching a specific date, completing a specific task, or the occurrence of a specific event'. The draft Regulations adopt a similarly broad definition for their own purposes, and indeed go further by amending unfair dismissal and redundancy law to include expiry of a task contract in the general definitions of 'dismissal'. On the other hand, although the coverage is wide, the principle of non-discrimination in the Directive is primarily aimed at requiring equal terms and conditions of employment for fixed-term workers, not at regulating the use of fixed-term contracts in the first place. What might have an effect, at least indirectly, in the latter part of the Directive which requires a member state to choose between imposing a requirement of objective justification for renewal of a fixed-term contract, a maximum total duration for successive fixed-term contracts or a maximum number of renewals. The proposal in the draft Regulations is that there is to be a rule that any employee kept on fixed-term contracts for four years or more should be deemed to be a permanent employee unless the employer can objectively justify retention of fixed-term status[10].

1   These are now contained in the ERA 1996, ss 95(1)(b) (for unfair dismissal purposes) and 136(1)(b) (for redundancy purposes).
2   *Dixon v BBC* [1979] ICR 281, [1979] IRLR 114, CA, disagreeing on this point with the earlier decision in *BBC v Ioannou* [1975] ICR 267, [1975] 2 All ER 999, CA, where this particular problem had not been apparent. Of course, one common law problem for the employee on this sort of contract would be that if the employer unilaterally terminated the employment part-way through the fixed term, wrongful dismissal damages would be restricted to wages during the notice period, not to wages for the rest of the fixed term.
3   *Wiltshire County Council v NATFHE* [1978] ICR 968, [1978] IRLR 301, CA.
4   *Weston v University College Swansea* [1975] IRLR 102.
5   See n 3, above.
6   [1986] IRLR 102, EAT.
7   ERA 1999 s 18, repealing the ERA 1996, s 197(1), (2).
8   In *Kingston-upon-Hull City Council v Mountain* [1999] ICR 715, EAT an employee with 21 years' service received no statutory redundancy payment because the *final* contract on which he was employed was a two year fixed-term contract containing an exclusion clause which was valid under s 197(3).
9   At para 2.16, above.
10 Contracts are to be considered 'successive' if they satisfy the normal continuity of employment rules in the ERA 1996, ss 210–219. Note that it is also proposed to repeal the ability of an employer to get the employee to sign away redundancy rights in a fixed-term contract of two years or more, see n 9, above.

6   Termination on insolvency

7.9   This is a curious area at common law, because it *sounds* to be of major importance (what happens to an employee's contract on the employer's insolvency?) but is full of uncertainty and covered only by old or very old case law. Also, there can be confusion in some areas as to whether the effect might be to put the employee under notice, or to operate as an instant, wrongful dismissal.

The basic position *appears* to be[1] that a compulsory winding up of a corporate employer operates as notice of dismissal. A voluntary winding up order may have the same effect if there is no intention of carrying on the business, otherwise it does not have this effect. The appointment of a receiver by the court, or an out of court appointment of a receiver as agent for the creditors is said to terminate employment contracts, whereas an out of court appointment of a receiver as an agent of the company does not do so (because it is not inconsistent with continued employment). It may be, however, that there are certain exceptions where even appointment as an agent of the company *is* inconsistent with continued employment, and so does terminate contracts. This complexity and uncertainty perhaps point to the fact that in most cases the common law position is of little practical importance, unless some incidental issue relies on it, particularly the continued validity of a restraint of trade clause (which would of course be negated by a wrongful dismissal)[2]. In most cases of employer insolvency, the involvement of the law will instead be concentrated on statutory matters, in particular (a) whether (if the business is eventually sold onTUPE safeguards the continuity of the employees' employment[3], (b) whether the employees have any protection under ordinary insolvency law, and (c) if not, whether they can claim payment from the Secretary of State[4]. Paradoxically, the only topicality that this subject has had in recent years was a change put urgently through Parliament[5] to increase protection for administrators and receivers, not employees. This was in response to *Powdrill v Watson*[6] which had shaken insolvency practice by holding that the general rule (that an administrator or receiver was not deemed to have adopted the contracts of those employed by the company because of anything done in the first 14 days of appointment) could be turned from a shield into a sword, so that adoption could be found readily *after* 14 days, and the administrator or receiver became directly liable for contractual debts to the employees, including (of importance for present purposes) wages during the notice period or damages for wrongful dismissal. Under the insolvency law provisions as substituted from 15 March 1994, even where the administrator or receiver adopts contracts, he is only liable for 'qualifying liabilities', namely wages or salary (including sick pay or holiday pay), or contributions to a pension scheme, in respect of services rendered after the adoption of the contract. Thus, wages for a missing notice period or damages for wrongful dismissal go back to being an ordinary unsecured debt, subject to the ordinary insolvency rules. In the light of this, perhaps it is not so surprising that the purely common law position attracts so little attention, and even less clarity.

1 Readers should construe this phrase as a *Hedley Byrne* exclusion clause. The rest of this paragraph is a precis of the position as set out in *Smith & Wood* p 357. See also *Harvey* A[882], [883].
2 *Measures Bros Ltd v Measures* [1910] 2 Ch 248, CA.
3 See McMullen, Business Transfers. Note particularly reg 4 which covers 'Transfers by receivers and liquidators', in particular the practice known as 'hiving down', and the purposive interpretation given to the regulation in *Re Maxwell Fleet and Facilities Management Ltd* [2000] IRLR 368, Ch D; at the time of writing the DTI consultation document on TUPE reform suggests dispensing with this particular provision, on the basis that it is now unnecessary.
4 Ie under the ERA 1996, ss 182–190. At the time of writing, the TUPE consultation document proposes extending this protection.
5 Insolvency Act 1994, amending the Insolvency Act 1986, ss 19 and 44.
6 [1995] ICR 1100, [1995] IRLR 269, HL. The legislation was in fact in response to the decision of the Court of Appeal, which was then largely upheld by the House of Lords. See *Harvey* para G[101] ff.

Chapter 8

Summary dismissal

1 Introduction

8.1   Summary dismissal for gross misconduct is one of those areas of employment law that one tends to take for granted, applying the old elephantine principle that it is normally easy to identify it, if not to define it; even where a case is arguable, the arguments tend to be about specifics, on the basis that here par excellence is the true home of the lawyer's escape clause 'it is all a question of fact', hence the lack of extensive reported case law on the subject. In many cases, all this will be true, but that does not obscure the fact that its legal basis is not free from difficulty, and that it may well be due for further consideration by the courts and tribunals. Three topics will be considered in this chapter – the meaning of and legal basis for summary dismissal for gross misconduct, whether it can be used in cases of negligence or under-performance, and finally the significance of contractual provisions expressly setting out the meaning of gross misconduct and the power to dismiss summarily. On the last point, it will be suggested that courts may eventually need to go beyond the wording of a particular contract and place extra-contractual limits on an employer's power of definition. Before going on to these topics, however, certain introductory points may be made by way of background.

8.2   The first, and most basic, is that 'summary dismissal' means a dismissal without the notice that is normally required by the contract or, as to minima, by statute[1]. The use of the phrase should be restricted to this. In particular, it should not be used to cover a dismissal with wages in lieu, even though the effect of such a dismissal is *instant* termination. Indeed, in a recent case considered below[2] the Court of Appeal had to construe the phrase 'liable to instant dismissal' in an employment contract (of some complexity) which caused a serious ambiguity. Preferably, phrases such as this should be avoided, to retain the basic division between dismissals with notice (whether or not actually worked out) and those without notice, ie true summary dismissals.

1   ERA 1996, s 86. There could also be a summary dismissal before the expiry of a fixed-term contract.
2   *T & K Home Improvements Ltd v Skilton* [2000] IRLR 595, CA; see para 8.13.

8.3   The second definitional point is that summary dismissal does *not* mean a dismissal without going through normal procedures. Clearly, it may arise in circumstances where the giving of warnings is not appropriate, but other than in extreme cases, the employer will normally still be expected to go through the appropriate procedures for investigation, the holding of a fair hearing of the allegations and the provision of an appeal. In fact, the drastic nature of the termination could be seen as making such procedures (or at least their availability[1]) more important, not less. If in a particular case there is an urgent need to remove the individual from the workplace, that may be better done by suspension with pay[2], rather than by proceeding directly to dismissal without affording basic natural justice rights to the accused employee. These points are made clear in the guidance on summary dismissal given in paragraph 7 of the ACAS Code of Practice 'Disciplinary and Grievance Procedures', which is worth setting out in full at this stage:

> 'Workers should be made aware of the likely consequences of breaking disciplinary rules or failing to meet performance standards. In particular, they should be given a clear indication of the type of conduct, often referred to as gross misconduct, which may warrant summary dismissal (ie. dismissal without notice). Summary is not necessarily synonymous with instant and incidents of gross misconduct will usually still need to be investigated as part of a formal procedure. Acts which constitute gross misconduct are those resulting in a serious breach of contractual terms and will be for organisations to decide in the light of their own particular circumstances. However, they might include the following:
>
> (i)   theft, fraud and deliberate falsification of records;
> (ii)   physical violence;
> (iii)   serious bullying or harassment;
> (iv)   deliberate damage to property;
> (v)   serious insubordination;
> (vi)   misuse of an organisation's property or name;
> (vii)   bringing the employer into serious disrepute;
> (viii) serious incapability whilst on duty brought on by alcohol or illegal drugs;
> (ix)   serious negligence which causes or might cause unacceptable loss, damage or injury;
> (x)   serious infringement of health and safety rules;
> (xi)   serious breach of confidence (subject to the Public Interest (Disclosure) Act 1998).
>
> As indicated earlier this list is not intended to be exhaustive.'

1   In a 'smoking gun' case, an employer might reasonably conclude that there would be little purpose in going through procedures; this was accepted in *Polkey v A E Dayton Services Ltd* [1988] ICR 142, [1987] IRLR 503, HL, the leading case on procedures in the context of an unfair dismissal claim. However, an employer may still be advised to consider the wise words of Megarry V-C in *John v Rees* [1970] Ch 345, [1969] 2 All ER 274, at 402, 309 (quoted in Smith & Wood, *Industrial Law* (7th edn, 2000) Butterworths, p 444) to the effect that often open-and-shut cases prove to be nothing of the sort on proper investigation; even though smoking, the gun could still have been planted. Moreover, the Employment Bill 2002 aims to make the use of the basic statutory procedure on dismissal (reasons; hearing; appeal) mandatory in all cases.
2   ACAS Code of Practice 'Disciplinary and Grievance Procedures' (2000) para 13.

8.4   The third point is that the modern law on summary dismissal has to be seen against the backdrop of the existence of the well-developed law of unfair dismissal. Technically, of course, unfair dismissal and summary dismissal (usually sounding in an action for wrongful dismissal if being challenged per se) are entirely separate and must not be confused. As Judge Clark pointed out clearly in a review of this area of law in *Farrant v Woodroffe School*[1], a case concerning breach of orders and incidental questions as to the lawfulness of those orders, in wrongful dismissal (and indeed in the area of constructive dismissal under the statute) 'the terms of the contract and breach of those terms is of the utmost importance', whereas in unfair dismissal questions of contractual correctness of orders are relevant but not decisive factors on the larger question of the overall fairness of the decision to dismiss in all the circumstances. Thus, to take one example, a summary dismissal might not be wrongful (because strictly within the terms of the contract), but might still be unfair (eg because hasty and lacking in proper procedures, see above)[2]. However, this formalistic division may not show the whole picture, because the very existence of the unfair dismissal action can have indirect effects. It is clear that its existence does not remove or diminish any rights to claim wrongful dismissal (based on a summary dismissal that the ex-employee claims was not warranted) which may still be more valuable in the case of a high earner on long notice, even after the increasing of the maximum compensatory award to £50,000 in 1999 (with further up-rating increases to £52,600 at the time of writing). Further, the employer's right to dismiss summarily is equally clearly retained under the modern legislation, as can be seen from its provision on minimum notice[3] and the ACAS Code of Practice[4]. On the other hand, it may be that the existence of an unfair dismissal entitlement in the background (where the employee has at least one year's service) will make an employer more nervous of dismissing summarily (as opposed to, say, with wages in lieu) except in obvious cases, if only for fear that the summary nature might make the dismissal *appear* more hasty, given that the form of the dismissal can be at least a factor for a tribunal to consider. Thus, while the following discussion will concentrate on summary dismissal in its contractual (wrongful dismissal) context, it cannot be wholly divorced from the law of unfair dismissal, at the very least because of certain cross-pollinations and analogies which help to explain its current position and use, as opposed to its origins in nineteenth century contract law.

1   [1998] ICR 184, [1998] IRLR 176, EAT.
2   For an interesting example of the opposite possibility, ie of a summary dismissal that was wrongful but not unfair, see *Treganowen v Robert Knee & Co Ltd* [1975] ICR 405, [1975] IRLR 247.
3   ERA 1996, s 86, which sets out minimum notice periods based on length of service. Section 86(6) states 'This section does not affect any right of either party to a contract of employment to treat the contract as terminable without notice by reason of conduct of the other party'.
4   ACAS Code of Practice, para 9(xi) suggests that a disciplinary procedure should 'ensure that, *except for gross misconduct*, no worker is dismissed for a first breach of discipline'. This is primarily in the context of the normal procedural reqirement of warnings prior to dismissal but can be seen more widely as sanctioning summary dismissal itself in appropriate cases.

2   Summary dismissal for gross misconduct

8.5   'The expression 'gross misconduct' is steeped in industrial history'[1]. It connotes the ability of the employer to dispense with the employee's services immediately and without compensation for lack of notice, due to the objective existence of sufficient misconduct; thus, it can apply (to defeat a wrongful dismissal action by the ex-employee) even on facts only coming to light after dismissal, unknown to the employer at the date of dismissal[2].

How does this power arise? Before the development of the contract basis for employment in the late nineteenth century, it was viewed as a necessary element of the legal relationship of master and servant. The classic statement was by Parke B in *Callo v Brouckner*[3], to the effect that there could be a summary dismissal for moral misconduct (pecuniary or otherwise), wilful dismissal or habitual neglect. Not only does this serve to illustrate the 'status' basis originally taken towards employment (ie as a fixed relationship, amenable to legal rules), it also arguably shows an emphasis on deliberate and culpable misconduct by the employee (even the reference to 'neglect' being qualified by the word 'habitual'), almost requiring what a criminal lawyer would refer to as mens rea (an approach which, we shall see, now needs qualification). As a result of this initial approach, we did see until surprisingly recently a tendency to try to isolate and categorise the various particular grounds on which an employee could be summarily dismissed[4], but ultimately this was a fruitless exercise (especially when very old case law was being cited) because even by the end of the nineteenth century the proper test was said to be a contractual one[5], heavily reliant on construction of the individual contract and application to the particular circumstances of the case[6]. Thus, factual precedents are of little use, especially as an area such as this is especially subject to changing influences in changing times and social background. As Edmund Davies LJ memorably put it in *Wilson v Racher*[7]:

> 'Reported decisions provide useful, but only general guides, each case turning on its own facts. Many of the decisions which are customarily cited in these cases date from the last century and may be wholly out of accord with the current social conditions. What would today be regarded as almost an attitude of Czar-serf, which is to be found in some of the older cases where a dismissed employee failed to recover damages would, I venture to think, be decided differently today'.

A good example of the courts having to adapt this law to evolving social realities was the decision of the EAT in *Denco Ltd v Joinson*[8], at a very early stage in the computer revolution, that *any* deliberate unauthorised abuse of the employer's computer system may (even in the absence of personal gain) justify summary dismissal for gross misconduct, which is likely to be held to have been fair. Contemporary employer concerns about the security and integrity of far more sophisticated systems, and possibly criminal or defamatory use of e-mail and the internet, show the continuing importance of such developments.

Once summary dismissal was seen in terms of the law of contract, it became a question of fitting it into the orthodox ideas of repudiation of contract by the employee and acceptance of that repudiation by the employer. In *Laws v London Chronicle Ltd*[9] Lord Evershed MR put it thus:

> '...since a contract of service is but an example of contracts in general, so that the general law of contract will be applicable, it follows that, if summary dismissal is claimed to be justifiable, the question must be whether the conduct complained of is such as to show the servant to have disregarded the essential conditions of the contract of service. It is, no doubt, therefore, generally true that wilful disobedience of an order will justify summary dismissal, since wilful disobedience of a lawful and reasonable order shows a disregard – a complete disregard – of a condition essential to the contract of service, namely, the condition that the servant must obey the proper orders of the master and that, unless he does so, the relationship is, so to speak, struck at fundamentally'.

Cases therefore revolve primarily around their facts, with questions of law being restricted to ensuring that the correct tests are applied, possibly enunciating *general* guidance (eg that, in a case involving loss of temper by the employee, the court should 'apply the standard of men and not angels'[10]), and if necessary interpreting the contract itself to see what was and was not required of the employee in the circumstances.

1   *Farrant v Woodroffe School* [1998] ICR 184 at 192, [1998] IRLR 176 at 179, EAT.
2   *Boston Deep Sea Fishing & Ice Co Ltd v Ansell* (1888) 39 Ch D 339, [1886–1890] All ER Rep 65, CA. This is, of course, a well known point of contrast with unfair dismissal law, where an employer can only rely on a reason known and acted upon at the time of dismissal: *W Devis & Sons Ltd v Atkins* [1977] ICR 662, [1977] IRLR 314, HL.
3   (1831) 4 C & P 518.
4   As late as the 1976 issue of volume 16 (Employment) of Halsbury's Laws of England, the subject of summary dismissal was covered by several paragraphs setting out ancient case law under headings such as 'disobedience to instructions', 'misconduct', neglect' and 'incompetence'. To take an extreme example, one footnote cited *R v Brampton Inhabitants* (1777) Cald Mag Cas 11 for the proposition that a maidservant can be properly dismissed for being found with child, and *R v Welford Inhabitants* (1778) Cald Mag Cas 57 as permitting the summary dismissal of a servant who was the father of a bastard child of a female servant in the same family. The footnote did add, however, that 'it is submitted that merely being the parent of an illegitimate child would not be a sufficient misconduct to justify dismissal from most kinds of employment today'. Controversial stuff.
5   'The true question is whether the acts and conduct of the party evince an intention no longer to be bound by the contract': *Freeth v Burr* (1874) LR 9 CP 208 at 213, per Lord Coleridge CJ, applied by the House of Lords in *General Billposting Co Ltd v Atkinson* [1909] AC 118 (the leading authority that a wrongful dismissal destroys a restraint of trade clause). See also *Clouston & Co Ltd v Corry* [1906] AC 122, PC.
6   *Re Rubel Bronze and Metal Co* [1918] 1 KB 315, QBD; *Jupiter General Insurance Co Ltd v Shroff* [1937] 3 All ER 67, PC.
7   [1974] ICR 428, [1974] IRLR 114, CA.
8   [1991] ICR 172, [1991] IRLR 63, EAT.
9   [1959] 2 All ER 285, [1959] 1 WLR 698, CA; see also *Denmark Productions Ltd v Boscobel Productions Ltd* [1969] 1 QB 699, [1968] 3 All ER 513, CA and *Pepper v Webb* [1969] 2 All ER 216, [1969] 1 WLR 514, CA, both decided subsequently, but before the introduction of the new unfair dismissal jurisdiction in 1971.
10 *Jupiter General Insurance Co Ltd v Shroff* [1937] 3 All ER 67, PC.

8.6   As is so often the case in modern employment law, this purely contractual analysis has been subject to some qualification and development. Three examples of this will serve to illustrate the point. The first is that there is a strong tendency in practice to run together the question in wrongful dismissal law of whether the employee's misconduct deserved summary dismissal and the question in unfair dismissal of whether that misconduct deserves dismissal without the giving of warnings. Technically, these are separate matters, and there could be a case of relatively serious misconduct which falls just short of meriting a summary dismissal, but which is serious enough to justify the employer resorting straight to a dismissal without going through a system of warnings; the result would be an immediate dismissal without warnings, but with notice (or, more likely, with wages in lieu). However, in many cases in practice that may be too subtle an approach, and the choice remains between going through the normal warnings system[1] *or* going for summary dismissal. This may have the beneficial effect of emphasising how serious the facts have to be to merit summary dismissal. It may also mean that, although there is little modern case authority on summary dismissal, the more extensive authority in unfair dismissal law on when an employer will act reasonably in dispensing with warnings[2] could be used instead, at least by way of analogy.

1   Under the 2000 revision of the ACAS Code of Practice it is possible that more use may be made in some of these cases of the device of a 'first and final' warning, which is now impliedly suggested in the redrafted para 15.
2   See *Harvey on Industrial Relations and Employment Law* paras D1 [1550] ff.

8.7   The second example is that we may be seeing more emphasis on the reasonableness of the employer's conduct, even in a wrongful dismissal case. Where the question at issue is disobedience of orders, a purely contractual approach to summary dismissal would simply ask whether the employer had the contractual power to issue that particular order. However, we have already seen[1] that in other areas of employment contract law (especially where arising in an unfair dismissal action, eg in the context of constructive dismissal) theories are developing that contractual rights may have to be enforced, if not always 'reasonably', at least in such a way as not to breach the essential obligations of trust and respect. We could also see that in a summary dismissal case. Even in the dictum set out above from *Laws v London Chronicle Ltd*, Lord Evershed referred to 'disobedience of a lawful and reasonable order'; this point was specifically picked up by Judge Clark in *Farrant v Woodroffe School*[2]:

> 'From [the Laws case] it is plain to see how refusal to obey a lawful and reasonable instruction may be regarded as gross misconduct entitling the employer to summarily dismiss the employee. Since wrongful dismissal is a purely contractual concept, the need for the instruction to be lawful, that is falling within the scope of the contract, is a prerequisite for a permissible summary dismissal at common law. Further, the instruction must be reasonable. Even if it falls within the strict terms of the contract, refusal to obey an unreasonable order may not amount to grounds for summary dismissal'.

1   At para 3.13, above.
2   [1998] ICR 184 at 193, [1998] IRLR 176 at 179, EAT.

8.8   The third example is that a recent case (in a most unusual jurisdiction, but directly relevant) has suggested that the basis for summary dismissal should now lie, not in unrefined ideas of repudiation and acceptance as such, but instead in the more contemporary area of trust and confidence. *Neary v Dean of Westminster*[1] concerned the high-profile summary dismissal of the organist of Westminster Abbey and his wife due to alleged (non-fraudulent) financial irregularities in the running of certain musical events and the adoption of inappropriate financial methods unknown to the Abbey authorities. Lord Jauncey was appointed by the Queen as a special commissioner to hear their appeal petitions, and determined that summary dismissal was justified. Setting out the principle to be applied, he stated that:

> '...conduct amounting to gross misconduct justifying [summary] dismissal must so undermine the trust and confidence which is inherent in the particular contract of employment that the master should no longer be required to retain the servant in his employment'.

This could be a significant development, not going as far as to cut summary dismissal free from its contractual basis (since trust and confidence is itself an implied term of the contract), but possibly moving away from ordinary repudiation and acceptance, towards a broader enquiry as to the overall effects of the employee's conduct on the employment *relationship*, through the medium of the equally broad concept of trust and confidence. In the case in question this was important in holding that the financial misdealing justified summary dismissal even though there was *no* allegation of dishonesty or personal gain, particularly given the nature of the employment and the employees' duties (the importance of which to an individual case was again emphasised, as a question of fact). We have already seen above[2] the quite remarkable development of the implied term of trust and respect, and its importance in allowing the law of employment to evolve away, when necessary, from strict contract law principles in order to fit present day realities. Its emergence here, in the realm of summary dismissal, shows its all-pervasive nature.

1   [1999] IRLR 288.
2   See para 4.8, above. Lord Jauncey was in fact able to cite previous authority relying on ideas of the employee's conduct being 'incompatible with the employment' (*Sinclair v Neighbour* [1967] 2 QB 279, at 286 per Sellers LJ) and, later, specifically referred to breaches by the employee of 'the implied obligation of trust and confidence of sufficient gravity' (*Lewis v Motorworld Garages Ltd* [1985] IRLR 465, at 469 per Glidewell LJ – in fact referring to constructive dismissal, but said by Lord Jauncey to be equally applicable in reverse).

3   Negligence and under-performance

8.9   Although the original formulation of the grounds for summary dismissal in *Callo v Brouckner* (para 8.5, above) concentrated on deliberate misconduct by the employee, it now seems clear that certain forms of neglect can also be included. The decision in *Neary v Dean of Westminster* (para 8.8, above) that financial irregularities *not* of a fraudulent or personally profitable nature could still constitute gross misconduct can be seen as a recent example of this. A problem could arise, however, in the case of a one-off act of negligence; would that be sufficient? Old authority suggested that such a one-off would not constitute gross misconduct, unless attended by serious consequences[1], but there lies the problem – should the law look at the nature of the negligent act[2] or at the consequences following from it? What about a case of a momentary slip causing vast damage? In one of the few cases to address this point, the court did say that it should look primarily at the negligent act, not the consequences, because to look at the consequences could be too harsh and involve too much hindsight[3]. However, it is not clear that this represents the law. As already seen, older case law had mentioned the relevance of serious consequences, and the relevant provision of the ACAS Code of Practice[4] refers to 'serious negligence which causes or might cause unacceptable loss, damage or injury' – this itself may give a mixed message because the adjective 'serious' is attached to the negligence itself, whereas the emphasis is also heavily on the actual or potential consequences. In many cases, this will be just semantics, because serious consequences will have been caused by serious neglect. However, the issue could eventually be forced in a case concerning an act of neglect in itself relatively slight or momentary but with awful consequences (eg multiple deaths or serious environmental pollution), especially if it concerned a highly publicised disaster. In such a case it might be extremely difficult in practice to hold a line that hindsight should not be used and that only the neglect itself should be taken into consideration – imagine the public reaction (let alone that of the tabloid newspapers) if a railway engineer whose one-off fault led to a major train disaster was seen only to receive a formal warning not to cause another one. On the other hand, more logically, to subject that employee to summary dismissal might suggest the making of a scapegoat, raising the same sort of unease that occurs in health and safety law when an individual is punished but the employing organisation (whose systems allowed it to happen) is not[5].

1   *Edwards v Levy* (1860) 2 F & F 94; *Baster v London and County Printing Works* [1899] 1 QB 901.
2   The concept of 'gross' negligence has recently been reaffirmed in criminal law, as a basis for manslaughter (*A-G's Reference (No 2 of 1999)* [2000] IRLR 417, CA, arising out of the Southall rail disaster, and affirming that an action would not lie for corporate manslaughter), but the concept has always caused problems in criminal law, and still requires an answer to the question – grossly negligent as to what?
3   *Savage v British India Steam Navigation Co Ltd* (1930) 46 TLR 294.
4   Paragraph 7 (ix); see para 8.3, above.
5   The obvious example here is the Zeebrugge ferry disaster where the individual employee who fell asleep without closing the bow doors was convicted but the ferry company was not.

8.10   The other area of potential uncertainty here concerns the availability of summary dismissal in cases of under-performance. According to venerable authority, a skilled employee warrants that he is reasonably competent for the work to be done[1], and this may mean that any immediate and dramatic discovery of lack of ability by a new employee would justify dismissal, particularly if there had been fraud in obtaining the employment. However, a more difficult case would arise if there were serious allegations of incompetence more generally during employment. In the case of an ordinary employee, incapability such as this would not generally give rise to summary dismissal, but would be amenable to a series of warnings (giving the employee a reasonable chance to improve)[2], with any eventual dismissal likely to be with notice or payment in lieu thereof. There might, on the other hand, be a case of a key employee or senior manager/director whose role is so vital that serious incompetence might come within the ambit of summary dismissal. This could, for example, be the case in an industry known to be volatile, operating on a 'high-risk – high reward' basis[3], where staff anticipate that continued employment depends on continually meeting targets.

The first point to note here is that this would fit in with the general approach that there are no fixed rules on what justifies summary dismissal, and that it may depend on the circumstances and demands of the particular job and the position of the particular employee[4]. Thus, the high risk nature of the job could be an important factor, possibly laying the basis for summary dismissal even though there would be no question of it in less frenetic circumstances. A rare reported example of such a case is *Jackson v Invicta Plastics Ltd*[5] where, after a boardroom struggle, the chief executive (also a director) was summarily dismissed. The company defended his claim for wrongful dismissal on the basis of misconduct and incompetence. The latter centred round objections taken to some of his business decisions (not closing down a subsidiary, not making redundancies, and making speculative investments). In fact, Pain J held that their defence failed on both grounds on the facts. With regard to the principle to apply on incompetence, he stated that the general tendency at common law had been for it to become increasingly difficult to justify summary dismissal on grounds of incompetence, and that this had been re-emphasised by the existence now of the law of unfair dismissal. Moreover, there was a particular difficulty where the job in question was generically defined ('chief executive') so that it was more difficult to define the standards to be expected than it would be, say, in the case of a skilled craftsman. Indeed, one might add that the incompetence alleged in the case could simply reflect a bona fide difference of opinion as to business desirability, as between accuser and accused. The conclusion that the judge came to was that:

> 'Although the right to dismiss summarily for incompetence still survives, it is difficult to imagine circumstances in which the necessary evidence would be available in the case of a chief executive, who had recently been appointed. The employer would have to show that his continued employment would be quite impracticable because of the harm he was likely to do to the company'.

Thus, the judge emphasised potential harm as a key factor, not just the incompetence itself. Even here, there may be a question as to whether that justifies *summary* dismissal, as opposed to an ordinary dismissal with notice or wages in lieu. One possible answer to that might arise if the employee was in fact on a fixed term contract or on long notice, where it might be unreasonable to expect the employer to continue to be bound by the contract, and/or *possibly* if instant termination was in fact the general expectation in that industry, especially in a case of failure to meet targets. Of course, these all remain questions of fact; the position appears to be in general that, while a summary dismissal for incompetence cannot be ruled out, in most foreseeable cases it would normally require special and pressing circumstances. One possibility is that an employer might seek to link failure to meet targets with summary dismissal in the contract itself, and argue that the special circumstance was that the employee was under no illusions. Would that be effective? It is to questions such as this that we now turn.

1   Harmer v Cornelius (1858) 5 CBNS 236.
2   See *Harvey* D1 [1125] ff.
3   As in *T & K Home Improvements Ltd v Skilton* [2000] IRLR 595, CA, considered below.
4   Clouston v Corry [1906] AC 122, at 129 per Lord James of Hereford.
5   [1987] BCLC 329.

4   Defining gross misconduct in the contract

8.11   An employer will frequently include in its disciplinary procedure a section covering summary dismissal; to do so has been advised for many years now in the ACAS Code of Practice, the relevant provision of which is set out above. Certain matters will be fairly immutable in all employments (theft, assault, etc), but the employer may use the occasion to spell out in addition any misdemeanours that are particularly unacceptable in the circumstances of the particular employment (the proverbial example being smoking in an armaments factory, a more practical example being breaches of hygiene rules in a food factory). The usual advice is that, in drafting such a provision, the employer should make it clear that the list is *not* exhaustive, so that there will be residual discretion to treat some novel and/or unforeseen misconduct as still warranting summary dismissal. Indeed, the ACAS Code of Practice specifically states that its suggested list is not intended to be exhaustive.

What effect does an express summary dismissal clause have? In the law of unfair dismissal it is well established that although breach of a clearly stated rule may be important evidence for the employer, it cannot per se make the dismissal fair, and certainly does not prevent the tribunal from going on to consider fairness in *all* the circumstances[1]. However, the point that arises for present purposes is whether the existence of such a clause and its clear breach by the employee will *always* validate summary dismissal at common law (and so defeat a claim of wrongful dismissal). This depends on whether one accepts a purely contractual approach to summary dismissal (ie the repudiation-and-acceptance theory, basing the repudiation simply on what the contract itself states expressly to be unacceptable conduct), or whether (if and when the matter is eventually pressed) a court or tribunal might construe 'gross misconduct' in a more objective manner, at least to the extent of requiring some minimum threshold of heinousness in the employee's conduct in order to justify the drastic remedy of summary dismissal, regardless of what it may say in the contract. As is often the case when a question such as this arises in employment law, it gives rise to two very distinct approaches – the pure contract approach is based on ideas of economic freedom and neo-liberalism, namely that both parties are free to make whatever bargain they want in a free market, and that if the employee signs a contract with a clear clause in it on summary dismissal, he or she must abide by it; the 'objective meaning' approach is based on the idea of the desirability of certain minimum standards, to protect an employee from disadvantage resulting from a pure contract approach, operating in an unequal labour market. This battleground has been well fought over in other contexts.

1   Laws Stores Ltd v Oliphant [1978] IRLR 251, EAT; *Taylor v Parsons, Peebles, NEI Bruce Peebles Ltd* [1981] IRLR 119, EAT.

8.12   In the area of employment contracts and summary dismissal clauses, the issue has yet to be tested in the courts. We have had one very interesting decision recently on summary dismissal, but it settles a different (though equally important) point. In *Macari v Celtic Football and Athletic Co Ltd*[1] a football manager was subject to a contract stipulating two years notice (or payment in lieu), with a clause specifically covering the power to dismiss summarily in six circumstances[2], where the board formed the view that the manager was in breach of any of them. In addition, the contract contained a clause requiring the manager to live close to the club. In fact, he did not do so, but this was not initially challenged because the club adopted a relatively 'hands off' approach, leaving the manager very considerable discretion in carrying out his functions. This all changed when the club was taken over, and a new, more aggressive management started to exercise more direct control, finding fault with the manager, including over the residence question. Matters came to a head over a holiday, which the management effectively tried to veto. The manager was summarily dismissed. His claim for wrongful dismissal raised several distinct issues[3], one of which was his argument that the express summary dismissal clause *supplanted* any common law on the matter; the point about this was that it could be shown that 'the board' had not met to decide on his dismissal, and therefore (under the clause) 'the board' could not have been satisfied that grounds existed to dismiss him. Holding for the employers (generally, and on this point) the Inner House of the Court of Session held that an employer is entitled to dismiss summarily under the general law of contract where there is a material breach by the employee, regardless of any stipulations in an express summary dismissal clause – such a clause *supplements* the general law, and does not exclude it. Thus, not only was there no need for the conduct itself to come within the enumerated headings, but it also meant that the employer was not bound to go through a procedure which (the manager had argued) it had set out in the contract.

This case gives strong backing to the point made above that such clauses are not to be construed as exhaustive; indeed, it is a particularly strong case because it accepts such a rule as to both substance and procedure. However, it does not directly address the question being posed here – can a widely drafted contractual clause *extend* the grounds that would normally be considered to be gross misconduct. To take one *reductio ad absurdum* example, what would be the position if an employer (for no particularly strong work-related reason[4]) put a clause into the contract that the employee agreed that being five minutes' late on any one occasion would constitute gross misconduct, for which he would be dismissed summarily? Would an eventual summary dismissal for that reason be lawful at common law? On its face, this example may seem far fetched, but cases not a million miles from it could be imagined in certain employments where the whole culture of the business is 'live-or-die' and results-orientated, and where employee relations are known to be run on 'robust' lines.

A purely contractual approach would be in the employer's favour – the employee has agreed the term, which the employer has effectively made into a condition, breach of which constitutes repudiation by the employee, permitting the employer to accept the repudiation and dismiss summarily. Would a modern court or tribunal allow that to happen? Three possible ways to avoid it are suggested, in ascending order of uncertainty and lack of authority.

1   [1999] IRLR 787, Ct of Sess (IH).
2   One of them, intriguingly, was where 'the manager shall have become addicted to intemperance'; the possible questions of interpretation are limitless.
3   See also para 4.8, above.
4   It is accepted that there could be an exceptional case where the particular nature of the employment could mean that there was a genuine business need for absolute punctuality, and this would fall into the category, mentioned above, where the employer has properly tailored the clause to the bona fide needs of the firm (as with absolute hygiene rules in food factories). By contrast, the example being used here is of an employer cynically using its contracting power to set up a lawful summary dismissal where that would not normally be possible.

(a)   A construction approach

8.13   We have seen one recent case which at least suggests that, where there is any ambiguity in the contract[1], a court should be slow to find a power of summary dismissal where it would not normally lie, because to do so goes against the usual implication that an employee has a right to receive notice, or pay in lieu thereof. *T & K Home Improvements Ltd v Skilton*[2] concerned the summary dismissal of a double glazing firm's sales and marketing director for not meeting his quarterly sales targets. His contract provided for three months' notice on either side, with a payment in lieu/garden leave option for the employer, and summary dismissal for 'gross misconduct, gross incompetence or other repudiatory breach of contract'. A separate clause covered dismissal for missing targets, stating that if he failed over any quarter to achieve his performance target, he might be 'dismissed with immediate effect'. It was this clause that the employers relied on, as justifying the summary dismissal, especially in a high risk/high reward industry such as theirs. However, a major ambiguity was caused by the words 'immediate effect' and when the employee claimed damages for wrongful dismissal his claim was upheld by the Court of Appeal (as it had been by the tribunal and the EAT). Viewing the targets clause in the light of the other, more standard, dismissal clauses, they held that it did *not* permit summary dismissal, but instead was consistent with allowing immediate termination of the employment, but without prejudice to other rights under the contract, in particular the right to receive payment in lieu of notice. On that basis the dismissal was wrongful and the employee was entitled to three months' wages in lieu.

This is only a relatively short judgment, largely concentrating on the construction of the individual contract, but it does suggest that a construction approach may be useful. However, as with construction arguments in other contexts[3], the problem is that ultimately such an approach by itself could not deal with a clause in the contract which, though inequitable in its application, was clear and unambiguous. What if, in *Skilton*, the clause had expressly said that failure to meet targets would lead to *summary* dismissal?

1   Perhaps this should not be underestimated, on the principle that, with a receptive bench, ambiguity is in the eye of the beholder.
2   [2000] IRLR 595, CA.
3   See in particular, the discussion at para 3.12, above of the reluctance of a court to find in a contract a valid power of unilateral variation by an employer.

(b)   Statute

8.14   Could statute help? In general, it does not because the ERA 1996 has little to say expressly about summary dismissal and gross misconduct, which are primarily left as common law matters. A rare reference to summary dismissal occurs in s 86. This lays down minimum periods of notice (based on length of service), but contains the qualification in sub-s (6) that the section 'does not affect any right of either party to a contract of employment to treat the contract as terminable without notice by reason of the conduct of the other party'. Ostensibly, that simply retains summary dismissal (or, conversely, the right of the employee to leave immediately in the light of repudiatory conduct by the employer), but a question could be raised as to the meaning of the 'conduct' of the other party. On a pure contract approach it could be argued that this simply refers to conduct which is contractually repudiatory, and that if the employer has indeed 'set up' that which is to be considered repudiatory (in our example, lateness on a single occasion), then that is the end of the matter and s 86(6) has no limiting effect. However, the opposite argument might be that, as s 86's function is to lay down *statutory* rules on notice (impinging on the employer's common law ability to put a provision into a contract requiring little, or possibly even no, notice), sub-s (6) should be viewed as establishing a statutory exception which must be viewed in its own terms, and having meaning in itself. This would lead to the further argument that the reference to 'conduct' means 'gross misconduct', which must itself have a minimum threshold of seriousness before it is allowed to remove the freestanding statutory right to minimum notice in s 86(1). This point remains open, though there may be two crumbs of authority in favour of the latter interpretation. First, there may be an analogy with the obiter remarks of Morison P in *Cerberus Software Ltd v Rowley*[1] that the statutory right to waive notice in s 86(3) might only apply to an ad hoc waiver, not to a formal payment-in-lieu clause in the contract. It was argued above[2] that (given the widespread use of such clauses) this may be unlikely to be accepted in its result, ie rendering such clauses in general invalid, but the reasoning is interesting – that the statutory exceptions in s 86 should be construed narrowly, in order to attain the Parliamentary intent which was to enact the right to minimum notice in s 86(1), which should apply in all except clear cases to the contrary. Secondly, in *Lanton Leisure Ltd v White and Gibson*[3] the Scottish EAT strongly disapproved an employer's argument that all that was required for the activation of s 86(6) (and thus the disapplication of the normal statutory notice provisions in s 86(1)) was that the employer had *purported* expressly to dismiss summarily for gross misconduct. Lord Mayfield held that, for s 86(6) to apply, it must first be shown, on an inquiry into the merits, that there had in fact been such conduct as would enable the employer to terminate by notice. Thus, gross misconduct must be shown as objective fact. Of course, that still begs the substantive question as to whether it is enough just to show repudiatory breach of an express stipulation of the contract (however unfair), but at the least the case might be seen as *some* validation of a more objective approach to gross misconduct under s 86(6).

1   [1999] IRLR 690, EAT, (reversed on other grounds: [2001] ICR 376, [2001] IRLR 160, CA).
2   At para 3.30.
3   [1987] IRLR 119, EAT. The case in fact concerned what is now the ERA 1996, s 97(4) which extends the date of dismissal by the length of notice that should have been given, for certain statutory purposes (including the qualifying period for unfair dismissal). The employer (who had dismissed instantly one week before the employees had served the necessary period) argued that s 97(4) did not apply because they had dismissed summarily within s 86(6).

8.15   One further statutory argument might be under the Unfair Contract Terms Act 1977; could an arguably inequitable summary dismissal power in the contract be attacked under this Act, and its test of reasonableness? As seen above[1], it has finally been held in *Brigden v American Express Bank Ltd*[2] that the Act can apply in an employment contract, by the linguistically dubious means of defining the employee as a 'consumer' for statutory purposes. However, it must be remembered that the challenge under the Act failed in *Brigden* (which concerned a provision in a contract of employment witholding the disciplinary procedure from employees in their first year of employment) for a reason that could well be material here too – the Act does not concern 'unfair' contract terms, but rather exclusion of liability terms, or terms purporting to give the dominant party a right to render performance different from that envisaged by the contract. In *Brigden* it was held that the clause in question was in fact one *defining* liabilities in the first place, not excluding or amending them. As stated above, this is likely to be the case with most provisions of a contract of employment; it could therefore be argued strongly that a broad summary dismissal clause was also one defining the relationship, and so not subject to the Act's reasonableness test.

1   At para 3.1.
2   [2000] IRLR 94, QBD.

(c)   A broader principle?

8.16   Given the limitations of the construction approach and the doubts surrounding any statutory intervention, could an inequitably broad summary dismissal power be challenged on any wider principle? This would depend on whether a court or tribunal could be persuaded to limit freedom of contract in this area, possibly by holding that at common law 'gross misconduct' has an inherent meaning. This could possibly be interpreted as meaning that there must be some minimum level of seriousness of the employee's conduct (especially in the sort of 'immutable' headings set out in the ACAS Code of Practice), *and* that any contractual provision purporting to allow summary dismissal for a lesser level of infraction must be specifically justified by the nature of the business (smoking in an armaments factory). The general argument in favour of such a development is that it would be consistent with other areas of modern

141

employment law where there have been moves away from a strictly contractual approach, at least to the extent that, although contractual rights are the starting point, a court or tribunal is given certain legal devices or qualifications to use where a purely contractual analysis leads to what it perceives to be an unfair and/or unrealistic result. There would, of course, be the irony that any such movement could be seen as moving back towards the original (pre-contractual) approach to summary dismissal in *Callo v Brouckner*[1] itself, which clearly envisaged the existence of common law rules as to when conduct does and does not justify summary dismissal. However, progress by way of wide and graceful circles is by no means unknown in employment law.

1   (1831) 4 C & P 518; see para 8.5, above.

Chapter 9

Remedies for wrongful dismissal

1 Introduction

9.1 The most common form of remedy for breach of the employment contract is the claim for damages arising from a wrongful dismissal. One major consequence of the recent widening of the jurisdiction of the employment tribunal to include claims for breach of contract has been to revive this cause of action[1]. In general terms the approach of the court or tribunal to the assessment of damages in such a case is to follow normal contractual principles and this should be relatively uncontroversial[2]. However, recent years have seen a suprising degree of development in this area and there is now a strong basis for contending that, in certain albeit limited instances, the classical contractual approach is no longer applicable to employment claims.

1 See the Employment Tribunals Extension of Jurisdiction (England and Wales) Order 1994, SI 1994/1623 and the Employment Tribunals Extension of Jurisdiction (Scotland)Order 1994, SI 1994/1624; see para 1.3, above.
2 For a detailed overview of these principles see *Harvey on Industrial Relations and Employment Law* Div A.

2 Basic principles of recovery

9.2 The classic statement of traditional contractual orthodoxy in this area remains the decision of the majority of the Court of Appeal in *Lavarack v Woods of Colchester Ltd*[1]. The decision remains instructive because of the powerful dissenting judgment of Lord Denning MR which clarified the two competing approaches to assessment adopted in that case. For a proper understanding of the legal issues some reference to the material facts is necessary: Mr Lavarack was employed in a senior position on an annual salary of not less than £4,000 per annum. A substantial part of his remuneration package was made up of bonus payments and the contractual provision dealing with such bonuses provided that he was entitled to 'such bonus (if any) as the directors . . . shall from time to time determine.' Mr Lavarack was wrongfully dismissed and brought a claim for damages as a result. The factual background was complicated by the fact that in the period immediately after his dismissal the employer altered its remuneration structure and ended the bonus scheme replacing it in the majority of cases with higher salary payments. In the meantime Mr Lavarack had mitigated his loss by taking employment at a lower level of salary. He had also purchased half of the share capital in his new employer. At first instance Mr Lavarack was awarded damages on the basis that he too would have received an increase in his basic salary if he had remained in employment with the defendant. On appeal the Court of Appeal was split on the proper approach to be taken to the withdrawal of the bonus scheme and the corresponding increase in salary.

The leading judgment of the majority was given by Diplock LJ who recognised that the issue in dispute gave rise to a 'question of law of some importance.' He analysed the wording of the contractual documentation and concluded that there was no contractual *right* as such to the bonus. Diplock LJ directed himself in accordance with the general proposition that in an action for breach of contract a defendant is not liable in damages for not doing that which he is not bound to do. It followed that where there are several ways in which the contract might be performed when assessing damages the mode is adopted which is the least profitable to the claimant and the least burdensome to the defendant. As the judge put it:

> 'The law is concerned with legal obligations only and the law of contract only with legal obligations created by mutual agreement between contractors – not with expectations, however reasonable, of one contractor that the other will do something that he has assumed no legal obligation to do. And so if the contract is broken or wrongly repudiated, the first task of the assessor of damages is to estimate as best he can what the plaintiff would have gained in money or money's worth if the defendant had fulfilled his legal obligations and had done no more.' ([1967] 1 QB 294C to D).

Applying these principles to the facts of the case Diplock LJ concluded that the employer was under no legal obligation to continue the bonus scheme which had been discontinued. Furthermore, Mr Lavarack had no contractual right to any higher salary payment which might have become due under some imaginary future agreement which the defendant did not make with him but might have done if it had wished. It followed that there could be no award to reflect the loss of bonus.

1   [1967] 1 QB 278.

9.3   As has been noted above the dissenting view was contained in the judgment of Lord Denning MR who felt that the task of the court when assessing damages for wrongful dismissal was to calculate the sums which the claimant might *reasonably* have expected to receive in his old employment and deduct from this sum any payments received by way of mitigation. With regard to the bonus issue the judge did not accept the contention that simply because the claimant had no legal right to receive a bonus in the relevant year he was not entitled to receive compensation for loss of future bonuses. The basis for refusing to accept that contention was that in wrongfully dismissing the employee the employer had deprived him of the chance of receiving such bonuses in the future and he was entitled to be compensated for the loss of that chance. Lord Denning MR also rejected the contentions based upon the principle that the mode to be adopted when assessing damages is that which is the least profitable to the claimant and the least burdensome to the defendant in the following terms:

> 'But that has no application here. There were not two ways in which this contract could be performed. There was only one way, namely, by the

claimant performing his service and the defendants paying him for it. In such a case the compensation is to be based on the probabilities of the case – on the remuneration which the claimant might reasonably be expected to receive – and not on the bare minimum necessary to satisfy the legal right.' ([1967] 1 QB 278 at 288 E to F).

As to the argument that the bonus scheme was discontinued and Mr Lavarack thereby lost the right to all future bonus losses Lord Denning MR said:

> 'I cannot see this. . ..The defendants, by wrongfully dismissing him, have deprived him of the chance of getting either future bonuses or their equivalent – an increase in salary in lieu of bonus: and he is entitled to compensation for loss of the chance. The value of the chance in this case was considerable. The master was satisfied that, if he had not been dismissed, he would have got £2,000 by way of increase in salary. So he has lost this sum. I think he should be allowed it . . . ' ([1967] 1 QB 278 at 289D to F).

In *Lavarack* we can therefore see a clear division being drawn between what may be termed the strict legalistic approach of the majority and the more practical and equitable approach of the minority. To the modern employment lawyer the approach of the majority does not dovetail well with the present understanding of the employment relationship and its legal obligations. There appears to be little doubt that the result in *Lavarack* was unduly harsh on the dismissed employee. In particular it is relevant to note that in practical terms the employer saw the bonus scheme as being more than just a system which could be withdrawn at its own whim. This is well illustrated by the fact that in the vast majority of cases its withdrawal was accompanied by a substantial increase in salary. Furthermore it is also relevant to note that in the year immediately preceding the dismissal Mr Lavarack received a bonus of £3,500 in the context of an annual salary of £4,000. In this context it was a wholly unrealistic assumption to conclude that his employment could ever have continued for a further period without either a bonus payment or a substantial increase in salary.

9.4   It is necessary to make a number of points here. The first is that Lord Denning's approach to assessment was also couched in the language of normal contractual principles the principal difference being that he was willing to deploy the principle that the courts may assess damages on the basis of the loss of a chance in an appropriate case in order to reach a just result. Secondly, and this may have some resonance in the modern context, Diplock LJ specifically recognised that there was no allegation of bad faith made against the employer. The bonus scheme was withdrawn as a matter of policy and this action was not directed at Mr Lavarack or his claim. Indeed as discussed below it may well be that this is the real basis upon which the decision can be reconciled with both the recent authorities on damages and the developments in implied terms in the modern context. It is also worth noting that the decision was reached before the implementation of the law on unfair dismissal. There is no doubt that the broader approach to the assessment of compensation for unfair dismissal would have embraced the bonus element in this case and it is the application of these broader principles on a regular basis which has led to both employers and employees being more familiar with the legal recovery of sums which are based more upon legitimate expectations rather than hard legal rights.

However, despite its limitations the traditional contractual orthodoxy has continued to be applied. A modern example of its application is *Focsa Services (UK) Ltd v Birkett*[1]. In that case an employment tribunal had arrived at the rather fantastical conclusion that it was entitled to sidestep the niceties of statutory qualifying periods by finding that it was an implied term of the contract of employment that an employee had the right not to be unfairly dismissed. Accompanying this was a factual finding that if the employer had followed a fair procedure the employee would not have been dismissed and the tribunal went on to assess damages on the same basis as a compensatory award for unfair dismissal. On appeal the EAT robustly applied the normal contractual orthodoxy and allowed the appeal following the decisions in *Boyo* and *Gunton*[2].

It is of interest to note that in *Focsa* no arguments appear to have been advanced on the basis that there was some suggestion from the tribunal that the employer had acted in bad faith and dismissed the employee on a whim. A further reference to bad faith was made in a later decision of another division of the EAT in *Janciuk v Winerite Ltd*[3]. In that case the appellant was seeking to argue that he was entitled to damages for the loss of the chance that if the contractual disciplinary procedure had been applied to him he would not have been dismissed. His claim was rejected by the EAT by reference to the decision in *Lavarack* holding that the proper measure for damages in such a situation was to assess how long the employment would have continued if the employer had performed the contract in the least burdensome manner. In the circumstances of that case the relevant period was simply how long it would have taken to go through the procedure and no account should be taken of the possibility that dismissal would not have resulted. However, although *Janciuk* is undoubtedly a robust application of the *Lavarack* principles, there is the tantalising reference to the absence of bad faith in the decision of the EAT. It was specifically stated that the result reached in that case was 'on the assumption that the employer has not been accused of acting in bad faith where other principles might apply.'

1   [1996] IRLR 325.
2   For a fuller discussion of these authorities see para 7.3, above.
3   [1998] IRLR 63.

9.5   It is therefore necessary when looking at possible future developments in this area to consider what precisely is meant by bad faith in this context. The starting point is the fact that *Lavarack* was decided before the modern developments in the implied term of trust and confidence began and it must obviously be assumed that Diplock LJ was not reserving the position on the basis of a breach of such a term. However, this does not necessarily mean that the breach of the implied term of trust and confidence should not have an impact in this area. Indeed we have seen in Chapter 5 a role for this implied term in relation to forms of post-termination remuneration such as share schemes and pensions. On this basis it appears difficult to justify the exclusion of the implied term in this context. Alternatively we may be in the territory of the category of bad faith identified by Burton J in *Clark v Nomura International plc*[1] as adopted by the Court of Appeal in *Mallone v BPB Industries Ltd*[2]. It is submitted that there is a potentially significant difference between the two implied terms which may be of relevance. In relation to the *Nomura* type term there would be no basis for creating a legal right to a particular payment simply on the basis of the perverse exercise of a discretion. It is clear that in both *Nomura* and *Mallone* there was a pre-existing contractual right to the payment in question so long as the discretion was exercised appropriately. To this extent the intervention envisaged by *Nomura* would not run against the approach of Diplock LJ in *Lavarack*. However the implied term of trust and confidence is arguably not so limited and may create a right to a payment where otherwise there was no such pre existing right[3]. A clear example can be made from the facts of *Lavarack* itself in the sense that it would be strongly arguable that a failure to have provided Mr Lavarack with an increase in salary in recognition of the termination of the bonus scheme may well have amounted to a breach of the implied term of trust and confidence[4]. In such a situation it would be strongly arguable that he would be entitled to recover his loss not on the basis of Lord Denning's loss of a chance or reasonable expectation but on the basis of a breach of the implied term.

Indeed there is some insight into the above debate in High Court decision of *Clark v BET*[5]. In that case the court had to assess two particular elements of loss in a wrongful dismissal claim which are of interest in this context. The first related to the exercise of an absolute discretion by the employer when assessing an upward adjustment of annual salary (there being a contractual right to an annual increase). The second related to a bonus payment where the contract set a maximum level but, importantly, no minimum level.

In dealing with the first issue Timothy Walker J said as follows:

> 'Accepting the principle that a defendant in an action for breach of contract 'is not liable for not doing that which he is not bound to do' per Diplock LJ in *Lavarack v Woods of Colchester* [1967] 1 QB 278, 294B-C, if the board had capriciously or in bad faith exercised its discretion so as to determine the increase at nil and therefore to pay Mr Clark no increase at all, that would have been a breach of contract ... the question I have to decide on the facts is what position Mr Clark would have been in had BET performed this obligation ... Nor should I assume that any discretion would have been exercised so as to give the least possible benefit to the claimant if such an assumption would on the facts be unrealistic ... ([1997] IRLR 348 at 349 para 11).

There would appear to be two legitimate ways of analysing the above passage. The first is to say that although the court paid lip service to the rule in *Lavarack* the reality is that the decision reached is no different in principle to that of Lord Denning's dissent in that case. There is certainly an uncanny degree of similarity between Lord Denning's reliance upon the bonus payments which the employee might reasonably expect from his employer and the realistic assumptions referred to in *BET*. Indeed *Lavarack* is open to criticism precisely because its point of reference is the legal minimum performance and not the realistic assumption. The second analysis would be that this is nothing more than a practical example of the impact of bad faith in this context which was also recognised by the majority in *Lavarack*. However this second analysis is perhaps more difficult to support when we consider the way in which the bonuses were dealt with in the *BET* case. Although the express terms of the contract did not give any right to a minimum bonus payment the court held that the employee did have the right to participate in the bonus scheme and it was on this basis that the judge felt able to distinguish the decision in *Lavarack*. However, he then commented as follows:

'Against this contractual background I have to assess what position Mr Clark would have been in had BET performed their obligation. Again I should not make unrealistic assumptions.' ([1997] IRLR 348 at 350 para 18).

Once again the above passage lends itself easily to the argument that what the judge has done is to effectively produce a hybrid of all three judgments in *Lavarack*. Although it remains necessary to prove some legal entitlement to the benefit in order to recover damages once this has been done it is no longer necessary to award the legal minimum which could be provided by the employer but rather to apply realistic assumptions to the facts on the basis of the application of good faith principles. If this approach is combined with developments in the implied term of trust and confidence it is not difficult to predict that the future will see a further undermining of the full blooded principle in *Lavarack*.

Before leaving this topic it may also be worth considering whether the decision of the House of Lords in *Johnson v Unisys* can be used to block further development of the implied term of trust and confidence in this area[6]. An argument may be raised on the basis that there is sufficient material in the speeches in that case to suggest that the implied term of trust and confidence does not apply to dismissal situations. It is difficult to see how such an argument can succeed in this context. This is because there is no attempt in this area to fetter the decision to dismiss. On the contrary the principles only come into play once a dismissal has been effective and the purpose of utilising the implied term would be to fix the appropriate level of damages on the basis of a proper analysis of the legal relationship between the parties which would have existed during the notice period. Against this background it is submitted that *Johnson* is no impediment to further moves away from the contractual orthodoxy of *Lavarack*.

1   [2000] IRLR 766.
2   [2002] IRLR 452, CA. For a detailed discussion of these authorities see chap 5.
3   In these circumstances there could be no objection raised on the basis that the implied term is being used to override an express term.
4   For a detailed discussion of the developments in the law of implied terms see chap 4. Failure to include the applicant employee in an enhanced redundancy scheme covering all others was held to breach the term (even though the result of a genuine mistake by the employer) in *BG plc v O'Brien* [2002] EWCA Civ 379 [2002] IRLR 444.
5   [1997] IRLR 348. By way of interest *Clark v BET* was one of the authorities relied upon by Burton J in *Clark v Nomura* – see further chap 5.
6   For a fuller discussion of *Johnson v Unisys* see para 4.9, above.

3   Further principles

9.6   Aside from the controversy which presently surrounds the modern application of the principles in *Lavarack* the remaining issues which need to be covered when assessing damages in a wrongful dismissal context are well established. The clearest and most detailed analysis can still be found in the High Court judgment in *Shove v Downs Surgical plc*[1]. In essence the approach of the court is to assess the level of remuneration which the employee was legally entitled to receive if the employment had continued for the relevant period of notice. From these sums must be deducted all money earned by way of mitigation with appropriate reductions for income tax. These principles are well known and are not dealt with further here[2].

1   [1984] ICR 532.
2   See *Butterworths Employment Compensation Calculator*.

4   Damages for injury to feelings or reputation

9.7   As has been considered elsewhere in this book the effect of the decision of the House of Lords in *Johnson v Unisys* has been to block any further developments of the law on the recovery of damages for injury to feelings or reputation on dismissal[1]. However, there remains a small residual category of cases where similar types of claim can be made. The most obvious example is where it is an express or implied term of the contract of employment that the employee will be given the opportunity to obtain publicity in their trade. In these circumstances the employee may make a claim for the lost opportunity of enhancing their reputation[2].

1   See further para 4.9, above.
2   See *Collier v Sunday Referee Publishing Co Ltd* [1940] 2 KB 647.

5   PILON clauses

9.8   A further area which has caused some considerable debate in recent years is the effect of contractual terms which give the employer the right to lawfully terminate a contract with immediate effect by making an appropriate payment in lieu of notice (commonly known as a PILON clause)[1]. These provisions have proved to be something of a double edged sword for employers and employees alike. The starting point was the decision of the Court of Appeal in *Abrahams v Performing Right Society Ltd*[2]. In that case the employment contract contained a PILON clause which provided that the contract could be terminated either on notice or summarily on payment of a sum in lieu of notice. The employment was terminated summarily and a dispute arose as to whether or not the employee was under an obligation to mitigate his loss or whether he was entitled to the relevant payment in lieu as part of a liquidated damages claim. The Court of Appeal held that the relevant clause was indeed a liquidated damages clause and there was no obligation on the employee to mitigate his loss. The employer's argument that it had wrongfully dismissed the employee and the normal principles as to mitigation applied was rejected in robust terms by Hutchison LJ as follows:

> 'In my judgment [the claimant] is plainly right about this and I conclude that the termination of the contract was lawful and left the [claimant] with a right to a payment in lieu. . ..' ([1995] ICR 1028 at 1037G).

However, it then became a hotly disputed topic as to whether, on a proper analysis, *Abrahams* was a decision based upon the specific contractual wording in that case or involved some wider proposition of law which could be advanced in any case which involved a PILON clause. The issue then came before the Court of Appeal again in *Cerberus Software Ltd v Rowley*[3]. Interestingly the judgment has echoes of *Lavarack* in that it involved a majority decision with a strong dissenting judgment once again purporting to be based upon traditional contractual orthodoxy. It is relevant to note that the contractual term which was considered in *Cerberus* was drafted in a different form to the one in *Abrahams*. Importantly the provision in *Cerberus* provided that the employer might make a payment in lieu of notice and in this respect it was materially different to the provision which applied in *Abrahams* where such a discretion was not reserved to the employer[4].

The majority of the Court of Appeal dealt with the matter as an issue of construction. In view of the fact that the relevant provision only provided that the employer might make a payment in lieu of notice it was considered to be inconsistent with the employee having a contractual right to such a payment. It followed that in the event that an employer elected not to exercise this right the dismissal was wrongful and the employee was under a duty to mitigate his loss as a result. As stated above, however, the decision in *Cerberus* is primarily of interest because of the terms of the dissenting judgment of Sedley LJ. As with *Lavarack* it is strongly arguable that the position had been reached in which the legalistic approach had brought about a result which was at odds with the reality and fairness of the position. Indeed Ward LJ himself stated when giving judgment for the majority that he could 'readily understand Mr Rowley's incredulity that his employers might be permitted to behave with bad faith yet not pay for it.'

In his dissenting judgment Sedley LJ remarked dryly that if this is the law, there is something wrong with it. He then went on to consider the legal basis upon which a conclusion could have been reached in Mr Rowley's favour. After expressing the general ethical principle that people ought to honour their contracts he said:

> 'Why then should it be the case that by breaking the contract rather than honouring it Cerberus have put the onus on Mr Rowley to find another job as quickly as practicable and to give them the benefit of what he earns in it? To say that it is because the breach has turned the debt into damages is to explain nothing: it is merely to make it possible to substitute one principle of law for another. The question is which should prevail. It is a question which arises in a context which is not morally neutral, for it is both a cogent and an ethically attractive analysis that an employee who does not voluntarily acquiesce in an entirely unjustified summary dismissal has not accepted the repudiation: he may not be able to force the employer to let him work out the period of notice, but what he can do is insist on being paid his salary. In this perfectly realistic manner he is affirming the contract and claiming a debt under it. This in my view is what happened with Mr Rowley.' ([2001] ICR 376 at 386 E to G).

Although Sedley LJ's powerful dissent has much to recommend it in terms of logic and principle it appears unlikely that its approach can be developed further in the near future absent any consideration by the House of Lords of the 'elective' and 'automatic' theories of termination which are dealt with elsewhere in this book[5]. It follows that judicial conservatism appears to have the upper hand in the area of PILON disputes which now appear to be limited to a consideration of the contractual term in question. If the term is sufficiently drawn to give the employer a choice as to whether or not to make the payment in lieu a wrongful dismissal and the accompanying duty to mitigate remains a legally permissible outcome. It follows that the effect of *Abrahams* appears now to be limited to cases where a more or less identical PILON provision is in place. However, the employer will need to recognise that if it wishes to retain the advantage of any post termination restrictions it will need to balance the desireability of requiring an employee to mitigate against the risk that post termination restrictions fall away. It may also be necessary for the relevant payment in lieu to be made on the termination itself[6].

1   There is some debate as to whether such provisions are lawful in the light of the statutory right to minimum notice under the ERA 1996, s 86; see para 3.30, above.
2   [1995] ICR 1028.
3   [2001] EWCA Civ 78, [2001] ICR 376.
4   Although see Sedley LJ's powerful dissent on this question too at [2001] ICR 376 at 389C.
5   See para 7.2, above. The House of Lords refused leave to appeal in *Cerberus* see [2001] ICR 1241.
6   See for example *Levett v Biotrace International plc* [1999] ICR 818, [1999] IRLR 375, CA.

6   Penalty clauses

9.9   In *Abrahams* an argument advanced by the employer that a PILON clause was unenforceable as a penalty was rejected by the Court of Appeal thereby confirming the application of normal contractual principles in this area. A further example of the law on penalty clauses being applied in an employment context is the decision of the EAT in *Giraud UK Ltd v Smith*[1]. In *Giraud* the relevant clause provided that a failure by the employee to give proper notice and work it out will result in a reduction from his final payment equivalent to the number of days short. The employee left his employment without notice and the employer refused to make payment to him of sums which were otherwise due and owing under his contract. The EAT dismissed the employer's appeal holding that the relevant provision was a penalty. This was on the basis that it was not based on any genuine pre-estimate of loss. It follows from the above that although it may be permissible for liquidated damages clauses to be enforceable in an employment context the courts and tribunals will be particularly wary of enforcing unjust provisions against employees in particular.

1   [2000] IRLR 763.

7   Account of profits

9.10   When considering the remedies which may occur on termination of an employment contract it is now necessary to have a brief consideration of the remedy of an account of profits after the judgment of the House of Lords in *A-G v Blake*[1]. It is important to recognise that the facts in *Blake* were, on any view, extraordinary involving as they did a traitor and a notorious and infamous spy. It is against this background that the controversial decision of the House of Lords that the remedy of an account of profits may be available in an employment context must be viewed. However, the House of Lords has determined that there is no reason in principle why such a remedy must in all circumstances be ruled out. In certain exceptional cases it may be the only means of the court achieving practical justice. However, it would appear that there is no legitimate basis for extending the availability of an account of profits into the general field of employment disputes. It is in this context that *Blake* can properly be seen as an extraordinary case based upon extraordinary facts[2].

1   [2001] IRLR 36.

2   The dissenting speech of Lord Hobhouse makes salutary reading in this regard: see [2001] IRLR 45 at para 55.

Chapter 10

Enforcing a contract of employment

1 Introduction

10.1 It is well known that the remedy of reinstatement or re-engagement in the statutory action for unfair dismissal has never worked to any significant extent. That is, however, nothing new because at common law a remedy of in some way enforcing the contract (either positively by court order, or negatively by striking down the dismissal) was very rare indeed. Three main reasons are cited for this. The first is that employment is viewed as a personal relationship which will not be enforced against an unwilling party[1]. The second is that in any event, the principal remedies of an injunction or specific performance are discretionary in nature and will not usually be granted where continuing enforcement would be difficult or impossible. The third is a 'parity of reasoning' argument, namely that as a court may not force an employee to work for a particular employer[2], so it should not force an employer to employ a particular employee. To these might be added the common law reality that if the dismissal was only wrongful through notice not having been given, and if notice was short anyway, all that would happen is that the employee would be put back into employment, only to be vulnerable to a lawful dismissal by being given the proper notice.

While it can certainly be argued that in modern employment conditions, where the employer is likely to be a large and relatively impersonal body rather than an individual (so that the 'personal relationship' to be enforced is now far less personal) the first argument ought to be less persuasive, and that care must be needed with 'parity of treatment' arguments because they do not take into account lack of parity of economic strength or bargaining position, nevertheless there has been no major movement towards contractual enforcement. The one longstanding exception has been the ability of an employer to enforce a valid, negative restraint of trade clause. Even here, however, the emphasis against enforcement can still be seen from (a) the sub-rule that an apparently negative clause will not be enforced if in reality it is a positive obligation on the employee[3], (b) as a variant, the sub-rule that even a negative clause will not be enforced if it is so strong that its practical effect is to force the employee to continue working for that employer, or starve[4], and (c) the recent decision in *Jack Allen (Sales and Service) Ltd v Smith*[5] by Lord Johnston in the Outer House of the Court of Session that in order to claim an interim interdict the employer must show not just breach by the employee of a valid restraint clause, but also that the employer is likely to suffer actual harm which needs to be prevented by the interim order (ie no enforcement as a matter of principle)[6].

1 *De Francesco v Barnum* (1890) 45 Ch D 430; *Whitwood Chemical Co v Hardman* [1891] 2 Ch 416, CA.
2 This rule could be seen at common law, particularly in the pre-TUPE law that an employee could not be made to transfer to a new employer on a business transfer: *Nokes v Doncaster Amalgamated Collieries Ltd* [1940] AC 1014, [1940] 3 All ER 549, HL. It is now put into legislative form in the Trade Union and Labour Relations (Consolidation) Act 1992, s 236 which states that no court may, by way of an order for specific performance or specific implement of a contract of employment, or an injunction or interdict restraining a breach or threatened breach of such a contract, compel an employee to do any work or attend any place for the doing of any work. On the other hand it could be argued that an injunction to prevent a strike may have that effect in practice.
3 *Davis v Foreman* [1894] 3 Ch 654; *Warner Bros Pictures Inc v Nelson* [1937] 1 KB 209, [1936] 3 All ER 160.
4 *Page One Records Ltd v Britton* [1967] 3 All ER 822, [1968] 1 WLR 157; *Warren v Mendy* [1989] ICR 525, [1989] IRLR 210, CA. Both cases concerned unsuccessful attempts by managers to prevent their clients from leaving them by trying to enforce apparently negative stipulations which would in practice have forced them to continue to employ the original manager, or no-one else; the latter case concerned the boxer Nigel Benn and the former case The Troggs, apparently a popular beat combo of the day.
5 [1999] IRLR 19, Ct of Sess.
6 The case is a strong one, because this was not merely dicta – an interim interdict was discharged because on the facts the employer had failed to show the necessary potential harm.

10.2 The question has always been whether the possibility of direct or indirect enforcement will be permitted to go beyond this established exception. This complex and difficult area will be considered in three ways – how the automatic/elective theories fit in here, whether a court will enforce a contract of employment or any particular part thereof in a private law action, and whether judicial review can be used to challenge a dismissal or other breach of contract in a public law action. The general picture seems to be that examples of a court, in one way or another, preventing a wrongful dismissal and enforcing continued employment as such are extremely rare; where we have seen some movement is towards possible enforcement of certain incidents of a contract of employment, particularly a contractually-binding disciplinary procedure[1]. If this is accepted, it is in itself interesting because it could be seen as the law in effect holding the ring and ensuring fair play and adherence to the rules procedurally, without going as far as positive enforcement of what is still regarded as a personal relationship. The relative rarity of successful cases is shown not just numerically, but also by the fact that each such case tends to be followed by enthusiastic journal articles and case notes, in each of which the phrase 'the new remedy' seems to figure prominently. What will be argued here is that even when added together these developments (so diverse in nature and results) cannot yet be said to justify any such assertion, and that we as yet have no *reliable* remedy of contractual enforcement. One irony is that that was supposed to be provided by the law on unfair dismissal with its remedies of reinstatement and re-engagement, but it is a measure of the failure of that aspect of the statutory scheme that lawyers are still trying to mine the common law instead.

1 Note in this context that the Employment Bill before Parliament at the time of writing proposes to make the basic 'statutory procedure' for dismissal (contained within it) automatically part of all contracts of employment.

2 The effect of the elective/automatic controversy

10.3 We saw in Chapter 7 the continuing uncertainty over the theoretical basis for wrongful dismissal at common law, the two contenders being the automatic theory (that the contract automatically terminates when the employer repudiates it, so that the employee does not have the choice of refusing to accept the repudiation) and the elective theory (that contracts of employment are not formally an exception to the usual contractual requirement of repudiation and acceptance, so that, in theory at least, the employee could refuse to accept the employer's repudiation). In general, the elective theory tends to have the preponderance of modern authority since *Gunton v Richmond-upon-Thames London Borough Council*[1], but this theory has to be hedged around with qualifications in order to make it realistic, in particular (a) that it will in practice be easy to find acceptance by the employee, especially where the practicalities are such that he or she really has no choice but to accept that the employment is dead, and (b) that there remains a strong emphasis (at the least) against enforcing a personal contract that will apply to most conceivable cases. The latter point is particularly important because the common law tends to approach this question very much as a matter of remedies, rather than approaching it from the standpoint of substantive rights. However, one can at least discern at this point the ultimate difference between the two theories – the automatic theory views the non-enforceability of an employment contract as a matter of law (subject to the specific exception of restraint clauses), whereas the elective theory views non-enforceability as the application of remedies rules to the facts of employment cases, with the arguments against enforcement normally being dominant in the large majority of cases, *but* with the *possibility* of enforcement proceedings in untypical cases. This then places all the emphasis on whatever rules may have evolved in the remedies context as to when a court will feel able to give consideration to some sort of direct remedy, rather than proceeding directly to awarding damages.

1   [1980] ICR 755, [1980] IRLR 321, CA, though see para 7.3, above for the reservations expressed more recently in *Boyo v London Borough of Lambeth* [1994] ICR 727, [1995] IRLR 50, CA.

3 · Enforcement in a private law action

10.4   It is to these rules (or, at least, considerations) on remedies that we now turn. *Hill & C A Parsons & Co Ltd*[1] has been the cornerstone here, with much of the dispute being as to what it does and does not establish. As pointed out already[2], it is important to see the case in its now-historical setting, and any analysis of it is made more difficult by the fact that there was a definite 'agenda' behind the decision of the majority, wanting to do justice to the individual as they saw it, and using the available law to that end[3]. One basis of this was to hold that the normal 'rule' against enforcement is not a fixed rule of law, but rather a question of (frequently-recurring) fact which therefore admits of the possibility of enforcement in untypical cases where the usual factors against it do not apply. At first, *Hill* was narrowly construed[4], at a time when the new law on unfair dismissal was coming on stream and seemed to be a much preferable way of developing employee rights. Subsequently, however, there have been a few notable examples of orders in some way enforcing contracts or elements thereof, but the problem has been, in the words of one judge, that 'such exceptional cases as there have been give no very clear picture of the criteria for intervention'[5]. In the light of this, and the above remarks on *Hill*, it may be helpful to consider the case law in two ways – to look first at the categories into which the cases fall (in the sense of what was being enforced or prevented), and then secondly to try to isolate the factors influencing judges in cases where orders have been made.

It is suggested that the cases can be seen as falling into five categories, in relation to what was being sought by the employee.

1   [1972] Ch 305, [1971] 3 All ER 1345, CA.
2   At para 7.4, above.
3   This was the case, for example, in which Lord Denning memorably remarked that the principle *'ubi jus ibi remedium'* allowed the court to 'step over the trip-wires of previous cases and to bring the law into accord with the needs of today'. How the great man would have loved the Human Rights Act 1998, though quite what his version of it would have entailed we can only guess!
4   *GKN (Cwmbran) Ltd v Lloyd* [1972] ICR 214; *Sanders v Ernest A Neale Ltd* [1974] 3 All ER 327, [1974] ICR 565; *Chappell v Times Newspapers Ltd* [1975] 2 All ER 233, [1975] ICR 145.
5   *Anderson v Pringle of Scotland Ltd* [1998] IRLR 64, OH, per Lord Prosser at 67.

(a)   Restraining a wrongful dismissal *per se*

10.5   This would be the most radical form of order, restraining a dismissal simply *because* it is or would be wrongful. As suggested above, there is the immense logical problem here of what it would be that was being enforced – long-term employment into the future would be out of the question, and so one would be thrown back on to the common law doctrine of notice[1]; if not, there would be the inherent unfairness that employee A, because not given the four weeks' notice under the contract would get an order keeping him in employment indefinitely, whereas employee B who happened to have actually been given his four weeks' notice would have no rights at all. Thus, the question arises whether ultimately it would ever be possible to enforce employment for more than the notice period (unless the contract contained some unusual stipulation supplanting notice as the proper form of termination). *Hill* itself is arguably the only decision to come within this widest category, but even here all that was being restrained was a dismissal without the proper notice, the point being that 'proper' notice (as quantified by the court, in the lack of an express provision) would then bring the employee under the new provisions of the Industrial Relations Act 1971; at that point, his protection (from any similar industrial action to get rid of him) would be under the Act, not under any further common law right to continued employment.

1   See para 3.29, above.

(b)   Restraining unlawful disciplinary action

10.6   In *Peace v City of Edinburgh Council*[1] a teacher was threatened with being disciplined under a relatively new disciplinary procedure imposed by his employers; he claimed that the correct procedure was the previous one (requiring a hearing by elected council members, rather than a senior local government officer) which formed part of his contract of employment, and which he had not agreed to vary. Lord Penrose in the Outer House of the Court of Session found in favour of the teacher's application for an interdict restraining the employer from proceeding in accordance with the new disciplinary procedure. The employer had argued that, even if the use of the new procedure was in breach of contract, the court had no power to restrain that use, but the court disagreed, for reasons considered below. This category is a good example of the use of enforcement proceedings in relation to a *specific element* of the contract. However, not surprisingly, one can point immediately to another case with a similar objective, which failed. In *Ali v London Borough of Southwark*[2] a care assistant, against whom serious allegations had been made, was the subject of an internal inquiry which found a prima facie case against her; when the council stated its intention to proceed to a disciplinary hearing on the basis of the inquiry's report but without further consideration of the evidence, she sought an injunction to restrain any hearing without adducing further evidence and witnesses, which she claimed was a breach of her contractually-binding disciplinary procedure. Millett J held that, even assuming a contractual breach, no injunction would be granted.

1   [1999] IRLR 417, OH. *Barras D'Sa v Unversity Hospital Coventry and Warwickshire NHS Trust* [2001] EWCA Civ 983, [2001] IRLR 691 (injunction to restrain chief executive from acting on grounds not considered by internal inquiry, as provided for in contractual procedures) can be seen as analogous.
2   [1988] ICR 567, [1988] IRLR 100, Ch D.

(c)   Restraining a dismissal decided upon in breach of procedure

10.7   This can be seen as a hybrid of (i) and (ii), seeking to restrain the dismissal itself, but on the specific ground of breach of procedure. In *Irani v Southampton and South West Hampshire Health Authority*[1], a case which at the time seemed significant in reviving and seeking to extend the decision in *Hill*, the claimant was an NHS ophthalmologist involved in a dispute with his superior; an ad hoc panel of inquiry, not operating according to Whitley Council disputes procedures, found that the differences between the two were insoluble and recommended the dismissal of the claimant, who was given six weeks' notice. He sought an interim injunction restraining the health authority from implementing the dismissal notice until they had carried out the necessary disputes procedure; this was granted by Warner J, who saw it as necessary to prevent the employer from 'snapping its fingers' at the rights of its employees under the conditions of service. Similar decisions can be seen in *Wadcock v London Borough of Brent*[2], where Mervyn Davies J granted an interim injunction restraining the dismissal by notice of a social worker (who was in dispute as to his contractual obligations) without having gone through the proper disciplinary procedure, and in *Robb v London Borough of Hammersmith and Fulham*[3] where Morland J granted an injunction restraining the defendant authority from treating the employee, summarily dismissed without exhaustion of the contractually binding procedure, as no longer in their employment. This third category is thus where most success has occurred, but one variant of it has caused judicial disagreement. This is where an attempt has been made to challenge a dismissal in breach, not of a disciplinary procedure (as above) but of an agreed *redundancy* procedure. Can this be restrained? In *Alexander v Standard Telephone & Cables Ltd*[4] employees selected for redundancy contrary to the redundancy procedure in the applicable collective agreement sought to restrain their dismissals, but failed. Aldous J first held that the provisions of the collective agreement relating to redundancy selection (based on LIFO) were *not* incorporated into the claimants' contracts of employment[5]; this alone was enough to wreck their interim applications, but the judge also held that in any event this was not an appropriate case for an order restraining a breach of contract – the normal rule against enforcement remained, *Irani* and *Powell* (para 10.8, below) were characterised as highly unusual cases, and an order would be inappropriate in a redundancy case because there would be by definition no work for a reinstated employee to do unless the employer dismissed another employee instead. A very different conclusion was reached, on the other hand in *Anderson v Pringle of Scotland Ltd*[6] where, on very similar facts (negotiated LIFO agreement for redundancy selection being ignored by employers, in favour of a selective scheme to which the employees had not agreed), Lord Prosser granted an interim interdict restraining the dismissal of employees selected under the selective scheme. A key difference was that here the Court of Session was prepared to hold (for interim purposes) that the redundancy provisions of the collective bargain *were* incorporated into the employees' contracts. The court then went on to decide that the normal rule against enforcement admits of exceptions, and that this was one, the judge commenting that the case was one, like *Irani*, where it was the mechanisms of dismissal rather than the principle of dismissal that were at the heart of the matter.

1   [1985] ICR 590, [1985] IRLR 203, Ch D.
2   [1990] IRLR 223, Ch D.
3   [1991] ICR 514, [1991] IRLR 72, Ch D.
4   [1990] ICR 291, [1990] IRLR 55, Ch D.
5   This was eventually the reason for the failure of the action for damages at full hearing: *Alexander v Standard Telephones & Cable Ltd (No 2)* [1991] IRLR 286, QBD.
6   [1998] IRLR 64, OH. The judgment contains an interesting 'balance of convenience' argument relating to the injunction – if not granted, the employee would lose his job before the issue could come to trial, but if it were granted the employers (though placed in a difficult position) would not on the facts face any risk of disaster.

(d)   Restraining a collateral breach of contract

10.8   The fourth category is where the employee is seeking to prevent an actual or intended breach of his or her contractual rights, short of dismissal and not concerning disciplinary proceedings[1]. *Powell v London Borough of Brent*[2] arose in most unusual circumstances. The claimant employee was interviewed for an internal promotion, and was informed that she had been successful. However, one of the unsuccessful candidates complained that the procedure had breached the council equal opportunities policy, and the claimant's appointment was cancelled, the post being re-advertised. Her solicitors wrote to the council to state that she did not accept this breach of contract and sought an interlocutory injunction restraining the re-advertising and requiring the council to treat her as appointed to the new post. The Court of Appeal granted the injunction in the terms sought, stating that this was an exceptional case, *not* trying to keep the employee in employment as such, but rather keeping alive her interest in the particular job for which she had shown herself to be qualified. Powell was cited shortly afterwards in *Hughes v London Borough of Southwark*[3] which arose from a more mainstream dispute concerning changes to work patterns to which the employees objected. These changes (to the responsibilities of social workers) were found by the judge to be in breach of contract; on the facts, the balance of convenience was in favour of preserving the status quo, of the claimants only being required to perform their existing duties, and an interim injunction was granted restraining the employees from implementing the changes.

By contrast, in *City and Hackney Health Authority v NUPE*[4] an attempt to split off a particular aspect from the main employment contract, for the purpose of enforcement, failed. An employee was suspended for investigation of allegations of gross misconduct in organising a protest occupation of a hospital. That employee was the accredited NUPE shop steward there, and the employers insisted that that accreditation was also suspended, meaning that he was barred from the hospital in that capacity too. He applied for an interim injunction to permit him to enter the hospital, but it was refused by the Court of Appeal, who considered that any shop steward rights (which could be contractual) were reliant on his overall employment contract which had been properly suspended.

1   There might in practice be a cross-over here, in that the employee may fear that, if the employer succeeds in forcing through a change of duties, terms, responsibilities, etc, through lack of

positive objection from the staff, the next stage might be disciplinary proceedings against individuals still unwilling to work under the new conditions.

2   [1988] ICR 176, [1987] IRLR 466, CA.
3   [1988] IRLR 55, QBD.
4   [1985] IRLR 252, CA.

(e)   Restraining dismissal pending trial of an existing action

10.9   In a sense, there is nothing particularly unusual about this category, in that it fits the very idea of, and rules relating to, interim relief as such, and several of the cases above are also examples of this. However, in the sense of actually enforcing the contract of employment as such (not just the notice period) there have been two cases which arguably pushed this category the furthest and have been criticised for departing too far from the normal rule against enforcement of an employment *relationship*. In *Wadcock v London Borough of Brent*[1] the council had reorganised its social work functions, in such a way that the claimant employee refused to comply with the new system, arguing that it was unacceptable, and holding himself ready to perform his 'usual work'. He was eventually dismissed with notice, not being required to work it out. He brought legal proceedings for a declaration that the new system was unlawful, claiming an interim?injunction restraining the council from acting on the dismissal. At the interim hearing, he gave undertakings to work under the new system for the time being. On that basis, an order was granted going much further in actually requiring the council to allow him to continue to *work* for them, at his usual rate of pay, pending full trial. Arguably, this goes beyond an order merely keeping the contract in being legally. The second case, *Jones v Gwent County Council*[2], is a very odd decision because of the granting of a declaration as to the status of a letter of dismissal at the interim stage (see below); challenging the procedure adopted for disciplining her, a college lecturer sought also an interim injunction, which was granted in two parts – a perpetual injunction preventing the employers from dismissing her pursuant to the particular letter of dismissal, and ('since the Council could not be relied on to act fairly and rationally in relation to the claimant's employment') an injunction until trial restraining the employers from dismissing her unless proper grounds exist and after carrying out a proper procedure in accordance with her contract of employment. The latter part of this was novel, to say the least.

1   [1990] IRLR 223, Ch D.
2   [1992] IRLR 521, Ch D.

10.10   Having considered the above categories of possible intervention, it is now necessary to look at the *grounds* on which intervention has been granted or refused in the cases. Again, a complicated picture emerges, with no obvious tie-up between any particular category and any particular ground. It is suggested that at least the following five grounds can be seen in the cases, in the sense of being *factors* for the court to consider in exercising its overall discretion:

(i)   Continuing trust and confidence between the parties

10.11   This has been the principal ground upon which enforcement has been ordered in the cases, stemming from *Hill's* case itself[1], where the argument was that the employer had not lost confidence in Mr Hill, but was being induced to be rid of him by the trade union (which objected to his non-membership). It is interesting to note that this development occurred before the development of the implied term of trust and respect[2], which resembles it but arose in a different context and in response to a different need. Moreover, the 'trust and confidence' theory is useful in explaining why in the vast majority of cases there is no question of direct enforcement, given that in most cases the parties are in fact at each others' throats (at least metaphorically). By way of analogy, it is also interesting to see a recent reaffirmation of its role in the law of unfair dismissal as one of the factors operating against the remedy of reinstatement or re-engagement[3].

The importance of arguments of continuing trust and confidence on the facts of the particular/exceptional case can also be seen in *Powell v London Borough of Brent*[4] (promoted employee was clearly thought worthy of the new job by the employers) and in *Wadcock v London Borough of Brent*[5] (court accepted that the employee was a good social worker who would perform properly in the new work, given his undertaking to do so pending full trial). Conversely, in *Ali v London Borough of Southwark*[6] an order was refused partly on the ground that the employers no longer had confidence in the care assistant because of the allegations of mis-treatment of patients, which had received prima facie backing by an internal inquiry, and in *City and Hackney Authority v NUPE*[7] the court, having held that the employee's role as shop steward could not be divorced from his overall contract of employment, went on to find an unequivocal breakdown of confidence in him by the employers, due to his alleged involvement in the hospital occupation, which made entirely inappropriate an order effectively amounting to specific performance of that contract.

Obviously, the question of whether (in an untypical case) there can be said to be continuing mutual trust and confidence will be one of fact, However, two questions of principle have arisen, causing acute disagreements. The first is whether the applicant employee has to show *actual* trust and confidence, or whether there is a wider principle that it is enough to argue that, although there may be an actual breakdown in trust and confidence, it is on irrational grounds which are rectifiable (especially where the employee is trying to oblige the employer to go through proper procedures, in order to be able to exonerate himself). The former view (actual trust and confidence) is the simpler and more natural interpretation, and so for example in *Ali* Millett J, although alluding to the 'irrational grounds' element, still refused the injunction on the ground that (in the circumstances of the unresolved disciplinary charges) it was sufficient for the employers to show that they had lost confidence in the employee for the moment, on reasonable grounds. On the other hand, to take this simpler view could be unfair on the employee, ruling out a remedy on the employer's intransigence and own say-so. On that basis, Taylor J in *Hughes v London Borough of Southwark*[8] held that where there is not clear evidence of an irrevocable breakdown, mutual confidence is not to be defeated merely by the fact that the parties are in dispute as to their respective contractual rights and obligations.

The second, more specific, question of principle is whether the employer is to be treated as having continuing confidence in an employee who is being dismissed for redundancy. The point is that the whole idea of confidence or lack thereof fits more neatly into a case where the employee is being dismissed for some kind of misconduct. A redundancy dismissal, however, does not normally connote fault on the part of the employee. In *Alexander v Standard Telephones & Cables Ltd*[9], one of the reasons for Aldous J's refusal of an injunction to restrain a redundancy dismissal (argued to be in breach of contract as to the selection method) was that it could not be said that the employers retained complete confidence in the employee because, *ex hypothesi*, they had *less* confidence in him than in other members of the workforce who had not been selected. Thus, where there was not the work there for him to do, this constituted *sufficient* breakdown in confidence to activate the rule against enforcement, especially as the result of putting him back into employment would have been the dismissal instead of another employee thought more valuable. However, such arguments did not prevail in *Anderson v Pringle of Scotland Ltd*[10] where, although *Alexander* was not cited, Lord Prosser specifically disapproved of an analogy between the employer's preference for other employees and the need for confidence which is inherent in the employer/employee relationship. His remark that the circumstances would be different if there were any element of 'mistrust' is telling, and this approach in the Court of Session accepts that there *can* be continuing trust and confidence in a redundancy situation; the employers may, as the judge stated, suffer inconvenience and difficulty if a selected employee successfully challenges his dismissal, but if that selection was in breach of contract the employers cannot consider it unfair to be held to their own bargain, and cannot avoid that by claiming a breakdown in confidence. The contrast between these two cases of *Alexander* and *Anderson* is stark, on this point as on others.

1   [1972] Ch 305, [1971] 3 All ER 1345, CA.
2   See para 4.8, above.
3   In *Wood Group Heavy Industrial Turbines Ltd v Crossan* [1998] IRLR 680, EAT a dismissal for serious drug-related misconduct was found to be unfair on *procedural* grounds, but re-engagement was refused because the employers still had a strong belief in his guilt of the actual offence.
4   [1988] ICR 176, [1987] IRLR 466, CA. Here it was said that the sufficiency of the confidence must be judged by reference to the circumstances of the case, in particular the nature of the work, the people with whom the work must be done and the likely effect on the employer's undertaking of enforced continued employment.
5   [1990] IRLR 223, Ch D.
6   [1988] ICR 567, [1988] IRLR 100, Ch D. See also *Wishart v NACAB* [1990] ICR 794, [1990] IRLR 383, CA where the court refused to enforce a job offer which was not backed up by satisfactory references, on the basis of lack of confidence (Powell distinguished).
7   [1985] IRLR 252, CA.
8   [1988] IRLR 55, QBD.
9   [1990] ICR 291, [1990] IRLR 55, Ch D.
10 [1998] IRLR 64, OH.

(ii)   Intervention possible before termination

10.12   Simply as a matter of practicalities, a court may be more disposed to giving direct interim relief if the intervention can come before a dismissal takes effect, there being a difference between restraining a throwing out and an order trying to put the employee back in. This has been said to be one important factor in the decision in *Hill's* case[1] and, for example, in *Anderson* Lord Prosser commented that in the contemporary world intervention *before* dismissal must be seen as a matter of discretion, rather than impossibility. By analogy, this point can also be seen in the statutory rules on unfair dismissal where there is available (in some of the more 'sensitive' areas such as dismissal for trade union, health and safety, working time, worker representation or whistleblowing reasons) the direct remedy of an order for interim relief, continuing the contract until determination of the complaint, so that the employee is not left on the outside, trying to fight his or her way back in.

1   *GKN (Cwmbran) Ltd v Lloyd* [1972] ICR 214, NIRC, per Sir John Donaldson P.

(iii) The case concerns actions short of dismissal

10.13   The rule against enforcement evolved primarily in the context of dismissal and the extreme difficulty of requiring unwilling parties to work together again after such an event. However, we have seen cases above where the purpose of the action has been to restrain a contractual breach less than dismissal, and here there has been some success. In *Peace v City of Edinburgh Council*[1], where the Court of Session accepted that there could be an interdict restraining the use of a new disciplinary procedure that the employee claimed was contrary to his contract, Lord Penrose said that the court could control certain anticipated breaches of contract while the employment relationship subsists, and that 'modern employment contracts may include a range of provisions which may be enforced as between employer and employee during the subsistence of the employment without prejudice to any general rule that the courts will not enforce implement or continuing implement of a working relationship as such between employer and employee'. Cases concerning changes of work responsibilities or patterns may fit most neatly into this category, because by definition the parties want the relationship to continue. *Peace*, therefore, is a particularly strong case because the employee was restraining an improper disciplinary procedure which could, presumably, have led to dismissal *but* Lord Penrose held that it was enough for these purposes that the parties intended him to remain an employee at least until the proceedings were brought to a conclusion.

1   [1999] IRLR 417, OH.

(iv) Damages are not an adequate remedy

10.14   Again, this was a feature of *Hill's* case, and can be seen for example in *Powell* where, if the withdrawal of the promotion was not restrained, the employee could sue for loss of earnings but not for the loss of a more stimulating and challenging job or for the distress and humiliation in having to return to her former job. This is an interesting approach, looking beyond purely monetary loss. However, much will of course depend on a court's view of what is an 'adequate' remedy, and there is scope for disagreement. The adequacy of damages as a remedy in a more normal case of wrongful dismissal was affirmed by Ferris J in *Marsh v National Autistic Society*[1], and a further argument along these lines may be that that adequacy is reinforced if, under the rule in *Gunton's* case[2], the employee can eventually obtain an award of wages for the notice period plus for the further period it would have taken to have gone through the disciplinary procedure properly.

1   [1993] ICR 453, Ch D; the case is also of interest for ruling out any remedy of continuing payment of wages, recoverable in debt, based on refusal to accept the repudiatory conduct, see para 7.3, above.
2   [1980] ICR 755, [1980] IRLR 321, CA.

(v) An enforcing order would in practice be effective

10.15   Potential lack of effectiveness has always been one of the factors behind the normal rule against enforcement. If, to the contrary, a claimant can show that on the facts of the case an order would actually work, that may be an important consideration for the court. In some cases, this may simply give more substance to other factors considered above, but in *Robb v London Borough of Hammersmith & Fulham*[1] it was envisaged as being a possible *alternative* to the factor of continuing trust and confidence, at least where the aim of the proceedings is not the enforcement of the employment as such, but rather the requirement that proper procedures be adopted. Indeed, this could be set alongside the wider view of trust and confidence, namely that it might be sufficient that it could be restored through the effective use of proper procedures.

1   [1991] ICR 514, [1991] IRLR 72, Ch D.

10.16   Three points are offered by way of conclusion. The first is that it must be reaffirmed that these matters are not principles or rules of law, but rather they are factors which may sway a court, either singly or in combination. One case is difficult to fit into this analysis. In *Jones v Gwent County Council*[1], in addition to granting the interim injunctions as seen above, Chadwick J also issued a declaration as to the contractual validity of the suspension and letter of dismissal of the employee that lay at the heart of the claim. This was done under RSC Ord 14 A (now Part 24 of the CPR) which allows a question of law or construction of a document to be adjudicated upon if it appears that to do so will determine the claim. The problem was that the judge held that this power could be exercised *without* having regard to the normal rules on enforcement, in particular to questions of trust and confidence. Technically, of course, a declaration does not 'enforce' the contract, but in practice it could have the effect of deciding the case one way or the other. It is submitted that this procedure should not be permitted to be used as a back-door method of enforcement, avoiding the need for the careful balancing exercise that the courts have to go through.

The second point is simply the observation that the more recent English cases have nearly all involved public sector employees, though there is no reason in law why this should be so. The cynic might say that whatever remedy may lie here, it is only in practice for the employees of certain London boroughs!

The third point is, in a sense, to state the obvious, which is that this is complex law, with little certainty of a remedy of enforcement being granted. If one views this as primarily a remedy aimed at protecting long-term job security, then it does not work. Taking up the point made in *Anderson* that there is more chance of success if the challenge is to the 'mechanisms' of dismissal rather than dismissal itself, what an employee might gain by some, more limited form of enforcement is a tactical advantage over the employer. Such an advantage should not be underestimated, and it may be that in some cases the advantage could in practice be determinative. That, however, will depend on circumstances and practical realities generally, not just the legalities of an enforcing order.

1   [1992] IRLR 521, Ch D.

4   Enforcement in a public law action

10.17   The final question is whether there can be a form of enforcement through the invocation of public law principles and remedies. This would apply almost entirely in the public sector, though technically there is no reason why, in an appropriate case, it might not arise in the private sector.

This area has a considerable pedigree, though again the overall point is that it has provided anything but a widespread or reliable remedy, and lawyers are left to pick over the bones of the carcasses of such case law as there has been. As before, in the case of enforcement by private law action, the odd successful case has caused great excitement and much academic interest, but it has to be said that the area has been fairly dead for the last decade. The remarkably complicated law here is considered in detail elsewhere[1], and it is not proposed to repeat it here. The basic position is that, in line with the general development of administrative law in the last four decades, we began to see some application of the new principles to certain forms of employment, subsequent to the decision of the House of Lords in *Ridge v Baldwin*[2] where a chief constable's dismissal without an opportunity to be heard was declared to be in breach of natural justice and void. A finding of invalidity has major effects here, constituting a form of reinstatement with full back benefits. Although other rules of natural justice might be relevant (especially ultra vires), the focus for development was the *audi alteram partem* rule; one historical facet of this was, of course, that this was before the enactment of the law of unfair dismissal, the procedural aspects of which now lend themselves to arguments similar to those on natural justice, if not necessarily called that.

The problem that immediately arose was that these novel remedies were never meant to be applicable to all employments, but deciding which were to be the favoured ones has proved almost impossible. It is one thing to say, as in the old authority of *Vine v National Dock Labour Board*[3], that the public law remedies do not apply to 'ordinary master and servant' cases, but quite another thing to apply such a distinction. Arguably, the nearest the courts came to an answer was in *Malloch v Aberdeen Corpn*[4] where a Scottish teacher whose employment was heavily regulated by statute was held by a majority of the House of Lords to be entitled to a hearing before dismissal. Lord Wilberforce's oft-quoted speech concentrates on elements of public service, statutory support and/or an 'office or status capable of protection'. This last is the elusive element, and the cases on it look distinctly odd when considered side by side.

1   See Smith & Wood *Industrial Law* (7th edn, 2000) Butterworths, pp 381–388; *Harvey on Industrial Relations and Employment Law* paras A [710] ff.
2   [1964] AC 40, [1963] 2 All ER 66, HL.
3   [1957] AC 488, [1956] 3 All ER 939, HL.
4   [1971] 2 All ER 1278, [1971] 1 WLR 1578, HL.

10.18   The position has been complicated further by two major factors. The first is that in our changed economy the public sector is much smaller, and within it the norm now is for people engaged in it (even at high levels) to be subject to much more ordinary employment contracts and relationships, with a decline in many areas of what traditionally were at least quasi-professional appointments and, indeed, 'offices'.

The second complication has been the development of specific rules on judicial review, especially since the introduction of the specialised Order 53 procedure. At this remedies end, the key test is not whether the applicant has the necessary *Malloch* 'status', but whether what he or she is complaining of is a 'public law matter'. Of course, a case could arise where the treatment of an employee was in breach of a statute or statutory instrument, in which case judicial review would be appropriate. However, most employment disputes (even at high levels in the public sector) are ultimately not questions as to the vires of their arrangements, but are questions simply of *breach* of their contract. This imports the well known problem of the public/private divide in administration law into the employment arena. Large-scale development here was largely stopped in its tracks by the decision of the Court of Appeal in *R v East Berkshire Health Authority, ex p Walsh*[1] where a senior nursing officer under a contract made pursuant to regulations was refused judicial review to challenge his dismissal as contrary to natural justice (no hearing) and ultra vires the prescribed procedure. The decision is a very strong one, holding that the nature of his complaint remained a private, contractual one. It was strongly based on the simple principle that such disputes belong in the tribunals or ordinary courts, *not* in the Divisional Court on application for judicial review. In *McClaren v Home Office*[2] (a case arising in the highly unusual context of prison officers) Woolf LJ tried to restate the position in four main principles, as follows:

- In relation to a personal claim against the employer, an employee of a public body is normally in exactly the same situation as other employees and can bring proceedings in the ordinary way for damages, a declaration or an injunction (except in relation to the Crown).
- An employee of a public body can seek judicial review and obtain a remedy which would not be available to an employee in the private sector where there exists some disciplinary or other body established under the prerogative or by statute to which the employer or employee is entitled or required to refer disputes affecting their relationship.
- In addition, if an employee of a public body is adversely affected by a decision of general application by his employer, he can be entitled to challenge that decision by way of judicial review on grounds that it is flawed.
- Judicial review will *not* be available where disciplinary procedures are of a purely domestic nature, albeit that their decisions might affect the public.

These principles underscore the narrowness of the approach to judicial review here. The reference to a declaration or injunction in (i) above shows that, in theory at least, there is still room for a non-judicial-review remedy in a case brought by claim (or treated as brought by claim under Ord 53, r 9(5) if wrongly begun as a judicial review action) relying on the public law concepts of natural justice, and here it seems that the old office/status-based principles in *Malloch* would still apply. This could, however, produce the odd results of (1) a claimant seeking what is basically a public law right in a case where the intended public law remedy of judical review is not applicable and (2) a public law right being in theory available to a private sector employee (albeit that this is highly unlikely in practice).

1 [1984] ICR 743, [1984] IRLR 278, CA.
2 [1990] ICR 824, [1990] IRLR 338, CA.

10.19   As stated above, this area has been largely dormant for some time now, and one of the few recent cases on it shows that the rules may be becoming even tighter. In *Blair v Lochaber District Council*[1] a council chief executive was suspended on full pay during an investigation into allegations made in an auditor's report. He brought judicial review proceedings on the basis that this decision was ultra vires, being in breach of the local government legislation and the council's own standing orders. Lord Clyde in the Court of Session dismissed the petition; the suspension was essentially concerned with the regulation of the contract of employment and so not a matter for the court's supervisory jurisdiction. In the course of his judgment the judge even cast doubt on the modern relevance of *Malloch* and the original case law:

'One factor which [counsel for the petitioner] highlighted was that the petitioner was a chief executive and could be seen as holding something like a public office. . ..The case was thus different from any ordinary case of employer and employee. [Counsel] referred to *Malloch v Aberdeen Corpn* and found some support. . .for the proposition that *at that stage in the development of this area of the law* the status of senior officials may have been considered significant. But I am not persuaded that the status of the petitioner, so long as he is an employee, is of particular relevance to the issue before me. The petitioner is not the holder of a public office in the sense of having an appointment outwith the ordinary nature of an employment contract. . ... The petitioner is subject to a personal contract between him and his employer and he has the ordinary remedies under contract law'.

It is submitted that this is the way the wind has been blowing ever since *ex p, Walsh*, and one is tempted to the simple conclusion – if a council's chief executive is not an officeholder able to claim the protection of public law remedies, who is?

1   [1995] IRLR 135, OH, following *West v Secretary of State for Scotland* [1992] IRLR 399, IH.

Chapter 11

Settlements

1 Introduction

11.1   This Chapter deals with the settlement of contractual employment disputes. Although on first impression this may be viewed as an area in which normal contractual principles apply there are two factors which have created particular difficulties for the settlement of such disputes. The first relates to the extensive development of the law in relation to implied terms as discussed elsewhere in this book[1] which has opened up wider categories of unforeseen liability and the problems which this brings for the conclusive resolution of disputes. The second is the impact of the statutory protections regarding the settlement of statutory employment claims such as unfair dismissal and race and sex discrimination. Although these statutory provisions do not apply directly to the contractual jurisdiction of employment tribunals[2] their impact is felt whenever there is a potential cross over between a statutory claim and an underlying claim in contract as will be the case in the vast majority of disputes.

The difficulties involved in the drafting of settlements which flow from the opening up of new categories of liability attendant upon the extension of implied terms is well illustrated by the extraordinary fact that a contest regarding the construction of a general release in an employment dispute has recently been considered by the House of Lords in *BCCI v Ali*[3]. It is also instructive to note that the judicial committee was divided upon the scope and effect of the settlement agreement in that case. Although the full ramifications of the decision in *Ali* are still to be played out there is little doubt that the need for prudence when seeking to secure finality to an employment dispute now requires that increasingly long and detailed forms of settlement agreement are adopted. When taken together with the impact of the various statutory provisions it would not be unfair to say that employment claims now represent a special category in which detailed and specific wording is required rather than all embracing generality in order to ensure a clean break between the parties. These developments have resulted in employment disputes being cut off from the general trend of contract law which is towards a more flexible approach to the construction of documents[4]. This is both regrettable and ironic since the employment field is one of the very areas which could be thought to benefit most from the modern approach.

1   Please see chaps 3 and 4.
2   For an interesting example of this see *Sutherland v Network Appliance Ltd* [2001] IRLR 12.
3   [2001] UKHL 8, [2001] ICR 337.
4   See *Investors Compensation Scheme v West Bromwich Building Society* [1998] 1 WLR 896.

2 The position at common law

11.2   At common law parties are free to settle their disputes by contract as they see fit. The position was succinctly summarised by Browne-Wilkinson J in *Gilbert v Kembridge Fibres Ltd*[1] as follows:

> 'As a matter of general principle parties to any dispute are capable of coming to an agreement out of court whereby they agree to compromise their dispute. The agreement to compromise once reached operates as a bar to the further pursuit of the dispute in courts or tribunals and the parties' rights thereafter become rights to enforce their compromise agreement. Such compromise agreements can be made either in writing or orally. There is no general provision in the law requiring such disputes to be made in writing.'

Over time a considerable body of learning has built up regarding the precise application of normal contractual principles to the settlement of disputes in all areas of the law[2]. However, this can realistically be seen as the development of a sensible body of rules and practices which reflect the special circumstances in which compromise agreements are entered into rather than being any retreat from normal contractual orthodoxy.

The law of contract also recognises that there may be certain circumstances which justify the setting aside of an agreement which has been made by the parties. The typical circumstances in which the Court may be willing to intervene in this way are where economic duress, undue influence or inequality of bargaining power can be established. However, these categories are of relatively limited utility in the employment field and are unlikely to provide much relief for the dismissed and vulnerable employee who lacks trade union support. The dismissed employee who is faced with the choice between signing away his rights at an undervalue or embarking upon the difficult and hazardous route of litigation may view his choice as unpalatable but in the eyes of the common law it represents a choice nonetheless.

1   [1984] ICR 188 at 189C.
2   Foskett *The Law and Practice of Compromise* (5th edn) Sweet & Maxwell remains the leading work.

3 Statutory intervention

11.3   It was against this common law background that Parliament felt it necessary to provide for special protections when dealing with the settlement of statutory claims. This willingness to intervene was no doubt in part because of the real possibility of undue pressure being placed upon vulnerable employees who are desperate to secure their financial survival. However, there is also a wider public importance in ensuring that statutory claims such as those alleging racial and sexual discrimination should be litigated in tribunals without unfair hindrance or pressure from the employer. Part of the legacy of this intervention by Parliament is that there is now unlikely to be any extension of the common law in this area. As stated above although the traditional basis for not recognising an agreement at common law had little or no role to play in the settlement of employment disputes there may well have been some mileage in an argument that Lord Steyn's formulation of the implied term of fair dealing[1] is now sufficiently advanced to give a court the power to set aside an unfair settlement of an employment dispute in an appropriate case. These arguments are now almost certainly sidelined by the decision of the House of Lords in *Johnson v Unisys*[2] in view of the present level of statutory intervention.

Statutory intervention has taken place in two distinct ways: first of all through the role of ACAS appointed conciliation officers; and secondly through the controlling mechanism of compromise agreements.

1   For an overview of the development of this term see chap 4.
2   [2001] UKHL 13, [2001] ICR 480.

4   Conciliation officers

11.4   The first approach adopted by Parliament was to provide that a settlement of a relevant statutory employment claim prior to a tribunal hearing could only be secured through the intervention of a conciliation officer. As a part of the general industrial climate in the late 1960s and 1970s the need for the fair arbitration of employment disputes was widely recognised. Accordingly ACAS was established with a pivotal role in the resolution of not only collective but also individual employment disputes. The statutory provisions dealing with conciliation officers are now contained in the ERA 1996, s 18[1]. These essentially provide for a conciliation officer to become involved in order to promote the settlement of employment disputes which can be litigated before employment tribunals. The involvement of the conciliation officer is mandatory where requested by both parties to the dispute. In other cases the conciliation officer may become involved if he considers that there is a reasonable prospect of settling the dispute even though his involvement has not been requested by the parties. The involvement of a conciliation officer is also not dependent upon a tribunal claim having been brought and it is sufficient if a dispute which *could* be brought before the tribunal is in existence. The public policy behind the involvement of conciliation officers was therefore not only to promote conciliation but also to ensure insofar as possible that a form of fair dealing took place between the parties.

The role and function of conciliation officers was strengthened by the fact that Parliament not only provided for them to become involved in employment disputes but also provided that an agreement to settle such a dispute would only be binding on the tribunal and the parties if it had been reached through the officer. Typically this would involve the officer incorporating the agreement of the parties in a 'COT3' form designed specifically for this purpose. This additional requirement was achieved by providing within the relevant statute which established the employment right in question that any provision in an agreement (whether a contract of employment or not) was void insofar as it purported to be a settlement of such a claim. The only major exception to this rule was where the agreement had been reached after a conciliation officer had taken action in accordance with his statutory responsibilities. It followed that the statutory regime not only impacted upon the nature of the context in which a settlement could be reached but also the *process* by which it was reached.

Although at first sight the statutory provisions represented a substantial assault on the common law position it is important to recognise the limits inherent in the statutory scheme. It was particularly striking that even though Parliament saw the need to intervene in the area of settlements its general approach was to build upon the existing edifice of contract law. Accordingly in order to validly settle a tribunal claim it was only necessary for the agreement to be reached *through* the conciliation officer and no requirements were laid down as to the precise form which that agreement should take[2]. A clear example of this is *Gilbert v Kembridge Fibres Ltd*[3] in which the involvement of the conciliation officer had brought about an oral resolution of the dispute between the parties. Before the agreement could be recorded in writing the employee had second thoughts and decided to continue with his claim. The EAT was required to consider whether the dispute had been validly compromised and had little difficulty concluding that it had. It considered that Parliament had adopted the term 'agreement' in the legislation without further embellishment and that accordingly there was no formal requirement that such agreements should be recorded in writing. It followed that if an oral agreement had been reached between the parties according to normal contractual principles that would be sufficient to bar the claim.

1 For a comprehensive overview of these provisions see *Harvey on Industrial Relations and Employment Law* para T [1726].
2 See, for example, the ERA 1996, s 203(2)(e).
3 [1984] ICR 188.

11.5   The role of the law of contract was preserved in other areas too. Although there is some confusion in the authorities it appears reasonably clear that the existing role of the law of contract was also preserved with regard to the setting aside of agreements even where a conciliation officer has been involved. It follows that the general contractual rules on duress, undue influence and inequality of bargaining power may also be utilised in order to override any settlement even where it has been reached through the offices of a conciliation officer. This was the view taken by the EAT in *Hennessy v Craigmyle & Co Ltd*[1] in which an employee was contending that he had signed a COT3 agreement under economic duress. Although his claim failed on its facts consideration was given as to whether or not the agreement would be void even if he could have established that he entered into the agreement in such circumstances. The EAT held that the term 'agreement' was subject to all qualifications by which an agreement could be voided at common law including economic duress. The approach of the EAT was adopted by the Court of Appeal[2] where Sir John Donaldson MR put the position as follows:

'The purpose of [the statutory provisions] is undoubtedly to ensure that employees shall not surrender their rights without first receiving independent advice and assistance from skilled conciliation officers of ACAS. Nevertheless, it does not follow that such intervention will, in all circumstances, eliminate the possibility that duress was such as to amount to a coercion of will vitiating consent, which is the basis of economic or physical duress as a ground for avoiding a contract. It must, however, make the possibility more remote. Accordingly I agree with. . .the EAT that we are concerned to consider both [the statutory provisions] and economic duress.' (at 465 B to C).

Although a later decision of the EAT in *Larkfield of Chepstow Ltd v Milne*[3] appeared to suggest that *Hennessy* was not authority for the proposition that there was a general jurisdiction to set aside an agreement reached through a conciliation officer at common law or in equity it is respectfully contended that the later decision is wrong and should not be followed on this point.

1   [1985] ICR 879.
2   [1986] ICR 461.
3   [1988] ICR 1.

11.6   In other areas the inroads into traditional contractual orthodoxy made by the statutory protections have been starkly revealed. A striking example is *Courage Take Home Trade Ltd v Keys*[1] in which the fact that an employee had accepted a payment from the employers in full and final settlement of his claim after liability had been determined by the tribunal but before remedy had been dealt did not prevent that agreement from being void. In a robust interpretation of the statutory provisions the EAT held that the phrase 'bringing any proceedings' was of wide ambit and included the pursuit of a remedy after liability had been determined. However, the employee ultimately gained no advantage from the result because the EAT upheld the tribunal's decision that it would not be just and equitable to award him any higher sum.

It is also important to recognise that the statutory provisions do not have any impact on settlements which are sanctioned in the form of a consent order of the tribunal itself. This is illustrated by *Times Newspapers Ltd v Fitt*[2] in which the employee had been included in a schedule of employees who had settled their claims in error. The error was not identified and the tribunal dismissed his complaint through the mechanism of an agreed order. Upon discovering the mistake the employee later sought an order that the tribunal should reinstate his complaint which it duly did. However, on appeal the tribunal's decision was reversed by the EAT on the basis that once a tribunal had made an agreed order it had no jurisdiction to vary that order in the absence of fraud or misrepresentation[3].

1   [1986] ICR 874.
2   [1981] ICR 637.
3   Although a consent order may be set aside if it is in restraint of trade: see *Gerrard Ltd v Read* [2002] NLJR 22.

5   Compromise agreements

11.7   The second form of statutory protection is the compromise agreement. The relevant provisions were introduced in order to overcome the shortcomings inherent in the conciliation officer framework. Often the parties to a dispute were keen to secure an early settlement but were prevented from doing so because of the unavailability of the officer. Accordingly Parliament provided that a dispute could be validly settled without recourse to a conciliation officer but only where other stringent conditions were met. Once again the approach of Parliament was to build upon existing principles of contract law with some statutory modifications.

The approach of repeating the relevant statutory provisions in virtually identical form in each statute which gives rise to the right in question was again adopted for compromise agreements. The removal of the requirement for the involvement of a conciliation officer was ameliorated by the requirement that the employee had to have been in receipt of some independent and competent advice. Accordingly one of the mainstays of the compromise agreement structure is that the employee can only enter into a valid compromise agreement if he has received advice from a *relevant independent adviser*[1]. This formulation represents a relaxation of the initial provisions which required that the employee had received *independent legal advice from a qualified lawyer*. Three categories of independent adviser are permitted for the purposes of the statutory provisions, namely: (a) qualified lawyers; (b) officers, officials, employees or members of an independent trade union who are certified by the union as competent for these purposes; and (c) advice centre workers who are certified as competent for these purposes. The Secretary of State also has power to add to these categories if he sees fit. In order for the compromise agreement to be valid it is also necessary for the relevant adviser to be covered by a current contract of insurance covering liability for the consequences of the advice which is given. In addition the compromise agreement must identify the adviser and state that the statutory conditions *of the particular statute* have been satisfied.

As has been stated above the statutory framework dealing with compromise agreements operates on the basis that the power to settle a statutory employment claim by such an agreement is contained in each relevant statute. This was a deliberate policy decision and was designed to prevent the use of compromise agreements as a way of settling a broad range of employment disputes without the clear agreement of the employee. This aim was further secured through the wording of the relevant provisions which adopted the phrase *the particular proceedings* in its various statutory formulations. When introducing the amendments in Parliament the government minister responsible stated that the purpose behind the structure was to only allow such agreements to compromise a specific complaint which had already arisen between the parties. The purpose was not to allow 'an individual to compromise his right to present, or to continue with, a claim to a tribunal in respect of any matter other than the particular complaint which is the subject of the agreement'[2].

1   For a detailed overview of these provisions see *Harvey* para T [728].
2   Viscount Ullswater (Hansard, 545 HL Official Report (6 May 1993) col 904).

11.8   It is perhaps in the area of the drafting of such compromise agreements where we see the major impact on the normal contractual approach to the construction of such agreements. This impact is neatly illustrated by the decision of the EAT in *Lunt v Merseyside TEC Ltd*[1]. In *Lunt* the employee made a number of complaints to her employer regarding her treatment and indicated a number of claims which she may have against the employer including unfair dismissal, harassment, victimisation and sex discrimination. She also indicated that she was keen to secure an early settlement of her claims and as a result terms were agreed between the parties and a compromise agreement was drawn up and entered into. Importantly that agreement *only* provided that the requirements of the ERA 1996 had been satisfied, there being no mention of the Sex Discrimination Act 1975. The agreement also included a form of general release and was said to be 'in full and final settlement of all claims that she might have, whether arising out of her employment, her contract of employment, or the termination of either.. . .including without limitation all and any claims which the employee may have to make for unfair dismissal, constructive dismissal, notice pay, salary arrears, holiday pay, employment benefits, company pension contributions, statutory and contractual redundancy, or otherwise howsoever arising. . .' The employee later presented a complaint to the employment tribunal claiming equal pay, sex discrimination, constructive dismissal, victimisation and breach of contract.

Adopting normal contractual principles the employer would have a very strong argument that the claims had been compromised by the employee and the wording adopted in the general release was sufficiently broad to encompass all of her claims. However the impact of the statutory provisions was that the claims brought under the Sex Discrimination Act 1975 had not been validly compromised. This is because no specific reference had been made to the necessary compliance with the provisions of the Act in the compromise agreement itself. It followed that the agreement was only effective to compromise the claims brought under the ERA 1996 and the claim for breach of contract. This was because the breach of contract claim was brought under the Employment Tribunals Act 1996 and was *not* caught by the provisions relating to compromise agreements at all and it followed that the normal principles of contract law applied to the settlement of that part of the claim.

Lunt is therefore a clear example of the impact of the statutory provisions on not only normal contractual principles but also the approach to the construction of settlement agreements. The requirement that each statute had to be identified in order to effectively bar such a claim had the inevitable consequence that the settlement of employment claims required relatively long and detailed agreements to be drawn up and general forms of release provided little comfort for the employer.

The impact of the statutory provisions dealing with compromise agreements has a further interesting twist in that it raises the question as to what happens to such an agreement if it subsequently transpires that it falls foul of the legislation. This issue was considered by the EAT in *Sutherland v Network Appliance Ltd*[2]. *Sutherland* was concerned with a compromise agreement which sought to compromise *any claim* but which failed to comply with the requirements of the ERA 1996. The employer nevertheless wished to rely upon the agreement as a bar to a claim for breach of contract and the EAT held that the employer could do so. This is because the impact of the statutory provisions was only to render void the relevant *part* of any such agreement insofar as it purports to preclude or exclude the complaint in question. It followed that the agreement is only struck down in part and is not void for all purposes. The approach of the EAT was to decide this issue on the basis of a construction of the statutory provisions. This, however, leaves open the question as to whether an employer who feels that they have paid over the odds for their bargain can seek repayment of sums paid where forms of general release have been ineffective. This question raises in a most focused way the interaction of normal contractual principles and the relevant statutory framework. Although the matter is not beyond doubt (and may well depend upon the precise wording adopted) it is unlikely that the law will provide any comfort to the employer in these circumstances. This is because of the impact of the statutory provisions on the proper construction of the general release itself. As will be seen by analogy with the decision of the House of Lords in *Ali* the very fact that the statutory provisions have not been complied with lends strong support to the argument that the general release was not intended to operate as a bar to those claims for which the statutory requirements have not been met. When coupled with the pure statutory construction arguments which found favour in *Sutherland* it appears unlikely that a court would be willing to entirely unravel any such agreement. This may not be the end of the matter, however, as the tribunal which determines the claim will no doubt take such issues into account when assessing what level of compensation which is just and equitable[3].

As can be seen from the above the present law regarding compromise agreements is capable of producing unjust results and of defeating the legitimate intentions of the parties in a manner which does not dovetail with the original purpose behind the various statutory protections. These concerns led to a proposed reform in the Employment Bill 2002 to, in effect, reverse *Lunt* (by removing the statutory reference to particular claims). However, at a late stage in the Parliamentary process, this clause came under sustained attack (the argument being that an 'all claims' settlement power would advantage the employer too much) and the government were persuaded to remove it. Thus, the *Lunt* case remains the principal authority in this area.

1   [1999] ICR 17.
2   [2001] IRLR 12.
3   For an example of this see *Courage Take Home Trade Ltd v Keys* [1986] ICR 874.

6   *BCCI v Ali*

11.9   Ironically even if the stautory reform had gone ahead, its impact on the drafting of settlement agreements would have been limited by the recent decision of the House of Lords in *BCCI v Ali*[1]. The *Ali* claim arose out of the general litigation surrounding the collapse of *BCCI* and involved the construction of a form of general release which was entered into before the fraudulent nature of the bank's activities had become generally known. The general release was not suprisingly drafted in very broad terms and provided for the terms to be 'in full and final settlement of all or any claims. . .of whatsoever nature that exist or may exist'. In response to claims made by the liquidators for the repayment of loans made to the employees the employees counterclaimed for damages for misrepresentation and breach of their employment contracts arising from the corrupt way in which the bank had been run. The liquidators not suprisingly contended that the counterclaims were barred by reason of the compromise agreements which had been signed. By a majority the House of Lords held that the claims were not compromised. In his speech Lord Bingham applied the modern approach to the construction of documents as set out in *Investors Compensation Scheme Ltd v West Bromwich Building Society*[2] and found that the wording adopted was insufficient to cover the type of claim identified because it was one which could not have been in the contemplation of the parties at the time at which the agreement was reached. Although he accepted that such claims *could* be compromised by way of a general release he considered that the court should be slow to infer that any such intention was present unless very clear wording to that effect was agreed upon. Adopting this *cautionary principle* he considered that the clause in question could not be read literally and that the surrounding circumstances were insufficient to give rise to the inference that the type of claim in question had been compromised by the employees. A major part of this reasoning no doubt flows from the fairly extraordinary nature of the events and practices which subsequently came to light and the subsequent development in the law on implied terms which they heralded. These factors also weighed heavily with Lord Nicholls who agreed with Lord Bingham's construction. He stressed that he considered it most unattractive to treat the parties as having intended to have compromised a claim which did not exist *as a matter of law* at the time at which the agreement was entered into.

Ali is probably most striking, however, because of the trenchant dissenting speech of Lord Hoffman who considered that the claims had been compromised through the general release. He stated the consequences of the decision of the majority as follows:

> 'Lord Keeper Henley's ghost (*Salkeld v Vernon* 1 Eden 64) will have struck back. I think it would be an unfortunate retreat into formalism if the outcome of this case were to require employers using the services of ACAS to add verbiage to the form of release in order to attain the comprehensiveness which it is obviously intended to achieve.' (at 359A to B).

Advisers in the employment field are now left to tiptoe their way through the debris left after the judicial sparring in *Ali*. Lord Hoffman's powerful dissent aside, it may have been possible to dismiss *Ali* as an extraordinary case involving extraordinary facts. However, the prudent view must now be that the impact of *Ali* is that not only must compromise agreements comply with the statutory requirements as to their form but it is also now essential to cover each head of claim in specific detail whether that claim be real, imagined or even unforeseen. These difficulties are further exacerbated because of the variety of sources of potential claims open to employees in the employment sphere[3] and the fact that many employee benefits are now provided through vehicles and arrangements which are arguably separate from the individual employment contract. Classic examples are occupational pensions and share schemes which may well require other parties to be included in the compromise agreements[4].

1   [2001] UKHL 8, [2001] ICR 337.
2   [1998] 1 WLR 896.
3   An interesting example as regards free standing claims under EC law is *Livingstone v Hepworth Refractories Ltd* [1992] ICR 287.
4   See further chap 5.

7   Conclusion

11.10   In conclusion it is fair to say that the prospects of a simplification in the law relating to the settlement of contractual employment disputes are bleak. The combined effect of the statutory provisions relating to the settlement of statutory claims and the judgment of the House of Lords in *Ali* leave the prudent adviser with little option but to draft the settlement of any employment claim in great detail.

Chapter 12

The Scottish dimension

1   Introduction

12.1   The Scots law position concerning contracts of employment is very similar to that of our English counterparts. This should come as no surprise given the first eleven chapters of this publication frequently cite Scottish authorities, being that decisions either of the Court of Session or in appeals therefrom to the House of Lords.

In what circumstances, will a party to a contract of employment subject to Scots law be placed in a different position to a party south of the border? Such differences as exist result not from statute: employment law emanating from Parliament has long been of UK-wide effect, with practically no distinctions being drawn between the jurisdictions[1]. This remains true today, with employment law being reserved by the British Parliament. It does not fall within the ambit of the Scotland Act 1998 and consequently it is not within the legislative competence of the Scottish Parliament[2].

Such practical differences as there are arise from the common law of Scotland having a quite different history and evolution to that of our Southern neighbours.

The common law of Scotland is of Roman-Canonical descent. The distinction between the two alternatives of a contract of service (or employment) and a contract for services, for example, extends back to Roman law and the difference between *locatio conductio operis* and *locatio conductio operarum*[3]. However, in the context of the employment relationship the two sets of common laws have become less distinct.

There have been instances of direct interference with Scots common law by the House of Lords. There is evidence ranging back to the middle of the nineteenth century of the common law of England 'influencing' the Scots position with regard to the employment contract to such an extent that a more apt description would be 'importation' of English common law into Scots.

In *Bartonshill Coal Co v Reid*[4], for example, the House of Lords imported into the Scots common law the doctrine of common employment. The doctrine dictated that a servant was deemed to have agreed, as an implied term of his contract of employment, that he would not sue his master to recover damages for injuries caused by the negligence of a fellow servant. Before this case, the

Scottish courts had refused to recognise such a legal position[5]. Indeed, as Lord Macmillan would later note, the doctrine was 'a principle as distasteful as it was alien to Scottish jurisprudence'.

However, there remains a small number of Scots common law nuances that have stood the test of time, that leave certain subtleties in the Scottish contract of employment.

Decisions of the Court of Appeal and the House of Lords in appeals therefrom, are binding in Scots law in so far as concerned with the interpretation of legislative provisions common to both jurisdictions. Such decisions, when relating to the substance of common law rules will be treated as persuasive authority in Scots law. Where a matter which relates purely to aspects of Scots law comes before an Employment Tribunal or Employment Appeal Tribunal, it will not regard itself as bound by decisions of any English appellate court[6].

It would be wrong to suppose that these differences and the basis of Scots law are only of consequence to Scottish employment lawyers. With such a cross-border flow, an English employment lawyer must be aware of the areas which are typically Scottish and, vice versa. Although the practical effects of the two common laws have been substantially assimilated, the 'route' at which a court or tribunal in Scotland arrives at a decision, will be based largely on Scots law principles. It would not be appropriate, without care, to seek to rely on, for example, Halsbury's Laws of England when arguing a point of law governed by Scots law, however similar the practical effect of law may be north and south of the border.

An employment lawyer, asked to advise on a point outwith his or her usual jurisdiction of practice, should be aware, at the very least, of the differing basis to each jurisdiction's laws and areas where assimilation has not occurred.

1   An example of one such distinction is the fact that there are different rules of procedure for Scottish Employment Tribunals and English Tribunals. The actual difference in practice, however, is limited.
2   See Scotland Act 1998, Sch 5, Pt II, Section H1.
3   See the comments of Lord Carmont in *Glasgow Western Hospitals Board of Management* 1954 SC 453 at 479, 1954 SLT 226 at 238.
4   See 1858 3 Macqueen 266.
5   See *Dixon v Ranken* (1852) 14 D 420.
6   See *Brown v Rentokil Ltd* [1992] IRLR 302, EAT.

2   Relevant differences in general doctrines of contract

(a)   Capacity to contract

12.2   Whilst the capacity to contract is now, in the main, a matter of statutory and not common law, the division is not absolute.

The capacity to contract for those who have not yet reached the age of majority, is regulated by the Age of Legal Capacity (Scotland) Act 1991. Generally, those under 16 years of age have no contractual capacity while those over that age have full contractual capacity[1]. Unsurprisingly, where a person under the age of

16 attempts to enter into a contract for which he has no legal capacity, the contract is void[2].

However, there is an exception, which applies amongst other areas, in the context of employment. A person under 16 years of age has full legal capacity to enter into contracts of a kind commonly entered into by persons of that age and on terms that are not unreasonable, and in appropriate circumstances[3].

Notably, a person under the age of 21 can set aside a contract entered into between the ages of 16 and 18 where that contract is established as having been, in fact, prejudicial[4]. It should be noted that there are circumstances provided for when this rule does not apply, for example, if the contract was entered into in the course of a trade, business, or profession[5].

As a general rule, no child under the age of 14 may be employed. It should be noted that this is subject to local authority bye-laws[6].

1   Age of Legal Capacity (Scotland) Act 1991, s 1(1).
2   Age of Legal Capacity (Scotland) Act 1991, s 2(5).
3   Section 2(1).
4   Section 3(1).
5   Age of Legal Capacity (Scotland) Act 1991, ss 2, 3(3)(f).
6   Children and Young Persons (Scotland) Act 1937, s 28 (amended by the Children (Protection at Work) Regulations 1998, SI 1998/276, reg 8(2)).

(b)   Notice and pay in lieu of notice

12.3   In England, where an employee is dismissed without notice, in circumstances where he or she is entitled to notice of termination of employment, then the employee is entitled to damages for breach of contract. This right to damages colloquially has become known as pay in lieu of notice[1]. The level of damages is to be fixed by reference to the unexpired portion of either the reasonable or agreed notice period. Since the award is for damages for breach of contract it is subject to the usual rules for mitigation of loss.

Since the position in English law is that, in the usual course of events, payment in lieu of notice is a payment towards damages for failing to give requisite notice, no employer's national insurance contributions are payable on such payments and they attract tax, not as a payment of emoluments under the contract but under the provisions for severance payments in ICTA 1988, s 148.

The proper characterisation of notice and payment in lieu of notice under Scots law is more difficult. This is principally because the reported cases are all of some antiquity and because what is said by the various judges in the cases regarding the nature of payments in lieu of notice is not entirely consistent.

The starting point is the case of *Moffat v Sheddon*[2] where Lord President Hope said:

> 'I apprehend that the connection of the parties might be brought to a close by either of them upon reasonable and equitable notice being given of the period of its termination. If such notice were not given then compensation must be due in respect of the failure to give it.'

The decision in *Moffat* was relied upon by the Second Division in the case of *William Morrison v Abernethy School Board*[3]. The case obviously troubled the judges in the Second Division because the four judges there consulted three further judges and the case was eventually determined by a bench of sevens. The principal opinion, for the majority of the judges, who came down 5 to 2 for the employee, was given by Lord Deas. His opinion is a classic of its time and warrants reading if only for the quality of the prose. What he said at 949 of the report was:

> 'The next question is does such a contract imply, in a case such as the present, an obligation on the master or employer to give notice or to make a pecuniary allowance in lieu of notice when he means to terminate the contract, without alleging fault on the part of the servant? My answer to that question is, that, by the law and practice of Scotland, such a contract does imply that obligation.'

Lord Muir at 961 of the report said:

> 'By the rules of the law of Scotland I have always understood that in all cases between master and servant there must be reasonable notice given of the intention to make a change or reasonable compensation.'

At 962 Lord Gifford said:

> '... I am of the opinion that a schoolmaster, although he holds his office simply "during the pleasure" of the school board, is yet entitled to reasonable notice on dismissal; or if the school board without notice insist upon his instantly giving up the school and ceasing to discharge his duties, that he shall have compensation equivalent to what he would have received had reasonable notice been given.'

Finally the Lord Justice Clerk at 964 of the report said:

> 'I think that a tenure at pleasure, whilst it implies the right of the employer to dismiss the employed at any time, without reason assigned, lays upon him an obligation either to give reasonable notice or compensation in lieu of notice.'

The final interlocutor pronounced by the court was:

> '... find that the Respondents were entitled to dismiss the Appellant from his office of headmaster of the public school of Abernethy at their pleasure, but were bound either to give him reasonable notice or to compensate for the want of it ...'

In the case of *William Forsyth v Heathery Knowe Coal Co and Thomas Brownlie*[4] the First Division pronounced an interlocutor holding that an employee 'should have received 3 months notice and was entitled to 3 months wages in lieu thereof'. Thus we see the distinction between the laws of England and Scotland in this issue. In Scotland, unlike England, it appears that payment in lieu of notice is not a payment on account of damages for breach of contract but is an obligation implied into the contract in the event the employer elects not to give the notice to which an employee is contractually entitled.

1   *Gothard v Mirror Group Newspapers* [1988] IRLR 396; *Delaney v Staples* [1992] IRLR 191, HL.
2   (1838) 1 D 468.
3   (1876) 3 R 945.
4   (1880) 7 R 887.

(c) Illegality

12.4   A contract will be unable to be relied upon by either party when the agreement is 'illegal'. Illegality can be through criminal or immoral purposes, or due to specific prohibition by statute.

An example of a statutory prohibition would be the Working Time Regulations[1] whereby an employee contracts to work in excess of the statutory maximum, without having been advised of the limit to which he can insist upon working and signing a waiver of his right therefrom.

It is more common, however, for the illegality to arise out of the actual performance of an otherwise legal contract. Such an example would be an operation that wilfully defrauds the Inland Revenue.

Acquiescence or active participation in such a fraud would render the contract of employment null and void, both for common law and statutory purposes.

But, a contract that is 'illegal' due to the manner of performance will generally only be struck down when the party seeking to rely on the contract knew or ought to have known of the illegality[2].

There then falls the question of an otherwise enforceable contract, which has certain terms which conflict with rules of public policy, and whether those rules may be struck out and the remainder of the contract preserved. It has been stressed by the Employment Appeal Tribunal in Scotland that as the rule of *ex turpi causa non oritur actio* has its foundation in public policy, it must be applied by the courts in a pragmatic and flexible manner, not rigidly and automatically[3].

1   See 1998/1833, reg 4.
2   See *Davidson v Pillay* [1979] IRLR 275.
3   But contrast *Salveson v Simons* [1994] ICR 409, [1994] IRLR 52, EAT, with *Annandale Engineering v Samson* [1994] IRLR 59, EAT.

(d) Frustration

12.5   The laws of Scotland and England share roughly the same effects, but the grounding upon which these practical effects arise from differ. Indeed, it appears an advanceable argument that English law is moving towards Scots law[1], for once, rather than the opposite.

In relation to 'commercial impossibility', Scots law would regard itself as bound by tighter constraints than English law. Whilst it is recognised that *Krell v Henry*[2] can perhaps be said to be at the more radical end of the spectrum of decisions on frustration by an English court, it is strongly doubted that it would be followed by Scots law[3]. The greater likelihood is that the presumption would be in favour of the contract being upheld, if all that had occurred was the non-occurrence of an expected event as opposed to the occurrence of an unexpected event. Indeed, there has been a longstanding and definite reluctance upon Scottish courts to even consider extending the concept of commercial impossibility[4].

In theory there should be less debate about whether a person employed in Scotland will be able to rely on PHI provisions in his contract, and even contractual sick pay, than if he were employed under an English contract of employment. It is submitted that it is harder for an employer to argue that the contract has been frustrated, through the employee's illness, when the contract clearly covers provision for such an event.

That all said, if the House of Lords clarifies and enshrines the present English stance to frustration, it is submitted that it would perhaps come as no great surprise if Scots law eventually ended up following the southern position, given past experiences in this area. The other half of the law of frustration in the context of the employment relationship, namely the concept of frustration through an employee's imprisonment, has developed due to English influence, resulting in law and effect which does not sit well with Scots principles[5]. In terms of Scots law, it is apparent that imprisonment should be properly termed as repudiation, requiring acceptance to terminate the contract.

1   See para 7.5, above, upon the development of frustration in relation to PHI in England.
2   (1903) 2 KB 740.
3   See Lord Cooper's comments, citing Professor Gloag, (1946) 28 J Comp L 1.
4   See *Hong Kong and Whampoa Dock Co Ltd v Netherton Shipping Ltd* [1909] SC 34.
5   See Lord Fraser, *Master and Servant*, (3rd edn) p 322 referring to the Bell's *Principles*, s 181, and RJ Pothier, *Louage* No 172. See also *McEwan v Malcolm* (1867) 5 SLR 62.

3   Form of contract

12.6   By virtue of the Requirements of Writing (Scotland) Act 1995[1], contracts of service or for services, of any duration, do not need to be constituted in writing to be valid. Indeed, it is possible to enter into such a contract orally, in writing, by implication, or by a mixture of all or any of these.

However, where a contract of employment, for a fixed term of one year or more was entered into on or before 30 July 1995, there is a separate regime that applies. At common law, such a contract (including contracts of apprenticeship) has to be either in probative writing, or improbative followed by *rei interventus*[2].

It has been commented that these rules, although essential for constitution and helpful for proof, have not the remotest connection with the current employment environment. However, for those fixed-term contracts that are still in existence today, which were constituted prior to 31 July 1995, these rules retain practical significance[3].

1   Chapter 7, ss 1, 11.
2   See *Grant v Ramage & Ferguson Ltd* (1897) 25 R 35 and Bell's *Principles*, ss 179, 190
3   See, for example, *Cook v Grubb* 1963 SLT 78 and more recently, *Heneaghan v Aero Technologies Ltd* 1990 GWD 13-692.

4   Offer, acceptance and payment of wages

12.7   When looking at the construction of a contract in English law and specifically in our context, the contract of employment, the doctrine of consideration would be relevant. This doctrine, however, is one of the few to have completely failed to make its way into Scots law.

However, it is arguable that the practical effect is negligible. The doctrine of consideration is that acceptance is made *by* conduct. Whereas, in Scotland, acceptance is said to be *implied from* conduct. The net effect is therefore, negligible.

Acknowledging the fact that within eight weeks of the commencement of employment, the employee should receive a written statement of terms and conditions[1], the question of whether an employee is working for wages or not should rarely arise, given that this statement must contain a term covering remuneration. However, there is a rebuttable presumption in favour of the employee that services are given for payment[2]. In the absence of neither an express nor implied term concerning the amount of remuneration to be paid, the parties can have resort to the equitable principle of *quantum meruit*[3].

In terms of wages paid during the illness of an employee, when the employee is absent from work, it would seem that the English authorities would be persuasive, given there has been practically no Scottish judicial pronouncement on the subject. When dealing with a fixed-term contract, however, it seems that the employer would be obliged by Scots law principles to continue paying the employee's wages during short periods of illness[4].

1   ERA 1996, ss 1(1) and (2).
2   See *Thomson v Thomson's Trs* (1889) 16 R 333.
3   See *Mackenzie v Baird's Trustees* 1907 SC 838.
4   See Stair, *Institutions*, I, 15, 2; Bell's *Principles*, s 179.

5   Implied terms

(a)   Reasonable care

12.8   An employee must perform his duties with reasonable care[1]. So, for example, the bank teller who had the misfortune/lack of attention to pay out £1,000 instead of £100 was held to account for the difference by the courts at the instance of proceedings raised by the employer[2].

The position concerning an employee's duty to indemnify his employer in the event of the negligent performance of a contractual obligation that injures a third party, is somewhat uncertain in Scots law. In practical terms the topic may rarely arise, given the 'gentleman's agreement' of British insurance companies to resist from exercising subrogation rights against employees[3]. Certainly, it is a matter for pure conjecture as to how the Scottish courts would react to circumstances such as in the famous English case of *Lister v Romford Ice and Cold Storage Ltd*[4]. It should be noted, though, there is no Scottish equivalent to the English Civil Liability (Contribution) Act 1978 by which a vicariously liable employer can recover a contribution from the negligent employee. Furthermore, the employer and employee are deemed to not be jointly and severally liable under Scots law, accordingly, the Law Reform (Miscellaneous Provisions) (Scotland) Act 1940, s 3(2) does not apply.

1   See Lord Fraser, *Master and Servant* (3rd edn) pp 68, 69.
2   See *Clydesdale Bank v Beatson* (1882) 10 R 88. A very substantial amount for the time!
3   See Glanville Williams 'Vicarious liability and the Master's Indemnity' (1952) 20 MLR 220, 437; G Gardiner 'Reports of Committees' (1959) 22 MLR 652.
4   [1957] AC 555, HL.

(b)   Fidelity

12.9   Whilst an obligation of loyalty, or fidelity, on the employee's part, is implied into the contract of employment, this branch of the law in Scotland is, as has been observed, 'somewhat obscured and not fully developed'[1]. Certainly, this may be due to a preference to seek to use restrictive covenants, which if properly constructed, will offer greater protection to an employer.

Whilst acknowledging there is no direct authority, it is likely that the Scottish courts would accord with the decision of the Court of Appeal in *Roger Bullivant v Ellis*[2]. There, it was held that the implied term of fidelity could be relied upon in the absence of an express enforceable covenant[3].

Inherent in fidelity is the concept of confidential information. Accordingly, it is convenient at this point to note that it is well established that the laws of Scotland and England are to the same effect[4].

1   See *Chill Foods (Scotland) Ltd v Cool Foods Ltd* 1977 SLT 38 at p 40, per Lord Maxwell.
2   See [1987] IRLR 491, CA.
3   See Craig and Miller *Employment Law in Scotland* (2nd edn) Butterworths Scotland, p 96.
4   See *Lord Advocate v Scotsman Publications Ltd* 1988 SLT 490 per Lord Justice-Clerk Ross at p 503.

6   Restrictive covenants

12.10   The drafting and enforcement of restrictive covenants are largely similar north and south of the border, but certain issues require consideration.

In Scots law the starting point is to examine the nature of the employers' business and the employee's position in that business[1].

There is no reported Scots authority concerning the enforceability of a contractual term which prevents an ex-employee from asking current employees to leave their employment. Whilst it is recognised that there have been decisions in the Court of Appeal[2], which it is submitted are conflicting, it is suggested that a Scottish court would need to consider the following questions[3]:

- Whilst anti-competitive covenants, against former employees, require consideration of whether there is a legitimate interest requiring protection, should the same criteria be used for anti-poaching covenants given the party seeking protection, the employer, is already in a contractual relationship, whereas that will rarely be true of his customers?
- Should the employer not protect his relationship with his existing employees through covenants in their contracts?

- Has the employee's 'value', in fact, been increased by training provided by the employer?
- Even in the absence of an enforceable express term prohibiting employment by a competitor, the employer can rely on the ex-employee's implied duty to protect and not divulge confidential information. Where does the justification lie for a restriction that casts a net further?

These questions are compounded against the background of the employer's existing delictual action to available to restrain the actings of an ex-employee in inducing the breach of a contract of employment, knowingly and without justification.

The Scottish courts agreed with the English decision that a restrictive covenant phrased so as to operate on the termination of the employment relationship, in whatever circumstances that come to happen and whether lawfully or not, is manifestly unreasonable and will not be upheld[4].

Recent decisions, however, have moved on to the extent that the restriction will not be held to be manifestly unreasonable unless the relationship was not only terminated by the employer, but terminated unlawfully[5].

1   *Scottish Farmers Dairy Co (Glasgow) Ltd v McGhee* 1933 SC 148.
2   See *Hanover Insurance Brokers v Schapiro* [1994] IRLR 82, CA; *Alliance Paper Group plc v Prestwich* [1996] IRLR 25, CA.
3   See Craig and Miller *Employment Law in Scotland* (2nd edn) Butterworths Scotland, p 102.
4   See *Living Design (Home Improvements) Ltd v Davidson* [1994] IRLR 69, OH (as applied in *Lux Traffic Control Ltd v Healey* 1994 SLT 1153, OH) – the English authority being *Briggs v Oates* [1990] IRLR 472, Ch.
5   See *Aramark plc v Sommerville* 1995 SLT 749 and *PR Consultants Ltd v Mann* [1996] IRLR 188, OH.

7   Rights under share schemes

12.11   There is an interesting divergence between the laws of England and the laws of Scotland, primarily due to statute. The effect, however, is contractual.

Harvey on Industrial relations and Employment Law states that 'It is a common feature of ESOPs that an individual's right to exercise their options will lapse on dismissal since it is a requirement of the statutory provisions that members of an ESOP must be employees'[1]. This is fairly straightforward. The interesting discussion comes when the relevant employment has been terminated wrongfully or otherwise brought to an end by the employer.

A case such as *Thompson v Asda-MFI Group plc*[2] would, it is submitted, have been decided the same in Scotland as it was, in England. The reasoning was straightforward and it is apparent therefore, the presiding judge was quite correct to find that it would be wrong to imply into a scheme that the principal employer should not sell off any participating subsidiary. The more complex case of *Micklefield v SAC Technology Ltd*[3] is of more interest to us, however, given the outcome and the fact that this contrasts with the position in Scotland.

In *Micklefield*, the court looked at the issue of Mr Micklefield's predicament in the context that he was wrongly dismissed some 10 days before his entitlement to shares mature and so, the consequent estimated £30,000 of realisable wealth. The scheme central to the dispute contained not one, but two relevant exclusion clauses. First, his options would lapse if he ceased to be employed ' . . . for whatever reason whatsoever . . . ' and secondly, there was a provision stating that on applying for an option, the employee was 'deemed irrevocably to have waived any entitlement to any sum or other benefit to compensate him for loss under the scheme'. Micklefield argued that to deprive him of his shares would be to allow the employer to benefit from its wrong. The claim was dismissed. The court held simply that both exclusions blocked the claim. First, the exclusion clause was drafted in broad enough terms so as to encompass circumstances in which the employee was wrongfully dismissed. The second clause was held as valid since it only exempted the employer from part of the liability for the wrongful dismissal. In the circumstances, the court said, neither clause could be said to be out with the ambit of a parties ability to expressly contract out of the general principle of construction, that a party is not entitled to benefit from its own wrong.

When considering the further question of whether either of the terms were contrary to the Unfair Contract Terms Act 1977, the court decided that the scheme was outside the reach of the said statute, due to their interpretation that it fell within the transfer of securities exception[4]. When faced with a similar claim, the Scottish courts took a contrasting view.

In *Chapman v Aberdeen Construction*[5], Mr Chapman was summarily dismissed from his position as Executive Director of the Aberdeen Construction Group. His claim, including the element that he was entitled to six months notice of termination (which would have led to an EDT of 8 January 1988) was for wrongful dismissal and damages accordingly. One part to the claim and the part that is of interest for our present purposes, was that he sustained a loss by being deprived of his right to exercise certain options granted to him under the company's executive share option scheme. In the Outer House of the Court of Session, before Lord Caplan, the employer's submission to have that part of the claim deleted was upheld and it was excluded accordingly. On Appeal to the Inner House, Mr Chapman was successful in having the share scheme claim restored.

The dispute centred round the fact that under the scheme, if an applicant was favoured and the Directors of the scheme granted the applicant the right to purchase options, the applicant could not then exercise those options until three years after the date the Directors had granted their assent. In Mr Chapman's case, the Directors made a grant on 9 November 1984, of an option in respect of 20,000 shares at £1.75 per share. Accordingly, at the time of dismissal, his three year period had not expired. If he had not been wrongly dismissed, he claimed, he would have acquired the requisite service, however. The employer relied upon an exclusion clause which bore remarkable similarities to that in Mr Micklefield's case, namely 'it shall be a condition of the scheme that in the event of the dismissal of a participant from employment he shall not become entitled to any damages or compensation or any additional damages or compensation by reason of any alteration of his rights or expectations under the scheme'.

On the claim that the exclusion clause was void by virtue of the terms of UCTA 1977[6] and the basis that a contract of employment was a consumer contract under that enactment, the Inner House of the Court of Session granted the reclaiming motion. It rejected the defender's argument that the share option scheme was not contractual. Importantly, the court concluded, the exclusion clause attempted to strike at a remedy arising under the contract of employment itself since it purported to restrict the employer's liability to pay damages for that breach of contract. The Lord Ordinary wrongly concluded that the exclusion clause had the effect of only restricting the employer's liability under the option contract and did not exclude or restrict their liability under the contract of employment itself. In a dissenting judgment, however, Lord Wylie ruled that since Mr Chapman had accepted the benefit under the share option scheme 'on the express condition that loss of the benefit in the event of dismissal would not sound in damages, no right or remedy arose which could be excluded or restricted, and accordingly, there was no scope for s 23 to apply'[7].

1   See *Harvey on Industrial Relations and Employment Law*, Div B [520]. See generally chap 5, above.
2   See [1988] IRLR 340, Scott J presiding.
3   See [1990] IRLR 218, at para 5.3, above.
4   As contained in para 1(e) to Sch 1 of UCTA 1977.
5   See [1991] IRLR 505.
6   See UCTA 1977, s 23.
7   See [1991] IRLR 505, at 506.

8   The English remedy of specific performance

12.12   In relation to the implied term of mutual trust and confidence that must exist between employer and employee, the reader will no doubt be aware that the English courts may, at their discretion, grant an injunction to restrain or at least, postpone, a potentially wrongful dismissal. The requirement is normally that the employer retains sufficient confidence in the employee's ability to do the job. Examples of this remedy in practice, can be found in the cases of *Hughes v London Borough of Southwark*[1] and *Ali v London Borough of Southwark*[2]. In the former there was 'no question' of the employer having lost confidence in the employee's ability to do the job and an injunction was granted accordingly. On the other hand, in the latter, it was plain that whilst the employer had not necessarily irrevocably lost confidence in the employee, they had lost it for the time-being on reasonable grounds and this was sufficient to persuade the court that an injunction was not appropriate. Indeed, it is acknowledged that procedures in English law allow for an injunction to be granted even when the trust and confidence in the relationship may well have broken down[3].

Traditionally there was no equivalent procedure available to an employee in Scotland. In the normal course of events and especially where the mutual trust and confidence is no longer apparent in the relationship, the only remedy for a wrongful dismissal or termination of employment by the employee in breach of contract will only be damages[4]. Where an employee is dismissed but receives payment in lieu for wages and other contractual benefits, no action for damages will be available to the employee at all, on the grounding that an employer has an implied right to terminate the contract of employment[5]. It should be noted that an employee has no equivalent right[6].

However, there is a developing relaxation of the traditional stance in cases where it is clear that the essential trust and confidence between employer and employee is intact[7].

With regard to breaches of contract other than those leading to termination, interdict (the Scots law equivalent of injunction) is an option. It's use will be practically in line with the use of injunction in English law[8].

1   See [1988] IRLR 55, QBD. See para 10.8, above.
2   See [1988] IRLR 100, Ch D. See para 10.6, above.
3   See *Jones v Gwent County Council* [1992] IRLR 521, Ch, where the Rules of the Supreme Court were invoked (RSC Order 14A, r 1).
4   *Skerret v Oliver* (1896) 23 R 468; *Murray v Dumbarton County Council* 1935 SLT 239.
5   See *Graham v Thomson* (1822) 1 S 309.
6   See *Wallace v Shishart* (1800) Hume 383.
7   *Anderson v Pringle of Scotland Ltd* 1998 SLT 754. See para 10.7, above.
8   *Peace v City of Edinburgh Council* 1999 SLT 712. See para 10.12, above.

9   Judicial review

12.13   In Chapter 9 to this book, concerning the enforcement of a contract of employment, there is discussion of the distinction between public law and the private law issues. There is no real distinction as such, in practical or real terms, north of the border.

In Scotland, the Court of Session exercises a supervisory power over administrative bodies, persons taking administrative decisions, lesser courts and tribunals, in the same way as the High Court operates in England, by way of judicial review. By Court of Session rules 58.3 and 58.4, the court may consider, review and make such order as it thinks fit, as could be made in any action or petition, including an order for reduction, suspension, declarator, interdict, specific implement, restitution and payment[1]. It should be noted that it is not the rule itself which limits the court's powers but the court itself, in that as the court can exercise any of these powers under a competent application, provided the application is accepted, the court can act accordingly.

The supervisory power of the Court of Session means, in theory, that it can review the decisions of tribunals or any administrative body relating to an employment matter. An example of an employee calling upon the power was the case of *Nahar v Strathclyde Regional Council*[2]. An important pre-condition to application to the Court for judicial review is there must be no other avenues of appeal or resolution available or the application will fail[3].

For a period the approach in Scotland to judicial review was similar to that in England, with decisions such as *R v East Berkshire Health Authority, ex p Walsh*[4] being followed north of the border in cases such as *Tehrani v Argyll and Clyde Health Board (No 2)*[5]. The analysis was that judicial review was suitable for the enforcement of public rights, whereas the employees in each case were seeking to enforce private contractual rights under their respective contracts of employment. However, the Inner House of the Court of Session comprehensively and authoritatively dispelled this approach, in holding that the availability of Judicial Review in Scotland was not based upon any public or private law distinction, but what is required is:

• the conferring of a decision-making power upon a body either by statute, agreement or some other tool;

- an allegation that the body has exceeded, abused or perhaps failed to exercise that power; and
- the existence of a tri-partite relationship constituted by the conferring of the decision making power upon that third party.

For the judicial review process to be available all three elements require to be present[6].

The effect is that for example, a prison officer's terms of employment will not be entertained by judicial review in the absence of a tri-partite relationship[7], but a school teacher's application was competent where she was seeking to challenge her employer's unilateral departure from the terms of her employment, where those terms were established by a body constituted by statute[8].

1 The English equivalent, it is believed, is the Rules of the Supreme Court, r 53.
2 See 1986 SLT 570, OH. The applicant sought reduction of the employer's decision to dismiss him on the grounds of misconduct.
3 See r 58.3(2).
4 See [1984] ICR 743, CA. See para 10.16, above.
5 See 1990 SLT 118, OH.
6 *West v Secretary of State for Scotland* 1992 SC 385.
7 See *Blair v Lochaber District Council* [1995] IRLR 135, OH; para 10.17, above.
8 See *Watt v Strathclyde Regional Council* 1992 SLT 324, IH; the statute in question being the Education (Scotland) Act 1980.

10   The criminal law

12.14   The existence of the crime of malicious mischief in Scotland and its application in cases of computer misuse illustrate differences between Scots and English law.

At common law, it is a crime wilfully and maliciously to destroy or damage the property of another, indeed there may be a sustainable argument that it will suffice to have a deliberate disregard or indifference for the property rights of others[1]. Physical damage is not a prerequisite to the crime[2]. Thus, there are a number of examples of employees' behaviour that could constitute malicious mischief[3].

1 See *Ward v Robertson* 1938 JC 32.
2 See *HM Advocate v Wilson* 1984 SLT 117.
3 See Craig and Miller *Employment Law in Scotland* (2nd edn) Butterworths Scotland.

Employment Contract

Prec 1

THIS Agreement is made on [   ]

BETWEEN:

(1)   [   ] [Limited] [plc] of [   ] ('the Company'); and

(2)   [insert name of employee] of [   ] .

IT IS AGREED as follows:

1   Status of Agreement

This document, which is legally binding, sets out the terms and conditions of your employment by the Company as agreed between us at the above date. It incorporates the written statement of particulars of employment which the Company is required to give you under sections 1–7 of the Employment Rights Act 1996 and therefore no separate written statement will be provided.

Notes:

This precedent is designed as a basic contractual document which could be adapted for junior administrative staff or for employees without managerial responsibility. It would not be suitable for more senior employees, such as executive directors, nor where the employment is subject to specific regulation (eg under the Financial Services and Markets Act 2000). As with all precedents it should be used as a starting point and will need to be amended to reflect the particular circumstances in a given case as well as any changes in the law. Please note that the precedent is drafted to comply with English law only.

It is often the case that the employee is sent an offer letter prior to the start of employment and the contract is only issued once the employee has started work.

---

*   Contributed by Helen Milgate, Solicitor, Pinsent Curtis Biddle.

Always check to ensure consistency between such documents and any other written material (such as staff handbooks) which may be relevant to the employment relationship to avoid subsequent disputes.

The contract incorporates the written statement of particulars of employment which most employees are entitled to receive from their employer within two months of starting work (see chap 3, para 3.2). For ease of reference *clauses which have to be included to comply with the written statement requirements are marked with an asterisk (*)*. It will therefore be relatively easy to convert the precedent into a pure written statement (commonly referred to as a 'section 1 statement') if this is what is required.

To comply with the rules relating to section 1 statements the contract should be issued within two months of the start of the employment (see the ERA 1996, s 1(2)), although in the interests of certainty it is much better if the parties sign up to the contract on or before the date the employment begins. Strictly speaking, as the law now stands, the clauses which constitute the section 1 statement have to be accurate at a date no more than seven days before the written statement is given (see the ERA 1996, s 1(4)). However, the contract is drafted on the straightforward basis that it is accurate at the date the contract is made.

The rules relating to section 1 statements provide that the statement must identify both the employer and the employee (ERA 1996, s 1(3)(a)). Although there is no legal requirement that addresses be given, these should be included for clarity. (The one exceptional case where an employer's address has to be given is where the employee is required or permitted to work at various locations; see the ERA 1996, s 1(4)(h)).

Important changes to strengthen the role of section 1 statements are contained in the Employment Act 2002, ss 35 to 38. These changes which are likely to take effect towards the end of 2003 reflect the Government's view that if clear information about the basic terms and conditions of employment is given at the start of the employment relationship, subsequent disputes are far less likely. As a result, under the Employment Act 2002, s 38 tribunals will, for the first time, be able to award compensation to employees where the lack, incompleteness or inaccuracy of the section 1 statement becomes evident during the course of certain tribunal claims. (The list of claims where such an award can be made is set out in the Employment Act 2002, Sch 5 and includes unfair dismissal and discrimination claims). Although this provision is parasitic in that compensation can only be awarded if one of the listed claims is successfully pursued, it clearly reinforces the need for clear written documentation at the start of the employment relationship. As a result the notion of an oral employment contract (discussed in chap 3 at para 3.3) may become much less meaningful in practice.

To avoid unnecessary duplication (and the inconsistencies that often result) Clause 37 of the Act will, when it comes into force, confirm existing practice by providing that the section 1 statement can be included in the employment contract, provided that (as now) the contract is issued within two months of the start date. Where this is done, the information required by the section 1 statement will have to be accurate either at the date of the contract or, if the contract is issued before the employment begins, on the first day of employment. As noted above the precedent conforms with the former approach, and is stated to be accurate at the date of the agreement.

Prec 2

---

2   *Commencement of Employment

2.1   Your employment by the Company began on [   ] and your period of continuous employment also runs from this date. No employment with a previous employer counts as part of your period of continuous employment.

OR:

2.2   Your employment by the Company began on [   ]. However your period of continuous employment (which takes account of your employment with [insert name of previous employer]) began on [   ].

Notes:

To comply with the rules relating to section 1 statements this Clause sets out the date on which the employment began (see the ERA 1996, s 1(3)(b)). In addition under the ERA 1996, s 1(3)(c), a section 1 statement has to specify the date on which the employee's period of continuous employment began and whether any period of employment with a previous employer counts towards continuity.

Continuity of employment is a purely statutory concept which cannot be modified by agreement between the parties (see *Collison v BBC* [1998] IRLR 238, EAT). The information given in this Clause must therefore reflect the governing provisions on continuity which are found in the ERA 1996, ss 210–219.

Prec 3

---

3   *Job Title

You are employed as [   ] and will be responsible to
[   ] . You are expected to be flexible in the duties you carry out
and the Company reserves the right to vary your duties from time to time
as it thinks fit. You may therefore be required during the course of your
employment to work in a different department and/or carry out any other
duties which are reasonable and within your capabilities should the
Company consider this to be in the best interests of its business.

Notes:

A section 1 statement *must* specify the employee's job title or give a brief job
description (see ERA 1996, s 1(4)(f)). This Clause adopts the first option as in
practice a job description may not be available.

The clause attempts to give the employer a reasonable amount of flexibility in
varying duties if there is a business need for this, thereby reducing the risk of a
constructive dismissal claim should it be necessary to transfer the employee to a
different role. The attitude of the courts towards such 'flexibility clauses', which
effectively give the employer a unilateral power of variation, is discussed in chap 3
at para 3.12. At the very least the parties should be aware that however clearly
drafted such a clause may be, it is unlikely to give the employer carte blanche to
alter the employee's job at will. So, for example in *Haden Ltd v Cowan* [1982]
IRLR 314, CA the Court of Appeal held that a clause requiring a divisional
contracts surveyor to perform 'any and all duties which reasonably [fell] within the
scope of his capabilities' did not give the employer the right to transfer the
employee to any quantity surveyor role within its organisation. Instead the employer
could only transfer him to duties commensurate with his role as divisional contracts
surveyor.

The difficult issue of whether changes to the method of performing a particular job
(as opposed to changes to the duties themselves) will amount to a breach of contract
by the employer is discussed in chap 4 at para 4.14.

Prec 4

---

4   Qualifications and References

4.1   Your employment is conditional upon you holding and retaining all the educational, vocational, professional and other qualifications which you listed in your application form. It is also expected that the examination grades and/or work experience claimed on your application form or at interview are accurate. The Company reserves the right, depending on the particular circumstances, to terminate your employment either summarily or with due notice [or by making a payment in lieu of notice] if at any time it is discovered that you do not have any of the said qualifications, grades or experience. [You will be required to bring the originals of all examination certificates and professional qualifications with you on your first day at work].

4.2   Your employment is also conditional upon receipt of [2] satisfactory references. Whilst every effort will be made to obtain all such references as quickly as possible your employment may start before some or all of your references are received. If so it is agreed that the Company may, depending upon the particular circumstances, terminate your employment either summarily or with due notice [or by making a payment in lieu of notice] if any reference falls short of our requirements. The Company's decision is final as to whether your references meet the required standard.

Notes:

Many job offers are conditional upon the receipt of satisfactory references and proof of qualifications. However, it may not be possible to take up references or check qualifications before the offer is accepted. This Clause therefore gives the employer a contractual remedy if, after the employment starts, it turns out that these conditions have not been fulfilled. Note that the employer's right to terminate the contract by making a payment in lieu of notice is contained in Clause 18.

Clearly the employer will have to evaluate any references which he receives. In *Wishart v National Association of Citizens Advice Bureaux Ltd* [1990] ICR 794, the Court of Appeal held that where receipt of satisfactory references was made a condition of the contract, the employer's subjective view of the references was final. This is reflected in the drafting of Clause 4.2. Nonetheless, particular care should be taken if an unsatisfactory reference is received or acted on more than a year after the employee starts work, as there is always the potential for an unfair dismissal claim in such a case, particularly if the employee has worked satisfactorily for the new employer. The legal duties surrounding the giving of references are discussed in chap 4 at para 4.22.

As well as verifying qualifications and references, the employer will also need to be satisfied that a prospective employee is entitled to work in the UK to avoid

195

committing an offence under the Asylum and Immigration Act 1996, s 8. This is usually achieved by a provision in the offer letter requiring the employee to produce appropriate documentation (such as a passport, birth certificate or evidence of their national insurance number) before the employment starts. It does not normally require any specific contractual provision. The Commission for Racial Equality has produced detailed Guidance for employers on how to avoid a liability under section 8 whilst still complying with the Race Relations Act 1976.

Prec 5

---

5   Freedom to take up Employment

You confirm that by taking up employment with the Company or performing your duties under this Agreement you will not be in breach of any contract or of any other binding obligation and you agree to identify the Company fully against any costs, claims or demands made against it arising out of any such breach or alleged breach.

Notes:

This Clause confirms that the employee is not fettered by prior contractual commitments owed to a former employer. If any such commitments exist and the Company (being the new employer) knows about them, it risks being held liable for inducing the employee to breach his previous contract.

Prec 6

---

6   Duties of your Employment

6.1   During your employment your duties will include:

    6.1.1   carrying out your duties diligently and to the best of your ability;

    6.1.2   devoting your whole time and attention to the Company during working hours;

    6.1.3   complying with all lawful and reasonable instructions of the Company;

    6.1.4   doing your utmost to promote the interests and reputation of the Company;

    6.1.5   refraining from making any false or misleading statement relating to the Company [or its suppliers/customers/clients]; and

    6.1.6   taking all possible care not to damage any of the Company's property or equipment.

6.2   [In addition during your employment you should report to the Company any material breach of Company rules or procedures or any other misconduct or dishonesty relating to the Company or its business which you reasonably and honestly believe has been committed or is being seriously contemplated by any other member of staff or by a third party (such as a customer or a supplier). You are encouraged to use the channels of communication set up under the Company's Whistleblowing Procedure for this purpose. The Company will treat any information reported in compliance with this duty in confidence as far as it is practicable to do so. Should you fail to act in accordance with this duty or should you make any report knowing it to be false the Company reserves the right to treat this as a disciplinary matter justifying summary dismissal under Clause 20 in an appropriate case].

Notes:

This Clause sets out a basic list of the employee's duties which can be expanded if appropriate. Some elements (such as the duty to obey instructions) simply reflect the implied obligations on employees discussed in chap 4. On the other hand, the duty to report the wrongdoing of third parties would not necessarily form part of the contract without express provision as there is no general duty to report a fellow employee's misconduct (see *Sybron Corpn v Rochem Ltd* [1984] Ch 112, CA). If Clause 6.2 is included it should be consistent with any whistleblowing policy operated by the employer.

Prec 7

---

7   Outside Interests

If during the course of your employment you wish:

7.1   to be engaged in any other paid employment;

7.2   to have any outside business interests (other than investments in shares or securities quoted on a recognised investment exchange such as the London Stock Exchange); or

7.3   to accept any public office (whether paid or unpaid)

you must seek the written permission of [your Manager] who will consider whether it is in the best interests of the company to agree to your request. If permission is given this may be subject to any conditions [your Manager] deems appropriate.

Notes:

Although the law is prepared, in certain circumstances, to imply a duty on the employee not to engage in competitive activities with the employer (discussed in chap 4 at para 4.16), this Clause is substantially wider, giving the employer an effective veto over certain activities whether competitive or not. It will clearly not be appropriate in all cases.

Prec 8

---

8   *Place of Work

8.1   Your normal place of work will be [   ] although you may be required to work from any of the Company's premises on a temporary basis should the need arise. You may also be required to travel to customer sites and premises in the course of your duties and on occasion to attend training sessions and meetings at such venues as the Company may reasonably determine.

8.2   During the course of your employment you may be required to change your normal place of work to any premises maintained by the Company from time to time. You will be given as much notice as possible of any such change.

8.3   If you normal place of work does change in accordance with Clause 8.2 you will be entitled to move home and will be given such financial assistance in relation to the expenses of the move [as the Company in its absolute discretion deems fair and reasonable in all the circumstances] [as set out in the Company's relocation policy]. [It is agreed that any sums paid to you or on your behalf by the Company to cover relocation expenses, other than sums paid to cover temporary accommodation costs, shall be repayable by you to the Company on demand or may be withheld from any sums due to you from the Company in accordance with Clause 15 if you should resign voluntarily from the Company's employment within [1 year] of the date of the said move].

OR:

8.4   You will have no normal place of work but will instead be expected to travel to visit [clients, customers, suppliers] as necessary. You will be required to report to [   ] on a [daily/weekly/monthly] basis [by telephone] [by e-mail] [in person at the Company's [   ] office] to discuss your progress. You will also be required to attend the Company's [   ] office [every month] to liaise with management and to attend [the Company's budgeting meetings]. [You will be permitted to carry out any administrative duties from your home].

Notes:

To comply with the section 1 statement requirements this Clause must specify the employee's place of work or, where the employee is required or permitted to work at various places, it has to give an indication to that effect together with details of the employer's address. In addition, if the employee is to be required to work abroad for a continuous period of more than one month then certain extra information must be provided, such as the currency in which he is to be paid (see the ERA 1996, s 1(4)(k)).

Clause 8.2 takes the form of a contractual mobility clause. Such clauses are, in effect, a form of flexibility clause, giving management considerable autonomy in this area (see the discussion in chap 3 at para 3.12). However, there are clearly limits on the extent to which an employer can rely on such clauses. In the first place, the Court of Appeal has held that mobility clauses could be subject to challenge on the grounds of indirect sex discrimination. (See *Meade-Hill v British Council* [1995] IRLR 478 where it was held that a mobility clause in the contract of a female middle manager could be discriminatory because women were more likely than their partners to be the second earner and so were less able to relocate. This argument would seem to have a greater chance of success where employment is at a junior level although it is always open to the employer to justify the mobility clause). Secondly, mobility clauses must not be used so as to 'destroy or seriously damage the relationship of confidence and trust between employer and employee'. In *United Bank v Akhtar* [1989] IRLR 507, EAT the employee was asked to relocate from Leeds to the Midlands at a few days' notice pursuant to a contractual mobility clause. However, at the time his wife was ill and he was offered no assistance with the expenses of moving. The EAT held the employer was in breach of the implied obligation not to destroy the relationship of trust and confidence. A similar approach was adopted in *Prestwick Circuits Ltd v McAndrew* [1990] IRLR 191 where an employer was held to be in breach of contract when he gave an employee just one week's notice of relocation. On the other hand in *White v Reflecting Roadstuds Ltd* [1991] ICR 733 the EAT said that there was no authority to the effect that a mobility clause had to be operated reasonably. The most that could be said was that an employer must not act capriciously. However, even this statement acknowledges that some (albeit minimal) standard does apply to the operation of such clauses. Thirdly it is now possible that such a clause will be subject to the reasonableness test imposed by the Unfair Contract Terms Act 1977, s 3 (see the discussion of this point in chap 3).

Clause 8.3 deals with the employer's contribution to removal expenses. Employers should be aware that in granting generous relocation packages, they may take on substantial obligations. For example in *French v Barclays Bank plc* [1998] IRLR 646, CA the Court of Appeal held that the employer was in breach of the implied term of trust and confidence when it tried to alter the terms of an interest free bridging loan, granted to the employee on relocation. Effectively this meant that once the loan had been granted, it was for Barclays to bear the burden of the collapse of the housing market, not the employee. In this context the parties should also be aware that some removal expenses and benefits can be paid to the employee free of income tax (see the Income and Corporation Taxes Act 1988, s 191A and Sch 11A).

Prec 9

---

9   *Collective Agreements

EITHER:

9.1   There are no collective agreements which directly affect the terms and conditions of your employment.

OR:

9.2   The following terms of the collective agreement entered into between [   ] and [   ] on [*insert date*], as varied from time to time, directly affect the terms and conditions of your employment by the Company and will take effect as part of this Agreement [*specify relevant terms*]:

Notes:

This Clause reflects the fact that details of any collective agreements which directly affect the terms and conditions of employment have to be included in the section 1 statement. Where the employer is not a party to the collective agreement particulars of the actual parties must be given (see the ERA 1996, s 1(4)(j)) but it is always advisable to include such details, together with the date of the collective agreement, for clarity. Where no relevant collective agreements exist this must also be stated (see the ERA 1996, s 2(1)).

The issue of whether particular terms of a collective agreement form part of the employee's contract needs to be considered carefully. Whilst there may be good reason for incorporating some parts of a collective agreement, it may not be appropriate for other terms – particularly where the collective agreement sets out procedural arrangements which are only intended as a guide to best practice.

Where incorporation is to take place it is best to refer to the relevant provisions 'as varied from time to time'. This ensures that subsequent amendments to the collectively agreed terms are reflected in the employment contract. However, even if such words are used, incorporation is unlikely to be affected by the termination of the collective agreement at a later date. In such circumstances the last version of the incorporated term is likely to remain binding as between employer and employee unless the individual contract is expressly amended. (See *Robertson v British Gas Corpn* [1983] ICR 351).

You may want to consider extending this Clause to cover the relevant provisions of any workforce agreements entered into under recent legislation, such as the Working Time Regulations 1998 and the Maternity and Parental Leave etc Regulations 1999. There seems no reason in principle why the terms of such an agreement may not be expressly incorporated into the individual contract of employment if the parties so agree. However, as such an agreement can only take effect for a maximum of 5 years (see for example the Working Time Regulations 1998, Sch 1) it will be particularly important to refer to future variations and/or to consider the effect of the workforce agreement terminating without being replaced.

Prec 10

---

10   *Hours of Work

10.1   The Company is committed to complying with the provisions of the Working Time Regulations 1998 ('the Regulations') and this clause is drafted accordingly. For your part you must comply with the policies and requirements of the Company from time to time in force in relation to your Working Time (as defined below) and the recording of your working hours. The Company reserves the right to treat any failure to comply with its record keeping requirements or the deliberate provision of false information about your working time as a disciplinary matter which could lead to summary dismissal under Clause 20 in an appropriate case.

10.2   Your normal hours of work will be [   ] am to [   ] pm Monday to Friday inclusive with a daily [lunch] [meal] break of [   ] minutes.

10.3   In addition to your normal hours of work:

EITHER:

   10.3.1   you will from time to time be expected to work additional hours [without extra remuneration and without any entitlement to take time off in lieu] where this is necessary to perform your job properly;

OR:

   10.3.2   you may choose to work overtime [up to a maximum of [   ] hours overtime per week] to be paid at the rate specified in Clause 11.3. However the Company has no obligation to make any overtime available to you;

OR:

   10.3.3   you will be required to work up to [   ] hours overtime per week where this is provided by the Company to be paid at the rate specified in Clause 11.3. However the Company has no obligation to make any overtime available to you at any time;

OR:

   10.3.4   the Company undertakes to provide and you agree to work [   ] hours overtime per week to be paid at the rate specified in Clause 11.3.

10.4 [By signing this Agreement you agree that the limit in Regulation 4(1) of the Regulations (which restricts Working Time including overtime to a maximum of 48 hours per week averaged over the reference period set out in Clause 10.6) does not apply to you with the result that your weekly Working Time may exceed the 48 hour average. [You may withdraw your agreement to work in excess of this limit by giving us [3 months] prior written notice]].

10.5 In this Clause 'Working Time' has the meaning given to it in Regulation 2 of the Regulations and in particular covers any time when you are working, at the Company's disposal and carrying out your activities or duties. [For the avoidance of doubt it is agreed that Working Time includes:

   10.5.1 time spent travelling between your home and any location which you attend (other than your normal place of work) in the proper performance of your duties;

   10.5.2 time spent travelling between any two locations (including your normal place of work) which you attend in the proper performance of your duties;

   10.5.3 time when you are on-call and present [on any of our premises] [at your normal place of work]; and

   10.5.4 [*include any other activities as appropriate*]].

10.6 The reference period to be used for calculating your Working Time is:

   10.6.1 any 17 week period during your employment by the Company; or

   10.6.2 the number of weeks for which you have worked for the Company if this is less than 17.

10.7 [You agree to notify us in writing on a [regular] [monthly] basis [using the form supplied for the purpose] of any hours worked for any other employer, organisation or concern].

10.8 [This Clause is subject to the provisions on lay off and short time working set out in Clause 22.]

Notes:

To comply with the section 1 statement requirements, this provision must give particulars of any terms and conditions relating to hours of work including any terms and conditions relating to 'normal working hours' (a term which is partially defined by the ERA 1996, s 234). The recent ECJ decision in *Lange v Georg*

Schünemann GmbH (C-350/99, [2001] IRLR 244, ECJ) makes it clear that the governing Proof of Employment Relationship Directive (91/533/EEC) requires details of compulsory overtime to be included in the section 1 statement. The provision therefore contains drafting to comply with this obligation.

The clause is drafted on the basis that the Working Time Regulations 1998 (as amended) apply to the employment. If the Regulations do not apply, hours of work will be a matter for negotiation between employer and employee unless there is an applicable collective agreement or some other form of regulatory control. The DTI Employment Relations website (www.dti.gov.uk) contains a useful summary of those sectors which are currently excluded from the Regulations and the progress which has been made towards extending regulation to cover them.

Assuming the Regulations do apply then, as discussed in chap 2, para 2.10 they represent a significant erosion of the parties' freedom of contract in this area with the effect that the employee's working time, including overtime, cannot exceed an average of 48 hours per week (unless he has entered into an opt-out agreement such as the one in Clause 10.4). The Regulations also contain restrictions on night working together with entitlements to daily and weekly rest periods. Clauses 10.2 and 10.3 should therefore be drafted with these provisions in mind. (It is assumed here that the 'managing executive exemption' set out in Regulation 20(1) which exempts workers who have considerable autonomy over their working hours from most of the provisions in the Regulations is unlikely to apply to a junior employee).

To try and clarify which activities are to be included in the calculation of working time Clause 10.5 gives scope for providing that certain borderline activities, such as on-call duties are to be counted in (although the ECJ has now confirmed that even without such a provision on-call time would count towards working time at least where the worker is obliged to be present and available at the workplace during on-call hours; see *SIMAP v Conselleria de Sanidad y Consumo de la Generalidad Valenciana* [2002] IRLR 845).

Clause 10.6 reflects the fact that the basic reference period set by the Regulations for calculating the average weekly total is a rolling 17 week period (see Regulation 4(3)). However, it may on some occasions be possible to modify this and you will need to refer to the Regulations if you propose doing so.

If the employee's average weekly hours (including overtime) are likely to exceed 48 then the employer will need to obtain an opt-out agreement such as the one in Clause 10.4 to avoid liability under the Regulations. However, the employee cannot be compelled to enter such an agreement and is protected from victimisation or dismissal if he refuses to do so (see the ERA 1996, ss 45(a) and 101(a)). If the employee does agree to enter an opt-out the following factors should be borne in mind:

(a) the employer has to keep a list of all workers who have actually signed opt-out agreements (see Regulation 4(2) as amended). This is now the only record keeping requirement in relation to opt-outs making the opt-out very attractive to employers;

(b) under the Regulations an employee can always withdraw his agreement to work long hours. If the contract is silent on the matter he need only give seven days' notice of the change. However, his contract may provide for up to three months' notice to be given and Clause 10.4 adopts this option;

(c) an opt-out agreement does not have to be included in the contract of employment and can exist as a separate document.

Clause 10.7 can be useful where the employee has not signed an opt-out and he is allowed to work for other organisations during his employment by the Company. The Clause enables the Company to monitor the employee's total weekly average and would be evidence to show that the Company is taking 'all reasonable steps' to ensure that the 48 hour average is being complied with as required by Regulation 4(2). The Clause could also be used where an opt-out has been signed, but the employer wants to be sure that any work for third parties does not become too onerous.

Note that under the Regulations special rules apply to the working hours of young workers (ie those over the minimum school leaving age but under 18). Further restrictions are likely to be introduced before the end of 2002 to comply with the UK's obligations under the Protection of Young Workers Directive 94/33/EC and you should refer to these provisions where necessary.

Prec 11

---

11   *Pay

EITHER:-

11.1   Your [basic] pay is £[   ] gross for each hour worked during the normal hours of work specified in Clause 10.2. You will not be paid for lunch or rest periods.

11.2   You will be paid in arrears [each Friday] [on or around the [   ] of each month] [by means of a weekly wage packet] [by direct credit transfer to your bank or building society account] in respect of the hours worked during the preceding [week] [month] after any necessary deductions for income tax and national insurance and any other authorised deductions have been made.

11.3   [Hours of overtime worked in accordance with Clause 10.3 will be paid at the rate of [1½ times] your [basic] hourly rate of pay. Any such payment will be made in arrears in the manner set out in Clause 11.2].

OR:

11.4   Your annual salary is £[   ] gross which shall accrue on a daily basis and shall be paid monthly in arrears by direct credit transfer to your bank or building society account after any necessary deductions for income tax, national insurance and any other authorised deductions have been made. You will be paid [on or about the [22nd] of each month] [on the [last day] of the month, although if this falls on a day when banking services are not available payment will be made on the last day on which banking services are available before that date]. The Company may change the date and manner of payment at its discretion but will give you as much notice as reasonably possible of any such change.

IN EITHER CASE:

11.5   [It will be your responsibility to ensure that a member of the Personnel Department is given the name of your current bank or building society, its sort code number and the number of your account and details of any changes to these items].

11.6   The Company will carry out a review of your [basic pay/salary] [and the overtime rate referred to in Clause 11.3] from time to time. The Company is under no contractual obligation to increase your [salary/pay] [or your overtime rate] following such a review.

11.7   [This Clause is subject to the provisions on lay off and short term working set out in Clause 22].

Notes:

This Clause reflects the requirement that the section 1 statement must specify the scale or rate of remuneration (or the method of calculating remuneration) and the intervals at which remuneration is paid (see the ERA 1996, s 1(4)(b) and (c)). It will of course be subject to the requirements of the national minimum wage (discussed in chap 2, para 2.10) which covers nearly all workers in the UK even if they are only here on a temporary basis. Pay rates may also be subject to statutory scrutiny as a result of the Equal Pay Act 1970 and various other anti-discrimination laws such as the Part-time Workers (Prevention of Less Favourable Treatment) Regulations 2000.

Clause 11.6 provides a pay review mechanism and makes it absolutely clear that any such review will not lead automatically to an increase. The employer could go further and include a provision allowing pay to be decreased after the review if this is in the interests of his business. However, notwithstanding such a provision, an unreasonable reduction in pay might well amount to a breach of the implied term of mutual trust and confidence (see *United Bank v Akhtar* [1989] IRLR 507, EAT where unreasonable reliance on a mobility clause was said to 'destroy . . . the relationship of confidence and trust between employer and employee'). Any such discretion should therefore be exercised with care.

Prec 12

---

12   *Pension Provision

EITHER:-

12.1 You will be permitted as soon as you are eligible to join the [*insert details of appropriate pension scheme*] or such other scheme as the Company may nominate for this purpose (in either case the 'Scheme'), subject to the rules of the Scheme in force from time to time. Details of the Scheme are available from the Personnel Department on request.

12.2 [No] [A] contracting-out certificate is in force in relation to your employment if you join the Scheme.

12.3 If you join the Scheme the Company will be entitled to deduct contributions from your salary [pay] for payment into the Scheme on your behalf in accordance with your instructions and subject to the rules of the Scheme from time to time in force.

12.4 The Company reserves the right at any time to withdraw or amend any of the rules or benefits of the Scheme and/or to terminate your participation in the Scheme.

Notes:

The section 1 statement must normally set out details of any terms and conditions relating to pensions and pension schemes unless the employee's pension is set up under statute and the statutory scheme already gives employees the right to information about their pension rights when they start work (see the ERA 1996, ss 1(4)(d)(iii) and 1(5)). It is possible to refer the employee to a 'reasonably accessible' document containing all or part of the relevant information and Clause 12.1 follows this approach (see the ERA 1996, s 2(2)). The written statement must also specify whether a contracting-out certificate is in force for pension purposes (see the ERA 1996, s 3(5)).

Employers and employees alike should always take detailed advice on the issue of pension provision. Generally speaking, in the case of junior employees, the most tax efficient way of providing a pension scheme is through an Inland Revenue approved scheme. This may take the form of an occupational scheme set up by the employer or a personal pension taken out by the employee whether on an individual or group basis. However, where an occupational scheme is set up the employee cannot be required to join; see Pension Schemes Act 1993, s 160, reflected in the wording of Clause 12.1. In addition, with effect from 8 October 2001, employers with five employees or more have to provide eligible employees with access to a new type of pension scheme, known as a 'stakeholder scheme' unless they already offer an occupational scheme or personal pension plan which meets certain statutory conditions.

Clause 12.4 gives the employer the right to withdraw or vary pension benefits. Despite the apparent width of this Clause the employer's room for manoeuvre may in practice be circumscribed by the implied terms of the contract (see discussion in chap 5, para 5.6).

Prec 13

---

13   Additional Benefits

The additional benefits to which you are entitled under this Agreement are as follows:

[*Insert details of benefits*].

Notes:

This Clause allows you to identify any additional elements of the remuneration package such as private medical expenses insurance, season ticket loans or free medical screening. If considering whether life insurance should be provided it is usually worth checking whether such insurance is provided under the Company's pension scheme. This is because many schemes provide life insurance of up to a maximum of four times pensionable salary.

Prec 14

14   Expenses

You will be reimbursed for all reasonable travel, accommodation, entertainment and other out-of-pocket expenses incurred on authorised Company business [excluding any car parking or road traffic offence fines] [subject to the production of such receipts or other evidence of expenditure as the Company may reasonably require] [in accordance with the procedure set out in the Staff Handbook].

Prec 15

---

15   Deductions

It is agreed that the Company may at any time deduct any sums which you owe to the Company from your [salary] [pay] or from any other payment due to be made to you by the Company. It is also agreed that you will at all times pay to the Company upon demand any sums which you owe to the Company. This provision does not affect the right of the Company to recover any sums or balance of sums owed by you to the Company by taking legal proceedings.

Notes:

This Clause authorises deductions to be made from the employee's wages in accordance with the ERA 1996, Part II. From the employer's point of view this Clause is essential. Note that under the ERA 1996, s 13(2) the employer must give the employee a copy of the contract containing this Clause before he makes the relevant deduction.

16   *Holidays

16.1   The Company's holiday year runs from [1 January to 31 December].

16.2   You are entitled to the following paid holiday:

    16.2.1   [25] working days in each holiday year; and

    16.2.2   the following [8] Bank and Public holidays: [Christmas Day, Boxing Day, New Year's Day, Good Friday, Easter Monday, May Day, Spring Bank Holiday, Late Summer Bank Holiday].

16.3   The amount payable in respect of any paid holiday period shall be calculated as follows: [insert relevant details].

16.4   You must not take any holiday unless you have [submitted a Company holiday form to and] obtained the prior [written] approval of your Manager. In addition it will not be possible to take more than [15] working days holiday at any one time without first obtaining the [written] authority of [your Manager]. In light of these arrangements, Regulations 15(1) to 15(4) of the Working Time Regulations 1998 ('the Regulations'), which require certain notices to be given before holiday can be taken or denied, do not apply to your employment. However you will be expected to give as much notice as reasonably possible of your intended holiday arrangements so that if they cannot be approved [your Manager] can let you know in good time. In addition during your first year of employment you will be able to take all or part of your holiday entitlement before it has accrued under Regulation 15A of the Regulations provided you have followed the procedures set out in this Clause and have obtained [your Manager's] prior [written] approval.

16.5   The Company reserves the right to require you to take all or part of your holiday entitlement during any period of notice given under this Agreement or on a particular day or days [including any of the Bank or Public Holidays set out in Clause 16.2]. The Company undertakes to give you as much notice as reasonably possible of any such requirement.

16.6   [Holiday entitlement should be taken in the holiday year in which it accrues. As a result any holiday entitlement remaining unused at [31 December] cannot be carried over into the following holiday year and there will be no entitlement to pay in lieu of unused holiday except on termination of your employment in accordance with Clause 16.7]. OR [If you do not take all the holiday to which you are entitled during a particular holiday year you will be permitted to carry forward up to [5] days to the next holiday year. Otherwise any unused holiday entitlement will be lost and no payment in lieu of unused holiday entitlement will be made except on termination of the employment in accordance with Clause 16.7].

16.7 On the termination of your employment you will be entitled to be paid in lieu of any outstanding holiday entitlement for that particular holiday year or, as the case may be, will be obliged to repay to the Company any payments received by you in excess of your accrued holiday entitlement for that year. A day's holiday pay for these purposes is [$^1/_{260}$ of your annual salary calculated on the basis of the number of actual working days in a year after deducting weekends and rounded to the nearest 10] [7 times your [basic] hourly rate of pay] except that, if you are summarily dismissed pursuant to Clause 20, the amount of any payment in lieu of outstanding holiday entitlement due to you from the Company shall be one penny.

16.8 If you are ill on any day or days previously booked or designated as paid holiday, such day or days must nonetheless be taken as counting towards your paid holiday entitlement unless sanctioned as sick leave by [your Manager].

Notes:

The section 1 statement must contain particulars of terms and conditions relating to holiday entitlement (including public holidays) and holiday pay and the precedent reflects this. Sufficient detail must be given to enable holiday pay, including any entitlement to accrued holiday pay on termination, to be calculated with precision (see the ERA 1996, s 1(4)(d)(i)).

As with Clause 10 (Hours of Work) this Clause is drafted on the basis that the Working Time Regulations 1998 (as amended) apply to the employment so that the employee is entitled to a minimum of four weeks' paid leave each year. However, the precedent reflects the fact that the entitlement can be increased by agreement between the parties. It also specifically refers to public holidays to avoid any ambiguity as employees have no automatic right to take such holidays unless there is an appropriate provision in the contract (see *Campbell and Smith Construction Group Ltd v Greenwood* [2001] IRLR 588, EAT).

Clause 16.3 allows the method of calculating holiday pay to be set out. This may simply reflect the mechanism for such a calculation as set out in Regulation 16. Alternatively there is no reason why the contract may not be more generous if the employer so wishes. Note that the legality of paying 'rolled-up' holiday rates, where the employer increases hourly rates to include an element for holiday pay, rather than make specific payments at the time holiday is actually taken, is currently in doubt (see *Blackburn v Gridquest Ltd (t/a Select Employment)* [2002] EWCA Civ 1037 [2002] All ER (D) 325 (Jul), where the Court of Appeal failed to give a definitive ruling on this point).

Clause 16.4 deals with the procedure for agreeing periods of holiday which in this precedent simply requires prior management approval. Without such a provision leave could only be applied for or declined on the relatively short notice periods in Regulation 15, which could cause considerable inconvenience in practice. In addition the Clause disapplies the clumsily drafted provisions on accrual of leave during the first year of employment, introduced by the Working Time (Amendment) Regulations 2001. These Regulations were formulated in response to the ECJ's decision *in R (on the application of BECTU) v Secretary of State for Trade and Industry*: C-173/99 [2001] IRLR 559 which ruled that the 13-week qualifying period for annual leave, originally required by the UK Regulations, was unlawful. However, it is generally better to give greater flexibility to the parties than the 2001 Regulations allow and the precedent reflects this.

Clause 16.5 is very useful for an employer as it allows him to insist that holiday be taken at a particular time (eg during a factory shut down).

The first part of Clause 16.6 reflects the fact that under the Regulations holiday must be taken in the leave year to which it relates and cannot be carried over (see Regulation 13(9)). However, there is no reason why any contractual entitlement over and above the statutory minimum cannot be carried over and alternative drafting to this effect is provided in the second half of the clause. Clause 16.6 also provides that a payment in lieu of unused holiday entitlement will only be made on termination of the employment. This accords with Regulation 13(9)(a) which states that statutory leave may not be replaced by a payment in lieu except where the worker's employment is terminated. However, there is nothing in the Regulations to prevent such a payment being made in respect of any leave granted in excess of the statutory four week entitlement and this could be reflected in the agreement if the parties so wished.

If the employment terminates during a leave year and the employee has not used his accrued holiday entitlement then, under the Regulations, the employer must make him a payment in lieu. This apparently applies even where the employee has been summarily dismissed (see Regulation 14). The payment due is calculated by reference to a formula set out in the Regulations or can be determined by agreement between the parties. Clause 16.7 adopts the latter approach and bases the calculation of a daily rate of pay on the number of working days in each year. Note that this Clause also specifies that on a summary dismissal payment in lieu of outstanding holiday will be one penny. (This would appear to comply with the Working Time Regulations which stipulate that a payment must be made whatever the reason for termination, but permit the *amount* of any payment in lieu to be agreed by the parties; see Regulation 14(3)(a) and *Witley and District Mens Club v Mackay* [2001] IRLR 595, EAT).

Under Regulation 14(4) a contract of employment may provide that if on termination the employee has taken more than his accrued holiday he can be required to compensate the employer whether by a payment or by undertaking additional work or otherwise. Clause 16.7 requires such a payment to be made and from an employer's point of view should always be included, otherwise no deduction for overpaid holiday may be made, see *Hill v Howard Chappel* (20 March 2002, unreported), EAT.

Prec 17

17   *Absence from Work and Medical Examination

17.1   If you are absent from work for any reason you, or someone acting on your behalf, must contact [   ] before [10 am] on the first day of absence to explain the reason for your absence and its expected duration.

17.2   If the absence is due to sickness or injury and lasts for 7 calendar days or less you must complete a self-certification form which will be provided by the Company on your return.

17.3   If the absence is due to sickness or injury and lasts for more than 7 calendar days you will be required to produce a medical certificate signed by your doctor stating the reason for absence by no later than the 8th day of illness. Medical certificates must cover the whole period of absence. If you do not provide such certificates your absence will be deemed to be unauthorised.

17.4   You may be required at any time during your employment to undergo a medical examination [including a health assessment for the purpose of night working in accordance with the Working Time Regulations 1998] at the Company's expense by a doctor of the Company's choice to help determine your fitness for continued employment [and/or your entitlement to contractual sick pay]. You agree to give your consent to such an examination, to co-operate fully in obtaining the doctor's report and to authorise full disclosure of the report to the Company. [Such an examination may include or consist of tests for alcohol or drugs (including controlled drugs as defined by the Misuse of Drugs Act 1971) where the Company has reason to believe that the use of alcohol or drugs is adversely affecting your performance at work or is posing a risk to health and safety]. If you unreasonably refuse to undergo such an examination you may be subject to disciplinary action.

EITHER:

17.5   Provided you meet all of the relevant statutory conditions in force from time to time the Company will pay you statutory sick pay. For statutory sick pay purposes your qualifying days will be [Monday to Friday] inclusive. Beyond this there is no contractual right to payment in respect of periods of absence due to sickness or injury.

OR:

17.6   Provided you follow the procedure set out in Clauses 17.1 to 17.3, you undergo any medical examination required by the Company under Clause 17.4 and provided the Company is satisfied that your absence is due to sickness or injury, then [subject to Clause 17.7] you will be entitled during your employment to the following contractual sick pay during any [rolling 12 month period] [calendar year]:

17.6.1   if you have between 6 months' and 2 years' continuous employment 5 days' full pay followed by 5 days' half pay; or

17.6.2   if you have more than 2 years continuous employment 10 days' full pay followed by 10 days' half pay.

Thereafter any payment of contractual sick pay will be entirely at the discretion of the Company. For the purposes of this Clause a day's full pay is [1/260 of your annual salary] [7 times your [basic] hourly rate of pay] and half a day's pay shall be calculated proportionately.

17.7   [Should you be unable due to sickness or injury to attend any meeting or hearing scheduled pursuant to the Company's disciplinary, grievance, capability or bullying and harassment procedures (as in force from time to time) then notwithstanding Clause 17.6 payment of contractual sick pay for any continuous period of absence which includes the date for which that meeting or hearing has been scheduled will be entirely at the discretion of the Company].

17.8   Any liability to pay statutory sick pay will be discharged by the payment of contractual sick pay of the same or greater amount. However if contractual sick pay is less than the statutory sick pay due for a particular period the Company will pay you the greater amount. To avoid any doubt all other state benefits which you receive or to which you are entitled whilst off sick (whether claimed by you or not) will be set off against your contractual sick pay.

17.9   For the avoidance of doubt the term 'sickness or injury' when used in this Clause includes any mental or psychiatric illness and any injury, whether or not this has been sustained in the course of your duties.

Notes:

The section 1 statement must set out any terms relating to incapacity for work due to sickness or injury, including any provision for sick pay (ERA 1996, s 1(4)(d)(ii)) unless the statement refers the employee to a 'reasonably accessible' document for these purposes (ERA 1996, s 2(2)).

Clauses 17.2 and 17.3 set out the Company's notification procedure on absence. Note that for statutory sick pay purposes an employer cannot require medical evidence for the first seven days of any period of incapacity for work (see the Social Security Administration Act 1992, s 14(1), (3)). The precedent reflects this. However, there is nothing to stop an employer requiring medical evidence earlier than this if he so wishes for the purposes of his own contractual sick pay scheme.

The employer cannot require the employee to undergo a medical examination without his/her consent. For this reason Clause 17.4 provides for the employee to give advance consent to any such examination. However, it is doubtful whether such a clause could be enforced by injunction and ultimately the employer is dependent on the employee giving written consent to a specific examination and physically attending the appointment. Nonetheless the inclusion of such a provision in the contract means that a refusal to undergo a medical will be a breach of contract and would therefore constitute a disciplinary offence. Note that Clause 17.4 allows the Company to decide which doctor will carry out the examination. Where this is done by the employee's own doctor the Access to Medical Reports Act 1988 applies. This Act requires the employee to consent to the preparation of any medical report by his doctor and gives him the right to see the report and request amendment of it before it is sent to the employer. As it is not clear whether any advance consent obtained in the employee's contract will satisfy the Act, specific consents should also be obtained at the time of the examination. Note that the Act only applies to reports obtained from a medical practitioner 'who is or has been responsible for the clinical care of the employee'. The employer may therefore prefer to appoint an independent doctor who prepares a report after a one-off examination.

Although medical testing may not, in itself, fall within the Data Protection Act 1998, if the doctor's report is subsequently kept or recorded (eg in a personnel file) it is likely that the Act will apply. The Information Commissioner is due to publish a Code of Practice on the processing of medical information which should give employers guidance in this area. One issue which may prove controversial is the area of drug or alcohol testing. An early draft version of the Code provided that such testing would only be justified on safety grounds or if it was part of a voluntary programme for the detection and treatment of drug/alcohol abuse. It is not clear at the time of writing whether the final Code will take such a restrictive approach.

It is important to specify whether any payment will be made for periods of absence due to sickness or injury. Employers are by law required to pay statutory sick pay to certain employees. However, the agreement may also provide for the provision of contractual sick pay in certain circumstances. Clauses 17.5 to 17.8 provide drafting to cover both situations. Note that the length of contractual sick pay entitlement may be relevant to the fairness of any dismissal for long sickness absence. This is because a tribunal may be less inclined to infer that a dismissal is reasonable if the employee is still receiving full sick pay. Equally it is possible that a generous contractual sick pay scheme may give rise to a wrongful dismissal claim if the employer gives due notice to the employee, but this expires within the sick pay period (see the discussion of this point in Chapter 4 at para 4.30). In addition, even where sick pay is expressed to be discretionary, the courts are prepared to intervene to impose some minimum standards on the exercise of that discretion. (See for example *Manchester City Council v Thurston* [2002] IRLR 319, EAT and also *London Club Management Ltd v Hood* [2001] IRLR 719, EAT where the possibility of challenging a failure to pay discretionary sick pay under the Disability Discrimination Act 1995 was discussed). Finally, some employers may find clause 17.7 useful, if only for its deterrent value. However, if a refusal to pay sick pay under such a provision were to be challenged it is likely that the courts would scrutinise the Company's decision very closely indeed.

Prec 18

---

18   *Notice and Termination of Employment

18.1   Termination by the Company

The Company may terminate your employment at any time by giving you the following periods of notice:

> 18.1.1   during the first 2 years of your employment - 1 week;
>
> 18.1.2   thereafter 1 week's notice for each completed year of service rising to a maximum of 12 weeks after 12 or more years service

and any such notice shall be in writing.

The provisions of this Clause do not affect the Company's right of summary dismissal under Clause 20.

18.2   Termination by the Employee

You may terminate your employment [at any time] by giving to the Company 4 weeks' [written] notice. [Your notice must be given so that it expires at the end of your [weekly] pay period].

18.3   Retirement

It is agreed that your employment will terminate automatically without the need for notice to be given by either party at the end of the month in which you reach the Company's normal retirement age of [   ]. Clauses 18.1 and 18.2 do not therefore apply in this situation.

18.4   Payment in Lieu of Notice

[It is agreed that the Company may at any time, if it so chooses, terminate your employment immediately by paying you a sum in lieu of the notice period due under Clause 18.1 (or any unexpired part of such notice period) such sum being the amount of salary payable to you under Clause 11.4 during such period or part period [excluding any bonus or benefits in kind]. Such a payment will be subject to deductions for tax and national insurance at source as required by law and to any other authorised deductions. The provisions of this Clause do not affect the Company's right of summary dismissal under Clause 20].

Notes:

The written statement must specify the length of notice which both employer and employee must give to terminate the contract (ERA 1996, s 1(4)(e)). Although such information will normally be set out in the statement itself the employee can be referred to any relevant statutory provisions (such as the ERA 1996, s 86, discussed below) or to a reasonably accessible collective agreement for particulars of the notice period. Note that if the employee's job is not intended to be permanent the statement should specify the expected length of the employment or, if the employment is for a fixed term, the date when the employment is to end (ERA 1996, s 1(4)(g)).

Where the employment is to be terminated on notice, the parties' freedom of contract is fettered by the ERA 1996, s 86 which provides for certain minimum periods of notice to be given, whatever the position under the contract. However, in this precedent the contractual notice due to the employee reflects the statutory provisions.

Any failure to comply with the notice provisions is a breach of contract, entitling the injured party to sue for damages to recover his loss. However, be wary of trying to pre-determine this loss in the contract, in case the courts view such a provision as a penalty clause. This is what happened in *Giraud UK Ltd v Smith* [2000] IRLR 763, EAT where the contract provided that a failure on the part of the employee to give and work his notice would result in a deduction from his final salary of a sum equal to the pay due for the number of days short. The EAT held that this was not a genuine pre-estimate of loss. It was therefore a penalty clause and as such was unenforceable (for further discussion of this case see Chapter 9, para 9.9).

Clause 18.3 allows for automatic termination of the contract when the employee reaches the normal retirement age. However, even where this Clause is included it would be possible to continue the employment after the normal retirement age if a new contract can be agreed.

Clause 18.4 contains a payment in lieu clause, the pros and cons of which are discussed in chap 3, para 3.30 and Chapter 9, para 9.8. Note that the clause is discretionary allowing the employer to make the payment 'if it so chooses'. The Court of Appeal in *Cerberus Software Ltd v Rowley* [2001] IRLR 160 has recently confirmed that such a discretionary provision gives the employer three options when considering how to terminate the contract (assuming there are no circumstances justifying summary dismissal):

(a)   he can dismiss on full contractual notice;

(b)   he can opt to terminate immediately by complying with the contract and making the full payment in lieu, so ensuring the continued validity of any restrictive covenants. However, if he chooses this course there will be no obligation on the employee to mitigate his loss; or

(c)   he can dismiss without notice and without making a payment in lieu, thereby breaching the contract and so forcing the employee to claim damages for the breach. Whilst this option might put any restrictive covenants at risk, it could be financially attractive as in this situation the employee will have to mitigate. As a result any earnings from a new job which the employee receives during his former notice period will reduce the value of the employee's claim.

In many cases – particularly where the employee has a short notice period, is not privy to any sensitive information and there are no restrictive covenants – a PILON clause may not be necessary. However, if such a clause is included to protect the employer's interests then the notice period should be as short as possible so that the size of the PILON is minimised. In addition it may be possible to build some form of mitigation into the PILON itself such as excluding fringe benefits from the payment.

Prec 19

---

19   Garden Leave

19.1 The Company may require you to cease performing your job and to stay away from its premises and to have no contact with any employees, officers, customers, clients, agents or suppliers of the Company during the whole or part of any period of notice, whether that notice is given by you or by the Company.

19.2 During any such period of garden leave:

19.2.1 the Company shall be under no obligation to provide you with any work although it will continue to pay your salary and provide all the benefits to which you are entitled under this Agreement;

19.2.2 you will continue to be bound by all of your obligations under this Agreement insofar as they are compatible with your being on garden leave including your duty of good faith and your duties under Clause 7 (Outside Interests); and

19.2.3 the Company may appoint someone else to perform some or all of your duties under this Agreement whether on a permanent or temporary basis.

Notes:

As discussed in chap 3, para 3.31, a garden leave clause can be very useful to an employer. However, as the employer has to continue paying the employee throughout the garden leave period he may prefer, instead of sending the employee home, to transfer the employee to other duties during the notice period (eg so that he/she will have less customer contact). If so Clause 3 (Job Title) should be drafted to give sufficient flexibility to allow this.

If the employer wants any restrictions on the employee's ability to work for third parties to continue during the garden leave period the wording set out in the latter part of Clause 19.2.2 should be included. This is necessary because of the Court of Appeal's decision in *Hutchings v Coinseed* [1998] IRLR 190, CA where it was held that a garden leave clause did not of itself prevent an employee taking a job with a competitor during the garden leave period. Express wording to this effect was necessary. This approach was subsequently reinforced by Sir Richard Scott at first instance, in *Symbian v Christensen* [2000] IRLR 77, CA where he expressed doubt whether the implied duty of fidelity and good faith survived during a period of garden leave. In addition there was considerable confusion in that case over which other provisions of the contract continued during garden leave. It is hoped that the wording in Clause 19.2.2 will help in this respect.

Prec 20

---

20   Summary Dismissal

The Company is entitled to terminate your employment without notice or payment in lieu of notice in any of the following circumstances:

20.1   you are guilty of any gross misconduct or wilful neglect in the discharge of your duties including, but not restricted to [*give particular examples*];

20.2   you commit a serious breach of any terms of this Agreement (whether that term specifically refers to the right of summary dismissal under this clause or not);

20.3   you repeat or continue any breach of this Agreement the cumulative effect of which, in the reasonable opinion of the Company, constitutes a serious breach;

20.4   you are guilty of any conduct which in the Company's opinion is likely to prejudice the interests of the Company whether or not such conduct occurs in the course of your employment;

20.5   you are convicted of any criminal offence [other than an offence under road traffic legislation in the United Kingdom or elsewhere for which a fine or a non-custodial sentence is imposed] which might reasonably be thought to adversely affect the performance of your duties;

20.6   [you are found during working hours to have taken or be under the influence of] [you become addicted to or are habitually under the influence of] alcohol or any drug (other than a drug prescribed for you by a medical practitioner for the treatment of a condition other than drug addiction) the possession of which is controlled by law;

20.7   [you lose your [UK driving licence] [HGV licence] for any reason]; or

20.8   you become a patient within the meaning of the Mental Health Act 1983.

Notes:

Summary dismissal is discussed in detail in chap 8 which makes the point that such a clause must not only give a clear indication of the types of conduct that will lead to summary dismissal but should also be wide enough to cover any unforeseen or novel misconduct. In addition the clause must be tailored to the circumstances of the particular employment. So, for example, the reference in Clause 20.6 to being under the influence of alcohol or drugs may be essential where the employee is operating dangerous machinery but not in other cases.

Dismissal under this provision is expressed to be immediate and without any entitlement to payment in lieu of notice. This avoids the problems experienced in *T & K Home Improvements Ltd v Skilton* [2000] IRLR 595 where ambiguous drafting meant that an employee was entitled to a payment in lieu of notice even though under the contract he could be dismissed 'with immediate effect' (see chap 8 at para 8.13 for further discussion of this case).

It is common to see a reference to the Mental Health Act 1983 in such clauses. However, in practice summary dismissal in such circumstances needs careful consideration as it may give rise to liability under the Disability Discrimination Act 1995. In addition, as an employee could be sectioned under the Mental Health Act 1983 for a relatively short period of time, any dismissal under Clause 20.8 might also be unfair, even though not in breach of contract.

Prec 21

---

21   Suspension

21.1   In order to investigate a complaint of misconduct against you, the Company may suspend you from your duties on full pay with full entitlement to all other benefits to which you are entitled under this Agreement for as long as the Company considers necessary to carry out a proper investigation of the complaint. During any such period of suspension:

    21.1.1   the Company will be under no obligation to provide you with any work;

    21.1.2   you may be required to stay away from the Company's premises and to have no contact with any employees, officers, customers, clients, agents or suppliers of the Company (except to the extent that such contact is necessary to enable you to investigate or defend any disciplinary charges, grievances or legal proceedings brought against you); and

    21.1.3   you will continue to be bound by all of your obligations under this Agreement insofar as they are compatible with you being suspended including your duty of good faith and your duties under Clause 7 (Outside Interests).

21.2   This Clause does not affect any right you may have to be suspended from work (or the terms of that suspension) under any legislative provision.

Notes:

As discussed in chap 4 at para 4.5 it is best to have an express clause dealing with suspension. This Clause provides for full salary and benefits to be paid to the employee during his suspension. However, if the employer wishes to be able to suspend without pay and benefits this would have to be set out very clearly in the contract, otherwise such a suspension would constitute a fundamental breach of contract by the employer enabling the employee to resign and claim constructive dismissal.

Although the power to suspend is expressed in broad terms in this Clause, it needs to be exercised carefully. In *Gogay v Hertfordshire County Council* [2000] IRLR 703, CA the Court of Appeal held that the unwarranted suspension of an employee pending a disciplinary investigation amounted to a breach of the implied term of trust and confidence. On the particular facts a transfer to another job or a period of leave would have been more appropriate. (For a more general discussion of the way the 'overriding obligation' of trust and respect has been applied to qualify the literal wording of the contract see chap 3 at para 3.19).

There are certain situations in which an employer is required to suspend an employee from work, eg, where their continued employment could expose them to a hazardous substance or where the working environment could pose a risk to the health and safety of a new or expectant mother or her baby. This Clause does not affect the employee's rights in such a situation.

Prec 22

22   Lay-off and Short Time Working

22.1   If there is a shortage of work or if the Company is unable to operate its business for any reason either generally or so as to prevent it giving you enough work to occupy you throughout your normal hours of work [and any hours of guaranteed overtime], then the Company has the right:

22.1.1   to lay you off from work without pay [or any other contractual benefits]; or

22.1.2   to reduce your normal hours of work [and/or any guaranteed overtime] and to reduce your pay proportionately

as the Company reasonably deems necessary for as long as the situation continues.

22.2   Nothing in this clause will affect any right you may have to a guarantee payment under section 28 of the Employment Rights Act 1996.

Notes:

This Clause gives the employer a right to lay-off the employee without pay or to reduce his hours of work and to alter his pay accordingly. This will often occur as a prelude to redundancy.

Prec 23

---

23   Searches

23.1 You agree to submit to a personal search and/or to a search of your office, locker, desk and other personal effects whenever the Company reasonably believes such a search to be necessary for safety reasons, for the protection of health (whether your own health or that of a third party), for the prevention of crime or for the protection of the rights of others (including the Company's rights).

23.2 [Such a search must take place in accordance with any policy laid down by the Company from time to time]. [Such a search will be carried out in a private room by a senior manager in the presence of another member of management and, if you so wish, a colleague of your choice. You may request that the search is carried out by a person of the same sex in the presence of individuals of the same sex].

23.3 If you unreasonably refuse to submit to a search authorised by this Clause you may be subject to disciplinary action, which could lead to summary dismissal under Clause 20 in an appropriate case.

Notes:

In the past powers of search were usually only seen in the contracts of manual workers in heavy industry. However in recent years there has been a change in culture and search provisions are now more common in the contracts of certain office workers (such as IT workers). However even where such a provision exists it is always prudent for the employer to obtain further written authority prior to a particular search. This guards against the risk of a civil action for trespass by the employee and possible criminal liability as well.

The Human Rights Act 1998 which incorporates the right to respect for private and family life into UK law is likely to have an impact in this area, particularly where the employer is a public authority and subject to direct liability under the Act. As a result the wording in Clause 23.1, which defines the circumstances in which a search may be undertaken, reflects Article 8(2) and the legitimate restrictions which may be placed on the right to privacy.

Employers should ideally have clear procedures in place to govern the conduct of employee searches and the first part of Clause 23.2 reflects this. However, if no such policy exists (and it may not) the second part of Clause 23.2 sets out some minimum standards which should apply to the search.

Prec 24

---

24   Confidentiality

24.1   You must not at any time (whether during or after your employment) communicate, divulge, use or exploit in any way any Confidential Information relating to the business affairs, trade secrets, management, personnel or administration of the Company or any of its current or former [clients] [customers] [suppliers] [without first obtaining the consent of the Company] unless such conduct is necessary for the proper performance of your duties or you have been requested or instructed to do so by the Company.

24.2   In this Clause 'Confidential Information' means:

24.2.1   any information which is designated by the Company as confidential;

24.2.2   any information which comes to your attention during your employment and which, by reason of its character and/or the manner of its coming, is evidently confidential

and includes, but is not restricted to the following [*give particular examples*] provided that information shall not be, or shall cease to be, Confidential Information to the extent that it comes to be in the public domain, unless this happens as the result of any unauthorised act or omission for which you are responsible.

24.3   Nothing in this Clause or in any other parts of this Agreement shall be taken to prevent you from making a protected disclosure within the meaning of the Public Interest Disclosure Act 1998 [and you are encouraged to refer to the Company's Whistleblowing Procedure for further information on the types of disclosure covered by the Act, as well as the channels of communication which are available within the Company for making such disclosures].

Notes:

An express confidentiality clause is useful not only because it reminds the employee of his duties in this area but also because such a clause can impose obligations over and above those at common law. The extent of the residual implied duty of confidentiality is discussed in chap 4 at para 4.19.

When drafting this clause you need to bear in mind the provisions of the Public Interest Disclosure Act 1998 discussed in chap 4 at para 4.21. The Act makes any contractual provision void insofar as it purports to preclude a worker from making a disclosure which is protected by the Act (see s 1 of the Act, inserting a new s 43J into the ERA 1996). This will clearly have a substantial impact on the scope of confidentiality clauses and is an example of the trend towards statutory intervention into freedom of contract discussed in chap 2 at para 2.10.

Prec 25

25   Post Termination Activities

25.1   [It is agreed that for a period of [   ] months after your employment terminates (the 'Relevant Period') you must not for any reason whether directly or indirectly and whether on your own account or with or on behalf of any third party:

25.1.1   canvass;

25.1.2   solicit;

25.1.3   endeavour to take away from the Company; or

25.1.4   deal with

any Relevant [Client] [Customer] of the Company [in relation to the supply of [*insert details of relevant goods and services*]].

25.2   For the purposes of this Clause a Relevant [Client] [Customer] is any person, firm or company who, either at the date of termination of your employment or at any time during the [   ] months prior to such termination was a [customer] [client] of the Company with whom you dealt directly other than in a trivial way.

25.3   The restrictions contained in this Clause are considered reasonable and necessary by the parties to protect the interests of the Company. However if any of these restrictions are held to be void but would be valid if part of the wording were deleted, then they shall apply with such deletions and modifications as may be necessary to make them enforceable.

25.4   You agree to draw this Clause to the attention of any third party who offers to employ you or engage you in any capacity during the Relevant Period].

Notes:

Restrictive covenants will only be upheld by the courts if they are designed to protect the employer's legitimate interests and go no further than is reasonably necessary to protect those interests. In addition the courts are likely to scrutinise restrictions on the activities of junior employees particularly closely. As a result in many cases it will be unrealistic to include any restrictive covenants in a contract of this type particularly if the employer's interests could be protected adequately by a garden leave clause. However, occasionally restrictive covenants may be necessary and this provision therefore contains a basic non-solicitation/non-dealing clause which seeks to protect the employer's customer connection. The courts tend to prefer such clauses to area covenants (which prohibit post-employment competition within a certain geographical area). However, an area covenant might be more appropriate if it would be difficult to identify customers (eg because customers tend to pay for their goods or services in cash) or if the employer is trying to protect trade secrets or confidential information which prove difficult to define.

When drafting a restrictive covenant it is essential to tailor it to meet the needs of the particular employment. This Clause therefore serves as an example only and should be used with care. In addition it should go no further than absolutely necessary to protect the employer's customer connection. As a result the clause does not cover all the employer's clients and is drafted to cover only those clients with whom the ex-employee has had meaningful dealings during a relatively short period leading up to termination. It is not wide enough to cover potential customers (such as those whom the ex-employee dealt with during the specified period but who never placed a firm order), although there seems to be no reason in principle why such a covenant would not be upheld in an appropriate case. However if you wanted the covenant to extend this far you would need to define potential customers with precision. In addition the covenant does not cover those who become customers after the employment terminates. This is because such a restriction is unlikely to protect a legitimate business interest of the employer and would normally be invalid.

To have the best chance of enforcement, the length of the covenant should be as short as possible, particularly if the employee is relatively junior. As a general rule, any period over six months is likely to be risky as far as enforcement is concerned, although it must be stressed that much depends on the facts of the particular case (such as the business cycle and order patterns).

The Clause prohibits a number of activities including a restriction on dealings. This can be useful as it is very easy for the ex-employee to assert that it was the customer who approached him and that there was therefore no solicitation. If dealings are prohibited this argument does not arise.

The Clause only applies after termination of the employment, primarily because the employer's interests are not necessarily the same whilst the employment relationship continues. The employer therefore needs to be sure that the duties of the employment (Clause 6), the restrictions on outside interests (Clause 7) and the confidentiality provisions (Clause 24) give the employer sufficient protection prior to termination.

Finally, when drafting any restrictive covenant be wary of trying to pre-determine losses caused by any subsequent breach. In *Taylor Stuart & Co v Croft* (1997) 606 IRLB 15, a case which concerned an accountancy firm, the employee's contract provided that if he breached a non-solicitation covenant then he would be liable for 'twice the aggregate fees derived from the client during the year immediately preceding the termination of employment'. However, the High Court held that this was a penalty clause and therefore unenforceable. Instead of being a genuine pre-estimate of the employer's loss of profit in this situation, the clause was an attempt to put a figure on the past capital value of the client. It paid no regard to the fact that the client may have ceased to use the company in any event, regardless of the employee's breach.

Prec 26

26 Return of Company Property

At any time during your employment (at the request of the Company) and in any event when your employment terminates you must immediately return to the Company all property in your possession or control which belongs to or relates to the Company together with any copies of the same whether such copies are in electronic, documentary or some other form.

For the avoidance of doubt such property includes, but is not restricted to, all safety equipment, protective clothing, uniform, keys, security and computer passes, credit cards, charge cards, documents, tapes, laptop computers and computer software [insert details of any other property that may be relevant].

27   Office Communications

27.1   During your employment you will be able to use the Company's telecoms and computer system ('the Office System') which provides for communication by various means including telephone, fax, e-mail, text message, voice mail [and video conferencing link] and which also allows access to the internet [and the Company's intranet].

27.2   The Office System (which, for the purposes of this Clause, includes any mobile phone or laptop computer belonging to or provided by the Company) is intended [primarily] for business use [only] and must be operated and used strictly in accordance with the Company's IT and Communications Policy ('the IT Policy') as amended from time to time. In particular you must not send any e-mails or other messages on the Office System which are of a defamatory or abusive nature, which constitute sexual or any other form of harassment or which are calculated to or may tend to prejudice or injure the interests of the Company. In addition you are prohibited from accessing or download-ing any pornographic or other offensive material from the Office System at any time. You hereby undertake to indemnify the Company fully against all liabilities, costs and expenses arising out of any breach of this Clause, whether such liabilities costs and expenses are incurred during or after your employment by the Company.

27.3   The Company reserves the right to treat a breach of the IT Policy as a disciplinary matter justifying summary dismissal under Clause 20 in an appropriate case.

27.4   [A public pay phone is provided on Company premises for employees' private use. Any private calls should normally be made during lunch and rest breaks only].

27.5   The Company may, at any time during your employment, where this is necessary in the interests of the Company's business, monitor or record your use of the Office System (whether this occurs during or outside normal working hours) including without limit:

27.5.1   the time, duration and contents of any communication whatsoever sent by you or to you via the Office System;

27.5.2   your access to and use of the internet; and

27.5.3   your access to and use of any computerised information retrieval system (such as an intranet) operated by the Company

and you hereby consent to such monitoring or recording taking place. [Further information on the purpose and extent of employee monitoring can be found in the Staff Handbook].

Notes:

This Clause deals with the appropriate use of office communication systems and employee monitoring. Until recently any monitoring of communications such as e-mails, faxes and telephone calls made by employees on office systems was not subject to specific regulation. However, since 24 October 2000 an employer can be liable if it intercepts communications made via its private telecoms system without having lawful authority to do so; see the Regulation of Investigatory Powers Act 2000 ('RIPA'), s 1(3). In the employment context lawful authority will usually arise in the following situations:

(i)   where the employer has reasonable grounds to believe that both the sender and the intended recipient consent to the interception; or

(ii) where there is no such consent, but the interception falls within the Telecommunications (Lawful Business Practice) (Interception of Communications) Regulations 2000. These Regulations authorise interception in a number of situations (eg to investigate unauthorised use of the system) but only if the employer has made 'all reasonable efforts' to notify everyone who uses the office system that communications may be intercepted.

Clause 27.5 is designed to reflect this position and has two main functions. First it contains a specific consent to interception. If such wording is included in all employment contracts then interception of communications between employees on the office system will not give rise to liability under RIPA because the employer will have all the necessary consents. Secondly it also serves as a warning to the employee that interception of his communications on the office system make take place. As noted above this is vital if the employer is to rely on the Lawful Business Practice Regulations to legitimise the interception (as may be necessary if the communication involves an outside third party who has not given express consents to monitoring). Of course a similar warning must be given to all those likely to use the system (ie not just members of the workforce but also independent contractors, customers and suppliers who may come onto Company premises and use the office system). However, as long as this generalised warning is given the employer may be able to rely on the Regulations to authorise interception. The Clause should therefore be inserted in the contract of any employee who is likely to use the Company's system, whether on a regular basis or not.

Note that Clause 27.5 is wider than is strictly necessary for the purposes of RIPA, which is only concerned with the interception of the contents of communications made on a private telecoms system. This is because the employer may want to carry out other forms of monitoring (such as call logging) which do not necessarily lead to the disclosure of the contents of messages but nonetheless provide useful information (such as the number of private calls made by a particular employee in a given period). Whilst such activities may fall outside RIPA they could infringe the right to respect for family and private life, home and correspondence guaranteed by Article 8(1) of the European Convention on Human Rights (which is now incorporated into UK law by the Human Rights Act 1998) if carried out without the employee's consent. The wide consent given in this Clause is therefore intended to deal with this point. Note that the consent is restricted to interceptions which are 'necessary in the interests of the Company's business'. This is designed to reflect Article 8(2) which allows derogations from the basic right, but only in strictly limited circumstances.

There is clearly some overlap between the restriction on interception of communications under RIPA and the requirements of the Data Protection Act 1998. This is because interception of e-mails, faxes and the like may well involve the processing of personal data. As a result it will be necessary to ensure that, if communications are to be monitored, both regimes are satisfied. So, for example, although monitoring staff e-mails to prevent abuse of the system may not contravene RIPA if a clause such as this one is inserted into employees' contracts, such conduct may nonetheless breach the First Data Protection Principle if any personal data which has been gathered is not processed fairly and lawfully. Guidance on appropriate conduct in such cases will be available when the Information Commissioner's long awaited Code of Practice on the use of personal data in employer/employee relationships is published. It is likely that the Code will require detailed information about monitoring (including the reasons why personal data is to be obtained and how it will be used) to be given to the employee. Clause 27.5 therefore refers the employee to further information on this issue.

Clause 27.4 refers to the provision of a public pay phone for the private use of employees. This reflects the guidance provided by OFTEL, the telephone industry regulator, in August 1999 to the effect that employers who intend to monitor phone calls should provide some lines at work for employees to use for private calls in the knowledge that their conversations on such lines will not be monitored or recorded. This guidance is not legally binding and Clause 27.4 is therefore optional. Nonetheless a public authority employer in particular may want to give the provision of such pay phones serious consideration, bearing in mind that such a body could be directly liable for a breach of Article 8 of the European Convention (see the Human Rights Act 1998 s 6). If pay phones are available and the employee also consents to telephone monitoring on the office system (as in Clause 27.5) then any Article 8 claim in respect of such monitoring would be unlikely to succeed.

Prec 28

---

28 *Disciplinary Procedure

28.1 The Company expects and will enforce reasonable standards of conduct and performance from its employees and a copy of the Company's disciplinary procedure ('the Disciplinary Procedure') which applies to your employment is set out in the Staff Handbook and is also available on the Company's intranet.

28.2 The Disciplinary Procedure [forms part of this Agreement] [is intended to be a guide to best practice only, to be operated at the Company's discretion. It does not therefore form part of this Agreement]. The terms of the Disciplinary Procedure may be changed from time to time by the Company and in such cases the most recent version will take priority.

28.3 Should you be dissatisfied with any disciplinary decision taken against you, you should take the matter up with the Personnel Manager in writing. You may appeal against the Personnel Manager's decision and the appropriate steps for doing so are set out in the Disciplinary Procedure.

Notes:

As the law now stands an employer is not required to adopt any detailed disciplinary rules or procedures. Instead the law simply requires that any rules which do exist are specified in the section 1 statement (either in the statement itself or by reference to a reasonably accessible document). In addition the statement must identify a person to whom the employee can apply if dissatisfied with any disciplinary decision and refer to any right of appeal available to him following such an application. Clause 28.3 is drafted accordingly although it should be noted these requirements do not apply if the employer has less than 20 employees (including employees of any associated employer) when the employment began; see the ERA 1996, s 3.

If the employer does adopt a formal disciplinary procedure he will need to decide whether to incorporate it into the contract and the drafting of Clause 28.2 reflects this. Many employers prefer not to incorporate disciplinary procedures because a failure to follow the procedure could put them in breach of contract (see *Dietman v Brent London Borough Council* [1987] IRLR 259; aff [1988] ICR 842, CA). In addition if a contractual disciplinary procedure is not followed and the employee is dismissed before he has sufficient continuous employment to bring an unfair dismissal claim there is a further risk. This is because in any wrongful dismissal action the employee could be awarded compensation for the lost opportunity to bring an unfair dismissal claim if due compliance with the procedure would have kept the employee in employment until the qualifying period had been reached (see *Raspin v United News Shops Ltd* [1999] IRLR 9, EAT).

For the future, the Employment Act 2002 will make substantial reforms in this area and the provisions of this Clause (together with any existing disciplinary procedures) are therefore likely to need some amendment when the new rules take effect, probably late in 2003. Under s 30 of the Act every contract of employment will be deemed to include a statutory disciplinary and dismissal procedure in the form set out in Schedule 2 to the Act. This will, in effect, require all employers (regardless of size) to have minimum procedures in place, which cannot be varied or amended by agreement, although there will be nothing to stop employers adopting or retaining more elaborate procedures as long as these are not inconsistent with the basic statutory standards. Unlike the statutory procedures, any such additional procedures would not necessarily form part of the contract. However, it may be that the arguments for incorporation become slightly stronger, if only to avoid the confusion caused by a two tier approach. It would certainly be very unfortunate (and risky for the employer) if an obligation to investigate misconduct prior to taking action, which forms a central part of most disciplinary procedures but which surprisingly does not appear as such in the statutory procedure, comes to be regarded in a manager's mind as somehow less important than the steps set out in the statutory procedure. Finally, under the new rules, the section 1 statement and any employment contract incorporating the statement will have to draw attention to the employer's disciplinary procedures, either by setting them out in the statement itself, or by reference to a readily accessible document. There will no longer be a small employer's exemption from this requirement.

In light of these changes ACAS is to revise its Code of Practice on disciplinary procedures. This should provide essential guidance when the reforms take effect.

Prec 29

> ### 29 *Grievances
>
> 29.1 If you have a grievance relating to your employment you should raise this with your immediate manager in writing at the earliest opportunity in accordance with the Company's grievance procedure ('the Grievance Procedure") which is set out in the Staff Handbook and is also available on the Company's intranet. If the matter is not resolved at this stage or you are not satisfied with the outcome you should follow the steps for appealing against your manager's decision as set out in the Grievance Procedure.
>
> 29.2 The Grievance Procedure [forms part of this Agreement] [is intended as a guide to best practice only and will therefore be operated at the Company's discretion and does not form part of this Agreement]. Its terms may be changed from time to time by the Company and in such cases the most recent version will take priority.

Notes:

Under current law, regardless of the size of the employer, the section 1 statement must specify the person to whom an employer can apply if he has a grievance. It must also set out the manner in which the grievance should be made (see the ERA 1996, s 3(1)(b)(ii)). Arguably this makes the adoption of a very basic grievance procedure mandatory but in any event there is an implied term in the employment contract that an employer will deal with employee grievances in a reasonable and prompt manner (see *Goold (W A) (Pearmak) Ltd v McConnell* [1995] IRLR 516, EAT discussed in chap 4 at para 4.7). If there are any further steps in the grievance procedure these should be set out in the section 1 statement or alternatively the employee should be referred to a reasonably accessible document for such information (see the ERA 1996, s 3(1)(c)). Strictly speaking reference to further appeals is unnecessary if the employer (together with any associated employer) had less than 20 employees on the date the employment began. However, in practice given that the written statement must set out the first stage of the grievance procedure whatever the size of the undertaking there seems little point in omitting any further stages on the strength of this exemption.

The introduction of statutory grievance procedures by the Employment Act 2002 will have an impact on this Clause, particularly as these statutory procedures, like the statutory disciplinary and dismissal procedures, will form part of every contract and will need to be reflected in the information provided in the section 1 statement. The provisions of this Clause, together with any existing grievance procedures, will therefore need to be reviewed when the new rules take effect which, in line with the new statutory disciplinary procedures, will probably be at the end of 2003.

30   Data Protection

30.1   You must at all times during your employment act in accordance with any policy or instruction introduced by the Company to ensure compliance with the Data Protection Act 1998 or any other applicable data protection legislation.

30.2   You explicitly consent to:

30.2.1   the Company Processing any Personal Data relating to you;

30.2.2   the Company Processing any Sensitive Personal Data relating to you [including, without being restricted to, any self certification forms or medical certificates supplied to the Company to explain your absence by reason of sickness or injury, any records of sickness absence, any medical reports or health assessments, any details of your trade union membership or any information relating to any criminal convictions or any criminal charges secured or brought against you. *Enter any other examples of Sensitive Personal Data that may be relevant*]; and

30.2.3   the Company collecting and disclosing your Personal Data (including Sensitive Personal Data) from time to time to and from third parties [including the situation where this involves the transfer of such Personal Data outside the European Economic Area]

provided that any such processing is necessary or reasonably required by the Company for the performance of this Agreement, the conduct of the Company's business or the proper administration and management of the employment relationship (both during and after your employment) or where such processing is required by law.

30.3   For its part the Company will take steps to ensure that it complies with its legal obligations in relation to the processing of your Personal Data and in particular will put procedures in place to ensure that all your Personal Data held by the Company is accurate and up to date and is not kept for longer than necessary. Measures will also be taken to safeguard against unauthorised or unlawful processing and accidental loss or destruction or damage to the data.

30.4   In this Clause 'Personal Data', 'Processing' and 'Sensitive Personal Data' have the meanings set out in sections 1 and 2 of the Data Protection Act 1998. [The European Economic Area ('the EEA') comprises the 15 Member States of the European Union together with Norway, Iceland and Liechtenstein and any other countries which are designated as part of the EEA from time to time.]

Notes:

A detailed commentary on the Data Protection regime is clearly beyond the scope of this book and these notes are therefore restricted to drafting points raised by the clause.

It should be used in conjunction with a detailed Data Protection Policy. Such a provision seeks to secure:

(i)   a generalised consent to the processing of personal data relating to the employee. (This should help to satsify the First Principle of the Data Protection Act 1998 which requires data to be processed fairly and lawfully);

(ii) an explicit consent to the processing of sensitive data (this is also relevant to the First Principle);

(iii) a consent to the transfer of the employee's personal data outside the European Economic Area (relevant to the Eighth Data Protection Principle). Such a consent could be relevant if, for example, the employer's parent company is based in the USA); and

(iv) an obligation on both the employer and employee to comply with the 1998 Act.

All contracts of employment should contain such a Clause, however junior the employee.

The Clause limits processing to that which is 'necessary or reasonably required by the Company' for the performance of the Agreement, the conduct of the Company's business or the proper administration and management of the employment relationship. This is because the Information Commissioner has indicated that a blanket or general consent to the processing of personal data is unlikely to be sufficient as a basis on which to process personal data, particularly sensitive personal data. It is hoped that the provision is therefore sufficiently specific to constitute a valid consent, although there is as yet no case law on this issue.

Note that even if personal data is processed with the employee's consent there will still be a breach of the First Data Protection Principle if the processing is in breach of any legal duty or responsibility. So, for example, if the processing breaches the common law duty of confidence or if it contravenes RIPA there will be a breach of the First Principle regardless of any employee consent to processing. Similarly if the employer is a public authority and the processing involves an infringement of a right guaranteed by the European Convention on Human Rights (such as where monitoring of e-mails breaches the right to respect for private life set out in Article 8) the processing will be unlawful under the Human Rights Act 1998 and contrary to the First Principle. It is therefore important that the consents contained in both this Clause and Clause 27 (which deals with Office Communications) are included in the contract.

---

31   Health and Safety

The Company is committed to ensuring as far as possible the health and safety and welfare at work of its employees. It is the duty of employees to ensure that they are familiar with and follow the Company's Health and Safety Policy as laid down from time to time. A copy of this Policy is set out in the Staff Handbook and is also available on the Company's intranet. Breach of the Company's Health and Safety Policy will normally be treated as a serious disciplinary matter which could lead to summary dismissal under Clause 20 in an appropriate case.

Notes:

This Clause reflects the fact that employers have a statutory duty to prepare and keep revised a written statement of the Company's health and safety policy and to bring it to the notice of all employees unless they have less than five employees (see the Health and Safety At Work Etc Act 1974, s 2(3)).

EITHER:

Prec 32

---

32 Third Party Rights (for use where no third party rights are to arise)

32.1 It is agreed that no term of this Agreement [including the terms of any documents incorporated into this Agreement] shall be enforceable by a Third Party in his own right by virtue of section 1(1) of the Contracts (Rights of Third Parties) Act 1999 [and to avoid any doubt this Agreement may be rescinded or varied in whole or in part by agreement between us or by the Company pursuant to Clause 35 without the consent of any such Third Party].

32.2 For the purposes of this Clause a 'Third Party' means any person who is not named as a party to this Agreement.

OR:

Prec 33

33 Third Party Rights (for use where limited third party rights are to arise)

33.1 It is agreed that section 1(1) of the Contracts (Rights of Third Parties) Act 1999 ('the CRTPA') shall apply to this Agreement but only to the extent that [*insert name of Third Party*] may enforce the terms of Clause [   ] in his/her/its own right despite the fact that [*insert name of Third Party*] is not a party to this Agreement.

33.2 [In accordance with section 2(3)(a) of the CRTPA the whole or any part of this Agreement can be rescinded or varied by agreement between us or by the Company pursuant to Clause 35 without the consent of [*insert name of Third Party*]).

33.3 For the avoidance of doubt Clause [   ] is the only term of this Agreement which it intended to be enforceable by a person who is not a party to this Agreement by virtue of section 1(1) of the CRTPA.

Notes:

Clauses 32 and 33 contain drafting to deal with the Contracts (Rights of Third Parties) Act 1999. This legislation partially abolishes the doctrine of privity so that a person who is not a party to a contract (known as a 'Third Party') can, in certain circumstances, acquire legally enforceable rights where a contractual term purports to benefit that Third Party. However the Act has a limited application to employment contracts because it provides that third party rights can only be created in such a contract as against an employer (or ex-employer). They cannot be created against the employee. This means that in practice the Act is likely to have most effect in relation to the benefits package where third parties, such as the spouse or dependants of an employee, may be able to obtain enforceable rights to certain benefits if the effect of the Act is overlooked. However, clearly the Act could also be relevant to other aspects of the Agreement and its effect on the contract as a whole, including any documents incorporated into the contract (such as company policies), should always be considered.

The precedent gives sample drafting for two situations. In Clause 32 the effect of the Act is excluded altogether. Such a clause is likely to be in the employer's interests as it prevents any third party rights arising against the employer. The wording in square brackets at the end of Clause 32.1 refers to the third party's right of veto in respect of any variation or rescission of the contract. Such a right will arise in certain circumstances where third party rights are obtained under the Act (see s 2). As Clause 32 prevents third party rights arising in the first place, technically such a reference is unnecessary. However, it is included to put the matter beyond doubt.

Clause 33 on the other hand creates some limited third party rights and is most likely to be of value to an employee, although it will obviously need adapting to suit a given situation. Clause 33.2 gives the option of excluding the third party's right of veto in respect of variation or rescission. As discussed, such a right will arise automatically unless wording such as this is used.

Prec 34

34   Change of Personal Details

You must inform the personnel and payroll departments promptly of any change in your personal circumstances such as next of kin, change of permanent address or change of bank details. The processing of such details will be carried out in accordance with Clause 30 (Data Protection).

Prec 35

---

35   [Variation

Subject to any overriding statutory provision, the Company reserves the right to vary any term of this Agreement unilaterally on giving you [4 weeks prior written notice of any such change] [reasonable notice in writing of any such change]].

Notes:

For a discussion of such clauses see chap 3 at para 3.12.

Prec 36

---

36   General

36.1 This Agreement (together with any documents incorporated within it), constitutes the entire agreement between us with regard to its subject matter, and supersedes any previous agreement (whether verbal or written) made between us at any time.

36.2 A reference to any legislative provision includes any subsequent amendment or re-enactment of that provision.

36.3 Clause headings are included in this Agreement for convenience only and do not affect its construction.

36.4 References in this Agreement to your employment means your employment by the Company under this Agreement as varied from time to time.

36.5 This Agreement is governed by English Law and only English courts and tribunals are to have jurisdiction in relation to any claim or dispute arising out of or relating to it.

Notes:

The provisions in this Clause are for the most part self-explanatory. Clause 36.1 is generally in the employer's interest as it promotes certainty. However it does reinforce the need for the contract to be clear and comprehensive. If such a clause is omitted the court may decide to look at external evidence to clarify ambiguities in employment terms (see *Tayside Regional Council v McIntosh* [1982] IRLR 272, EAT where the contents of a job advert were referred to for this purpose).

Prec 37

SIGNED by or on behalf of the parties on the date set out at the beginning of this Agreement.

SIGNED by [   ] (Director/Secretary))
for and on behalf of the Company   ) . . . .
SIGNED by [insert name of employee]   ) . . . .

Notes:

Normally there will be no legal requirement for the contract to be executed as a deed. However, if the contract contains a power of attorney a deed should be used to ensure the validity of the power (see Powers of Attorney Act 1971, s 1). An employment contract is not subject to stamp duty and the same is true of the section 1 statement.

Index

249

ELI-2002
December